A One-Year Devotional
for Teens and Young Adults

A One-Year Devotional
for Teens and Young Adults

Ruth Chesney

John Ritchie Publishing

40 Beansburn, Kilmarnock, Scotland

ISBN-13: 978 1 912522 96 5

Copyright © 2020 by John Ritchie Ltd.
40 Beansburn, Kilmarnock, Scotland

www.ritchiechristianmedia.co.uk

Typeset by John Ritchie Ltd., Kilmarnock
Printed by Bell & Bain Ltd., Glasgow

This book provides simple, spiritual sustenance every day of the year from the Scriptures. Each page can be read in a few minutes. Teenagers have specific issues to face and the carefully selected material will be helpful on their spiritual journey. We all need a varied diet to help us develop and grow and the daily devotional thoughts range across multiple issues and topics. This interesting book will instil desires to meditate more fully upon God's Word and follow in the footsteps of the Master.

Craig & Hannah Munro

Ruth displays a real insight into the mind-set and problems of the modern Christian teenager. She addresses many issues in a colloquial style that would appeal to the teenage mind without in any way compromising reverence for God. Reading the book will instil into the young believer respect for God, love for the Saviour, and commitment to the Word of God.

Jack & Lillian Hay

A wonderful collection of concise, appealing daily readings, each based on a Bible verse, explaining foundational truths in diverse ways. It includes biographical stories, everyday examples, scientific facts, and personal anecdotes. I loved reading through this book; readers will find it easy to understand, practical, personable, humorous at times, and soundly Biblical with helpful references and supporting evidence throughout. This book will undoubtedly be a great support to spiritual growth for younger Christians through the year.

Eunice Wilkie

Before You Begin...

Thank you for picking up *Climb*! I'm so glad you have chosen to join me as we climb together this year. Nothing is more important than living for the glory of our Lord Jesus Christ and giving Him first place. If you are a young Christian, these daily devotional readings were written especially for you. Christians are people who have realised that, as sinners, we have fallen short of God's holy standard (Romans 3:23) but have trusted in the Lord Jesus for our eternal salvation (Acts 16:30,31). We have been fully forgiven through His death for us on the cross. He arose from the dead, so He is alive today.

In this book, you'll find a number of different topics – creation and apologetics, biographies, practical lessons for everyday Christian living, and studies of Bible teaching and characters. Some of the subjects will be light reading, others will stretch your brain a little. Some will be encouraging, others convicting. And although not every devotional will be relevant to every reader, each one was written with your spiritual progress in mind.

While this book is designed to be read daily, **it is not a substitute for the Bible!** Reading the Word of God and praying are vital for a Christian and shouldn't be neglected. These devotionals are only supplements to help you in your Christian life. If you must make a choice between reading your Bible or this book, choose your Bible, every time.

If you aren't yet a Christian – if you have never accepted Christ as your Saviour – I fully recommend Him to you. He is not only a great Saviour, He is the best friend any young (or older) person could ever have. He will change your life and give it purpose and meaning, and you will have gained a home in heaven forever.

As you read *Climb*, my hope and prayer for you is that you will do as the apostle Paul did – forget what lies behind and strain forward to what lies ahead, and 'press on toward the goal for the prize of the upward call of God in Christ Jesus' (Philippians 3:13,14 ESV).

Christ, alone, is worthy!

For Him, and for His glory,

Ruth

An Introduction to Climbing

The quiet path winds gently uphill through leafy forests and beside a gurgling stream. The birdsong in the trees matches the joy in your heart as you stroll along. Your backpack doesn't feel too heavy and you're enjoying the pleasant shade from the warm sun. Then you reach a fork in the path. You pause. Should you follow the track which runs alongside the stream? It looks pleasant, a lot like the path you've been following. Or should you turn to the right? This way is narrower, rougher, and steeper. It leads out of the forest, towards the rocky, grey mountain. Both paths are uphill, but you know that the mountain one will test you and try you. You will need to climb, to push yourself to your limit. The temperature will fluctuate between extremes of scorching heat and chilling cold. Your backpack will begin to feel like a heavy burden. The gradient may be so steep in places that you will find yourself clinging by your fingernails. But the higher you climb, the purer the air will be, and the more magnificent the view. At some point, you will haul yourself over that final ledge and find yourself in breath-taking wonder at the awesome vista before you. The arduous, gruelling, and oftentimes dangerous climb will have been worth it all. When someone asks, "Would you choose the same path if you were to do it over?" your answer will be a resounding "Yes!"

The Christian life is a lot like climbing a mountain. When we trust Christ for salvation we begin on the gentle slopes, but it's not long before we are faced with a choice. Are we going to leisurely make our way to heaven, gliding along and living how we please? Or will we choose the steep and difficult path, the path of self-denial, of living wholeheartedly for God? Every true believer in the Lord Jesus Christ will be in heaven, but wouldn't it be tragic, when we arrive, to realise that we totally wasted our lives? God left us here for a purpose – to glorify Him.

It's never too late to decide to live for God. Maybe you once began to climb, but wandered off the path, or turned back. Past failures don't need to hinder you. When we wander away, God stands ready to forgive and restore. And whether we've been on the path a while or we've just started, the great thing is that we are never alone. He is always with us as our helper, protector, and guide. So adjust that backpack on your shoulders, take a deep breath, and step up onto that stony path.

Let's climb!

JANUARY

They began to consecrate on the first day of the first month.

2 Chronicles 29:17 ESV

Today we're standing at the gateway of another year. The unknown, untrodden path lies ahead. We can't see very far; a bend at the beginning of the path hides the rest of it from our view. As we move forward, each step will reveal a little more that is presently hidden from us. There will be many twists and turns; we will need to tread carefully and make wise decisions. But maybe the biggest decisions come right now, before we've moved at all.

Hezekiah was one of the better kings of Judah. Before he reigned, conditions in the land had deteriorated, and many of God's commandments were disobeyed. The temple had been defiled and worship had ceased. So Hezekiah began the new year with a clear-out. Everything that defiled the house of the Lord was removed, the altar, table, and utensils were cleansed, and the temple was consecrated.

It's a good way to begin the new year! We all have things in our lives that defile us. You know what the defiling things are in your life – films, social media, song lyrics, certain people you choose to spend time with. Maybe it's time for a clear-out.

It's certainly time for cleansing. 'Wherewithal shall a young man [or woman] cleanse his [or her] way? by taking heed thereto according to Thy word' (Psalm 119:9). Each day, we need the cleansing that reading the Bible brings to our lives.

What about consecration? Is this going to be the year that we set ourselves apart to put our very best – our all – into living for God? He loved us so much that He gave us His best, His beloved Son. How can we do less than give all that we have – time, talents, possessions, energy, even our very bodies – for Him? 'I beseech you therefore, brethren, by the mercies of God, that ye present your bodies a living sacrifice, holy, acceptable unto God, which is your reasonable service. And be not conformed to this world: but be ye transformed by the renewing of your mind, that ye may prove what is that good, and acceptable, and perfect, will of God' (Romans 12:1-2).

'Consecrate yourselves today to the Lord' (Exodus 32:29).

There is a friend that sticketh closer than a brother.

Proverbs 18:24

Everyone loves having friends. It's great to have people who share your interests, friends you can laugh with, and those with whom you can talk over your problems. Some people make lifelong friends at nursery or primary school. For most of us, though, our friends change over the years. Maybe we transfer to a different school or move away to university.

More often, we grow apart because we discover that we don't have so much in common anymore. This is especially true for those who are believers in the Lord Jesus Christ. Friends who aren't saved won't understand our desire to read God's Word and pray, to attend gatherings where Christ is the centre, and to live for God. Sometimes even those who profess to be Christians don't understand us either. It can be easy for a young believer to feel lonely. I know – I've been there.

You do have a friend though – One who sticks closer than a brother. He's the very best friend that it's possible to have. He even died for you. This friend will never let you down. He'll never mock you, never talk about you behind your back. The best bit is that He's always with you, no matter where you go.

When I was a teenager, I was given the good advice that I should get to know my Best Friend better, by reading His Word and telling Him everything that happens, because He's interested in every detail. Tell Him about your loneliness! Ask Him to guide you to people who will be the best kind of friends – those who will help you draw even nearer to the Lord Jesus Christ. In His time, He will answer those prayers.

It is a good thing to give thanks unto the Lord.

Psalm 92:1

Have you heard of 'practising gratitude'? It's a term which has become very popular in recent times, and is cropping up online, in books, and in podcasts, mainly in relation to improving mental health. According to one secular psychology website, being grateful can improve our physical health, our sleep, and our mood. But isn't it interesting that thousands of years ago the psalmist already knew that being thankful was a good thing? Practising gratitude isn't a new idea at all.

The problem with the world's idea is that they often have no object for their gratitude – no one to thank. They can be as grateful as can be, but without someone to address, it is merely an exercise in positive thinking. As Christians, we don't have this problem. We know where every blessing and gift comes from and we know exactly who to thank! For us, being grateful is something that should be as natural as breathing.

Sometimes being grateful isn't easy. There are days that, from the minute we wake up, everything seems to go wrong – we sleep in, drop toothpaste on our clothes, or we have the worst of bad hair days. Or maybe there's something ahead that we're dreading – an assessment, a presentation, a class with a cross teacher or lecturer, an interview – and the last thing we feel is gratitude.

Those are the days when it's even more important to be thankful! I have discovered that writing down a few things that I'm grateful for every morning helps me to get a better perspective and recognise what's truly important. I remember that we have a good God who loves to give good gifts to His children. Everything we receive is undeserved and given in grace. In thanking God, I see what He has already done for me, and it encourages me to know that He will be with me during the difficult day ahead.

I recommend that you find a notebook or journal and take a few minutes each morning during your regular Bible reading and prayer time to jot down what you're grateful for. Remember – it is a good thing to give thanks unto the Lord!

I have created him for My glory.
Isaiah 43:7

JANUARY

4

Truly satisfied people are hard to find in our society. There are teenagers aiming for the 'perfect' number of social media followers, students striving for top grades and a place at a prestigious university, fitness fanatics expending time and effort to obtain the ideal body, and people from all walks of life diving into the search for ultimate pleasure and gratification. But as they pursue their goals, their targets keep shifting, drawing them along in a pointless chase after fulfilment and contentment.

Many don't know what they are looking for. The conclusion of atheism, which is so popular in our western world today, is that we are each a cosmic accident, here by chance. All we do, all we strive towards, is only for here and now. The emptiness people feel drives them to work hard and play harder to find satisfaction. Earthly things might stifle emptiness in the same way sugar suppresses hunger, but they will never provide deep and lasting satisfaction.

Why? Because, as human beings, we were made for more. A preacher used to tell the story of two little boys who bought a trombone case from a second-hand shop. They knew it had been made for something, but they didn't know what. So they tried to use it as a suitcase, then a lunch pail, and lastly a fishing tackle box. Nothing worked, so they took it back. One day, as they were passing the shop, they saw the opened trombone case in the window with a trombone inside. Every indentation, mark, and groove finally made perfect sense. The case had been made for a specific purpose![1]

We, too, were made for a purpose. Look again at our verse for today. We were created for God's glory. Although many activities and pursuits are harmless and legitimate, no matter what we try to fit into our lives, we will never have full satisfaction until we find it in loving God and living for Him. As the unsaved people around us watch us live our lives, let them see someone who has discovered the secret of true satisfaction.

_____

1. https://www.heaven4sure.com/2006/12/21/peter-orasuk-from-drugs-to-christ/

Then drew near unto Him all the publicans and sinners for to hear Him.

Luke 15:1

How popular are you? Are you in a group of friends that everyone else looks up to with awe and admiration? Or do you feel that no one really notices that you exist? Maybe you even wish you could be invisible, because then you wouldn't get so much unwanted attention or bullying. How popular we are can depend on many factors, but often there's no logic at all why certain people are popular, and others aren't.

No matter where on the scale we land, it would do us all good to think about the Lord Jesus Christ's attitude to people. He wasn't at all swayed by other people's opinions. He ate with Pharisees – those proud, religious leaders. He also ate in the homes of publicans and sinners – those who were unpopular and despised. He did not hold one group above the other, and others' opinions made no difference to how He treated anyone. If the Lord was at your school, He wouldn't always sit with the popular crowd at lunchtime. I think, instead, He would pick out the loneliest people and eat with them. He had time for everyone and loved each one equally. He even shocked the disciples, because He talked to those that they didn't think He should be speaking with – like the Samaritan woman in John 4.

We can all take a lesson from this. No matter how popular or unpopular we are, I'm sure we can find someone who looks lonely. Maybe there's a person you know, and for some reason (that no one can actually explain), no one ever wants to bother with them. Sometimes these 'outcasts' are a little bit unique. Or maybe they have problems interacting with others. Perhaps they come from homes where they don't receive the same care from their parents as you have enjoyed. Maybe they're from a different country and struggle to communicate or integrate. Whatever it is, let's be more like Christ. Forget about what others will think, and let's treat that individual as Christ would. It might take courage and work, but when you show that you are like Christ, you will please God.

I have treasured the words
of His mouth more than my
necessary food.

Job 23:12 NKJV

6

JANUARY

I trusted the Lord Jesus Christ as my Saviour about three months before I finished primary school, and I wasn't saved very long when I received some really good advice – always take time every morning to read and pray. I can't remember where I started in the Bible – possibly the gospel of Matthew – but I tried to make an effort to read and pray before I left for school.

It's a really good habit to get into. Some mornings I didn't feel like it, sometimes I ran late, and my reading was very rushed. Occasionally, I was horrified to discover, later in the day, that I'd forgotten to read and pray at all! But the habit that I developed from the age of eleven, right through my teenage years, has been a good one. Spending time with my Bible and praying every morning is a valuable and necessary part of my day now.

Are you making time to read and pray? Whether you're at school, university, or work, mornings can be really busy, and sometimes it's hard to be alert, especially if you've been up late the night before. Reading your Bible and praying, however, is so important! Every day we face many temptations, and we are dependent on God for help to get through each day. Even if you struggle to understand what you've read, simply reading the Word of God has a cleansing effect, although it's also good to look up the passage in a relevant commentary when you have time. Talk to God about your day ahead; listen to Him as He speaks to you through His Word.

You might need to get up a little earlier. You'll possibly have to make decisions about how much time is spent on your personal appearance. You may even need to cut down on time spent at the breakfast table (look at the verse at the top of this page!), but one thing is sure – any 'sacrifices' you make to spend time with God will be well worth it. You will never lose out.

In the beginning God...

JANUARY

Genesis 1:1

Nowadays, at least in the Western world, believing that there is a God is not at all popular. Atheists like to scoff at the very notion, and so we often find ourselves on the lookout for arguments and proofs that we can use to explain to others that God really does exist. The problem is that we can get so caught up in finding evidence *for* God that we neglect to spend time learning *about* God.

And what a lot there is to learn! In preparation for writing today's reading, I've just opened a concordance and read through all the references to God, concentrating especially on the references to 'God is'. It'll be worth your while taking a few minutes, maybe on your bus journey, or over coffee or a snack, to open up the Bible app on your phone and search for 'God is'. I promise you'll learn a lot, even with only a quick scan through the various verses.

The first thing we need to remember about God is that He was there right at the beginning. It's not that He existed *from* the beginning, but He was there *in* the beginning. So before the world ever began, God was there. In Deuteronomy 33:27, we learn that God is eternal – He didn't begin a few years or millennia before the earth was created, He was always there. It's impossible for us to wrap our brains around, because we have only known the limitations of time, but just because we cannot understand it doesn't mean it's not true. God never had a beginning – He always existed and, what's more, He will always exist.

Don't you find this truth reassuring? I know I do. We probably all have people – friends or family members – that we cannot imagine life without. The problem is that someday, sooner or later, we will have to say goodbye to them. No matter how much they love us, they cannot always be around for us. Not so with God. God is eternal. There will never come a day when His contract expires, or His time is up. This eternal God is our God – forever!

> Except a corn of wheat fall into the ground and die, it abideth alone: but if it die, it bringeth forth much fruit.
>
> John 12:24

You may be familiar with the quotation 'He is no fool who gives what he cannot keep to gain what he cannot lose', but how much do you know about the young man who wrote it in his journal when he wasn't a great deal older than you are now?

Jim Elliot was born in Portland, Oregon, in 1927 and had a happy, fun-filled childhood. He was saved at the age of six, and the rest of his life was characterised by one burning desire – to live for God. This desire influenced various choices he made, both in spiritual things and in practical down-to-earth matters.

Maybe you're thinking that it doesn't sound as if he was a whole lot of fun to be around, but his biography shows that he was a normal young man, full of life and laughter. Yet, in another sense, his desire to always put God first, his knowledge and insatiable love of Scripture, and his burden for those still unsaved, could not be called ordinary. He often wrote of his willingness to give his life for God, almost as if he expected that this was the very thing he'd be asked to do. And it was.

On 8th January 1956, he, along with four other young missionaries, was speared to death by members of a tribal people in the jungles of Ecuador. They had gone to try to contact them, hoping one day to be able to explain the good news of God's love for them. But instead of the tribal people arriving to meet them as friends, they had a different plan. In a short time, all five missionaries were with Christ.

Jim Elliot was a young man with so much energy and zeal, yet he had early learned that we cannot keep our lives for ourselves. The impact of his death reverberated around the globe, with many answering the call of God to go and preach the gospel to every creature. Truly his death brought forth much fruit. Was he a fool to give his life? Of course not! Jim Elliot is with Christ – he has truly gained that which he will never lose.[2]

---

2. *Shadow of the Almighty* tells the story of the lives and death of Jim Elliot and his fellow missionaries. I consider it a must-read for every believer. It was written by Jim's widow, Elisabeth Elliot, and published by Hodder & Stoughton Ltd in 1958.

Bear ye one another's burdens, and so fulfil the law of Christ.
Galatians 6:2

"What's wrong?"

"Nothing!"

How many times have you had this conversation, either as the questioner or as the one being questioned? Most people aren't very good at hiding their feelings, and those closest to us can generally guess that something is up. In fact, the more vehemently the word 'nothing' comes out, the more likely it is that it isn't true at all! Sometimes we're looking for a reason to vent, to spill everything that's been going wrong in our lives, and it doesn't take many more questions before all the hurts, injustices, and complaints come gushing out.

There are other times when the hurt seems too deep for words, when we feel too fragile to bring our problems into the open and let the light shine on them. We'd rather bottle everything up inside and hope it goes away. Maybe something has happened that, for whatever reason, you feel you couldn't possibly tell anyone. And so it sits there, fermenting and growing, until you don't know how you can live with this secret any longer.

If you find yourself in this situation, please remember that God is still there. He loves you, and He cares about your problem. Your feelings can never change the reality of God's love for you. God has also put people into your life to help you. He has instructed every one of us to bear each other's burdens, and this includes listening to your problems. Find a believer you can talk to. Think outside the box and don't rule out older age groups. They may not be able to relate to some parts of your story, but they are still able to give sound, godly advice and, most importantly, pray for you. If you find it hard to talk about, write it down. Don't let shame keep you from sharing your burden – not one of us is sinless.

So look up, and look out. Sometimes it may not feel like it, but this difficulty will pass. And if you find that you are totally unable to find a sympathetic ear, remember that God loves you and nothing reaches you that isn't known by Him. He *will* bring you through.

Think on these things.

Philippians 4:8

hen I was twelve, a friend sold me a hamster called Timmie. We didn't have this tiny ball of fluff for very long before it became clear that, apart from stashing food in his bed, Timmie's favourite activity was exercising on his wheel. Round and round and round the wheel went, as he raced along on his little, short legs. While I was glad that Timmie had something to occupy him, I felt sorry for him because he wasn't going anywhere, just using all that energy and staying in the same spot!

Often our minds are a bit like Timmie on his wheel. They go round and round and round, and when they eventually stop we discover we haven't actually gone anywhere. This is especially true when it comes to worry. In Philippians 4, Paul instructs the believers in Philippi not to be anxious, but to commit everything to God, who will give us peace and keep our hearts and minds through Christ Jesus. God wants us to step off the hamster wheel of anxious thoughts.

But what are we to replace these thoughts with? I often find that the mind is like a vacuum. I'm sure you've tried to think about nothing. If you manage not to get distracted by what you see or hear, you soon find yourself wondering what thinking about nothing should feel like. Or you begin to focus on ridding your mind of thoughts one by one, the way people bale out a sinking boat with a bucket, with the water pouring in as quickly as it's scooped out! It doesn't really work very well, does it?

That's why Paul has listed commendable qualities for believers to focus on. In fact, the word he uses is 'meditate', but this isn't the meditation that people are keen to practise nowadays, where they sit with their eyes closed, maybe in a cross-legged pose, focussing on their breathing. Instead, it is to 'carefully reflect' or 'make... things the subjects of your thoughtful consideration.'³ So when anxious or negative thoughts of any kind begin to intrude, we must displace them by carefully reflecting on the qualities Paul goes on to list, which we'll look at over the next few days.

---

3. The Bible dictionary I refer to most often is the *Expository Dictionary of New Testament Words* by W. E. Vine, published by Oliphants in 1940. I'll abbreviate it to *Vine's Dictionary* from now on.

11
JANUARY

Whatever is true.
Philippians 4:8 ESV

If you were to make a list of things that we should think about to replace anxious thoughts, what would you put on it? Whatever is happy, whatever is comforting, whatever is amusing...? Actually, none of these things feature on Paul's list. Instead, he begins with something very basic and yet absolutely vital. Things that are true.

You see, most of our worry comes from dwelling on things that aren't true. Think about it for a minute. We worry about things that might happen, things that, most of the time, will either never take place or, if they do, won't turn out to be as awful as we imagine. Until they happen, our imaginings are not true. So, to guard against worry, we must think about what is true – that God is in control, that He loves us, and that He has promised never to leave or forsake us.

Knowing the truth about ourselves will guard against anxious thoughts. Some people are affected by a great deal of self-importance, others by low self-esteem – neither attitude is God's mind for us. In His Word, we read that we are loved by God and precious to Him, but we are also warned about pride.

There's also the truth about others. Some people we envy because we think that their lives are perfect. Others we despise and look down on because we believe they aren't as good as we are. Sometimes we even attribute to other people thoughts and actions which aren't true. How many of us have believed that someone was talking about us behind our backs without any evidence to back it up? We can get so caught up with trying to guess or thinking we know the thoughts and motives of other people, when only God knows the heart. If we think true thoughts about others, it will free our minds from many of the worries we carry around with us.

So how can we replace those negative thoughts and meditate on what is true? John 17:17 says, 'Thy word is truth.' Reading and memorising Scripture will give us a store of truth to choose from when we need to expel worry from our minds.

Whatever is honourable.

Philippians 4:8 ESV

The second word in the list of qualities we should meditate on is translated as 'honest', 'honourable', or 'noble', depending on which Bible version you read. The thought behind the Greek word Paul used is 'worthy of respect'[4], or 'inspiring reverence and awe'[5]. It's the opposite of dishonour, which is a state of shame or disgrace.

Is there anyone you know whom you would describe as honourable? When we hear the word, we automatically think of someone older – maybe an elder in the church, or a grandparent – but being honourable is something that everyone can be, no matter what age we are. One of the main characteristics of honourable people is that their word is dependable. You won't catch them saying one thing and doing another. They won't be conniving, scheming, or trying to wriggle out of their duties. To have honour is to have a commitment to what is right, no matter the personal cost. Someone who is honourable will be living in a way that will please God and won't bring reproach on His name.

In the word honourable, there's also the thought of dignity. Honourable people won't be thoughtless or flippant, tossing around offhand comments that don't add anything profitable to the conversation, and which might even be damaging.

There are so many dishonourable things in this world – things which are shameful, disgraceful, dishonest, insincere, and underhand – the complete opposite of what should draw our attention and occupy our minds. Isn't it remarkable that this verse doesn't ask us to *be* honourable? Instead, we're to *think* on whatever is honourable, because whatever occupies our minds will affect our lives – for good or bad.

---

4. In this book, I often refer to Warren W. Wiersbe's Commentary, *The Wiersbe Bible Commentary*, published by David C. Cook, 2007.
5. *Vine's Dictionary.*

Whatever is just.
Philippians 4:8 ESV

I love the prophecy of Isaiah. Yes, there are many parts that are difficult to understand, but it's an exciting book, because we get a glimpse of how the Lord Jesus Christ will come as King in a future day, and everything will be put right. But I'm sure you're wondering why I'm writing about Isaiah when we're looking at a verse in Philippians! The reason is that throughout Isaiah's prophecy, we learn that justice is lacking. Widows and orphans are being oppressed and the poor are being robbed, but the One who is promised is absolutely just. When He comes to earth, all injustice will end.

People in the world are concerned about justice and equal rights, but the sad truth is that they're often being selective. Some feel that they are being treated unfairly when they don't get their own way. But being just doesn't mean giving people what they want or making them feel important. It's being fair, so it's essential to have an unchanging standard of right and wrong, which can only be found in God's Word, rather than us deciding for ourselves what's fair and what isn't.

God is absolutely just. To Him, everyone is on the same level – all sinners, deserving nothing at all, yet loved equally and perfectly by Him. God doesn't let some people away with certain sins, nor does He have favourites. While we don't have the all-knowing capacity of our Creator, we are still expected to be like Him. How many of us are guilty of preferring some people above others? Of letting people away with certain things? Maybe you could excuse something that your friend says about your little brother, but if the annoying guy who lives two doors down from you said the same thing, you'd never forgive him. Or you're planning to go on a shopping trip with all the girls in your class, but no one has asked the quiet, slightly peculiar girl who sits on her own. She wouldn't want to go anyway, you reason. Maybe you see someone get bullied, but they're usually so insufferable that you don't feel like intervening for fear of what others might think.

Being just isn't easy. It takes courage and conviction, but meditating on 'whatever is just' will keep our minds right, and then our actions will follow.

Whatever is pure.

Philippians 4:8 ESV

Right now, as I'm writing, fluffy flakes of snow are falling outside. While it may seem clichéd, it's easy to see why snow and the concept of purity are inseparably linked, especially when the dull winter landscape is covered by a blanket of white without even a footprint to ruin its perfection. To be pure means to be free from contamination, and, like snow, purity is fragile and can be easily defiled. We might start off the day by reading the Scriptures and praying, but we don't get very far before there's a dirty footprint here, a spray of mud from a passing car there, marring the purity.

Some contamination is unavoidable. We can't help it when someone on the bus uses bad language, or when we are shown adverts that use sin to promote products. Other times we stomp right through that muddy puddle instead of going around it. Or could it be that we even deliberately go out of our way to enjoy the muddy puddle?

Purity can be compromised using almost all of our senses. Our speech can be impure. It's tempting to sink to the same level as others as we talk with them, but God values purity of speech. Purity can be affected by what we listen to – music, podcasts, even other people. We might not be able to hop off a bus mid-journey, but oftentimes we can and must take steps to protect ourselves from impure words. What we see has a huge bearing on our purity. Screens are everywhere, and much of what is available to watch constitutes filth. Guard your eyes! Once you've seen something, it is impossible to unsee it. Take steps to protect yourself, and make sure you don't actively go looking for something which is sure to defile you. The sense of touch takes defilement to a physical level. Don't do anything that you know displeases God, and don't rationalise it. Guard against it, both for your own purity and that of others. God has put standards in place for a very important reason.

But not only should we protect our senses, we should use them to focus and actively meditate on what is pure. Listen to good, biblically sound Christian music, saturate your minds in the Word of God, only watch what is clean and wholesome, and treat others with purity and respect.

Whatever is lovely.
Philippians 4:8 ESV

Of all the qualities that we are to think about, this is likely the one which has most of us scratching our heads! The word 'lovely' is used often in our everyday lives, at least in the part of the world where I live, but it's hard to define without peeking at a dictionary. Vine's Dictionary gives the meaning as 'pleasing' or 'agreeable'[6]. I think we all know people who fit this description – people who are easy to get on with, good to be around, unselfish, and kind. Of course, some might be so eager to be agreeable that they may be as changeable as the tide – one minute agreeing with one person, the next agreeing with someone who holds the opposite opinion. It's possible to disagree with someone, but in an agreeable manner. Honour and justice shouldn't be smothered by loveliness.

We also know people who are the opposite of lovely – those who are disagreeable. No matter what you say to them, it's never right. They're never happy, always grumbling, starting arguments. They're the sort of people who can foul your good mood quicker than an alligator can snap his jaws. When you meet them, it's as if the sun has gone behind a thick, black cloud. Your day is as good as ruined because moving on from an encounter with this type of person is almost impossible.

But God doesn't want us to either be, or think about, disagreeable people. He knows that spending time and mental energy ruminating on them and their difficult ways will only lead to anxious thoughts. We think about what they said, what we said, what we should have said, what we'll say next time, and before we know it, we've spent most of the day wasting good brainpower on a situation which certainly doesn't merit it.

Instead, we are to think about what is agreeable and pleasing. In the Bible, many traits are mentioned which please the Lord, and there many Bible characters who come under the definition of lovely. Spend time with those in your circle of friends, family, or church who are pleasant and agreeable, who help you grow in the Lord and influence you to live for Him. For when we meditate on what is pleasant and spend time with those who are agreeable, we will be transformed into someone who can be called lovely by God.

---

6. *Vine's Dictionary.*

Whatever is commendable.

Philippians 4:8 ESV

Commendable. This has the distinct flavour of a word you might find on a school report – 'Julie's effort in art class this year was very commendable.' But it's not only a word used by teachers, and it can certainly have a much wider application than schoolwork. 'Commendable' means 'to be worthy of praise', or 'well reported of'. Warren Wiersbe, in his commentary on the New Testament, gives the meaning as 'worth talking about'.[7] We will be able to discuss what is commendable without feeling as if we are wasting our time or breath. Dwelling on praiseworthy things is good for us and will build us up spiritually, as well as help to dispel thoughts which aren't helpful.

There is a danger that we might spend too much time thinking about things that are not at all commendable, things which are 'scandalous or dubious'.[8] There's so much out there that isn't worth talking about – all sorts and flavours of sin and scandal. We can't escape out of this world, so at times we're exposed to things that we'd rather avoid. But this doesn't give us licence to dwell on them and churn them over in our minds.

How do we avoid sin and meditate on what is commendable? Why not start with Proverbs 31? There you'll find a number of admirable features about a virtuous woman that all of us, male or female, can take to heart. Make a list of these qualities and see how many you get – there will be quite a number! And when you get to the end of the chapter, you'll see that this truly was a lady who was worthy to be praised and who displayed what was commendable – features well worth thinking and talking about.

7. The *Wiersbe Bible Commentary*.
8. From *Philippians, Colossians, 1&2 Thessalonians* by John Riddle, published by John Ritchie Ltd in 2015.

If there is any excellence, if there is anything worthy of praise...

Philippians 4:8 ESV

As a younger believer, when I read Philippians 4:8 I always thought this line meant that if we received any praise from other people, we shouldn't dwell on it, but instead think about all the qualities we've looked at over the past few days. And while that would be a really good idea, it isn't what this sentence actually means. Instead, these words are more of a summary. It includes the qualities which have already been named in the verse but covers everything that is good and wholesome. Focussing our minds on excellent and praiseworthy things will guard against worry and care, as well as helping us live to please God.

Is there anywhere we can find every single one of these qualities? Any person who perfectly displays each godly feature in their lives? I'm sure your mind is turning to our Lord Jesus Christ. He is the only One who is perfectly true, honourable, just, pure, lovely, and commendable. Not only was He true, He could say in John 14:6, "I am... the truth." His life was absolutely honourable and worthy of all honour – "All men should honour the Son" (John 5:23). Zechariah foretold of the Lord riding into Jerusalem on a donkey. He said, "He is just, and having salvation" (Zechariah 9:9). His purity was evident to the apostle John, who later wrote in a letter, "In Him is no sin" (1 John 3:5). In the Song of Solomon, where we get a picture of the Lord Jesus Christ in all His incomparable beauty and worth, we read, "He is altogether lovely" (Song of Solomon 5:16). And in the book of Revelation, we find the One who is commendable and worthy of all praise – "Worthy is the Lamb that was slain to receive power, and riches, and wisdom, and strength, and honour, and glory, and blessing" (Revelation 5:12).

We could meditate on no better subject than Christ – the One who displays every excellence. Like a precious gem being examined by a jeweller, no matter which aspect of His life and character we view, we will never find a single flaw in Him. Instead, we will discover enough to occupy our minds from now until we are with Him in glory.

Be strong and courageous...
the Lord your God is with you
wherever you go.
Joshua 1:9 ESV

18

JANUARY

What type of person travels by train across two continents in wartime? Who confronts a madman brandishing an axe in a prison? Or what about leading one hundred children over mountains whilst avoiding a cruel enemy? Surely someone strong and tough, with a commanding and fearless presence. Not a tiny, five-foot-tall woman!

Yet this was the very person God used – Gladys Aylward, former parlour maid, uneducated, older than the average missionary trainee, and poor. No missionary society would accept her, except for one on a trial basis, and they then rejected her because she hadn't made sufficient progress in that time. Gladys was on her own, but she still firmly believed that God was calling her to China. "Oh God!" she said. "Here's my Bible. Here's my money. Here's me. Use me, God." For years, Gladys saved money for the fare to China – a train trip right across Europe and Russia. It was a journey fraught with many dangers, but God miraculously brought her to China to work with an old Scottish missionary called Jeannie Lawson. Together they opened the Inn of Eight Happinesses in order to tell the muleteers the good news about Jesus Christ. When Jeannie passed away, Gladys found herself the only British woman for miles, never hearing English spoken.

Gladys agreed to be the inspector of women's feet during the time that the custom of foot binding was being outlawed, so that she could travel around the whole area spreading the message of the gospel. She also began to take in needy children. But when the Japanese arrived, life became more difficult – and terrifying. She was badly mistreated by them, and on one occasion notices were posted offering a reward for her capture.

Her journey over the mountains with around one hundred children took twelve days, with many dangers and obstacles. When they finally made it to safety, Gladys was admitted to hospital and didn't recover for a long time. After the communists gained control of the country, she returned to England, before moving to the non-communist Chinese island of Formosa (now Taiwan) where she passed away at her orphanage at sixty-seven years of age.[9]

This remarkable lady once said, "I am very weak; my courage is only borrowed from Him... I am at peace within, because I know that He never faileth."[10]

---

9. From *Never Say Die – The Story of Gladys Aylward,* by Cyril Davey, published by Lutterworth Press in 1964.
10. https://www.azquotes.com/author/42416-Gladys_Aylward

Be content with such things as ye have.
Hebrews 13:5

Who hasn't looked at someone's pictures on social media and felt at least a touch of envy? It could be over the person's appearance, their brand-new car, their holidays, or any number of covetable possessions and experiences. Our lives can start to feel bland and underwhelming by comparison.

Because we become accustomed to viewing so many details about people's lives, we might think we know more about them than we actually do. It's easy to look at others and assume that their lives are perfect. But don't forget that a picture or video is only a snippet, and there's usually so much more going on underneath the surface.

In social media, many succumb to the temptation of sugar-coating reality. The holiday to the Seychelles that your friend had this summer might have looked amazing, but what you don't know is that her parents are at the point of getting a divorce and each day in paradise was accompanied by angry words and frosty stares.

Or maybe that popular, outgoing guy who loves to show off the results of his bodybuilding is actually terribly insecure beneath his toned exterior and perfect image.

The sparkling, brand-new car makes for a pretty picture, but it's no good sitting in the drive, while the owner keeps on failing his or her driving test!

And even if others' pictures do show reality, we still aren't to give in to envy. Next time we scroll through social media and find ourselves wishing that we have what someone else has, let's give ourselves a little reminder to be content. God knows us better than we know ourselves and He has given us everything we need. Joy is not found in possessions or experiences. Instead, it is found in Christ. After all, if we have Him, nothing else really matters.

I will praise Thee; for I am
fearfully and wonderfully made.
Psalm 139:14

As an optometrist, I may be biased, but I'm convinced that the eye has to be the most amazing organ in the human body. This fragile little globe gives us the ability to view our surroundings in great detail and in vivid colour. And right at the very front of the eye is a small, clear film called the cornea, which is a little over one centimetre in diameter. This important structure refracts light to help us focus and also protects what's inside the eye.

The cornea has five layers which are made up of different types of cells and collagen fibrils. The epithelium, the outside layer, consists of cells with a fantastic ability to regenerate, which helps prevent scarring. The middle layer, the stroma, is the one I'm especially in awe of. Think about it – despite all those cells, fibrils and other components, the cornea is perfectly clear! This is due in part to the uniform, orderly arrangement of the collagen fibrils in the stroma. If they were thrown in there any old way, we'd never be able to see clearly.

Have you ever poked yourself in the eye? You'll have discovered that the cornea also has an extremely high concentration of nerves. They are there for your eye's protection, along with a lightning-fast blink reflex when something comes towards you.

No one has ever been able to even come close to developing a fully functional human eye, yet our Creator knew exactly how to form the dust of the earth in such a way that His creation would have the privilege and precious gift of sight.

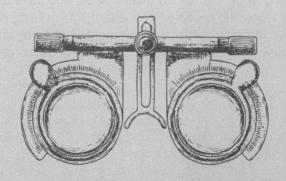

He is not afraid of bad news; his heart is firm, trusting in the Lord.

Psalm 112:7 ESV

Are you a worrier? Someone who is scared of what they're going to hear next? If so, I completely understand. After all, this world is an uncertain sort of place, and anything can happen. It's easy for our hearts to tremble and for us to give way to 'what ifs'. Perhaps you worry about exam results, and whether or not you will be able to continue with a subject or get accepted on to that university course. Maybe you can't decide which career path you should follow, and you're worrying that you will make wrong choices. Or you have a job that provides much-needed income and you're afraid you'll be told that you aren't needed anymore. Maybe you have worries about health – yours or that of a family member.

In the verse at the top of the page, we read about a man who isn't afraid of bad news. Just imagine! He's able to go through life without worrying about what he's going to hear next. What's his secret? Is it because he's wealthy, so he doesn't need to worry about money? Or does his family have a great doctor, so health problems aren't a cause for concern? Actually, it's neither of these things. His secret is his trust in the Lord! This man's heart is firm, fixed, and steady. It doesn't falter. He knows that the Lord is able to be trusted and he's happy to have full confidence in Him.

But does that mean that our reason for being unafraid is the knowledge that the Lord will keep anything bad from happening to us? Not at all! The Lord is absolutely able to preserve us from problems, and many, many times He does so, but nowhere in the Bible has God promised us continuously smooth seas and sunny, trouble-free days. Instead, He has promised to be with us, no matter what. God loves us dearly, so we needn't worry. He knows what is ahead, and nothing is out of His control. Like the man in the verse, we ought not to be afraid of bad news, because our hearts can be firm, trusting in the Lord.

O the depth of the riches both of the wisdom and knowledge of God!

Romans 11:33

I think we'd all agree that, as believers, knowing God is vitally important. But do you know *why* it is so important to learn what the Scriptures say about Him?

First of all, God is our Creator, and the One who loves us and gave His Son to save us. We are going to be with Him for all eternity. If there was no other reason than simply to know the One who did so much for us, this would be enough. To know Him is to lift our hearts in worship to Him. The more we know of Him, the more cause we have to *praise Him* and bring glory to Him.

We shouldn't need convincing that God is great. We know He is perfect. Therefore, being like Him and conformed to Him – walking in His ways and developing godly characteristics – should be the goal of every believer. The better we know God, the more we will learn how we should behave and act to *become like Him*.

God's characteristics are also a great encouragement to His children. We can take comfort from attributes such as His love, His mercy, His faithfulness, His omniscience. God is who He is, whether we know about His attributes or not, but the more we know, the deeper our *trust in Him* will be.

Knowing God will also affect our *service for Him*. We will learn what is important to Him, and what we ought to be focussing and spending our time on. We will discover His values and learn to see things from His perspective. Emulating our Creator will affect our treatment of other people, both saved and unsaved.

So, as you come across readings in this book which talk about the character of God, please take time to meditate upon them, and allow each characteristic to affect your worship, your walk, your trust, and your time.

And they glorified God in me.

Galatians 1:24

While reading your Bible, you probably come across words such as 'glory' and 'glorify'. But what do they actually mean? W. E. Vine, in his great Bible dictionary, says that glory is 'the honour resulting from a good opinion', and that 'magnify', 'extol', and 'praise' are words which help to give the meaning of 'glorify'.[11] It's certainly not an easy word to get your head around!

Many of the references in the Bible are to do with giving glory to God, so, amongst other things, praising Him will bring Him glory. But there are other times when the Bible instructs us to cause others to glorify God. I have to admit that this has often made me pause. How does this work in everyday life?

I once heard a short sentence in a Bible teaching meeting which helped me understand how we can bring glory to God in our everyday lives. It was this – 'We are here on earth to make God look great!' Think about that for a moment. God has left us here, on this earth, to show Him as He is in His greatness!

Of course, we know that God is great. Our actions cannot alter the sure fact of God's greatness. But what we do, or don't do, on this earth can cause others to view God in a certain light. Think for a moment about the Lord Jesus Christ. He said in John 17:4 that He had glorified God on the earth: He had finished the work God gave Him to do. He was obedient to His Father's will. He had showed the character of God, and given mankind a glimpse of the Divine. He glorified God.

This is what we have been asked to do. How does that look for you? Maybe it's showing kindness to someone who isn't really all that loveable. Maybe it's taking those taunts and sneers patiently and without retaliation. Maybe it's being obedient when being obedient isn't very popular. In other words, it's being like Christ.

As you go through the day and face all the challenges ahead, remember why you're here on earth – you're here to glorify God, as the Lord Jesus Christ did.

---

11. *Vine's Dictionary.*

He no longer should live... in the flesh to the lusts of men, but to the will of God.

1 Peter 4:2

24

JANUARY

Believe it or not, tomorrow is Opposite Day – the day when you can apparently say and do the opposite of everything you mean. You can wear your clothes inside out or back to front and choose two different shoes! You can even walk backwards if you decide to risk it!

Did you know that, for a Christian, every day is opposite day? Not in the sense that we say the opposite of what we mean – that's never good! – or that we go around looking as if we've dressed in a hurry in the dark – that's not good either! – but because that, when we trusted Christ, our lives changed dramatically. When we got saved, we repented of our sin. This means we changed our minds about how good we thought we were, and agreed with God that we were nothing but guilty sinners who only deserved eternal punishment. We acknowledged that God is right, and we were wrong. And we *still* believe that God is right.

This belief will affect every aspect of our lives – our thoughts, our speech, our actions, our habits. Those who have never trusted Christ often live for themselves. A little further on in the chapter from which I've quoted, we find a list of actions and habits that unsaved people may indulge in – things like promiscuity, drunkenness, and idolatry. Peter goes on to say that these people will think it strange when we don't join in with them 'in the same flood of debauchery' (1 Peter 4:4 ESV), and they will speak evil of us.

Maybe you've already felt the sharp edge of evil speaking. It's not easy. We long to fit in with everyone else, especially when we're young, and we soon discover that choosing God's way can often be a lonely path. It will mean refusing to attend certain events where promiscuity and drunkenness will be present – I had to do that when I was your age. It could mean spending less time with certain people. It will involve controlling what we watch or listen to. It will probably cost us, and it will probably hurt, but let us never forget why we are doing it – because it is the will of God. He notices, and it pleases Him.

Pride goeth before destruction, and an haughty spirit before a fall.

Proverbs 16:18

On this day in 1759, Scottish poet Robert Burns was born. Over his short and colourful lifetime, he wrote hundreds of poems and other literary works which have resonated with many people, whether Scottish or not. At school, we had to learn the last verse of *To a Louse*, which I've never forgotten.

Much of the poem is addressed in indignation to a louse which is crawling on a lady's bonnet in church. How dare the louse set foot on such a fine lady! Surely the place for this loathsome creature is in a beggar's hovel. But the creature climbs higher and higher, not content until it reaches the very top of the bonnet. What an obnoxiously proud little insect!

The penultimate verse addresses the lady herself, who is proudly tossing her head, oblivious to the progress of the louse climbing up her hat. People are pointing and staring, but she doesn't seem to notice – or if she does, she thinks they are only admiring her beauty.

Burns finishes off with a warning. Would that God would give us the power to see ourselves as others see us! For if our eyes were opened, we'd be preserved from a lot of folly and mistakes. We certainly wouldn't be so tempted to put on airs.

Burns wasn't a Christian – a quick glimpse at his life story will tell you that – but the truth contained in this poem echoes what the Bible has to say about pride. Both the louse and the lady suffered from a great deal of pride. Neither realised how others were really viewing them – one with revulsion, the other with mockery and amusement. While we shouldn't have the mistaken belief that we are worthless, it certainly does no harm to step back sometimes and take a look at ourselves through the eyes of others. If we persist in putting on airs, thinking we're somebody important, we might discover like the lady in the poem, that, while it might not involve a louse, God often has a way of letting us be brought right down to size.

"You'll never guess what Ethan did this summer!" Lucy whispered.

"What was it? Tell me!" Her friend's eyes grew large with anticipation.

Is there anyone who hasn't been in this situation, either as the one passing along information, or the one receiving it? Human nature loves to hear news about other people, especially things that we know the person would rather no one knew about. The wise man who wrote this proverb got it right – gossip is like a delicious morsel, maybe a rich, smooth Belgian chocolate truffle. The problem is that, like chocolate, gossip won't satisfy us, and it's not good for us either.

Although there are times when things have to be brought out into the open and someone held to account, these aren't very frequent. Much of what we listen to is either a story which has been made up to discredit the person, a skewed version of a true event, or an account of a failing which is really none of our business.

Have you ever been told something about someone which you really didn't think was true? What they were supposed to have done was completely at odds with what you knew of the person's character. And yet, no matter how much you tried, you couldn't quite dismiss the nagging feeling that perhaps the person who shared the gossip was right. You struggled to have the same respect for that person. Gossip hurts the teller and the listener, and especially the victim.

So how can you prevent hearing gossip without resorting to sticking your fingers in your ears? Firstly, try not to gossip yourself. People who spread news are less likely to share with those who don't participate in the same activity. If someone does launch into a juicy story in your presence, show no interest at all. They won't get the satisfaction of an intrigued response. Changing the subject is a good idea, or you can stop them before they get too far in their tale and, in a pleasant way, tell them you'd rather not hear anything that doesn't directly affect you.

Indulging in gossip doesn't please God. Let's resolve to only listen to wholesome words. They're much better for us!

A whisperer separates the best of friends.

Proverbs 16:28 NKJV

Yesterday we overheard Lucy begin to tell her friend some gossip about Ethan. I hope we walked away rather than trying to hear any more. Gossip hurts, as we can see from our verse – separating even the best of friends. But haven't many of us been tempted to whisper some interesting nugget to another person?

Why do we love to gossip so much? The main reason is that it makes us feel good. If we discredit someone else, we make ourselves look better. We also love to feel popular, the centre of attention. We might not know if there's any truth to the story, but the reaction we get is worth it. At its root, gossip is a very self-centred activity.

During the school holidays, my brothers and I often went to stay with our aunt and uncle on their farm. We loved it and felt very much at home there, chatting away about anything and everything. I'm not sure what I'd been talking about, but one day, when I was in my teens, my aunt told me that before I said anything, I should pass my words through three sieves. The first – Is it true? The second – Is it needful? The third – Is it kind?

I once made crab apple jelly. It's a long, drawn-out process involving boiling the little apples and then straining the mixture through a fine cloth. The skin, seeds, and pulp get left behind and the clear, red-orange juice drips into the bowl. This is then turned into a jelly-type jam. What would have happened if I'd decided to skip the straining step? Can you imagine spreading the jelly on your pancake and finding some seeds, or skin, or even a stem? It wouldn't be very pleasant.

Our words about others need to go through the same type of process to take out all the hard bits, the sharp bits, and the generally unpleasant bits. Only the clear things – that which is true, needful, and kind – will go through. So, today, when we're tempted to say something about someone else, let's get those sieves and put them to good use!

David and Goliath – names which many people, even those without a Christian background, instantly recognise. The story of how the lad David, with only a sling and stone, defeated the armed and experienced giant warrior, is one that many people know. Perhaps they recognise some weakness and smallness in themselves, so they enjoy a story where the 'underdog' wins.

Did you notice I put 'underdog' in inverted commas? You see, David wasn't really the underdog. Instead, he was in the majority, with a mighty force behind him. But I'm getting ahead of myself! Let's go back to the beginning of the story.

We learn of David when the prophet Samuel was sent to a man called Jesse to anoint one of his sons to be the next king. One by one, Jesse's sons passed before Samuel, but the Lord had not chosen any of these tall, strapping, handsome men. After all seven of them had been refused, Samuel asked Jesse if there were any more. There was – the youngest, who was keeping the sheep. Jesse hadn't even thought it worthwhile to bring him.

In those days, the oldest in the family was most important – he would be the one to receive special blessings – so you can imagine how insignificant son number eight would be! David had been given the task of keeping the sheep, a menial job back then. But he was the one God had chosen to be the next king. To say that God had big things in store for David would have been an understatement.

Yet, after this anointing, David went right back to keeping sheep. You'd have thought his lowly job would have been assigned to someone else, and he'd have been brought home and given special treatment until his time to reign. Instead, he was humble and submissive, content to wait God's time. He didn't walk around with an air of self-importance or a look-at-me attitude. In many ways, David reminds me of the Lord Jesus. While here on earth, He was greater than people realised, yet He exhibited perfect humility and submission to His Father. Humility ought to characterise believers. It doesn't come easily, yet God appreciates it in His people.

Who is this uncircumcised Philistine, that he should defy the armies of the living God?

1 Samuel 17:26

Philistines were fierce, and the fiercest of all was their champion, Goliath. He was huge, heavily armed, and undefeated – not someone you would want to provoke! Morning and evening, he roared across the valley, "Give me a man, that we may fight together." Who would go? Forty days went by, but no one responded.

One day, David's father sent him to the camp with food for his brothers. David heard the words of the enemy. I know what I'd have thought: 'If none of the tough soldiers in this army are able to fight the giant, well, I'm certainly not the person to do it.' But David was different. Instead of hearing the words of the giant as a challenge to the army, he recognised that Goliath was despising the living God. His desire to fight for God overrode any fear he may have had and eclipsed any ambition for earthly gain. David's chief concern was that God would be glorified. He was righteously indignant that Goliath would dare to attempt to undermine the greatness of God.

God doesn't need anyone to defend Him. In fact, He could easily have dealt with Goliath without using David. Instead, He chose to use him to bring glory to Himself. Throughout our lives, there will be times when God chooses to use us. Some of these times may, as in the case of David's fight with Goliath, be in a very public role. We need to be sure that our motivation is not that we will get glory for ourselves. Like David, our chief concern should be the glory of God.

That's not to say it will all go well, and everyone will be right behind us. Read verse 28 to see what Eliab, one of David's older brothers, said! You'd think that a member of his own family would support him, wouldn't you? When you do something for God, you will receive opposition from many sources – sometimes even from fellow believers. I'm sure if David had known the hymn, he'd have sung, 'Misunderstood by all, I dare to do what Thine own heart would prize.'[12] Yet he didn't let the opposition stop him, but moved on, confident that what he was doing would please God.

---

12. *The Sorrows of the Daily Life*, author unknown.

Thy servant kept his father's sheep.

1 Samuel 17:34

Do you remember two days ago we learned that, after David was anointed, he went back to keeping sheep? It certainly wasn't an occupation we'd have expected a king to have. Future kings should be winning great victories on the battlefield, or leading their people, not being out in the wilderness with the sheep! But we also learned that God had a great purpose for David. He *would* become a great leader and have many victories in battle. We're about to discover that those years David spent in obscurity in the wilderness with the sheep were also in God's plan.

Maybe you feel that there is something great that you would like to do for God, but for whatever reason, you're unable to. Maybe your everyday life – school, work, gatherings of your local church, household chores – seems humdrum and boring, and not very worthwhile. Keep going! If the years in the wilderness proved anything about David, it was his faithfulness to God. God greatly values faithfulness. Luke 16:10 says that he that is faithful in that which is least is faithful also in much. David proved that those who are faithful in little things show they can be trusted with the big things too.

Something else David learned in the years of obscurity was how to prove God. In the passage, we discover that he'd fought with a lion and a bear. Shepherding wasn't all sitting on a rock, playing a harp, while the sheep calmly grazed close by – it was a life-or-death matter! And now there was a greater enemy. The safety of the whole nation of Israel was at stake, not only that of one little lamb. Could David do it? Could he defeat the enemy? Let's listen to what he's saying – "The Lord that delivered me out of the paw of the lion, and out of the paw of the bear, *He will deliver me out of the hand of this Philistine.*" Why was David so sure that God would deliver him? Because David had proved God in the years in the wilderness. He'd learned that God was able to deliver.

And so it will be with you and me. Those times when we feel hidden and insignificant can be times of pleasing God, of preparing for a future day, and of proving God by learning more about Him.

The battle is the Lord's.
1 Samuel 17:47

It was settled. David, although young and inexperienced in battle, would rise to Goliath's challenge and deliver Israel. But first he needed kitted out; he couldn't possibly go dressed as he was! Armour, a helmet, and a sword would be needed: that's the way it was always done. But it didn't take David long to realise it was never going to work. David had proved God, but he hadn't proved Saul's armour. Gaining the victory isn't a one-size-fits-all approach. What might have worked for Saul wouldn't work for David. After all, David had something better than manmade armour – he had the presence of the Lord.

It can be tempting to look at other people, especially those who seem to be more experienced in battle, and rather than turning to God's Word for ourselves, attempt to copy their methods against the enemy. There was nothing borrowed about David's confidence – he had proved God himself, and he was leaning solely on Him. We can only win victories by the power of God.

David had confidence in the Lord. Notice in verse 48 how he *ran toward* the army to meet Goliath. When Goliath saw him, he sneered. Victory would be certain and far too easy, he thought. He was insulted. But Goliath's vision was deficient. He saw a young man, probably in his teens, with no armour or sword. His eyes were blind to the sight of the great God of Israel, the One who had delivered David in the past and would deliver him again. In our day, we often meet people with poor vision. Not physical vision, but spiritual. The world looks at believers and sees a feeble people with strange, outdated views and beliefs. Despite the scorn we may face, never forget that we have the mighty God with us. The story isn't over yet.

Goliath's end came swiftly. The giant never expected that a small stone would bring him down, or that the young man would use Goliath's own sword to take off his head. Before it had properly begun, the battle was over, and victory had been won. Why? Because David knew this wasn't his battle – he was only a tool in the hand of the Lord. This battle was the Lord's, and He would have the victory.

FEBRUARY

Then they that gladly received his word were baptized...

Acts 2:41

Who's up for learning some Greek today? Just one word, and it's not too difficult, I promise! It's the word βαπτισμα – baptisma, in our alphabet. And if you're thinking that it's very like an English word that you're familiar with, you're right! It comes from the word 'bapto', which means 'to dip', and it's where we get our English word 'baptism'.[13] When we dip something in liquid, it is immersed and lifted out. In a similar way, to be baptised is to be put completely under the water and brought out again.

Who should be baptised? Let's take a look at our verse for today. In this chapter, Peter has been preaching the gospel. He has told his audience of the death and resurrection of the Lord Jesus Christ and has preached that they must repent. Those who accepted the message of the gospel and have been saved are now baptised. Baptism is not necessary for salvation (for example, the thief on the cross beside the Lord Jesus never had any opportunity to be baptised, yet the Lord assured him he would be in heaven), but in the Bible it is expected that all believers are baptised.

Why should we be baptised? Firstly, because God commands it. If we refuse, we are being disobedient. But there is a deeper significance to baptism that we can't miss. If we turn to Romans 6:3-4, we learn something really important about baptism. Baptism is a picture of the death, burial, and resurrection of the Lord Jesus Christ, so when we are baptised, we are identifying ourselves with Him. We are showing to others that when we were saved, we died with Christ, we were buried with Christ, and we rose with Christ. Look at the end of verse 4 – we are raised to walk in newness of life. When we got saved, our lives changed. I was baptised as a teenager, and I was often told that baptism is 'an outward sign of an inward change.' Life doesn't change after baptism; it already changed at conversion.

When should we be baptised? The Bible says that it should be after salvation, and it gives no more guidance than that. Christians in the New Testament certainly didn't wait very long. The Philippian jailor in Acts 16 was baptised the very night he was saved. What about you? Have you been baptised yet?

---

13. *Vine's Dictionary.*

Unto Him that is able to do exceeding abundantly above all that we ask or think.

Ephesians 3:20

FEBRUARY

2

Have you ever been disappointed in someone? Maybe they promised you they would do something, and you were so excited, but then they didn't follow through. The oftener it happens, the lower our expectations become until we sometimes wonder if there's anyone out there who can keep their word.

God is not like that. When God says He'll do something, He does it – you can always depend on Him. He is faithful and trustworthy and will never go back on His word.

But there's more. Often, we ask God for certain things, and He kindly and graciously grants our request. Then there are occasions when He gives us far more than we asked for. More, in fact, than we ever dreamed! Maybe a tricky situation from which you could see no easy way out was resolved in the most miraculous way. Or you might have asked for help to scrape a pass on a test in your worst subject... and instead of merely passing, you ended up with a fantastic grade.

Take a moment to consider – have you ever been in any situations where God did exceeding abundantly above all that you asked or even thought? I have, many times. Once, when I was training to be an optometrist, I had to attend a course in a large city in England. This meant taking a flight, then travelling from the airport to the hotel by myself. I'd rarely travelled on my own before and I was nervous. So much could go wrong! But not only did I arrive safely, God arranged for a fellow student to be on the same flight *and* staying in the same hotel! I wasn't alone after all. And there have been numerous similar instances of God's love and care for me.

We sometimes allow our let-downs by human beings to influence how we view God, but we should never, ever underestimate Him. He is a gracious God and loves to display grace and kindness to His children. He is able!

Pray for the peace of Jerusalem: they shall prosper that love thee.

Psalm 122:6

Corrie ten Boom is a name that many people instantly recognise. She was a Dutch lady who, along with some of her family members, was arrested and sent to a concentration camp for hiding Jews during World War II. After her miraculous release, she travelled the world, telling people about her experiences and how she was able to forgive those who had treated her so badly.

You may not have heard of her father – a truly courageous hero. Casper ten Boom was a very old, snowy-bearded gentleman when the war broke out. He had been brought up in a home that had a deep love for the Jewish people. His father had started a prayer meeting many years before, to pray for Jews and for Jerusalem, as the Scriptures command.

When the opportunity arose to shelter Jews, Casper had no hesitation in playing his part. People told him that he should stop having Jews in his house as he would be sent to prison, but he replied that it would be an honour to give his life for God's ancient people, the Jews.

When the family was arrested, Casper was given the chance to go free if he gave his word that he wouldn't cause any more trouble. His reply – "If I go home today, tomorrow I will open my door again to any man in need who knocks."

Casper died ten days after he was arrested. He became ill and was transferred to hospital, where he died alone and unknown in a corridor, before being buried in an unmarked pauper's grave. But his soul made its swift flight to glory, right into the presence of his Saviour, the Lord Jesus Christ, the Jew who gave His life for Casper long before Casper gave his life for the Jews.[14]

---

14. The story of the ten Boom family and the part they played in saving the lives of Jews in the Netherlands during World War II is told in *The Hiding Place* by Corrie ten Boom, published by Hodder and Stoughton in 1972.

> If we say that we have no sin,
> we deceive ourselves.
>
> 1 John 1:8

Do you remember the joy you had when you first trusted Christ and were saved? Remember how glad you were to know that your sins were all forgiven, and that you were sure of being in heaven forever? Wanting to live to please God because He'd given His Son to die on the cross for you? But then do you remember, sooner or later, doing something wrong? Maybe you told a lie, had a spiteful thought, lashed out at your brother or sister, or were cheeky to your parents. You were probably filled with a great deal of remorse, and maybe even shock. As a Christian, you didn't think you would, or even could, sin like that anymore. You might even have begun to doubt whether you were really saved or not.

I know how you feel; the same thing happened to me. Sadly, when we got saved, we didn't become perfect. Believers are new creations in Christ (2 Corinthians 5:17), and we have the Holy Spirit indwelling us to help us, but the flesh, that which responds to temptation to sin, is still very much there. When we get to heaven, we will be like Christ and we won't struggle with sin ever again, but here on earth it's a different story. Look at the verse at the top of this page!

So what happens when we sin? First of all, it's good to remember that when Christ died for our sins, He died for them *all* – past, present, and future. They are all forgiven, and we will never be punished for them. But not only did the Lord Jesus Christ take the penalty for our sins, 1 John 2:1 tells us that He is an Advocate for us with the Father. An advocate is someone who pleads for someone else. When we sin, communion with God is broken. But when we confess our sins, communion with God is restored. We are cleansed from all unrighteousness (1 John 1:9).

Love ye therefore the stranger: for ye were strangers in the land of Egypt.

Deuteronomy 10:19

When I changed schools from primary to secondary, a couple of weeks before my twelfth birthday, I was taken aback by the attitude of the older pupils to the 'first years', as we were known back then. We were treated with disdain. Some scathingly called us 'the wee first years', and I even found scrawled on a desk the words 'I hate first year people!' Of course, I took all of this personally, even though I had no idea who wrote the words or what prompted them.

When I was learning to drive, I faced the same contempt from a handful of other drivers. Being in control of a car on a public road can be daunting enough without other cars driving closely behind you, or zipping past with hardly a moment's notice.

You'll each have your own experiences when you've been the newbie and others have been less than patient. Or maybe right now you're feeling convicted because you know that you're not being very kind to others who are in a place where you once were.

In the above verse, God tells the Israelites to be kind to the strangers. He reminds them that they were once strangers. They had known what it was to be different from others, away from home, and out of their comfort zone. It's not always easy putting yourself in someone else's shoes, especially if that person's situation or background is very different from your own. But when you've actually owned those shoes and walked in them yourself, it should be much easier to show sympathy and kindness. Don't forget what you went through, when you were where they are now – how you felt, what you thought, what your fears were. Be kind, be helpful, and be patient.

The human body is totally amazing! No matter which body part or system you learn about, you'll always come across facts which are mind-blowing. Take DNA, for instance. You probably learned about it in school, but have you stopped to really think about it?

DNA is present in the nucleus of each of our trillions of cells and consists of two strands which are wound together in a spiral. If the DNA in one tiny cell was unravelled, it would stretch over two metres in length, and the combined length of all the DNA in your body would reach from the earth to the sun and back six hundred times. The four chemical bases that DNA contains are found in different combinations, and this gives us our unique code.

DNA contains all the information needed for development, survival, and reproduction. That's a vast amount of data! A sample of DNA the size of a pinhead contains so much information that, if it was put in books, it would take one million million of them to hold it all (and no, that isn't a typo!). Technology today is more advanced than our ancestors could have imagined, yet not even the most brilliant and clever people have ever invented anything that can compare to DNA.

An interesting fact about DNA is that, due to a number of factors, it cannot survive in natural environments longer than ten thousand years, yet intact strands of DNA have been found in dinosaur fossils which were supposedly much older than that. It looks like the world isn't as old as many people say after all!

But where did DNA come from in the first place? If it had evolved, so many errors would have arisen that it would never have survived. Therefore, it had to have been created, or not exist at all. And it was created! We have been intricately designed and carefully created by our all-wise, all-powerful God.[15]

15. Some of the information here is found in *Creation's Story* by Robert W. Cargill. This book is full of fascinating facts about God's amazing creation and was published by John Ritchie Ltd in 2008. Material is also based on presentation notes from the Apologetics Conference (2019) at Hebron Gospel Hall, Bicester, by David Vallance. The audio and powerpoint presentation can be accessed at https://hebrongospelhall.org/sermons/dna-design-60-min/

I am the Lord, I change not.

Malachi 3:6

We humans are so changeable. Our moods, behaviours, attitudes, and appearance all change, sometimes on a daily basis. Over time we may even find that once strongly held opinions or convictions have changed. None of us stays the same.

God is the very opposite. The verse at the top of the page is one of many in the Bible which speak of God's immutability, or changelessness. The psalmist in Psalm 102:27 says, 'Thou art the same.' God does not and cannot change. As He always was, He always will be. In future days we will learn about other attributes of God, including His righteousness, His mercy, His love, and His wrath. His characteristic of changelessness means that none of His other attributes change either.

However, while God doesn't change, you might be wondering why God's dealings with people seem to change. For example, in the Old Testament, He commands the Israelites to slay certain wicked nations, yet in the New Testament, the Lord Jesus instructs us to turn the other cheek. But have God's attributes changed? Absolutely not! In one we see His righteousness, in the other we see His mercy and grace. God's ways of dealing with people differ for many reasons, but His character cannot change.

And what about the references in the Bible to God repenting, or relenting? Isn't this changing? Let's think about the story of Jonah. Jonah was sent to warn the wicked Assyrian nation of the judgment which was to fall on them for their sin, but when the people heard the message, they repented, and so God spared the nation. Did God change? Of course not! Instead, the people of Nineveh changed. God's righteousness was seen in His impending judgment, but His mercy was seen in the withholding of that judgment. For God to have punished the Assyrians even though they had repented would have been inconsistent with His character.

God's immutability is something that we can rejoice in as believers. With some people, we never quite know where we stand from day to day – not so with God. What He was yesterday, He is today, and will be tomorrow. His promises will never be changed or revoked, so we can have full and absolute confidence in what we read in His Word.

How sweet are Thy words unto
my taste! yea, sweeter than
honey to my mouth!

Psalm 119:103

FEBRUARY

8

Trudi is our liver and white, extremely exuberant, and somewhat immature springer spaniel. She is full of energy and there's nothing she loves better than running through muddy fields, nose down, sniffing out birds or other wildlife. Except, perhaps, for food. Trudi *loves* her food. And our food. And everyone else's food. The problem is that if we gave her everything she wanted, she'd be too roly-poly to run anymore. So, for her own good, we give her the right amount of dog food for her size, along with the odd little treat. A balanced diet.

How's your diet? I'm not talking about your physical diet, but about your spiritual one. What are you feeding on? In the human world, sugary foods tend to make us feel full without proper nourishment. A diet of certain movies, songs, books, or even spending time messaging friends may seem to give us momentary fulfilment, but instead what it may really be doing is causing us to lose our appetite for wholesome food. Be honest, after watching that movie, did you feel like praying? Have you noticed the Word of God losing its appeal after you spend time on social media?

I try to monitor Trudi's weight and adjust her food accordingly. When her diet isn't right, she puts on weight, and hasn't the same level of energy. Is your diet doing the same? As far as living for God is concerned, how's your energy level? Could it be that indulging in 'junk food' is causing you to become lethargic and not so energetic in your walk with God?

The difference between you and Trudi is that she can't make rational decisions for herself – she'd choose the tasty bacon rind every time. But you can. So next time you go to watch a movie, or select your favourite playlist, pause and consider. Is what I'm about to consume junk food or wholesome food? Will it help me or hinder me in my Christian life?

Behold, He that keepeth
Israel shall neither
slumber nor sleep.

Psalm 121:4

The more I read my Bible, the more divine paradoxes I come across. (In case you're not sure what I mean, a paradox is a logical statement that seems to contradict itself.) Throughout the Bible, we learn a lot about God. Take, for instance, the verse at the top of the page. Here we learn that God never sleeps but is always attentive and watchful over those He loves. But then we turn to the New Testament and read the story of the storm, when the Lord Jesus Christ was asleep on a pillow in the hinder part of the ship. We know that He is God. God does not slumber or sleep. Yet the Lord Jesus slept!

Many people get muddled when they think about the Lord Jesus' humanity and deity. Some think that He was part man and part God, and they attempt to assign His various actions either to His humanity or to His deity. Some even outright deny that He was God at all! There are many other errors which we wouldn't be wise to dwell on. Instead, we should focus on the truth – that the Lord Jesus Christ is fully human, yet without sin, and fully God. When He was sleeping in that boat, He was no less God than He ever was, and so was still watching over the distraught disciples.

So how do we know that the Lord Jesus was absolutely God and absolutely human? There are many passages you can turn to, but to start you off, here are some verses, all from different chapter twos, which show His deity and humanity. 'Christ Jesus... did not consider it robbery to be equal with God, but made Himself of no reputation... coming in the likeness of men' (Philippians 2:5-7 NKJV). 'In Him dwells all the fullness of the Godhead bodily' (Colossians 2:9 NKJV). 'Inasmuch then as the children have partaken of flesh and blood, He Himself likewise shared in the same' (Hebrews 2:14 NKJV).

Can you fully understand this – how He can be God, with all the power and majesty of deity, yet taking a physical body, with all its limitations? Neither can I. Yet while it's outside the limits of our earthbound minds, it doesn't change the reality, or the reason for His coming – to save you and me!

We must not... grumble.

1 Corinthians 10:9,10 ESV

There are four commands in this little section. The first has to do with idolatry. We don't bow down to idols, so we give ourselves a little pat on the back. Immorality? That's not really our way of life either, nor do we consider that we put Christ to the test. We're feeling pretty good about this checklist. But then we read that we must not grumble. Oh dear. Now, that's a different story!

I don't believe that we're as justified in feeling that we're doing okay with the three previous instructions as we might think (not all idolatry involves little figurines, for instance), but when we're told not to grumble, I'm sure that most of us feel greatly convicted. Grumbling seems to be a common trait of human beings, right from the very beginning of life – babies do cry a lot, don't they? And have you ever met a toddler who didn't whine about something ridiculous – square sandwiches versus triangles, for example?! Old people like to tell you all about their aches and pains, and the rest of us? Well, you know what you like to grumble about – homework, parents, not having enough money. I've my own list of grumble-inducers too.

The danger with grumbling is that, as with the children of Israel, we tend to grumble about things that God has very intentionally given us or has withheld from us. The Israelites grumbled about the food in the wilderness, contrasting it with the Egyptian food they'd enjoyed, and they grumbled about their leader, Moses – all things that God had put in place for their blessing.

Because God has ordained everything for our blessing and growth, when we grumble, we are grumbling about what God is doing. We think that we know better than God, and we are actually accusing Him of being less than loving, kind, and just. How serious!

There will be times when we face difficult situations and need to talk through them with someone. But for each of these occasions, there are probably many more times when all we are doing is indulging in whining, which cannot and will not bring glory to God. So next time we feel like grumbling, instead, let's accept the situation as part of God's wise plan for our growth and His glory.

I have surely seen... and have heard... I know their sorrows.

Exodus 3:7

Suri dropped her head, letting her hair shield her face, and tried to blink back hot tears. She didn't know what she had done to cause Cassidy and her friends to be so nasty to her. She always tried to keep a low profile and be polite to everybody, so why they had picked on her, she couldn't understand. It wasn't even what they said. Most of the time, her name was never mentioned. It was all so devious that she knew she'd have trouble proving to anyone that she was the object of their mockery. In fact, when she'd tried to explain it to Dad last night, he had told her to cheer up, that she was only imagining things. There was no one – no one at all – who understood her situation...

"Be quiet!" Aunt Em said as Carl stepped through the door. "Your mum had a really difficult day, but she's finally sleeping, so don't disturb her." Carl slid off his shoes and grabbed a packet of chocolate biscuits from the kitchen before tiptoeing upstairs. Ever since his mum's cancer diagnosis last year, life had been a nightmare. Her numerous appointments, hospital stays, and the side effects of treatment hadn't left her with much time or energy for all the things that mums normally do. He missed normal. He missed her chatting to him after school about his day, planning fun outings for the school holidays, helping him with his homework. He even missed her scolding him about the state of his bedroom. And, to devastate him totally, she wasn't going to get better. His friends tried to be nice to him, but they didn't understand. Life would never be the same, and there wasn't one thing he could do about it...

Maybe you are going through a very tough time right now, and you feel like Suri or Carl – that no one really understands. But take heart – no matter how awful you feel, there is One who knows all about it. He cared about the Israelites when they were in bondage for four hundred years in Egypt. He sees what you are going through, He has heard your cry, and He understands – perfectly! Run to Him – the God of all comfort – pour out your heart to Him and lean all your weight on Him. He cares *so much* for you!

The king held out to Esther the golden sceptre that was in his hand.

Esther 5:2

12

FEBRUARY

Esther took a deep breath and stepped through the doorway. The king, regal and resplendent on his throne, hadn't yet noticed her. Dressed in her royal robes, and with the prayers and fasting of all the Jews in the city taking place on her behalf, she waited. What she was doing was extremely risky. It was a known fact that to arrive unannounced in the king's presence could mean death. Unless the king held out the golden sceptre to her, she would die. But her message was so important that she had to take the risk.

After what probably seemed like an age to Esther, the king looked up. Would he hold out the sceptre, or would this spell the end for the beautiful Jewish girl who had miraculously become queen? For one heart-stopping moment, he paused, then lifted the sceptre and held it out to her. In relief, Esther moved forward and touched the top of it. She was safe. The king would now listen to her petition.

Each time I read this story, I can't help but think of the contrast between the Persian ruler and the mighty God of all the universe. Ahasuerus was a mere man, ruling over a tiny area of the globe. Yet the way into his presence was tightly controlled. God is the Creator, the Controller, and Sustainer of everything, but we can come with confidence right into His presence, wherever and whenever we like, and tell Him all about our worries, cares, and needs. We have no need to fear, for He loves us and cares for us. What a marvellous blessing! How privileged we are!

'Let us... come boldly unto the throne of grace, that we may obtain mercy, and find grace to help in time of need' (Hebrews 4:16).

Neither is man independent of woman, nor woman independent of man.
1 Corinthians 11:11 NKJV

We need each other! This message, found in 1 Corinthians, is hotly contested by society today. After years of varying levels of oppression and suppression of women, many have now risen up in radical feminism. To hear some of them speak, you'd wonder why men are on this planet at all!

It's true that oppression of women is wrong. Read the Bible carefully and you'll find that it never advocates it, as some may claim it does. Men and women are equal in God's sight, but God has given different family roles to each – the man is to lovingly lead, and the woman is to be submissive to his leadership. And in case you're thinking that this sounds like suppression, remember that the Lord Jesus Christ is submissive to His Father, and the Bible makes it clear that He is equal with God. Often, women and men have different strengths, suited to their roles. It's how God designed us. What determines whether we are male or female, however, isn't our interests or abilities, but what God has made us. Never think that a man who bakes exquisite birthday cakes is any less of a man, nor that a woman who has only ever wanted to be a mechanic is any less of a woman.

So, girls, although we don't need to wait around helplessly for a handsome prince to rescue us, at the same time let's not flex our muscles and conclude that males are dispensable in everyday life. We need men every bit as much as they need us.

And, boys, make sure you have a right view of females. This world has always suffered from men viewing women as objects for their lust. Females were not put on this earth to satisfy men's base desires – either physically, or online. Steer well clear of treating and using them as such. Instead, do as Paul exhorted Timothy – treat the younger women as sisters, with all purity. Value women as they are – made in the image of God, and worthy of honour and care.

God's design is always perfect. Men and women were made to complement each other, and His will is that we should have mutual respect for each other.

You shall love the Lord your God with all your heart... soul... mind, and... strength.

Mark 12:30 NKJV

14

FEBRUARY

Valentine's Day – a day when we show our love to those who are our nearest and dearest, usually in the form of pretty cards, heart-shaped chocolates, red roses, or fluffy heart-holding teddy bears. Things which are nice to look at, but useless, really, and generally extortionately overpriced. For some, these novelties are only cute add-ons which won't make much of a dent in their bank account. For others, that one little teddy bear might cost them a few months' savings.

There was a lady in the Bible like this. When it came to giving, the people threw into the treasury out of the abundance of what they possessed, but the Lord Jesus says of this lady that she "put in all that she had, her whole livelihood" (Mark 12:44 NKJV). It wasn't very much, not in comparison with the others, but the Lord knew what others didn't – that she had given until she had nothing left. She gave wholeheartedly.

When it comes to our love for the Lord our God, we ought to be wholehearted as well. The Lord Jesus Christ has instructed us to love Him with *all* our heart, *all* our soul, *all* our mind, and *all* our strength – every milligram of each. No locked rooms in our hearts to which He does not have full right to enter. No secret corners of our minds hung with a 'Keep Out' sign. He must have our full affection, our full intelligence, our full energy, and even our very being. And if that sounds too excessive, we only need to remember what He did for us.

Will it be easy? No. Our fleshly desires kick against the surrender of ourselves to Another. Like the rich in the story, we're happy to give, but only so much, hoping to hold back a part for ourselves. But what does giving all to God look like – living in a monastery and reading the Bible all day? Of course not. God doesn't expect us to become hermits. It means to live as God would have us live, giving Him His proper place in every choice we make and in everything we do. For unlike some sacrifices made today, this is certainly a sacrifice worth making for Someone worth loving.

15

FEBRUARY

Thou, being a man, makest Thyself God.
John 10:33

When we are searching for good apologetics arguments, either to use in discussion with others, or to further settle in our own minds the truth and reality of God and the Bible, we tend to look at archaeological and scientific evidence of events mentioned in the Bible, or answers to the problem of pain, and other moral arguments. While these are great ways of demonstrating that God and the Bible are true and trustworthy, sometimes we overlook the prophecies about Christ in the Old Testament and how He fulfilled them. While there are always going to be people who, despite solid historical evidence, deny that the Lord Jesus Christ existed, the majority of people accept that, at the very least, He was a historical figure. It's whether He was actually who He claimed to be that causes issues with atheists and those from other religions.

Someone might say to you that the Lord Jesus never actually said He was God. Although He never stated the words, "I am God," those who know their Bibles will have no difficulty recognising His claims. For example, we know from Exodus 3:14 that *I Am* is a divine title, belonging only to God Himself. And yet, in John 8:58, the Lord Jesus Christ calls Himself *I Am*. The Jews' reaction of taking up stones to cast at Him leaves us in no doubt that they too recognised the divine title and realised that the Lord Jesus was claiming to be God. Earlier, in John 5:17-18, the Lord Jesus had claimed equality with God which had provoked a similar response from the Jews.

If He wasn't actually God, why was He claiming to be God? An old argument, used by C. S. Lewis, asks if He was bad, mad, or God. On examination of His life, neither of the first two options can stand. His life was perfect, without flaw. His reasoning was so sound that those who came to catch Him out were silenced. When we read through the gospels, we cannot come to any other honest conclusion than that He was, is, and forever will be God.

Behold! My Servant whom I uphold, My Elect One in whom My soul delights!

Isaiah 42:1 NKJV

FEBRUARY 16

The Lord Jesus Christ claimed to be God, and His life showed it. He was utterly perfect, without a single sin, either in thought, word, or action. He also fulfilled all of the prophesied characteristics of the Messiah, the One God would send from Himself.

In Psalm 40:8, we read that He would delight to do God's will, and in John 6:38, we read that He said that He came, not to do His own will, but the will of the Father who sent Him. Not only would He be One who would delight to do God's will, God would delight in Him, as the verse at the top of the page says. At the Lord's baptism (Matthew 3:17), and at the transfiguration (Matthew 17:5), God verbally stated before those present that this was His beloved Son, in whom He was well pleased.

We learn about how the coming One would teach. Preaching would be a big feature of His ministry (Isaiah 61:1), but we also learn that He would use parables in His teaching. Matthew 13:34-35 says, 'All these things spake Jesus unto the multitude in parables; and without a parable spake He not unto them,' before explaining that this is a fulfilment of Psalm 78:2 – 'I will open my mouth in a parable.'

The Messiah would also be One who would have perfect self-control – He would not cry, nor lift up, nor cause His voice to be heard in the street (Isaiah 42:2). He would be compassionate and tender, like a shepherd (Isaiah 40:11). In Matthew 9:36, we read of the compassion He had on the multitude because they were like sheep without a shepherd, and in John 10:11 we learn that He said, "I am the good shepherd: the good shepherd giveth His life for the sheep." Not only would He have compassion on them, He would give His life for them.

It takes someone who is greater than sinful man to fully and completely fulfil these prophesies. Every single one of us would fall desperately short, should we try to live the life of the Messiah foretold in the Old Testament. Only One could do it, and He is truly God, the Lord Jesus Christ.

Go and show John again
those things which ye do
hear and see.

Matthew 11:4

John the Baptist was a remarkable man. His coming was foretold in Scripture and his birth was miraculous. The Lord Jesus Christ said that there hadn't been anyone greater than John the Baptist. But John was still human. When he was in prison, it seems he began to doubt whether the Lord Jesus really was the Messiah after all, so he sent some of his disciples to Him to find out. Instead of saying, "Tell John, yes, of course I'm the Messiah!" the Lord pointed him to where we should all go when we have doubts – back to the Scriptures.

John, brought up in a good Jewish home, with a priest for a father and a godly lady for a mother, would have been familiar with the Old Testament and all that it said about the coming Messiah. John would have known that Isaiah 35:5-6, along with other passages, would foretell the opening of the eyes of the blind, the deaf person's ears being unstopped, the lame man leaping as a young deer, and the dumb beginning to sing. John would have been familiar with Psalm 103:3 which speaks about the healing of all diseases, and of the hope of the dead being raised in Isaiah 26:19. The preaching of good news by the Messiah was clearly prophesied in Isaiah 61:1.

If we look at the early chapters of Matthew, before John's doubts are mentioned, we'll see how many times most of these foretold miracles were performed. Many people were healed – in chapter 8 a leper was cleansed, the centurion's servant was healed, and Peter's mother-in-law was restored to full health. Chapter 9 gives us the account of a lame man being made to walk, a dead girl being raised to life, two blind men receiving their sight, and a dumb man beginning to speak. Mark 7 tells of a deaf and dumb man being made to hear and speak. And, towards the end of Matthew 9, we read of the Lord preaching good news to those who were as sheep without a shepherd.

The Bible doesn't tell us whether this was enough to answer John's question; I don't think it needs to! The assurance of the Word of God would have been more than enough, as it still is for us today.

The Old Testament is full of Christ! There are prophecies about His birth, life, death, resurrection, exaltation, and, still to be fulfilled, His coming to the earth in glory. We also have types, shadows, and pictures throughout the whole of the Old Testament.

Let's look at a few of the prophecies about His death and see from the gospels how they were fulfilled. There isn't space to quote all the verses in full, so please look them up for yourself.

In Isaiah 50:6, we read, 'I gave My back to the smiters... I hid not My face from shame and spitting.' Matthew 26:67; 27:30, and John 19:1 show that this was fulfilled when He was before the religious leaders and Pilate. Micah 5:1 says 'they shall smite the judge of Israel with a rod upon the cheek,' which is recorded in Luke 22:64.

Crucifixion involved nailing the victim's hands and feet to a cross, foretold in Psalm 22:16 – 'they pierced My hands and My feet.' Bear in mind that when this prophecy was written, crucifixion hadn't even been invented!

As our Lord Jesus Christ hung on the cross, He was mocked for His trust in God (Psalm 22:8, Matthew 27:43). 'They... parted His garments, casting lots' (Matthew 27:35), in fulfilment of Psalm 22:18. When He said, "I thirst," He was offered vinegar mingled with gall (Matthew 27:34) – 'They gave Me also gall for My meat; and in My thirst they gave Me vinegar to drink' (Psalm 69:21).

During the hours of darkness, under the weight of God's judgment for sin, He was forsaken by God and cried, 'My God, My God, why hast Thou forsaken Me?' Psalm 22 opens with the very same words.

After His death, the soldiers came, and John is careful to tell us in his gospel (19:33,36) that they did not break His legs, because no bone was to be broken, in fulfilment of Scripture. There is a clear allusion to the Passover lamb here (a topic for another day) and also the fulfilment of Psalm 34:20 – 'He keepeth all His bones: not one of them is broken.'

In light of all this, is there any doubt that the sinless One who hung on the middle cross was any other than He who was prophesied in the Old Testament?

The Lord hath laid on Him the iniquity of us all.
Isaiah 53:6

If you were to ask me what my favourite portion of the Bible is, I'd probably say Isaiah 52:13-53:12. I love to read it and ponder all that the Lord Jesus Christ suffered for sinners... for me. What I sometimes tend to forget, though, is that these words were written as a prophecy about seven hundred years before the events took place. In fact, this is also a prophetic account of what the nation of Israel will say in a future day when their eyes are opened, and they understand that the Messiah was crucified for them. Because of that, these words are full of deep meaning and pathos.

To those who would have read this portion of Isaiah's prophecy before the Lord Jesus Christ came to earth, they would have concluded that this passage was speaking of someone wise (52:13) and humble (53:2), yet despised, One marked by sorrow and grief (53:3). These characteristics are totally in keeping with what we learn about the Lord Jesus in the gospels.

As the pre-coming-of-Christ reader would have continued to read, they would have discovered that this person was going to die. He would be treated brutally – wounded, bruised, oppressed, afflicted – but would be silent in His suffering (53:5,7). The injustice of the death of this perfect person is undeniable. And, what's more, even God Himself would punish Him – the Lord laid the iniquity on Him (53:6), and it pleased the Lord to bruise Him (53:10). Why would such a One bear so much?

The answer is clear. By His stripes we are healed (53:5). The Lord has laid on Him the iniquity of us all (53:6). He shall bear their iniquities (53:11). He bore the sin of many (53:12). He wasn't bearing His own sin, but that of others – not only for the Jews of a future day, but for us, right here, today!

This truth is expanded and developed in the New Testament, where we see clearly what was partially revealed to the Old Testament saints. The prophecy of gospel truth strengthens our faith and causes us to thank God for His plan of salvation.

In the fulfilment of many of the prophecies in the Bible, the people, kings, and nations involved weren't aware that their actions were so significant. They didn't realise that they were fulfilling a foretelling of something which had been written many, many years earlier. After all, if someone was aware of a prophecy and set out to bring it to pass, would it still be a prophecy?

What about the Lord Jesus? He knew each and every one of the prophecies about the Messiah. Is it possible that He was only an ordinary man who set out to make it look as if He was fulfilling prophecy?

Let's look at His birth. The Bible stated that the Messiah would be born in Bethlehem Ephratah (Micah 5:2) of a virgin (Isaiah 7:14). I think we'd all agree that it's ridiculous to believe that either of these events could be controlled by a mere human being. What about the miracles He would perform? These prophesies could only be fulfilled by One who has power to order world events, and power over the natural creation. And could an ordinary man, no matter how hard he tries, be able to live in such a way that God could say that He delights in him (Isaiah 42:1)?

What about the crucifixion? Would a mere man be able to arrange events involving the Jewish leaders and their enemies, the Romans, to tie in so seamlessly with everything that happened during the Lord's trial, suffering, and death? And, maybe more significantly, why would he want to? After all, the Jews in the Lord Jesus Christ's day were convinced that the Messiah would come to deliver them from the Romans, not to be put to death by them.

So did the Lord Jesus Christ knowingly fulfil all the prophecies about the Messiah? Yes, He did, as only One who is truly God could do, proving Himself to be truly the Messiah.[16]

---

16. If you'd like to read more about the topic of Messianic prophecies and proving the Bible is God's word, I recommend *The Prophets Still Speak – Messiah in Both Testaments* by Fred John Meldau, published by Friends of Israel Gospel Ministry in 1988; and *Prove It: How you can know and show that the Bible is God's word* by Paul McCauley, published by Decapolis Press in 2017.

God... knows all things.
1 John 3:20 NKJV

God is omniscient. If you're not sure what that means, take another look at the verse at the top of the page. *Omniscient* is one of those words which is made up of two smaller words. Put together, it translates something like 'all-knowing'.

I think we'd agree that a God who doesn't know everything isn't really God at all. For us to gain knowledge, we have to work at it – read books or articles, watch documentaries, listen to experts – but God's knowledge isn't acquired or learned.

The Bible contains many references to and examples of God's knowledge. Take the story of Job, for instance. You'll remember that Job was a faithful and righteous man, yet God permitted many severe trials to come his way. Although we get a little inside glimpse in the first few chapters of the book, Job was totally in the dark as to why he was having such an awful time.

Finally, after Job suffered through the 'comfort' of his friends, God speaks – about His power and knowledge. Over and over, He asks Job questions about creation. "Do you know this, Job? Do you know how or why it happens?" Job is speechless. It doesn't take him long to realise that God's knowledge is so far above ours that we couldn't even begin to compare it. Was Job ever told why these tragic things happened to him? Scripture doesn't say. My guess is that after God had finished speaking to him, the reasons didn't matter anymore. What did matter is that God is omniscient. That was enough for Job.

God's omniscience is an important truth for us to learn too. If He knows all about us, better than we even know ourselves, He also knows our motives. We might be able to fool other people, but we can never fool God. Yet isn't it comforting that we don't have to pretend with God? As well as being all-knowing, He is also loving, patient, merciful, and gracious.

It's also comforting to remember that, as was the case with Job, God knows what we are going through, and the reasons why. He also knows what lies ahead. As a popular quote reads, 'My unknown future is in the hands of the all-knowing God.'

They shall see His face.

Revelation 22:4

In my work as an optician, people often tell me that the sense that they fear losing, above all others, is their sight. The prospect of experiencing darkness instead of light and colour, needing help for simple tasks, and being unable to read or recognise faces can be terrifying.

And yet, for many, this has been and will be their reality. Some have lost their sight for various reasons, while others never remember being able to use their eyes at all. One such individual was the famous hymnwriter, Fanny Crosby. When she was only six weeks old, she became ill, and an inappropriate treatment caused her to become totally blind. Fanny never knew what it was to see the faces of her family, or the world around her. To have become permanently blind due to a preventable error was a tragedy, but instead of giving way to bitterness, Fanny determined to be content.

As time passed, it became clear that Fanny had a great gift for poetry. When she entered the Institution for the Blind in New York, at the age of fifteen, she wrote many poems, honing the skills that would later make her world famous in Christian circles and be a blessing to so many.

Her first hymn to be published, by a Mr Bradbury, was what she viewed as the beginning of her work as a hymnwriter, and by the time she died, aged ninety-five, she had written over eight thousand hymns and poems. Some of her best-known and loved include 'Safe in the Arms of Jesus', 'Rescue the Perishing', and 'Blessed Assurance'. Some hymns were inspired by stories she heard, others were written for pieces of music, and on other occasions she was asked to write on a particular theme.

Fanny Crosby lived in the sphere in which God had placed her, and used her gift for Him. God alone knows how many people will be in heaven because of the scriptural truth of her hymns, and how many others have been encouraged, comforted, and blessed by her words.[17]

When my life's work is ended and I cross the swelling tide,
When the bright and glorious morning I shall see;
I shall know my Redeemer when I reach the other side,
And His smile will be the first to welcome me.

17. S. Trevena Jackson recounted Fanny Crosby's story in *This is My Story, This is My Song*, first published in 1915 and republished by Ambassador Productions Ltd. in 1995.

I give unto them eternal life; and they shall never perish.

John 10:28

There's nothing better than being safe and secure! Right now, while I'm writing this, the wind is howling outside, and the rain is battering against the windows, but I'm sheltered safely inside a sturdy house. Of course, something could happen to the house. Perhaps a tree might fall on it, or if there is enough rain, it could flood. I'd be very foolish to have complete trust in a mere building, no matter how solid it might seem.

But when it comes to our salvation, we can be totally sure that we are safe. The Lord Jesus Christ is God, so He is absolutely trustworthy. When we accept His sacrifice and death on the cross for our sins and put our trust in Him, He gives us eternal life. And once He gives us eternal life, He will never take it from us. He couldn't put it much more plainly – 'they shall never perish'!

What if we sin? Maybe the devil whispers to you, "You've lost your salvation! You couldn't have done that and still be saved." Look at the rest of the verse. It says, 'neither shall any man pluck them out of My hand.' Think for a moment about the hand of Christ. He formed the universe – every gigantic star, right down to every tiny atom. He touched the leper and healed him. He lifted the little children into His arms. And He bore the nails for us. His hands are powerful, healing, tender, and saving. The Lord Jesus is very clear that other people cannot pluck us from His hand. And if that is so, why would we ever imagine that we somehow could remove ourselves? It's totally impossible. Once we trust Christ, we are absolutely and completely secure – eternally!

The task Joshua was facing must have seemed immense. For about forty years, the great leader Moses had guided the large multitude of Israelites through the wilderness. It hadn't been an easy task, and Joshua, his assistant, knew it. But now Moses was dead, and Joshua was the one whom God had chosen to pick up where Moses left off. Joshua would lead the children of Israel across the Jordan so that they could settle in the promised land. There would be battles to be fought, cities to be conquered, and great problems to be solved. Hard work and difficult days lay ahead. Was Joshua able?

Is there some task ahead that you don't feel up to? Maybe there's something you firmly believe God has guided you to do, but it seems far beyond your capabilities and is well out of your comfort zone. You don't know how you could ever hope to succeed.

God understands our fears. He knows our limitations much better than we do, and He won't ask the impossible from us. God commanded Joshua to be strong and courageous, and He repeated this message three times. He would say the same to you. *Be strong! Be courageous!* But where does this courage come from? Where can we find the confidence to carry out such a difficult task? From Him! The rest of Joshua 1:9 reads, 'for the Lord your God is with you wherever you go' (NKJV). The reason that we can be strong and courageous is because He is with us. He will never leave us nor forsake us. Joshua knew that God had never let Moses down, and this gave Joshua the confidence that God would be with him too.

God is still the same God. In another part of this devotional, we will learn more about Joshua. There we will see how God was with him, as He promised He would be. Whatever task is ahead of you, you can take fresh courage because He has promised to be with you too.

I am the Lord, I change not.

Malachi 3:6

As I write this, the Covid-19 pandemic is raging across our world. The future is scary. People are dying, and financially things seem bleak. This coronavirus appears to be spiralling out of control.

On the other side of the pandemic, you will have your own anxieties. They may not involve a contagious global illness, but they are very real all the same. They scare you. They cause you to question where God is. Does He see? Does He hear? Is He still in control?

I can assure you without a doubt that, yes, God is still very much in control. He still hears, He still sees, He still cares. After all, He is Jehovah, always and forever. And He does not change. He is the same God who preserved Noah in the worldwide flood. He is the same God who saw and delivered the children of Israel from bondage in Egypt. He is the same God who stopped the mouths of the lions in the den with Daniel. He is the One who calms the storm with a word; who can feed more than five thousand hungry mouths with only five loaves and two fishes; who can heal the sick, cause the blind to see, the dumb to speak, the lame to walk, and the dead to live. He may not prevent the difficulties from arising – He has His own purposes – but He can preserve and rescue in any and every circumstance. Nothing was too hard for Him in the past, and nothing is too hard for Him in the present, or in the future.

So whatever it is you are facing today, take courage. Our God has always been in control, and He has not changed!

Follow Me.
Matthew 16:24

I don't need to explain to you that the word 'follow' has had an extra dimension added to its meaning since social media was invented. It's big business! The concept of following and followers is what fuels all forms of social media. For ordinary people like you and me, it's never been easier to keep up with inside information on the lives of thousands of people – one tap and you will receive a regular stream of updates, posted by anyone from your best friend to A-list celebrities.

Did you know that the Bible talks *a lot* about following? Look up the word, and you will discover people who made choices about who to follow. Some made bad choices, like those who followed Absalom. Absalom was quite a celebrity in his day – he had striking good looks, great hair, and a charismatic personality. However, he was a rebel who tried to usurp the throne of his father, King David. He didn't end well. Think carefully about the celebrities you follow on social media – they may be attractive in many ways, but what kind of lives are they living? Many of them, sadly, like Absalom, are heading to a disastrous end.

So whom should we follow? If you've looked up the word, you will have come across the phrase 'Follow Me,' spoken by none other than the Lord Jesus Christ Himself to many different people. As Christians, we too must follow Him. Imagine spending as much time observing the life of the Lord Jesus as many do their favourite celebrity. The more we observe, the more we become like that person. Spend time in the Bible, reading about the Lord Jesus, and following Him.

There are also characteristics that we should follow, such as love, peace, faith, patience, and meekness. Take one of these words and think about how you can apply it in your life. Maybe it will mean biting your tongue rather than getting involved in an argument, or making the right choice when your friends want to do something which you know is wrong. It could even include unfollowing some of those celebrities we mentioned earlier.

So, next time you tap that social media app, think about what the Bible has to say about following, and choose to 'follow that which is good' (1 Thessalonians 5:15).

Be... followers of me, even as I also am of Christ.

1 Corinthians 11:1

Yesterday we thought about who and what we should follow – Christ, first and foremost, as well as all those characteristics that please God, such as peace, love, and patience. But did you ever consider that there may be people who are following you?

Maybe you're the sort of person who thrives on attention – the greater the audience you have, the better – but you figure that nobody really takes you very seriously. Or perhaps you've just had a little laugh at the idea that others are following you. You might feel you're not very important, and you certainly don't think that anyone will really be influenced by you. But never forget that, whether you're the centre of attention or tucked into a corner of the room, there's always someone looking on and taking note of your actions – a younger brother or sister, someone in your class or circle of friends whom you barely notice, maybe some of your followers on social media. The pictures you share, the posts you like, the language you use, the way you dress, and how you behave, can all have an impact on that person – for good, or bad. Be careful! Something you deem to be harmless and feel you can keep under control may turn out to be a snare to someone else.

The apostle Paul could say to the Corinthians, 'Be followers of me,' or, as other translations have, 'Be imitators of me.' Could we say that? Are we living in such a way that we would be happy for others to do what we do? Of course, Paul wasn't saying that others should imitate him because he felt his own life was impeccable. Instead, it was because he was a follower of Christ, the only One who ever lived a perfect life. Every thought, word, and action of His were absolutely faultless. So the only way we will be a good example to others, someone who can be followed, is if we too are following the Lord Jesus Christ.

Behold, your King is coming to you, lowly, and sitting on a donkey, a colt, the foal of a donkey.

Matthew 21:5 NKJV

28

FEBRUARY

Y ou've probably seen footage online of a monarch making his or her way to a destination in a cavalcade of luxury top-of-the-range vehicles, complete with bodyguards, a police escort, and lots of pomp and ceremony. Sometimes horses and carriages are used, but in past days the monarch would have ridden on a majestic, well-groomed horse, with special tack for the occasion.

I'm sure the readers of Zechariah's prophecy must have puzzled over the unusual lines in what we now know as chapter 9. A king riding on a *donkey*? And a colt, the foal of a donkey?

Donkeys are still used for work in various countries. I've seen them in the mountains of Mexico, carrying people and water supplies up and down hills. Their small size, wide girth and plodding gait certainly don't make the rider look very majestic. And yet the Lord chose a donkey for His entrance. The mother and the colt weren't anything special – only ordinary donkeys tied up, probably at the side of a house, waiting until the owner needed them again.

But instead of the owner, Someone else needed them. Animals know their owner (Isaiah 1:3) and I'm sure that they would have recognised the Lord Jesus as Master. The colt, who had never been broken in, or even had anyone on his back before, was totally submissive and obedient – just one proof of the greatness of the One who rode upon him. But not only were the donkeys quite ordinary, the Lord Jesus had no special tack – the coats of the disciples were His saddle. No red carpet – cut-down branches sufficed. And yet, in this lowly entrance, He fulfilled the prophecy given so many years before.

The end of the passage in Matthew's gospel states that all the city was moved. Some asked who He was; others answered that He was the prophet from Nazareth. They may not have known, but something big was about to happen in Jerusalem – this wouldn't be the last that they would hear of the King who rode into the city on a donkey, fulfilling Zechariah's ancient prophecy.

Look carefully then how you walk... making the best use of the time.

Ephesians 5:15,16 ESV

It's Leap Day – a very special day! There wasn't one last year, or the year before, or even the year before that, and there won't be another one for a while. Because each revolution of the earth around the sun is approximately 365.24 days, every four years an extra day needs to be added to our calendar to keep the seasons right. If we didn't have it, within a few centuries the seasons would be totally on their heads. You might even get snow on your summer holiday!

So this year we have 366 days instead of the usual 365 – a whole extra day. What are you going to do with yours? Maybe you've shrugged and answered, "Just the usual!" Of course. It's not usually a holiday, unfortunately. But that's not what I meant.

Each day of our lives is a gift, which is given to us by God so that we can live for Him. During the course of a day, we will face situations, we will meet people, and we will have opportunities that may never come our way again. Every day brings its own unique combination of events, and even if our lives follow the same pattern day after day, no two days are ever identical. Sometimes we seize the opportunities and use them for God, but often we fail and let God down. Yet He is gracious, forgiving us, and giving other opportunities to live for Him. Our lives will probably not be made up of great and noble acts, but, day by day, we can live a life of quiet faithfulness and obedience to God.

So let's take this gift of an extra day and live it for His glory, doing what we know will please Him and making the best use of time.

MARCH

You do not know... how the bones grow in the womb of her who is with child.

Ecclesiastes 11:5 NKJV

MARCH

Y ou are a miracle! Have you ever thought about that? A number of years ago, you didn't even exist. But now, here you are. You'll have already learned how babies develop. The very first stage is the fertilisation of the ovum by the sperm, but even for this to happen, many obstacles need to be surmounted. Then when fertilisation does occur, it's only the beginning of a long and treacherous journey for the little life. The fertilised ovum must divide properly and make its way to the uterus, then be implanted in the lining. So many things can go wrong.

After it is implanted, the little body gradually develops so that the baby can survive outside the uterus. By the time the embryo is three weeks old, the brain, spine, and heart will already have begun to develop, and five weeks later, the heart is fully formed. Ears also develop at this stage, and when the embryo is ten weeks old, all major organs will have formed. Two weeks later, urine is produced. The following week, they will begin to hear. Fifteen weeks after fertilisation, the little one will have his or her own individual fingerprints.[18] Within a relatively short space of time, a new human being is created and equipped with everything they need to survive.

A while ago, I watched a short video of the process. It was amazing. If I had never known that babies were formed in this way, I wouldn't have believed it was at all possible. And yet, I'm living proof. So are you!

Evolutionists like to tell us that this process developed over many years and finally, one day, it worked. There are many problems with that view, and, quite frankly, it would take a great deal more mental effort to believe it than the wonderful truth that God created us. Psalm 139:13 tells us that God formed our inward parts and knit us together in our mothers' wombs. Only a divine Creator could perform such a miracle. His fingerprints are upon each one of us.

---

18. https://www.nhs.uk/conditions/pregnancy-and-baby/pregnancy-week-by-week/

D id you know that each believer, including you, has a spiritual gift?

First of all, what is a spiritual gift? Warren Wiersbe says that 'a spiritual gift is a God-given ability to serve God and other Christians in such a way that Christ is glorified and believers are edified.'[19] In other words, God has given every believer a gift that he or she can use to bring glory to God and build up other Christians in the local church.

In 1 Corinthians 12, the human body is used as an example of the local church. Our bodies have many parts, which look different from each other and have different purposes. Yet they all work together for the benefit of the whole body. If we're missing one, we know about it!

During the late 1950s and early 1960s, some pregnant women were given a drug, called thalidomide, to help with morning sickness, not knowing that it led to congenital malformation. Many of the babies were born with missing limbs. On the whole, the ones who survived adjusted. Those without arms learned to use their feet to open doors, type on the computer, drive, and even blow their noses. They managed – but often it wasn't easy; arms and hands have a special function that isn't easily replaced.

So does every believer. We each have a special function, but to carry it out we must use the spiritual gift that God has given us. We might not consider our gift to be spectacular, but it is of vital importance. If we don't use our ability, the church suffers, and God doesn't get the glory He deserves.

What sort of gifts does God give? There are three main passages about spiritual gifts which I recommend you read – Romans 12, 1 Corinthians 12, and Ephesians 4. In these, you'll find lists of spiritual gifts. Some of them are what we call sign gifts, like tongues and healing, which were to be a sign to unbelieving Jews in the early days of the church. Others, for example, prophecy, we no longer need because we have the full word of God. But many other gifts are still in use today – such as teaching, giving, exhortation, helping, leading, and evangelism.

---

19. *The Wiersbe Bible Commentary.*

Having then gifts... let us use them.
Romans 12:6 NKJV

We were each given a spiritual gift when we trusted Christ... but the age-old question of each believer is *What is it?* Recognising our gifts may take time. Although natural talents can often be used for God, spiritual gift is different. It is not necessarily something we were born with, and it needs to be developed. A believer with the gift of teaching won't be able to teach from a difficult portion of Scripture at the first church gathering they attend after they get saved. Studying God's Word will take work!

You may not have the opportunity to fully use your gift yet. Someone with the gift of hospitality who lives at home with their parents won't have the same scope to exercise that gift as someone who has their own house. Or maybe your gift is teaching children, but you need to wait until you're old enough to have a Sunday school class. Waiting doesn't mean that you don't have the gift – it means that God is developing you and training you. Maybe you can look for opportunities to use your gift in an innovative way – showing hospitality by treating someone to a coffee, or perhaps telling Bible stories to your little cousins or neighbours.

Other gifts can be exercised at any age and stage of life. One gift is simply being a help – something all of us should do. How about carrying out acts of mercy? Or giving, not necessarily money – maybe your time and effort?

But what do you do if you have no idea what your gift might be? Firstly, do what you can, including those things just mentioned. As you develop as a believer, people will begin to recognise the gift that God has given you, but no one, yourself included, will ever know what it is if you hide in a corner and do nothing. Spend time in the Word of God. This will give you a good foundation for what the Lord would have you do in the future, and you will personally gain much benefit from it.

Be teachable and open to guidance and correction. Just because we have a certain gift, it doesn't mean that we'll know everything and won't need to learn from other believers who may be older and wiser.

And, finally, when you know what your gift is, keep humble. Some people have more public gifts than others, but every gift is absolutely vital for the proper functioning of the local church.

He gave... apostles... prophets...
evangelists... pastors... teachers;
for the perfecting of the saints.
Ephesians 4:11, 12

MARCH

4

What are your thoughts on those in your local church who teach the believers? Maybe you're not too keen on some of them because they are too direct. Maybe there are those who seem a bit boring to you. And maybe there are others you love listening to, because you always learn something new and helpful.

In the third passage which deals with gifts in the Bible, we discover that gifts are not only those God-given abilities which every believer has, but they include people as well. Paul lists various groups of individuals which God has given. Some of these, as we noticed the other day, we no longer have. Apostles were those who had personally seen the risen Christ, so it's clear that we don't have any nowadays. We have the full Bible today, so there is no need for prophets, and so this gift is no longer given.

Evangelists, pastors (shepherds), and teachers are still very much needed. Every believer is expected to share the gospel, but evangelists have a particular gift for this. Shepherds are those men who care for the believers of the local church, and this care will involve teaching, although not all teachers are shepherds. Shepherding and guiding Christians isn't easy work; people need even more attention than sheep do!

How do you respond to these believers whom God has given to the church? Do you only listen to those you like? Or do you appreciate that every teacher given to the church is a gift from God? If we really understood this, wouldn't we take more notice of what they have to say? As always, everything that is taught must agree with the Word of God, and we need to recognise that when it does, it has the authority of God, so should be obeyed. What about shepherds? Do you only respond to praise but resent the gentle words of correction?

God has given gifted men to the church for 'the equipping of the saints for the work of ministry, for the edifying of the body of Christ' (Ephesians 4:12 NKJV). In other words, the teaching and guidance we receive is to equip us to serve, and to build us up. When this happens, God is glorified.

The paths of the seas.

Psalm 8:8

Some Christians think that we need to prove that the Bible is true, or at the very least take scientific discoveries and make them fit into Scripture. Matthew Fontaine Maury did the opposite. Growing up in a Scripture-saturated home, he often heard the verse at the top of our page. Matthew believed that if the Bible said that there were paths in the sea, there were paths in the sea, and he was going to find them!

At nineteen, Matthew joined the United States Navy as a midshipman. His goal was to learn all about the sea, but he met with disappointment in the education he'd hoped to receive, so he studied by himself, and ended up puzzling the examiner of the Board of Naval Education with his brilliant answer to one of the questions.

When Matthew, on a voyage around South America, discovered that information on winds and currents didn't exist, he began to keep thorough records and later gathered information from other captains. These were used to compile pilot charts, which helped shorten the time of sea journeys. Further information led to him being able to produce charts of the Atlantic, Pacific, and Indian Oceans – the paths of the sea, of which the Bible speaks! It was also Matthew's work on the Atlantic seabed that helped to determine that a transatlantic telegraph cable could be laid.

It wasn't all plain sailing for Matthew – many criticised his firm stance on biblical truth and authority, and yet it was his belief in the Bible as the unerring Word of God that led to his great discoveries. In a speech he gave towards the end of his life, he stated, "The Bible is true and science is true... When your men of science, with vain and hasty conceit, announce the discovery of disagreement between them, rely upon it, the fault is not with the witness of His records, but with the worm who essays to interpret evidence which he does not understand."[20]

---

20. Information taken from https://www.britannica.com/biography/Matthew-Fontaine-Maury and https://creation.com/matthew-maury

> None of us lives to himself, and none of us dies to himself.
> Romans 14:7 ESV

MARCH 6

This morning, I went for a walk around a lake. Everything was calm, and the lake was still, until a little fish decided to rise to the surface. At once, the disturbance made a tiny ring in the water, which created a slightly bigger one, which led to another, and another, until the largest ring was over a metre in diameter. I wonder did the little fish know what a large impact he had just made?

Sometimes we make decisions that we don't think will have any impact. We move in a particular direction, decide to satisfy certain appetites, or choose to interact with someone. What we don't realise is that seemingly tiny decisions can have an impact beyond what we ever considered. Those rings that spread out when the little fish moved reached places where other fish were to be found. In the same way, maybe those decisions you make are affecting other people.

What if you choose to go somewhere? You know your parents wouldn't be happy, so you don't tell them. But maybe someone sees you, and figures that if you're going, it must be okay, so they go too, also against their parents' wishes. You've not only disobeyed your parents, you've influenced someone else to disobey theirs too. But then your parents find out and are disappointed. Your decision has also affected them, along with the other person's parents. And who knows who else has gone as a result of the other person following your example? You see how your decision can affect so many others?

Good decisions work the same way – by affecting people positively. A choice to read your Bible will lead to a more Christlike attitude and a love for others. A decision to do what you know pleases God will influence others for good.

Many people like to think that their decisions don't affect anyone else, and that they can do what they like, but the Bible is very clear that this isn't true. So next time you have a decision to make, take a moment to think about all the people who will be affected by your choice, and only move in a way that will glorify God and bring good to others.

Do not I fill heaven and earth? saith the Lord.

MARCH

Jeremiah 23:24

7

God's omnipresence is a truth that is either of great comfort or great discomfort, depending on your relationship with Him. You see, omnipresence is a word that is used to explain how God is present everywhere at once. He is too great to be confined to one particular place; instead, as Solomon said, the heaven and heaven of heavens cannot contain Him.

Those who try to hide from God will soon discover that it is useless to try. In Psalm 139, David writes that no matter how far away or to how remote a location he might go, God would be there. There is no escaping from Him, as Jonah found out. When we think we are alone, with no human eye to see what we are doing, we must remember that God is there.

But for the believer who is living in the light, God's presence is a great comfort. No matter in what situation you find yourself – whether amongst an ungodly crowd at school or university, in a home where angry words are often hurled through the air, or in dangerous and perilous situations, God is there. He is with you always – with you through the waters and with you in the valley of the shadow of death. When you feel alone, He is with you. When you feel downhearted, He is with you. When you feel afraid, He is with you.

When you can't even feel His presence at all, He is still with you. Sometimes God's presence isn't experienced as fully as at other times; this can be due to unconfessed sin. At other times there is no reason that we know of. In times like this, God may be giving us an opportunity to lean in simple faith on His Word. If He said He would never leave us, we must believe it, whether we feel it to be so or not. Nothing changes the great fact of His omnipresence. So let's step into today with confidence and assurance that no matter where we go, God is there.

He shall gather the lambs with His arm, and carry them in His bosom.

Isaiah 40:11

MARCH

8

There are very few animals as defenceless as sheep. With no way of protecting themselves, except to group together and run, they can easily find themselves at the mercy of cruel predators. Even more vulnerable are their little lambs. When born, they are weak and helpless, susceptible to hypothermia, infection, and, in some cases, rejection from their mothers. And then there are animals like wolves, coyotes, bears, mountain lions, and birds of prey, including eagles and ravens.

Here in the British Isles, lambs are often in danger from foxes. Foxes are cunning animals, stealthily creeping towards their target before moving in for the kill. Twin lambs are especially susceptible because the fox knows that the mother will struggle to protect both of her babies.

As Christians, we all have an enemy on our track who, like a fox, would love nothing better than to attack us and bring us down. We learn more of the Word of God as we grow, which enables us to fight against the wiles of the devil. But he is a cruel enemy, and often targets the newborn lambs – those who have recently been saved. How many of us had doubts about whether or not we were really saved, within hours or even minutes of our salvation?

In this country, the shepherd can't be continually with his sheep. Each night, he will need to leave them, hoping that the fox will stay away, and the little lambs will be preserved. Our Shepherd will never leave us. He is always with His sheep, every minute of every day. Take another look at our verse for today – not only is He with His sheep, He gathers up the little lambs with His arm, and carries them close to His heart. He doesn't choose only one to carry, leaving the others at greater risk. Instead, our Shepherd protects and cares for every single lamb, holding it close to Himself where the enemy cannot attack. Sheltered in His arms is the safest place to be.

The last state of that man is
worse than the first.
Matthew 12:45

In America, in the late eighteenth century, the Society of Friends, also known as Quakers, began a movement to abolish slavery. They rightly believed that owning slaves was wrong, so they encouraged people to free their slaves. In order to legally do this, the slave owners transferred ownership to the Society, and let the slaves go free. They would no longer live a life of slavery. By the 1820s, six hundred slaves had been freed in this way and a poll revealed that over half of them wanted to relocate to Liberia, Africa. The Society gathered the funds for the journey and began to convey the people to their country of choice. Tragically, one of the boats bound for Liberia docked in New Orleans, where the freed slaves were taken and auctioned off. Once again, they found themselves in bondage.[21]

There are many sad cases like this, not only in the world of nineteenth century America, but today. How often do you hear of people in bondage to vices such as alcohol, drugs, or gambling, who seem to have been freed from their sinful habits, either through their own efforts, rehabilitation, or a false religious experience? From all outward appearances, they seem to have changed – maybe they look more respectable or are living a more upright life. But often, like those poor slaves who thought they were free, they find themselves once more in bondage, deeper than they ever were before.

What happened? The sad truth is that, in many cases, they were never truly delivered. The heart itself is desperately wicked, so reformation and self-improvement will never adequately work. In the story that the Lord Jesus told, an unclean spirit leaves a man, but when he cannot find anywhere that he would rather be, he returns with seven other spirits who are more wicked than himself. If the man was in a bad condition before, he is much worse now. The power of God is needed in salvation, not only to break the chains of sin – forever! – but to fill the life and give the forgiven sinner something worth living for. And when that happens, the person will be indwelt, not with an unclean spirit, but with the Holy Spirit, who is given to every believer when they trust Christ.

---

21. This story is found at https://www.ncpedia.org/manumission-societies

He went out and began... to spread the matter.

Mark 1:45 NKJV

It was so exciting! Kelsey was bursting to tell someone. She turned to her best friend and enthusiastically whispered the news. At lunch, a girl Kelsey hardly knew gave her a smug smile. "So what's this interesting news I hear?" Kelsey's mouth fell open; her best friend had betrayed her!

Has anything like this ever happened to you? I thought so – me too! Our secrets don't always stay secret. Some people aren't very trustworthy, and it's often hard to know who those people are until they've let us down. It's crushing to realise you've been betrayed.

Did you know that the Lord Jesus Christ had problems with people who spread around what He had told them not to talk about? In Mark 1, a leper came to Him, and asked to be healed. The Lord was moved with compassion, and He healed the man. Afterwards He gave him very straight instructions – the healed leper was to say nothing to anyone. But what did the man do? Read the verse at the top of the page. After all that the Lord Jesus had done for him, he did exactly what He told him not to do! The healed leper might have tried to justify his actions, but the consequence was that the Lord Jesus was no longer able to go openly into the cities. It seems that the man's words actually hindered the Lord's ministry.

The Lord Jesus knew beforehand that the man would do this, yet in His marvellous kindness He healed him anyway. However, we don't have the ability to see into the future. How are we to know who to trust?

Look for wise friends. People who spread others' secrets are probably going to do the same with yours. And don't forget that the best listeners might be closer to you than you realise – in your own home or extended family, or your church. They might not even be your age at all.

But what if someone has let you down, spread your secret? It's hurtful, but we should forgive that person; we, ourselves, may have done the same thing to others. We can learn from the experience – how to guard our words and our hearts; how to choose a good friend, and how to be faithful friends ourselves.

You are not your own... for you were bought at a price.
1 Corinthians 6:19,20 NKJV

A quick scan through social media will give us the distinct impression that, at least in the western world, we live in a body-conscious society. Many people work hard to make their bodies look as attractive as possible; others endeavour to accept and celebrate theirs just as they are. You will also come across those who choose to satisfy their various cravings, even if these choices cause harmful physical effects. Whatever attitude people have towards their bodies, the common theme of each is "It's *my* body; I'll do what I like with it!"

It can be easy to fall into the same mindset. That's why it's good to remind ourselves of the verse at the top of the page. God doesn't only have claim over our souls; even our bodies belong to Him. He has bought us at a price for Himself, so we are not our own. The believer can't say, "It's my body; I'll do what I like with it."

If you read the passage, you'll learn that our bodies are the temple of the Holy Spirit. Consider for a moment how a temple of the Holy Spirit ought to be treated. Not idolised, of course, but care should be taken as to how it's handled, what's carried into it, and how it's used. In the same way, our bodies aren't to be idolised, but looked after. The Bible is often clear as to what we can or cannot do with our bodies. Take a look at the previous verse, for instance – it tells us that sexual activity outside of the biblical definition of marriage is wrong. Ephesians 5:18 instructs us not to be drunk with wine, but instead to be filled with the Spirit. There are many substances, not only alcohol, that may hinder or remove self-control, and which can be damaging to our health. Because our bodies are temples of the Holy Spirit, we will not want to mistreat them, either by what we do to them or put into them.

This truth will affect the choices we make every day – what we do, where we go, what we say. As we make our way through this world, let's remember that we aren't our own, for we were bought at a price, and are to glorify God in our bodies.

Present your bodies a living sacrifice, holy, acceptable unto God...

Romans 12:1

12

MARCH

Yesterday we learned that our bodies are the temple of the Holy Spirit, and because of this, we should look after them. Today's verse is also about our bodies, but instead of looking at what we *shouldn't* do with our bodies, we will see what we *should* do with them.

In the epistle to the Romans, Paul has been considering the mercy of God towards guilty sinners. This leads him to urge believers (including us) to present our bodies a living sacrifice to God. After all, it is our 'reasonable service' when we consider the great salvation we have received.

What will 'presenting our bodies' involve? Perhaps you are imagining a life spent giving medical care to those in a remote poverty-stricken village, or in spreading the gospel amongst unreached tribes deep in a rainforest. Maybe you are even envisaging martyrdom – giving your life for Christ.

While some of you may be called to serve God far from home, the truth is that, no matter where we spend our lives, presenting our bodies a living sacrifice is a very day-by-day and down-to-earth matter. It will involve little, everyday things – maybe sacrificing the comfort of the cosy armchair and stepping out into the cold, dark evening when your mum asks you to take out the bin; taking an hour or two out of your busy day to visit your elderly grandfather when you could be occupied with any number of other activities; providing a listening ear when one of your friends is unburdening his or her troubles to you. A sacrifice involves cost, so opportunities for sacrificial living will likely be inconvenient and not very pleasant. Your actions will probably be noticed by only a few, or maybe by no one at all. But people's praise isn't what matters. The sacrifice is for God. He sees it, and it is acceptable to Him.

Antipas was My faithful martyr, who was slain among you.

Revelation 2:13

"Have you grace to be a martyr?" someone once asked D. L. Moody.

His reply – "No, I have not. But if God wanted me to be one, He would give me a martyr's grace."

There are certain scenarios in life that we dread. The more we think about them, the more we convince ourselves that we will never be able to cope if, or when, they occur. The death of my grandparents and the notoriously difficult final year of study before I could qualify as an optometrist were only two of the situations that made me fret. But when the time came that I had to walk these paths, difficult as they were, I knew without a doubt that God was with me, helping, comforting, and guiding every step. You've likely had to face dreaded circumstances of your own, and I'm sure you'll agree that when there is a need, God meets it, perfectly and with impeccable timing.

And yet, no matter how much we've known the help of God in the past in difficult and fearful situations, there are many possible experiences that we sincerely hope won't be in our future. Some events, such as the loss of loved ones, we're unlikely to escape; other scenarios may only happen to a handful of us. In general, though, none of us knows what is ahead – either for good or bad. Mr Moody wasn't saying that he wouldn't be able to cope with being a martyr, or even that only certain individuals have a special ability to suffer – martyrs are human, like you and me. Instead, what he was explaining was that God would never ask us to go through a trial without giving us all the resources to face it. Even more importantly, He will give us those resources right when we need them – not a moment before, nor a moment too late. We've proved this in the little things we've faced so far. God doesn't want us to live anxiously, so why not trust Him to do the same in the bigger things?

God hath chosen the weak... that no flesh should glory in His presence.

1 Corinthians 1:27,29

MARCH **14**

What type of people do you think God uses? Those who are confident and charismatic? Intellectual types with extensive vocabulary? Brave and courageous people, who can calmly face down either a bear or a gun-toting thug and never blink?

Open your Bible to 1 Corinthians 1 and read from verse 26 to the end of the chapter. There you'll find the type of people God uses. Foolish, weak, base (ESV – low), and despised. Not many wise, not many mighty, not many noble.

If you're anything like me, you'll look at others and think that they are much better than you are. They have natural abilities that you don't have, they can easily accomplish things that you struggle to do even in a mediocre way. Why bother trying? You're scared to attempt something, knowing that there is a very real possibility that you'll let God down.

But God doesn't see things the way you do. Instead, He can use people like you and me. Those who feel their weakness and inability have the opportunity to depend on Him, whereas people with natural ability for the task may depend on their own strength. When God gives *His* strength, the outcome will far exceed that of someone who is doing it in *human* strength. You see, when someone uses their natural ability to do something great, they often receive praise. But when God calls us to do something for which we have no natural talent, others will see that He is working in us and through us. This will lead to God – the only One who really deserves praise – receiving all the glory.

So the next time God asks you to do something that you feel you aren't fitted for, remember that He has plans to be glorified, and He has chosen to use you – weak and despised – to bring Him glory. What could be better than that?

Daniel purposed in his heart.

Daniel 1:8

As a young Christian, many of the choices you must make will be as a result of pressure and temptation. Maybe some of them are because of the environment in which you find yourself. In the Bible we read of young people who found themselves in a foreign environment and were faced with great pressure and temptations that they wouldn't have had if they'd lived somewhere else or in another era. Maybe this is the same for you – are you being faced with pressures at school, at work, or even online, that others haven't had to face?

Today, let's visit ancient Babylon and meet one of these young people – Daniel.

Daniel lived in Israel but was taken captive to Babylon when Nebuchadnezzar invaded the land. Because of his looks and intelligence, Daniel was one of a number who were handpicked for an elite Chaldean education. The group were to be given a portion of the king's meat and of the king's wine. Daniel had a choice to make. Would he take what the king had prescribed and defile himself by doing what would displease God? Or would he refuse, and risk the wrath of the king? Daniel was under pressure to conform.

Are you under pressure to conform? 'Everybody does it,' has always been a common phrase among teenagers, but it isn't usually true. Even if everybody is doing it, that is no reason for you to join in. As a Christian, you need to be very careful with your diet – what you take in – what you watch, what you read, what you listen to. Your friends might think you're strange for not doing what they do. I'm sure the other young men thought Daniel and his three friends very odd for insisting on eating pulse (things like lentils) rather than meat and wine.

Did Daniel miss out? Take a moment to read Daniel 1. There you'll discover that not only did Daniel and his three friends look healthier, they also had greater wisdom than all the wise men of the kingdom! God noticed their decision and it pleased Him. As a young person, the temptation to conform is huge, but lift your eyes and look a little higher. There's much more to life than what you're experiencing right now, and God still honours wise choices.

How then can I do this great wickedness, and sin against God?

Genesis 39:9

16

MARCH

Every day she asked. Day after day after day. Wouldn't it have been easier to do what she wanted? Why keep saying no all the time?

Joseph, another young person in a foreign environment, ended up working in the house of Potiphar, an important man, where he encountered a very serious temptation. Joseph was an extremely handsome young man... and Potiphar's wife noticed. One day, she came to him with a blatant and immoral suggestion. There are times when a choice needs to be made right there and then, without delay. This was one of those times, and Joseph handled it perfectly with a firm 'no'.

Unfortunately, it made no difference. 'Day by day', Potiphar's wife continued in her attempts to wear him down. I think we'd all agree that it's usually easier to say 'no' once than to have to continue saying it. Every day, Joseph faced the pressure to compromise.

Are you under pressure to compromise? Maybe it's in a moral issue, like the type Joseph was faced with. Don't forget that God's standards are unchanging. It wasn't any easier for people in history to live moral lives, but today we have the added pressure of the internet. Are you tempted to compromise? To open that page or follow that link? Don't! Be like Joseph and flee instead. The long-term effects of going down such a route are truly dreadful.

When the situation finally came to a head, the accusation of Potiphar's wife landed Joseph in prison for many years. He knew that to comply with her request would have been a great wickedness and sin against God. God's assessment of Joseph was more important to him than anything else. He lost his freedom and reputation but retained his blameless character and his communion with God. He had his values right, and that was what mattered.

There's more to the story – the choice that Joseph made had consequences far beyond anything he could ever have imagined when he decided not to compromise. God used him in a mighty way in the preservation of many lives. Never forget that the choices you make as a young person aren't as insignificant and unimportant as you might think. Don't compromise. Put God first in every decision. You will never miss out and God will be glorified.

Greet... all the saints.
Hebrews 13:24 NKJV

At school, I once heard of a heated argument over whether Saint Patrick was Catholic or Protestant. It may seem like a strange thing to argue about, but at that time the relationship between the two groups in Northern Ireland was tense. Each side seemed to want to claim the Patron Saint of Ireland as its own!

The important thing, though, isn't whether Patrick was affiliated with any particular religious denomination. Instead, what really matters is whether or not he was saved. Many today have the mistaken belief that saints are people, already dead, who are declared saints by religious men. There is one thing they are absolutely right about, and that is that saints go to heaven. You see, saints are believers who have put their trust in the Lord Jesus Christ for salvation and so have been *set apart* for Him. The word 'saint' is linked to the word 'sanctify', which means 'to set apart'. I'm a saint. If you're saved, so are you. As our verse at the top of the page would show, it's not a title reserved for what are perceived to be miracle-working holy people who are already dead. So never mind whether Patrick was Protestant or Catholic (actually, the term 'Protestant' didn't even exist until over one thousand years after he lived) – was Patrick truly a saint?

He never called himself a saint, but he did call himself a sinner. He begins his writings, called The Confession of Saint Patrick, with 'I, Patrick, a sinner...' He'd understood the truth of Romans 3:23 – 'All have sinned, and come short of the glory of God.' He then goes on to say that he turned with all his heart to the Lord his God, and further on he says, 'Jesus Christ is Lord and God, in whom we believe.' Patrick truly was a saint – one who had trusted in the Lord Jesus Christ for salvation.

So, on the day which bears his name, while many celebrate with all things green, leprechauns, and lots of alcohol, I'm personally thankful that Patrick ever came to the shores of my native land with the gospel, so that many more people could understand that they were sinners but could become true saints through the death of our Lord Jesus Christ.

That every mouth may be stopped, and all the world may become guilty before God.

Romans 3:19

MARCH

18

If you'd have known ten-year-old Harry, you'd have thought that he was saved and on his way to heaven. In fact, when the Scottish preachers who often stayed in his home asked if he was born again, he told them of his gospel leaflet distribution, his Scripture memorisation, and his Sunday school attendance. Later, his widowed mother moved the family from Toronto to California, and Harry started a Sunday school for the children in the area. By this time, Harry had read the Bible through ten times, but he still couldn't say he was saved, even though it seemed to him that he had always believed.[22]

When he was almost fourteen, one of the Scottish preachers visited his home in California. As before, to Harry's discomfort, they asked if he was born again. His uncle replied for him, telling them that Harry himself now preached. This wasn't enough to satisfy the godly evangelist. He asked Harry to fetch his Bible, which he eventually did, and then asked him to turn to Romans 3:19 and read it aloud. After he had done so, the preacher asked him if his mouth had ever been stopped. "When God makes a preacher," he said, "He stops his mouth first.... When he trusts, he is born of God and his soul is saved. Then God opens his mouth."[23] Harry was convicted and gave up his Sunday school work, but instead began to live for himself.

One evening, while Harry was out at a party, God spoke to him from Proverbs 1:24-32. Harry realised that he had been guilty of refusing God's offer of mercy. Later, as a guilty sinner on his knees by his bed, he trusted the Lord Jesus Christ for salvation. No thrill of joy or sudden rush of love for Christ came, and he wondered if he was really saved. He later said, "There could be no mistake. God loved the world, of which I formed a part. God gave His Son to save all believers. I believed in Him as my Saviour. Therefore I must have everlasting life. Again I thanked Him, and rose from my knees to begin the walk of faith. God could not lie. I knew I must be saved."[24]

Finally, at fourteen years of age, Harry Ironside was born again.

---

22. As told in https://www.wholesomewords.org/biography/bioironside2.html
23. From http://www.plymouthbrethren.org/user/378
24. Also https://www.wholesomewords.org/biography/bioironside2.html

Love one another.

John 13:34

My five hens had always got along well. No squabbling, no pecking, no bossiness. Until one day Philomena turned on Eilish. I've no idea what triggered it, but Philomena flipped! She chased her, pounced on her, and pulled the feathers from her head. And if that wasn't bad enough, the other three hens joined in. Poor Eilish spent most of her days running away from Philomena and her accomplices, until finally we found Philomena a new home. Immediately the ringleader was removed, the bullying ceased. Harmony reigned once again.

Does this sound familiar to you? This pattern of behaviour doesn't only happen in the hen world; in fact, I'm hazarding a guess that you might find it at school, or even at work. Maybe there is someone who, for whatever reason, doesn't fit the perceived 'normal' mould. All of a sudden, someone begins to give them a hard time, either verbally or physically. There's no reason for it – they haven't said anything or done anything to deserve the treatment. They're vulnerable, an easy target. Then others join in too. The victim becomes more and more withdrawn and fearful, while the bullies feed their ego and try to feel important.

Is it possible that you've been tempted to join in? Throw a comment or a blow the victim's way, trying to gain approval and acceptance with the popular crowd? Don't! For a start, this isn't how God would have you treat your fellow human beings. We're commanded to love one another. And secondly, stop and consider what impact the bullying may be having on the victim. It's quite possible they're feeling that life isn't worth living. This is the time that they really need a friend. So instead of hiding with the popular people, why not stand up, cross the room, and show that person the love of God. The impact of your actions might be more than you could ever imagine.

I'm sure you've heard of Goldilocks and the three bears. In the story, the pretty, blonde-haired intruder visits the Bear Family's house, while they are out, and attempts to make herself at home. In each case, after finding fault with Papa Bear's and Mama Bear's bowls of porridge, chairs, and beds, she proclaims Baby Bear's 'just right'.

It's easy to see why the term 'The Goldilocks Enigma' is sometimes used when speaking of the way that conditions on earth are ideal for life. Our planet is exactly balanced – neither too hot nor too cold – due to its optimal distance from the sun. This distance allows the water on our planet to exist as a liquid. Too close, and it would be gas; too far away, and it would be solid.

Even the length of our day is precisely ordered. If the earth took longer than twenty-four hours to spin on its axis, extremely hot days and extremely cold nights would result. A near-circular orbit also helps keep temperatures more consistent than an elliptical orbit, which would give extremes of temperature, depending on how close the earth was to the sun at any point.

Our atmosphere also helps regulate the earth's temperature. If it's too thick, the insulating effect causes the temperature to rise; too thin, and it fluctuates by hundreds of degrees Celsius.

The gravitational pull of earth keeps important elements in the atmosphere, thus shielding and protecting the earth from the sun's rays. Gravitational pull is also important for ocean tides, to maintain a balance between the recycling of nutrients and pollutants, and coastal stability.

So before we've even moved past the first verse in the Bible, a little research about the wonderful earth God created for man gives us cause to wonder and praise Him who designed it so perfectly.[25]

---

25. From *Creation's Story*, by Robert W. Cargill.

I am the Almighty God.
Genesis 17:1

God's power is one of the most obvious of His characteristics. In fact, a reason that many give for not believing that there is a God is that they expect Him to be powerful enough to prevent all the bad things which happen. The issue is not that God hasn't the power – He does! – but that He has given mankind free will and holds him accountable for his actions.

Omnipotent is a word that is often used to describe God. It means 'all powerful', or a word you've probably come across in your Bible, 'almighty'. God's power, however, is consistent with His other attributes.

No matter what we look at – creation, history, future events, and even ourselves – God's power is visible and manifest. We get a glimpse of it when we consider the galaxies and the stars. It is equally visible when we focus on the tiniest components that make up our universe. Events in nature – volcanoes, earthquakes, hurricanes – also clearly show God's power and might. If you are privileged to be studying any of the sciences or geography at school or university, don't let evolutionist and atheistic teaching rob you of the wonder of God's great power manifest in His creation.

God's power is visible in His dealings with nations. Men have made self-serving decisions, and God has used those decisions to accomplish His purposes. The recent situation in Venezuela means that people are leaving for other lands, and they are sharing the gospel with those who have never heard it. Never forget that 'the king's heart is in the hand of the Lord... He turneth it whithersoever He will' (Proverbs 21:1).

God will also show His hand in judgment. People often accuse God of letting evil men get away with their wickedness, but a day is coming when those, like Hitler, who seemed to escape justice on earth, will be judged by God.

God's greatest demonstration of power is the resurrection of Christ. Ephesians 1:19-20 talks of God's mighty power, 'which He wrought in Christ, when He raised Him from the dead.'

Finally, God's power is also seen in us and for us. He has taken poor sinners and made us fit to dwell with Him. How great is our God!

Is thy God... able to deliver thee?

Daniel 6:20

I'm sure you're familiar with the story of how Daniel came to be in the lion's den – how that the king gave a command that no one was to pray to anyone but him, and Daniel disobeyed. Daniel knew what the king didn't seem to realise, that God alone is to be worshipped, and He alone is all powerful. Because of Daniel's obedience to God, he ended up being thrown into a pit full of lions.

Can you imagine? I've only ever seen a lion in a zoo, and it was enclosed behind a very strong glass wall. Lions may be majestic, but they are dangerous animals, especially when they are hungry, as these ones most likely were. One solitary, unarmed man wouldn't stand a chance against such ferocious beasts.

That didn't put Daniel off! He highly valued prayer to God because he knew the might and power of the One to whom he was praying. God's power far exceeded that of the earthly monarch. If the king had fallen into the pit, the lions wouldn't have taken one bit of notice of the royal robes. He had no power whatsoever over the lions. But Daniel knew who did. He knew the One who had created those lions, who had given them their instincts, and who knew the individual characteristics of each. Not only that, they were under His control. Those lions wouldn't open their mouths without God's permission. And they didn't. When the king called to Daniel the next morning to ask if His God was able, Daniel replied that God had shut the lions' mouths.

God is still able. Throughout life we face impossible situations, times when disaster looms and there is no way out. The whole thing can seem hopeless. Could it be that we have even dared to whisper the question, "Is God able?" Remember what we learned about God yesterday? He is omnipotent, all powerful, and almighty. If God is able to put His hand on the natural instincts of dangerous and hungry lions for a whole night, surely He is able for your situation. Never let us doubt the power of God. What was true in Daniel's day is equally true today. God is able to deliver!

Unto Him that is able to do
exceeding abundantly...
Ephesians 3:20

My husband insists I'm a pessimist. (I prefer the word *realist!*) Others are always optimistic. But no matter where on the scale you fall, this verse applies to you.

Let's start with a whittled-down version of the verse. 'God is able to do [what] we ask.' It's a basic truth of Christian life, but do we truly believe it? Sometimes we pray, and deep in our hearts we don't believe that God will actually answer. We know that there is nothing wrong with what we are asking for, but we feel it's an impossible request. Nothing is impossible with God, however, and we must continually remind ourselves of that.

'He can do [what] we ask *or think.*' Have you ever thought about something you desired, but because of a lack of faith, didn't go as far as praying for it? Take courage – God can do what we haven't even dared to voice.

Let's add in the little word 'all'. It's not 'some' of what we ask or think – it is 'all'. God can answer every single one of our prayers and desires if they are in keeping with His will.

It gets better! '*Above* all that we ask or think!' Even those things that we didn't know to ask for, or even to think about, God can do those too.

There's more. 'Abundantly'. I love this word! It brings to mind a fruit tree heavily laden with the most luscious, juicy fruit. God's gifts are generous – ample, plentiful, copious, exuberant, and luxurious.

You might think that you couldn't get better than 'abundantly above all', but you'd be wrong. God loves to shower His blessings on His children, so He tells us that He is able to do '*exceeding* abundantly above all that we ask or think.' There is no limit to God's gifts and ability.

And how is He able to do all this? Because of His power – the power which raised His Son from the dead. The very same power which is at work in us through the Holy Spirit. So next time you pray, remember that God is able to do exceeding abundantly above all that we ask or think.

When people are no longer able to visit the optician for an eye test, the optician goes to them and carries out the test in the person's home. One day, I visited a little old lady whose family had asked me to test her eyes. Putting it mildly, she wasn't one bit pleased that I was there. I figured that the best plan of action would be to do the test as quickly as I could and get out of there. So I hefted the large case with all the little lenses in it onto the sofa and opened it... upside down! Those lenses went everywhere. Trying to do an eye test with the lenses out of order is extremely difficult, so each lens had to be located and put in the correct place. I never opened the case upside down again.

This world is like my opened-upside-down lens case. Values and morals and order that once were taken for granted have been totally mixed up, and it feels as though it could never be put right. Good is called evil, and evil is called good. People are so confused; they hardly know which way is up anymore.

The verb 'to subdue' in our verse can be translated 'to subject'. It is a military term, with the thought of arranging in ranks. When Christ comes again and rules over this earth, everything and everyone – both creation and mankind – will be subdued and subjected to Him, put in order and in their proper place. All that is wrong with this world will be put right. He is the only One who has the power to do this.

This phrase from Philippians is actually the very end of a section which talks about the believers' bodies. The power by which Christ will subdue all things to Himself is the very same as that which will transform our earthly bodies to become like His body of glory. Isn't that a great thought? Not only will the world be put in order, but we will be like Him. So as you head out into this crazy, mixed-up world, don't forget that there is One who is able to subdue all things unto Himself... and we are going to be like Him!

He is able to succour them that are tempted.

Hebrews 2:18

Now and again, I visit homes where a little baby is asleep in another room. All is calm, then a loud cry breaks the silence. Immediately, the child's mother springs to her feet and rushes to the baby in order to soothe it and meet its needs. This is the meaning of the word 'succour' in today's verse – running to help one who calls. But this passage isn't talking about a mother and her baby. Instead, it's the Lord Jesus Christ who runs to the aid of the believer.

Sometimes, despite a mother's best efforts, the child cannot be consoled. Milk, a clean nappy, medicine – no matter what she does, nothing works. She might run to its aid, but she cannot truly help the little one. The Lord Jesus isn't like that. The Word of God is clear that He *is able* to succour! But for what reason is He able? Let's read the rest of the verse. 'For in that He Himself hath suffered being tempted...' The Lord Jesus Christ knows what it is to suffer. He became a man. He could never sin, but He knew the normal human experiences that we go through, because He went through them Himself. He knew what it was to be rejected, to be falsely accused, to be tested. He felt the attacks of Satan. He faced the scorn of men. He experienced the high cost of choosing to obey God. And because He suffered, He knows what you are going through.

Each mother was once a baby herself, but she cannot remember what it was like. The Lord Jesus Christ, however, fully remembers His days on earth as if He were still here. His memory cannot be dimmed. And so He is able to succour. When you cry to Him, He immediately hears you. He understands what you are facing, and He runs to your aid, bringing the help that you need.

He is able to save to the uttermost.

Hebrews 7:25 ESV

MARCH **26**

When you got saved, what were you thankful for? Probably that your sins were all forgiven, that the burden was gone, and that, one day, you'd be in heaven. But did you know that, while those things are truly wonderful, there is so much more to salvation?

The fact that 'He is able to save' is a great example of God's omnipotence. As sinners, our *righteous* deeds were filthy before God. How much more abhorrent were our *sins*? We could never be in His holy presence, and the only place we deserved was hell forever. Yet God in His mercy and great power, through the death of His only Son, was able to cleanse us and save us from our sins.

If God had only saved us from hell, that would have been amazing. But the verse says that He is able to save *to the uttermost* – completely and perfectly. There is nothing lacking in our salvation – no sin that He has not forgiven, no part of our character that He is not working on to make us more like Christ, no promised future blessing that He will hold back from us.

There is also no part of our salvation that depends upon us. If He saves to the uttermost – completely and perfectly – then how could we do anything to make ourselves any more saved? It's impossible! Living to please God is just that – pleasing Him, not earning some part of our salvation.

Also included in the word 'uttermost' is the thought of 'forever'. When God saves us, He saves us forever. When we sin, He doesn't change His mind and 'unsave' us. Communion with God may be broken, but our salvation will always be secure.

And the reason why we are saved completely, perfectly and forever? Because we are saved through the Lord Jesus Christ, whom God raised from the dead, the One who always lives. Unlike the sacrifices in the Old Testament, which had to be offered multiple times, the sacrifice of the Lord Jesus was a one-time sacrifice, which never has to be repeated.

Let's allow the word 'uttermost' to sink into our souls, and revel in our complete, perfect, and forever salvation!

To Him who is able to keep you from stumbling.
Jude 24 NKJV

One minute I was running as fast as my little seven- or eight-year-old legs could carry me, faster than I'd ever run before. The next I was sprawled on the ground, just short of the finish line. My pride hurt much more than my knees, especially the following week when the whole class watched the video of the only recorded sports day that I remember in my eight years at primary school. I squeezed my eyes tightly shut and tried to block out the laughter of my classmates as my ignominious tumble was shown on the screen.

Everyone knows what it is to stumble and fall. Maybe due to uneven paving, a lack of concentration, or a cat who insists on walking where you are about to set your foot. The Christian walk is no different. Stumbling is a very real possibility. Sometimes the path is so rocky that we need to take utmost care. Other times we're so engrossed in other things that we fail to concentrate on each step. And, of course, Satan is always out to trip us up. Maybe you even feel that there are so many dangers on the Christian pathway that stumbling is unavoidable.

That's not what the Bible says. We have an omnipotent, all-powerful, almighty God... who is able to keep us from stumbling! It doesn't have to be an unfortunate but inevitable part of a believer's life. With His help, we can take each step as surefooted and unfaltering as a mountain goat.

But what we must not do is think that we can manage in our own strength. 1 Corinthians 10:12 NKJV warns, 'Let him who thinks he stands take heed lest he fall.' Did you ever explore a rocky beach as a little child? Maybe the big rocks were slippery with seawater and seaweed, so you took your dad's hand. When you began to slip, his big hand and strong arm held you up and kept you from stumbling. Your dad was able, but you needed to be right by his side.

So, take courage. Stumbling is not an inevitable part of the Christian life. God is able to keep you from stumbling, but remember, you need to stay close to Him.

No man... was able to open the book.
The Lion of the tribe of Judah...
hath prevailed to open the book.
Revelation 5:3,5

28

MARCH

Over the past week, we have looked at divine omnipotence and have seen it illustrated by the phrase 'He is able'. Today we're going to take a journey into the future, right into heaven itself. As we stand quietly and observe with awe, we see the apostle John in great consternation. An angel is holding an exceedingly important scroll – most likely the title deeds of the whole earth – but no one is able to take it and open it. There is not a single person in heaven or on earth or under the earth who has the power or the authority to take the book.

As John weeps, we see one, called an elder, come to instruct John to stop weeping. There *is* One who is worthy to take and open the book. He is called the Lion of the tribe of Judah, the Root of David. This is none other than the Lord Jesus Christ. He is King and He is Messiah. But as the focus moves to Him, we realise that He is described as a slain Lamb, bearing the marks of death, yet living. Often, the lamb in the Bible is a picture of the Lord Jesus Christ. And here, almost at the end of the Bible, we see the Lord again depicted as a sacrificial lamb. We also learn that this lamb has seven horns (seven is the number of perfection and horns signify power, so this is power in complete perfection) and seven eyes (signifying knowledge in complete perfection). This One – the King, the Messiah, the Lamb – is the only One who has the power and the authority to open the book. He is able!

Who could help but worship One who is so worthy? Those in heaven begin to praise Him, singing of His death and shed blood which redeemed us to God, out of all nations of the earth. The chorus of praise swells and grows. Every creature joins in worship to the Only Worthy One. Let us join our voices in praise and worship to the One who has all power and authority, the One who is worthy, the One who redeemed us to God by His blood.

For to me to live is Christ.
Philippians 1:21

Robert Cleaver Chapman was born in Denmark in January 1803 into a wealthy family. When he was still young, they moved back to England, and Robert was sent to school in Yorkshire, before studying law and becoming a solicitor. Robert was a religious young man, believing he could get to heaven by his good works, but after a while he realised that he was a sinner. At this time, he was invited to a church service where he heard that all his good works could never earn favour with God, and he rested on Christ's finished work.

Robert continued his work as a solicitor, but now spent his evenings in the slums, sharing the gospel with people at the very bottom of society. He became convinced that God would have him give up his job to devote all his time to the Lord's work, but his friends told him he would never make a preacher. His response to them was, "There are many who preach Christ, but not so many who live Christ; my great aim will be to *live* Christ."[26]

Robert moved to Barnstaple and, despite his friends' glum predictions, he did become a preacher. His humble home, chosen because he knew he was susceptible to pride, was always open to anyone who needed it. This great man even insisted on cleaning the shoes and boots of all his guests, saying that it was the nearest thing in that day to washing the saints' feet. He had a desire to see people saved in other lands and visited Ireland in 1848 during the potato famine. He covered over six hundred miles, mostly on foot, preaching the gospel to those who had never heard of salvation by grace alone and helping to alleviate the distress of the poor and hungry. He also had a great interest in Spain and made a number of visits there to help spread the gospel.

Robert died when he was ninety-nine, but the great focus of his life was always the Lord Jesus, evidenced in the hymns he wrote, such as *O Our Saviour Crucified*, and *The Lamb of God to Slaughter Led*, which show a deep appreciation of Christ's suffering and death. R. C. Chapman was truly a man who lived Christ throughout his long and interesting life.

---

26. Information taken from https://bibletruthpublishers.com/r-c-chapman/henry-pickering/chief-men-among-the-brethren/hy-pickering/la129640

As we read through the Bible, we'll discover that the Old Testament and New Testament are closely linked. We will come across things in the Old Testament that we only really understand the importance of when they are viewed through the lens of the New Testament. The Passover, which we first read about in Exodus 12, is one of them.

You'll remember that, in the book of Genesis, Joseph's brothers sold him, and he ended up in Egypt. Eventually he became a great ruler, second only to Pharaoh, and saved many people's lives due to his wisdom in preparing for a great famine. Eventually, his whole family moved to Egypt, but, as time went on, the company grew so large that the new Pharaoh was alarmed, so he made them his slaves.

Pharaoh wasn't going to let them go without a fight, but God had plans to deliver them. If you didn't know the story already, you might have wondered if God would send an army of angels to swoop down and defeat Pharaoh. Instead, God's plan involved a lamb.

As we read through the chapter, with the benefit of our viewpoint from this side of Calvary, we recognise that the lamb is a type of our Lord Jesus Christ. The Passover was an important occasion in the calendar of the Jewish people, but it meant even more to God than it did to the people of Israel. He instructed them to keep it every year for a memorial, yet they couldn't see the significance of it the way we can. When John the Baptist proclaimed, "Behold the Lamb!" in John 1:29, I wonder if pieces of the jigsaw began to slot into place for those who heard him. By the time we reach the end of the New Testament, with its many references to the slain Lamb, we are in no doubt as to who the Passover lamb signified. Paul said in 1 Corinthians 5:7, 'Christ our passover is sacrificed for us.' Peter says, 'Ye were not redeemed with corruptible things... but with the precious blood of Christ, as of a lamb without blemish and without spot.' (1 Peter 1:18,19).

In your Bible reading, look out for references to the Passover. It's a central theme in the Word of God and important to know about.

Ye were... redeemed... with the precious blood of Christ, as of a lamb without blemish and without spot.

1 Peter 1:18,19

Yesterday we began to look at the Passover through the lens of the New Testament, and today we're going to take another look, learning some lessons along the way. You see, like the Israelites, we were once in bondage, slaves to a cruel tyrant with no hope of escaping by ourselves. In fact, we were in a worse condition than the Israelites ever were because we were bound by chains of sin, in the grasp of Satan. And when we read about the firstborn, we discover that not only was he in bondage, he was also condemned, as were we.

Like the Israelite firstborn, it took the death and shed blood of a spotless One to redeem us. The firstborn wouldn't have been saved unless the blood had been applied to the doorposts and lintel of the house. In the same way, we would never have been saved had we not 'applied the blood' – trusted in the Lord Jesus Christ and accepted His sacrifice. It was the applied blood that made those inside safe and secure, not their feelings. Our salvation doesn't depend on our feelings either.

The first Passover was a new beginning – God even changed Israel's calendar so that this month would be the beginning of months for them. When we got saved, there was a new beginning.

God also wanted this momentous event to be remembered, so He commanded that the feast would be kept each year in memory of their deliverance. Even the Lord Jesus Christ – the One whom the Passover lamb typified – kept the Passover the night before He was crucified. The sacrifice and death of Christ should never be far from our thoughts, but we have been asked by the Lord Himself to remember Him in a special way by partaking of bread and a cup with other believers in the local church at the Lord's supper (1 Corinthians 11:23-26).

There were periods in Israel's history when the Passover wasn't kept, but when recovery and restoration took place, the feast recommenced. Frequent remembrance of our redemption will keep our hearts warm, and when we grow spiritually cold, remembering the sacrifice and shed blood of the Lamb will draw us back to Him.

APRIL

Give attendance to reading.
1 Timothy 4:13

When you pick up your Bible, how do you decide where to read? Do you follow a plan, or do you flick through the pages until you find a verse that catches your eye? Maybe you have favourite passages you like to turn to, depending on your mood. What way should we read the Bible? Is there a right way and a wrong way?

It's good to keep in mind that the Bible is a collection of books. Some of them are history books, some prophecy, some poetry, and others are letters to churches or individuals. Because of this, we don't have to begin at Genesis and read right through to Revelation (although there are advantages to this, which we'll see in a minute). We can choose any of the sixty-six books – but read all of the book, not only your favourite parts. The books of the Bible have been arranged in a certain way and grouped together – law together, prophecy together, poetry together etc. In fact, did you know that Paul's letters are all grouped together, with the letters to churches first, followed by letters to individuals?

Some books of the Bible are easier to read than others. You'll likely be able to understand the gospels better than some of the books of prophecy in the Old Testament. But does this mean we forget about those more difficult books? Of course not! As we'll see tomorrow, all Scripture is profitable, and by reading it, you are laying a foundation of biblical knowledge which you will build upon as you grow as a believer.

So how do we make sure we're reading all of the Word of God? One valid method is, as I mentioned, to read from Genesis to Revelation. You'll not skip any books by mistake using this method. There are also plenty of good Bible reading plans out there – reading through the whole Bible in a year, for instance. Or plans to help you read the books of the Bible in chronological order. This way, you'll be able to see where the prophecies fit into history. Find a plan that works for you and keep at it. It doesn't really matter which method you use as long as you're reading your Bible – all of it!

All scripture is given by
inspiration of God, and is
profitable.

2 Timothy 3:16

APRIL

2

We've learned that we should be reading our Bibles, making sure we have some system in place so that we're covering the whole Word of God. But why exactly is it so important to read all of the Bible? Surely, since we are Christians who are living after the Lord Jesus was here, the New Testament is most relevant to us? It is – the teaching in the epistles was specifically written for believers in this day and age. We should read it, study it, and obey it.

But the Old Testament isn't any less important. It may not have been written primarily with us in mind, but it still has much value for us. First of all, in Genesis we have the history of the creation of the world, and we can read about the first people to occupy this planet. In another few chapters, you'll read about the flood in Noah's day – a significant event with geological consequences right to the present day.

Another reason the Old Testament is important is because you'll find prophecies about the Lord Jesus. There are many types and pictures of Him, especially in Exodus and Leviticus where we read about the tabernacle, the sacrifices, and the feasts. Reading a good commentary alongside your Bible will help you a lot here. Many books also cover the history of God's dealings with His people, Israel. We can learn many lessons from their actions and how God dealt with them – in judgment and in mercy. From these events, we find out so much about God's character.

You'll find wisdom and instruction in Proverbs and comfort and help in Psalms. We can marvel over the fulfilment of the prophecies and learn about those still to be fulfilled. There are many interesting characters in the Old Testament, and we can learn lessons from their triumphs and failures. In fact, the Old Testament is full of people! The lists of names may be hard to read, but God has seen fit to include them in Scripture. If we learn nothing else from these lists, we can rest assured that individuals are important to God.

Don't be afraid of the Old Testament. Read it and learn from it. After all, God has said that *all* Scripture is profitable!

Our God whom we serve is able to deliver us... but if not... we will not serve thy gods.

Daniel 3:17,18

It looked to be an impossible situation. Shadrach, Meshach and Abednego had been taken captive in the land of Israel, given a Babylonian education and, through extraordinary circumstances, had been promoted. Now they were being asked to bow down to King Nebuchadnezzar's golden image. If they obeyed Nebuchadnezzar, they'd be disobeying God. If they obeyed God by not bowing down, Nebuchadnezzar would throw them into a fiery furnace. For these three men, obeying the king wasn't an option. God had commanded that they should not worship any graven image.

Could God really deliver them? Look at the previous chapter. They had been threatened with death, but God stepped in and worked a miracle, revealing to their friend Daniel the king's dream and the meaning of it, thus saving their lives and the lives of many others. They knew what God could do. Despite them living in this ungodly land, He had never let them down. They also knew that God never changes. If He was able to deliver them before, He could do it again. They had full confidence in Him.

Has God ever delivered you? It's unlikely you've been threatened by a pagan king, but there have been other deliverances in your life, of which your deliverance from sin is the greatest. Our God is great!

So God could deliver and had delivered in the past, but look at the next part of the verse – 'but if not'. What? Haven't we just discovered that these men had full faith in God and His power? That's true. They had proved His delivering power before and knew He could deliver them again, but they also recognised that sometimes God lets His children face trials. Don't forget that He permitted Nebuchadnezzar to take these young men captive to begin with. The men had learned that sometimes God delivers, and sometimes, in His great love and wisdom, He doesn't. Whether God would deliver or not had no bearing on their trust in Him. Like these young men, it's good for us to have faith in God that He can deliver. But having full trust in God, whether He delivers or not, is even better!

W e've all seen simple depictions of Noah's ark – semi-circular-shaped base, little roofed area poking up in the middle, and happy-looking elephants, giraffes, and monkeys on the deck beside a jolly Mr Noah. I don't think any of us are convinced that what is shown in children's picture books is anything close to reality. For a start, Genesis 6 tells us that the ark was three hundred cubits long, and only thirty high, so it probably had the appearance of a barge – long and low. And it really was long! Because we don't use the measurement of cubits today, we can get a bit lost when it comes to dimensions in the Bible unless we look them up.[27] The ark was actually about 160 metres long – longer than two of the biggest passenger jumbo jets lined up nose to tail, and approximately 1.5 times the length of the football stadium, Old Trafford. It was huge!

But how did it ever stay afloat? Wouldn't you think that such a massive, oddly shaped vessel would toss and roll about in the middle of a violent storm? Actually, hydraulic engineering experts have worked on the given dimensions of the ark and have concluded that it would have been almost impossible to capsize. The ratio of length:breadth:height also meant that, not only would it have been stable, it wouldn't have been subject to pitching and rolling in the great waves either.

It was a huge vessel, but then, it had to be. Not only did it need to be spacious enough for Noah and his family, it had to have enough room for two of every type of animal, and seven of those specified by God, not to mention all the food that they would need for the time they would be there. Calculations have shown that the ark would hold over 125,000 sheep-sized animals. A very generous estimate puts the number of animals in the ark at 50,000. The One who made the animals knew how much space each would need, and there was plenty of room.

It's clear to see that the ark was perfectly designed – but should that cause us any surprise, when we remember who the Great Designer was, and consider the previous marvellous works He had already done?[28]

---

27. You'll find a useful chart on Bible weights and measures at https://www.webtruth.org/charts/bible-weights-and-measures-chart/

28. Material based on Chapter 15 – The Amazing Ark in *And God Said*, by Dr Farid Abou-Rahme, published by John Ritchie Ltd in 1997.

He who loves God must love
his brother also.
1 John 4:21 NKJV

There's a little poem I've often heard that never fails to make me smile. It goes like this –

To dwell above with saints we love, oh yes, that will be glory.
To dwell below with saints we know... Well, that's another story!

Have you ever felt like this? I sure have! We look forward to being in heaven with those believers we love so much. But then there's the reality of actually getting along with fellow believers right here on earth. And that can certainly be a challenge at times.

The wonderful thing about God's saving grace is that it's for everyone. He makes no distinction, and so people are saved from every background imaginable. There are different cultures, ethnic backgrounds, social classes, levels of intelligence, and personalities all represented in the family of God. This inevitably means that there will be other Christians whom we struggle to relate to or understand.

In your local assembly or church gathering, you may or may not have a wide range of cultural backgrounds, but you will certainly have a range of personalities. There will be those you naturally warm to, and others who never fail to rub you up the wrong way. Don't forget, though, that others may feel the same way about you!

What are we to do with those for whom our love doesn't come naturally? We must remember that Christ died for them every bit as much as He died for you. We are each loved with the greatest love possible, so no one is that little bit closer to God's heart than anyone else. Don't forget to pray for them. You might not develop any warm fuzzies towards them, but it will help you see them as God sees them. And, by the way, brotherly love isn't about warm fuzzies anyway; it's a deliberate choice. Recognise that you share a love for the Lord. If nothing else, you've got at least that one thing in common.

And pray for help. God knows if you're struggling with negative feelings towards others. He is able to change our hearts, if we are willing to be changed. Wouldn't it be wonderful if we could experience a little bit of heaven on earth?

A few years ago, my brother's best friend was a liver and white English springer spaniel named Heidi. As is typical of the breed, she was lively and playful, but, with training, that energy and intelligence were harnessed, and she became a skilful working gundog. She was the most obedient dog I've ever known. She stayed when she was told to stay, ran to fetch when she was instructed to fetch, and stopped and sat immediately when the whistle blew, even if she was only halfway to her goal. She jumped onto walls, over hedges, and plunged through undergrowth at my brother's instruction. Really, there was nothing she wouldn't do for him.

I often wonder why we Christians are not so keen to obey God! Heidi loved my brother; you could see the affection for him in her expressive brown eyes, and the feeling was mutual. Dogs don't really require much reason to love their owners – a little kindness, and they are your loyal companions. God did much more than show us a *little* kindness. Instead, He gave the very best He had – His only Son – and continues to heap grace upon grace every day. His giving has no limit. You'd think, really, that whatever God asked of us, we would almost trip over ourselves to do. So why don't we? Why do we run ahead when God wants us to wait, stay where we are when we have instruction to get on with something, and ignore His signal to go in this direction or that?

My brother had his reasons for asking Heidi to wait, to run, and to stop. He knew where she should be heading and was able to guide her, but it only worked when she let him take the lead and trusted his guidance.

Is that our problem when it comes to obeying God? Is it an issue of trust? Sometimes the things that God asks of us don't seem to make sense. It's possible for a Christian to lose trust in the greatness and goodness of God. In times like this, we must cling to the truth – that God loves us. My brother would never have asked Heidi to do anything that would be harmful to her. How much less would God ask anything of us that isn't for our good?

The exceeding riches of His grace.
Ephesians 2:7

mazing Grace, written by ex-slave trader John Newton in 1772, could well be the world's best-known hymn. It has been recorded by hundreds, maybe even thousands, of artists from many time periods and genres of music. But how many of these talented people were able to fully appreciate the beautiful words they were singing? And what exactly is grace anyway?

There are many references to grace in the Bible, especially in Paul's writings. In Ephesians 2:8 NKJV we read, 'For by grace you have been saved through faith, and that not of yourselves; it is the gift of God.' Here we learn that grace is not something that we can obtain in our own strength or do anything to earn. It's not even that we do the best we can, and God will do the rest. If that was the case, it would still be of ourselves, and the Bible states plainly that it's not. Grace is totally unmerited.

We can't earn grace, nor do we deserve it. We are sinners through and through, and only deserve punishment. One of the marks of a Christian is that we are more conscious of the vileness of our sin and our unworthiness than we were as unbelievers. When we see sin as God sees it, we don't need to be convinced that what we have been given as believers is all of grace. In fact, the more obnoxious sin is to us, and the more we realise how unworthy we are of receiving anything from God, the more we will appreciate His grace to us.

Grace is not God shrugging at sin and saying that it no longer matters. Sin needed to be dealt with righteously – it needed taken away – which is why God's grace shines so brightly. You know that to show grace to us, the Lord Jesus Christ had to die on the cross, but what amazes me is that He didn't only come to save us from our sins. That would have been truly wonderful, but think about how much more we have received. God has lavished blessings on us – we have been made rich. 2 Corinthians 8:9 NKJV says, 'You know the grace of our Lord Jesus Christ, that though He was rich, yet for your sakes He became poor, that you through His poverty might become rich.'

Let the little children come to Me.

Matthew 19:14 NKJV

There are many wonderful conversion stories! The apostle Paul met the Lord on the Damascus Road, and the Philippian jailor was awakened by an earthquake. You've probably heard countless modern-day conversion stories of those saved out of a life of drugs, immorality, and crime.

I was saved when I was eleven. I was a sinner – my disobedience to my parents and the lies I'd told, along with my bad temper, all ensured that I didn't need to be convinced of it – but I hadn't been involved in the depths of sin that are rampant in the world. Many of you likely had a similar experience. It can be tempting to think of your own testimony as, well, a little bit boring. We'd never admit it, but maybe, in our heart of hearts, we kind of wish we had some amazing tale of deliverance to recount.

Each soul saved is a miracle! It doesn't matter whether we were five or six, fifty or sixty, when it happened. It doesn't matter how deep into sin we'd sunk. Every single one of us was lost. If God hadn't given His Son to save us, we'd have been in hell. It took Christ's death on the cross to save each of us, even those of us who were still very young. We were totally helpless and hopeless without Him.

Do you ever think about what would have happened had you not got saved when you did? Where would you have been today? What about ten years' time? We will never really know, but what we can be sure of is that, in trusting Christ at an early age, God has preserved us from many of the evils in which we may have participated, had we not belonged to Him. Many who have been saved after years spent chasing worldly enjoyments still carry scars, both physical and psychological. They are a new creation in Christ Jesus, but their greatest regret is that they did not trust Him sooner.

So, instead of wishing our stories were a little more exciting, let's praise God and thank Him all the more for saving us when we were young, and preserving us for His glory.

9

APRIL

A friend loveth at all times.
Proverbs 17:17

I wonder how many people over the years have taken comfort from the old, well-known hymn 'What a Friend We Have in Jesus'? The words reassure us of the love and care of the Lord Jesus Christ for us, and encourage us to pray, especially when trials and temptations beset us and we're burdened, forsaken, and discouraged.

The writer of the hymn, Joseph Scriven, certainly knew all about trials. He was born in Banbridge, County Down, in 1819, and graduated from Trinity College, Dublin, in 1842. He was to be married in 1843, but the night before the wedding, his fiancée tragically drowned. Joseph then emigrated to Canada, but after a short time returned to Ireland and joined the Royal Dragoons. Poor health meant he could not continue, so a few years later, he returned to Canada and settled in Ontario, working as a private tutor, and giving what he had to help people in need. People were critical of his generosity, and he was often misunderstood.

Joseph fell in love once again, but a few weeks before the wedding, his fiancée passed away from pneumonia. His best-known hymn was written after this and was included in a letter to his mother to comfort her when she was ill. He never intended it to bring him praise or fame.

Joseph Scriven's hymn was written out of the deep, unforgettable sorrows of his heart. He knew all about pain, trials, temptations, discouragements, being despised and forsaken, but he knew the only One to whom he could turn in such circumstances – to the faithful Friend who always cares, who will shelter and shield us in His arms.

We may become overfamiliar and perhaps a bit bored with old, traditional hymns, and their impact is lost on us. But many of them, including this one, are full of comforting truth which will do our hearts good each time we sing and consider the words.[29]

> Have we trials and temptations?
> Is there trouble anywhere?
> We should never be discouraged
> Take it to the Lord in prayer.

---

29. Information taken from https://www.imdb.com/name/nm3772784/bio
https://www.belfasttelegraph.co.uk/news/northern-ireland/banbridge-honours-joseph-scriven-writer-of-famous-hymn-200-years-on-38489445.html
https://www.stempublishing.com/hymns/biographies/scriven.html

Walk by the Spirit, and you will not gratify the desires of the flesh.

Galatians 5:16 ESV

APRIL

10

As you read through the Bible, you'll have come across the word 'flesh'. But what does it mean? Normal English dictionaries aren't much help here, as we know the Bible isn't literally talking about the soft tissue between our skin and bones. Often, the word refers to the physical body, but in this passage it is used to describe our old, sinful nature.

There are many things that appeal to this nature, and they won't all be the same for each person. The section in verses 19-21 gives a long list of different works of the flesh, which a believer – one who is going to heaven – should not do. When you got saved, you may have been shocked to realise that you still sinned, even though you had turned to Christ for salvation. Believers often discover that when they commit sin, it bothers them much more than it ever did before they trusted Christ. Sadly, our old nature, as the old preachers used to say, 'was neither removed nor improved' upon conversion. In heaven, we will be free from sin, but right now we still have that nature within us that responds to sin and temptation.

So what can we do? An illustration that I often heard when I was your age was of two dogs. One is an angry, ill-tempered, vicious dog, the other is warm and loving, and we can only feed one of them. I'm sure it's obvious which one we should choose! Your two natures are like the two dogs, and the one we feed will be stronger. If we spend time feeding the old nature – gratifying the desires of the flesh – we will show the awful characteristics described in verses 19-21. But if we spend time feeding the new nature, for example, reading and studying Scripture – and so walking in the Spirit – we will manifest the characteristics in verses 22-23. These are the characteristics that we are going to look at over the next few days to see how we can live in such a way that the fruit of the Spirit is clear to all who observe us.

The fruit of the Spirit is love.
Galatians 5:22

The first fruit of the Spirit is love. In fact, some writers say that the other fruit grows out of this one. But if you're like me, you'll have discovered that 'love' is an easier word to say than to put into practice!

One of the best-known chapters in the Bible is 1 Corinthians 13. As it is all about love, it's commonly read at weddings, even those of people who aren't Christians. But you're not married, and you're wondering what on earth it has got to do with you! Quite a lot actually. 1 Corinthians 13 wasn't written to be read at weddings and it's not even talking about the love between a husband and a wife. Instead, it was written because there were problems in the church at Corinth. Paul was teaching the Christians that they should be motivated by love and show love to one another.

Let's take a quick look at 1 Corinthians 13 to see what love ought to look like. In the ESV translation, we read that love is patient, kind, doesn't envy or boast, isn't arrogant, rude, irritable, or resentful. It doesn't rejoice at wrongdoing but rejoices with the truth. It bears, believes, hopes, and endures all things.

Wow. Do you measure up? I sure don't! How often do we become resentful or envious? Are we always patient and kind? Or do we become irritable or rude? When reading a list like this, it can be easy to despair that we will ever be the type of believer God would have us to be. But don't forget that we are not trying to produce the fruit solely by our own effort. Instead, we have the Holy Spirit indwelling us, who will produce these characteristics in us, if we walk in Him.

One great way to walk in the Spirit is to spend time reading and thinking about the only One who ever lived a flawless life – the Lord Jesus Christ. He demonstrated all of these characteristics of love absolutely perfectly. The more time we spend reading and thinking about Him, the more like Him we will be – the One who loved us and gave Himself for us.

The fruit of the Spirit is... joy.

Galatians 5:22

I'm sure you can think of at least one children's Sunday school song that is all about joy. They're usually cheerful little choruses, and easy to sing with a smile. But what about those days when everything goes wrong, when life takes an unexpected turn, or when you wake up feeling grumpy? It's not so easy to display joy then, is it?

One of the common misconceptions of Christian life is that happiness and joy are the same thing. We have the mistaken notion that if we don't run around with huge grins on our faces, we are letting God down. The truth is that hard times come, and happiness isn't always possible. You see, happiness depends on happenings. Joy, however, is independent of our circumstances. While it may seem hard to believe, it's actually possible to have joy in the middle of difficult and trying times.

There are so many reasons why the Christian should be joyful, not least because we are saved. Isaiah 12:3 says, 'With joy shall ye draw water out of the wells of salvation.' Even if our entire life consists of one tough day after another, filled with loneliness and devoid of physical comfort, having the knowledge that our sins are forgiven is enough to give us joy in the darkest days.

But just because we have so much to be joyful about, it doesn't mean that we will always experience the joy we ought to have. Giving way to the desires of the flesh – for example, neglecting to read the Bible, unconfessed sin in our lives, or having a grudge against a fellow believer – will rob us of joy. But when we walk in the Spirit, living as we should as God's children, the Spirit will produce the fruit of joy in our lives. And as joy isn't something that can easily be hidden, God will be glorified in us.

The fruit of the Spirit is... peace.

Galatians 5:22

As my grandfather lay on his deathbed, a few days before he died, someone in the room began to sing. *When peace like a river attendeth my way, when sorrows like sea billows roll...* Everyone joined in, some of us struggling to force the words past the lumps in our throats at the realisation that Granda was soon going to leave us. *It is well... with my soul, it is well, it is well... with my soul.* Granda had lost his ability to sing years before when he had suffered a stroke, and he was now so ill he wasn't able to speak, but we all knew without a doubt, that could he have joined in, he would have – heartily.

I never hear this hymn without thinking of that moment. How that despite the billowing storm of great weakness and pain, Granda was at peace because he knew it was well with his soul.

Very often, peace doesn't come easily. Our circumstances can cause us to toss and turn at night. Anxiety seems to reign in our hearts and minds during the day. We might have trusted God for our eternal salvation, but we're struggling to trust Him for the temporal situations on earth. It doesn't really make sense, does it?

That's where the Spirit comes in. If we are walking in Him, trusting in God will be a natural thing to do. We will be praying and spending time in God's Word, learning and growing in the realisation that He is absolutely trustworthy. He didn't promise to take us to heaven, and then abandon us to muddle along on earth as best we can in the meantime. Instead, He promised to be with us. Romans 8:28 says that all things work together for good to those who love God, so we can take each situation as something He will use for good.

Peace isn't something that is unattainable, or only something we can experience during sunny days. Instead, it is a fruit of the Spirit. It will be displayed by those who are walking in Him and can be the experience of every one of us.

The fruit of the Spirit is... patience.

Galatians 5:22 ESV

APRIL

14

There's the little child who can't wait for Christmas... or maybe that's not only little kids! Maybe some of you are counting down the days until you finally get behind the wheel of a car. Parents might be excitedly looking forward to taking their children to Disney World for the first time. Or an older person is anxiously awaiting the arrival of a new grandchild. I don't think there is anyone, from babies to centenarians, who has never known what it is to struggle with exercising patience. Even my dog is severely patience-challenged when it comes to walks or food. When we want something, we want it *now*!

Patience is also required when dealing with certain people whose personalities rub us up the wrong way. We almost bite our tongues clean off in an effort to prevent ourselves saying something we regret. But don't forget that these people might be trying to exercise as much patience in dealing with us.

In this passage, the word 'patience' can also be translated as 'longsuffering', which, to be honest, doesn't sound like something we'd be too keen to have to put into practice! One commentary gives the meaning as 'courageous endurance without quitting'.[30] It means to keep pressing on, even though the road is uphill and you can't see the end. Some situations are temporary. Maybe you have a teacher who loves to pick on you, a subject you can't make sense of, a work colleague who makes your life a misery. The road may seem long, but it *will* end. Keep pressing on.

Other times you may not see an end to a situation. Life can look bleak and difficult, and sometimes you might even be tempted to feel that it isn't worth living. It's especially then that you must have patience. God hasn't let you experience your particular set of circumstances for no reason. He knows what He's doing, and He has a bright future ahead for you, when you will look back and thank Him for His wisdom. Keep walking in the Spirit and the fruit of patience will be produced in your life.

---

30. *The Wiersbe Bible Commentary.*

The fruit of the Spirit is...
kindness.
Galatians 5:22 NKJV

W e all know what the word 'kindness' means. It doesn't require an explanation, although, if you're wanting one, it has in it the thought of being considerate, helpful, and gentle. Admittedly, kindness may come more naturally to some people than it will to others. One thing is clear – you may have kind thoughts, but you cannot be truly kind unless you have some object on which to bestow kindness. In other words, you cannot live shut up like a hermit in a little house in the mountains, miles away from anyone, and say you're a kind person!

Some people are easy to show kindness to. Maybe they've been kind to you, or they tell you how much they appreciate all you do for them. Helpless creatures often arouse pity in us, and so we're kind to them. But what do you do when people are ungrateful, and never stop to thank you? Or when they even seem to resent your help?

In all of the characteristics we are looking at this week, the Lord Jesus Christ was the perfect example, especially when it came to dealing with fellow humans. Think of what He did, coming to earth, living amongst people (John 1 tells us that His own people didn't receive Him), healing the sick and lame, and finally giving Himself to the death of the cross so that sinners could be saved. He was mistreated and misunderstood, yet nothing that men said or did altered the kindness He displayed.

Walking in the Spirit will result in our becoming more like Christ, so the fruit of kindness will be produced in our lives. It won't happen automatically. We need to strive towards becoming more like Him, not because our salvation depends upon it, but because we will please God.

As you go about your daily life, look for opportunities to show kindness. It might involve walking across the classroom to sit beside someone who is viewed as an outcast, or it could be as simple as refusing to say some unkind thing that was on the tip of your tongue. Let's live in such a way that people will see the fruit of kindness in our lives.

Goodness is closely linked to kindness. Is kindness the thought which prompts goodness, or is goodness the characteristic which inspires kindness? My Bible dictionary says that the word goodness 'signifies not merely goodness as a quality, rather it is goodness in action, goodness expressing itself in deeds.'[31]

As believers in the Lord Jesus Christ, we are expected to be characterised by goodness. Why wouldn't we be? God, our Father, is good and only ever does good. Since we are His children, we ought to be good too. This world has so skewed our thinking that often we feel that goodness isn't something to aspire to, that there is something desirable in having a little bit of naughtiness in us. We agree wholeheartedly when sinners are told that even one sin is serious enough to keep them out of heaven, yet so often we have a little giggle when we do things, minor in our eyes, which God calls sin. If we are walking in the Spirit, we will have a correct view of how we should be living, and goodness will be displayed.

But not only are we to *be* good, we are to *do* good. Many passages in the Bible talk about doing good – both to believers and unbelievers. Sometimes opportunities come naturally – maybe when we're talking with someone and they open up to us, needing a listening ear. Other times we must actively seek ways to do good. It will often require some planning – Isaiah 32:8 NKJV says, 'A generous man devises generous things.' We can all do something. Helping older people with their shopping, housework, or gardening; maybe helping out a weary young mother by babysitting or amusing her children for a couple of hours; spending time with someone who is lonely... I'm sure you can think of many ways you can show goodness.

We should all keep our hearts prepared and our eyes open to display the fruit of goodness in our lives.

---

31. *Vine's Dictionary.*

The fruit of the Spirit is... faithfulness.

Galatians 5:22 NKJV

Faithfulness. Of all of the fruit of the Spirit that we have been learning about, this is the one which probably inspires us least. I mean, there's something very noble about being loving, kind, and good to others. Being patient, and displaying peace or joy feels worthwhile. But faithfulness? Plodding along, doing the same thing day after day, with hardly any recognition or praise? *Blah*, we might think. I'm not sure that we can really put these characteristics in any order of importance, but I suspect that God thinks a lot more of faithfulness than we do.

Faithfulness is one of the attributes of God that we often value most. We depend on His faithfulness in His love and care for us, His protection of us, and most of all for our salvation. We know and love the fact that He will always keep His word, no matter what happens. He will never, ever slip and let us down, not even once.

But do we value our faithfulness to Him as much? Scripture is very clear on what is expected of a believer in the Lord Jesus Christ. We have a good idea of how we ought to live. Often, we start off a new year with great resolutions, or we decide to make changes in our lives after a particularly inspiring or challenging message we've heard. In all likelihood, what we've decided to do is good, worthwhile, and what God values. And for the first while, we do well. We start off with great gusto, and a smile on our face, but then our steps start to drag, and it takes effort to keep going. Is it worth continuing? If it's for God, it's *definitely* worth continuing! Don't let laziness, selfishness, or lack of praise from others keep us from living faithfully for Him.

In fact, if you've been following along this past week, you'll know this by now – if we are walking in the Spirit, and not in the flesh, many of the self-centred barriers to faithfulness will be removed, and the fruit of the Spirit will be produced in our lives. Keep going!

People nowadays are really into talking about love. They're pretty keen on peace too, so using words like kindness and goodness won't cause any offence. But what about gentleness? Already some of you are beginning to wince! Unless we're dealing with babies or fluffy animals, gentleness, or as the King James Authorised Version puts it, meekness, isn't what we're supposed to show in this modern world. Instead, we're told to stand up for our rights, shout loudly, trample over whoever happens to be in the way in our fight to be seen and heard. It's not only what we've been told to do by society, it's what is in our very being as well. We hate it when someone gets the better of us, and for some of us, losing an argument isn't an option, no matter what. Using cutting words is viewed as fair play, and if someone snaps at us, we feel we have the right to snap back with as much force as we can muster.

Doesn't sound very much like our Lord Jesus Christ, though, does it? When He was reviled, He did not revile in return, when He suffered, He did not threaten (1 Peter 2:23 NKJV). Did those who surrounded Him that day view Him as weak? Probably. If you don't stand up for your rights, will you be seen as weak? Most likely. You see, those who don't love the Lord Jesus don't see the whole picture. They are living as if this world is all there is, and they are at the centre. Since we trusted Christ, we have a different viewpoint. We know the reason for the gentleness and meekness of our Lord Jesus Christ – that He was bearing our sins in His own body on the tree. We know that God is patient and gentle towards sinners and desires that they should be saved, but we also know that in a future day, this world will be righteously judged for rebellion against God. This should fill us with compassion for sinners and should give us the desire to be like our Saviour, displaying the gentleness that walking in the Spirit will cultivate in our lives.

The fruit of the Spirit is... self-control.
Galatians 5:22,23 NKJV

Oops! I just couldn't help it! Whether it's buying yet another pair of heels, finishing off a whole packet of chocolate biscuits, or binge-watching an entire series or box set on a school night, we humans aren't too great at self-control. Out of all of the characteristics of a believer who walks in the Spirit, this is probably the one I was least looking forward to writing about. Why? Because it hits very close to home. I can resist shoes, biscuits, and box sets, but there are many activities and interests that steal my time and attention, and which I find hard to resist.

Take a moment to think of your own temptations. Some are tangible, but they can also be emotional. It's not only a matter of putting the lid back on the box of Quality Street at Christmastime, although that's exercising very necessary self-control too. Many of us are easily ignited when something doesn't go our way, or when someone says or does something that annoys us. Indulging in tears, tantrums, and threats isn't limited to toddlers.

To an extent, we can manage the situations which lead to the breakdown of self-control. Asking someone to help us if we're struggling with temptation is a good idea. Or all it might take is resisting the temptation to buy that family-sized bar of chocolate or sharing bag of crisps in the first place. And we need to avoid substances such as alcohol and drugs which can cloud judgment and swiftly remove any self-control a person may have had.

As with all of the characteristics we've looked at, there is One who perfectly and completely exhibited total self-control, no matter the situation or who He was dealing with – Pharisees who did not want to hear what He had to say; disciples who didn't seem to understand when He talked about His crucifixion, arguing instead about who would be the greatest; cruel Roman soldiers who spat on Him and mocked Him before nailing Him to a cross. The Lord Jesus said, 'I came... not to do Mine own will, but the will of Him that sent Me' (John 6:38).

Walking in the Spirit will produce Christlikeness, which leads to a desire to do only what God wants, denying self. As we do this, the Spirit will produce the beautiful fruit of self-control in our lives.

I believe God.

Acts 27:25

When I was in my late teens, I read a book that made a great impression on me. It's one thing to learn about older people losing their lives because of their faith in Christ, but when it's a young person around your own age, it can have a much bigger impact.

Cassie Bernall was a pretty, blonde-haired seventeen-year-old from Colorado, United States. Looking at pictures of her, you would never have guessed that a few years earlier she had been involved in the occult, fascinated with self-mutilation and witchcraft. Her parents had been horrified to discover that Cassie was exchanging gruesome letters with a friend in which they discussed plans to kill them, as well as their teacher.

When she was fifteen, Cassie's life dramatically changed when she was born again. The truth of the words 'if anyone is in Christ, he [or she] is a new creation' (2 Corinthians 5:17 NKJV), was evidenced in her life. A week before Cassie died, she told her mother that she wasn't afraid to die, because she would be in heaven. Earlier, she'd written on a scrap of paper, 'I will die for my God. I will die for my faith. It's the least I can do for Christ dying for me.'

That's what happened.

On 20ᵗʰ April 1999, two students, armed with guns, entered the library of Columbine High School. One of them asked Cassie if she believed in God. She said, "Yes." In an instant, she was in heaven.

What was the secret to her willingness to die for Him? I believe it was her appreciation of what Christ had done for her. She had been rescued from the darkness of sin and the bondage of Satan, and she was truly grateful for her salvation.

What if gunmen had entered my school? Would I have had the courage to do what Cassie did? Could I have answered, "Yes," to their question as simply and confidently as she did? Could you? Do we have the life-changing appreciation of Christ that Cassie had? Are we living for Him? For as the sentence Cassie underlined in one of her favourite books says – 'All of us should live life so as to be able to face eternity at any time.'[32]

---

32. Cassie's mother, Misty Bernall, wrote her story in *She Said Yes – the unlikely martyrdom of Cassie Bernall*, published by Plough Publishing House in 1999.

When you pass through the waters, I will be with you.
Isaiah 43:2 NKJV

When I was a little girl, a preacher used to visit our home. I was very fond of him. I mean, who wouldn't like someone who bought lots of chocolate bars and filled your tiny red wellies with them? Then when I was fifteen, I had my appendix removed, and the same preacher came to visit me in hospital, this time with a carton of grape juice and a Scripture reading from Isaiah 43. As he read the passage, I couldn't help thinking that those verses were for older people – those with real problems, not a teenager who'd had a fairly common surgery like what I'd just had. I felt that I was too young to apply those verses to my situation.

I'm not sure where I got that notion from, but I'm very thankful to the preacher for reading those verses to me. For, in doing so, he helped me to realise that God's promise to be with His children in difficulty is for *all* of His children, no matter what age we are. Young people are often told that if they haven't had any trials yet, that they'll come, sooner or later. This gives the impression that only things like disease, death, and financial hardship – mostly, although not exclusively, grown-up issues – are the real trials, and nothing else counts.

Let me tell you that that is *not true*! Your trials may seem small in the eyes of others, but God knows exactly what you are going through. I was only saved a few weeks when I hit a difficult, humiliating situation and had my first opportunity to lean hard on God. At the time I wouldn't have called it a trial, but looking back, I know it was.

So read the first few verses of Isaiah 43, and all the other passages relating to trials in the Bible, take them to yourself, and bask in the promises of God for *you*!

God... is rich in mercy.
Ephesians 2:4

I have two younger brothers and I seem to recall quite a few wrestling matches in our house when we were growing up. They usually concluded with the winner pinning the other boy to the floor, while the loser yelled, "Mercy! Mercy!" until the victor decided it was time to let him go. Or until he got his breath back to thrash him in another round – I'm not sure which!

There's something very humbling about receiving mercy. The word may be translated various ways in your Bible, maybe as *lovingkindness* or *steadfast love*, but the basic meaning is the same. It is a word which denotes pity or compassion. It assumes that there is need on the recipient's part, but that the one who shows mercy has adequate resources to meet that need.[33] If we were able to meet the need ourselves, we wouldn't need mercy.

Often, mercy is given when it is least deserved. Look at the fragment of verse at the top of the page. Even better, get your Bible and read the first ten verses of the chapter. You will discover that the mercy that God has shown to us was totally and utterly undeserved. As sinners, we only deserved His wrath eternally, yet He has shown pity and compassion towards us – He has been merciful to us – and has saved us.

Not only must we never forget how merciful God has been to us, it is important that we also show mercy to others. It's a trait of human nature that we like things to be fair. Think for a moment what would have happened if God had decided to be fair and only given us what we deserved, both in a physical and spiritual sense. We would have had nothing – because we deserve nothing. So when we have an opportunity to show mercy to others, let's not allow our sense of fairness to colour our mercy, and instead display, as best we can, the same lovingkindness that God has shown to us. We serve a merciful God.

---

33. *Vine's Dictionary.*

Thou hast made... the earth,
and all things that are therein.
Nehemiah 9:6

" **F**lying snakes!" my husband exclaimed in horror. We were enjoying a delicious meal of chicken satay and fried rice with some Christians at an outdoor café in Malaysia. One of them was a missionary in a different area of Malaysia, and we were fascinated to learn about the rainforests there, complete with all sorts of wildlife. Flying snakes, we were told, are part of that wildlife!

Flying snakes are scientifically known as Chrysopelea and their home is in the rainforests of Southeast Asia. They can measure over a metre in length and are mildly venomous, though harmless to humans. In the rainforest, trees are very tall – the canopy can be around thirty metres in height – so rather than the snake taking the time to slither down one tree and back up another, it uses its God-given ability to glide. By doing this, it can catch prey and escape predators.

The mechanism by which the snake is able to glide is fascinating. It slithers to the end of a branch, then hangs off it in a J shape before propelling itself off. The natural shape of the snake should mean that it would head straight to the ground. Instead, as it jumps, it flattens out its body, rotating its ribs towards its head and upwards towards its spine. The flatter body produces an aerodynamic force, trapping air, in a similar way to an aeroplane wing. This provides the ability to glide, and coupled with its mid-air movements, it soars down through the jungle until it reaches its destination of another tree, or some food.

Isn't it remarkable how God has created even a snake, one of the least-liked animals, with the ability to travel swiftly and easily through the leafy canopy of the rainforest? He has provided for the needs of many of His creatures in various ways – and how much more does He provide for us as we travel around from day to day?

Jesus wept.

John 11:35

Losing someone you love is really hard. It doesn't matter if it's a grandparent, parent, sibling, or friend – there's nothing easy about it. Death is an enemy, a result of sin. In a day to come, it will be overruled and will come to an end, but in the meantime, death is still here and very painfully real.

The Lord Jesus Christ lost a good friend. Many times, while here on earth, he visited Mary, Martha, and Lazarus – two sisters and a brother. He enjoyed their company and loved this family dearly. But then Lazarus took sick and died. The Lord Jesus made the long journey to the village of Bethany, where Mary and Martha were waiting for Him. In their pain and sorrow, the person they most wanted to see was the only One who could help them.

When the Lord Jesus arrived and saw their sorrow, He was deeply moved, and He wept. He's the same Lord Jesus Christ today, you know. Nothing about His character changed when He ascended into heaven. Just as He felt Mary and Martha's pain, He still feels the pain of His children when they experience the sadness and separation of death. If you are mourning, He is right beside you. He understands exactly what you are going through, He knows the pain you're feeling, and He is deeply moved.

Tell Him all about it. Lean hard on Him. Hold on to His promises in the Bible. Keep going, day by day. Learning to live without your loved one isn't easy, but He has promised to be with you – every single hour of every single day.

Not as I will, but as Thou wilt.

Matthew 26:39

T here are certain times in the gospels when we read of our Lord Jesus Christ and we feel, like Moses, that we are standing on holy ground. Times when God draws back the curtain and gives us a sight of what is sacred. Occasions when we can only stand in wonder and amazement. The baptism of the Lord Jesus. The Mount of Transfiguration. And now, Gethsemane.

We don't know what we may have to face in this life, either of good or bad, but the Lord Jesus Christ knew in graphic detail what was ahead for Him – the cross, with all its suffering, shame, and death. As He made His way to the Garden of Gethsemane, He knew exactly where Judas, the betrayer, was. He knew that soon a group of men would arrive to arrest Him. As they entered the garden, He asked most of the disciples to wait for Him there, and took Peter, James, and John, the three disciples who had previously witnessed a glimpse of His glory, further into the garden. The Lord went further still: no one could fully share in the sufferings that He would soon face.

We almost feel as if we should hold our breath. The Lord Jesus Christ kneels, falling on His face and praying to His Father. The agony of what is ahead causes sweat, as great drops of blood, to fall from His head to the ground around Him. He knew all the derision, mockery, and scorn that would be thrown His way. He knew each pain and all the physical agony that He would soon face. And, the greatest horror of all, He knew the full weight of the vilest sins that He would bear, that would be laid on Him, while God would forsake Him in His deepest suffering.

No wonder He could cry, "If it be possible, let this cup pass from Me." Was there any other way for sins to be forgiven? If there was, He would never have had to die. No alternative presented itself; there was no other way. He had to die. And so He cried, "Not as I will, but as Thou wilt." He was willing to bury His will in His Father's, to suffer all that it would take to bring about salvation for guilty sinners. For you. For me.

Who do you know who has great wisdom? Maybe a teacher, an aunt, a friend, or someone from your church who, no matter what problem you have or decision you need to make, is able to give great advice. If you didn't know better, you might even think that they can look into the future and see how certain courses of action will turn out, with consequences you never imagined. My granda was like that. I remember at times thinking that he was getting unnecessarily worked up about some situation, only to watch things playing out as he had known they would.

Much of the time (although certainly not always) wisdom increases with age. When you've lived eighty years, you've seen and learned a lot. But do you know what's even better than a wise old person? A wise young person! I think we probably all aspire to being wise someday, but what about now? Do we sit back and wait for wisdom to come to us, hoping that when we're old and wrinkly we'll discover that we've turned out wise after all? (That's not a good plan, by the way. I've known quite a few unwise old people too!)

I love the verse at the top of this page. So often, I feel my lack of wisdom. What should I do in certain situations? What's the right thing to say? When someone asks my opinion, what should I tell them? It's so good to have the assurance that we can come to God, the One who has greater wisdom than we could ever comprehend, and ask of Him. The rest of the verse says, 'it shall be given him.' It's a simple promise. Because God says it, we can claim it.

But there's no point in asking God for wisdom if we aren't willing to obey the wisdom that He has given us in His Word. Proverbs 9:10 says that the fear of the Lord is the beginning of wisdom and the knowledge of the Holy is understanding. God is worthy of our obedience and respect. The closer we walk in communion with Him, the more we will see things as He does and become more like Him, and the greater our wisdom will be.

Joy shall be in heaven over one sinner that repenteth.
Luke 15:7

One dark evening, you are in your living room. Your parents are reading or catching up on household tasks, you're in the middle of a geography homework, and your little brother is building something out of Lego, when all of a sudden there is a loud, urgent knock at the door. You jump from your seat, but before you get a chance to open it, the person knocks again, shouting, "Hurry up! I've got great news!" When you pull open the door, there stands your neighbour, his clothes terribly muddy and torn, his face and hands scratched and battered, but with a great, beaming smile. He beckons with his hand. "Come! All of you," he says, looking over your shoulder at the rest of your family staring open-mouthed at the sight. "I've found my sheep – the one which was lost. Come and rejoice with me!" You follow your neighbour down the road and up his lane. You can hear the sounds of festivities, and your stomach growls at the delicious smell of barbecued food. As you come closer, you can see everyone from your district, all happy and smiling, and full of joy.

Have you ever been invited to an I've-found-my-lost-sheep party? It sounds like a great place to be! This type of party isn't exactly common, and I'm sure if you ask a sheep farmer why they don't have one when a sheep is found, they'll think you're crazy. After all, sheep are valuable enough, but not so valuable as to warrant a party when they're found, especially when it's only one of a large number. A party for a lost sheep is a bit excessive, isn't it?

How about when a sinner repents? After all, he or she is only one of a countless number of sinners in this world, surely not very valuable! But that's where we're wrong. When one soul gets saved, the Lord Jesus tells us that there is great joy in heaven. Just think, when you trusted Christ, maybe as a little child, there was joy in the presence of the angels of God because of your salvation! Might this have seemed a little excessive? To people on earth, probably, but not to God. After all, the Lord Jesus tells us in Mark 8:36 that one soul is of more value than all the world.

I am with you always.
Matthew 28:20

On the 28th of April 1988, Aloha Airlines Flight 243 set off from Hilo, en route to Honolulu in Hawaii. It was a regular route for the airline and for many of the passengers, who depended on air travel to go from island to island. Twenty minutes into the flight, the cabin crew were serving drinks when the entire top half of a large section of the fuselage tore away. It was terrifying! Everyone was convinced the plane was going to crash. How much was damaged? The plane seemed out of control, and the air stewardess was unable to reach the pilots via the intercom system. Were the pilots still there?

Has your life ever felt like Aloha Airlines Flight 243? Maybe everything is going great – you're comfortably flying along, relaxed, enjoying your surroundings, and then the roof is torn off, leaving you gasping for air and not sure if you're going to make it out unscathed. Maybe, like these passengers, you've been wondering if anyone is in control at all.

Unknown to the passengers, the pilots were still there and very much alive. Not only that, they were doing the best they could to land the plane safely, and land safely they did. With the exception of one cabin crew member who'd been sucked from the cabin when the hole opened in the roof, everyone else miraculously survived.

The circumstances of your life might be causing you to doubt. There was plenty to discourage and frighten the passengers on Flight 243. *That hole in the fuselage is huge! The plane might break apart at any moment. Is a safe landing even possible in the notorious Hawaiian high winds?*

The difference between Flight 243 and your life is that the One who is in control, unlike the pilots, is never taken by surprise. He knows exactly what you are facing, all the difficulties you are up against. He knows exactly how it will end. Don't focus on the torn-off roof. Instead, turn to Him. Because, after all, He is totally in control.

I say... to everyone... not to think of himself more highly than he ought to think.

Romans 12:3 NKJV

'How we see ourselves impacts how we behave.'[34]

I came across this quote in a Christian magazine a year or two ago. The sentence was in relation to our position in Christ, holy and righteous in Him, but the more I pondered it, the more I realised how relevant it is to other aspects of our lives as well. You see, image and self-esteem are two huge topics in our world today. People are obsessed with how they look, but many also feel anxious and insecure.

I'm sure we've all known someone who thought they were the most beautiful person God ever created. Their social media feed is full of pouting, sultry-eyed gazes into the camera, silky hair perfectly arranged over a slim, bronzed shoulder. When you see them in the flesh, you learn to your surprise that filters had been hard at work. The lack of them in real life, however, hasn't affected their self-absorbed attitude. Or perhaps we've known people who had greater confidence in their abilities than they actually merited. We've winced when we heard less-than-inspiring singing, or we've patiently listened to a hundred and one excuses why sports day turned out to be a disaster for them. These people see themselves totally differently to how everyone else sees them, and it's impacting how they behave.

Then there's the other extreme – those who believe they aren't any good at something, or they won't amount to anything, so they quit. Maybe they aren't even going to try in the first place. Why would they? Sure, they reason, they will only fail. How they see themselves impacts how they behave too.

Which attitude is better? Neither, actually. What God wants is for us to see ourselves as we are – forgiven sinners, who need God's help in everything we do. This would adjust our mindset – we would no longer think of ourselves more highly than we ought to think, and neither would we live a life of defeat with a no-point-in-trying attitude. The danger is found in making up our own minds as to what we are or aren't. If we see ourselves as God sees us, we will behave as He would have us behave.

---

34. Quote from *Spiritual Warfare (4): Breastplate of Righteousness* by Brian Joyce in Truth and Tidings magazine, September 2018.

People will be lovers of self.
2 Timothy 3:2 ESV

There are no selfies in the Bible! Graven images, but no selfies. In fact, the invention of photography was still a long way off when the Bible was written. And it's only in very recent history that the trend and means of taking pictures of oneself has developed. How long this craze will last is anyone's guess.

As human beings, we get a lot of pleasure from reliving good memories, and photos are an effective way of transporting us back to certain times and places. Selfies have their advantages – they're a great way to include everyone in the group in our picture. But they can often be used for totally narcissistic purposes. Many people use them to feel good about themselves.

In an online article I recently read, a professional photographer pointed out that nowadays everyone loves photography – we all have cameras on our phones which we regularly use. The problem, he said, was that the instinct of most people seems to be to take pictures of themselves or their friends and nothing outside of that. He also made a fascinating observation, that rarely in the worthwhile things in his life have the people involved been particularly interested in themselves.[35] As believers, that's obvious, isn't it? Anything worthwhile has someone or something outside of ourselves as its focus. But maybe that's something we often forget. Taking a few pictures of ourselves and our friends to look back on with nostalgia is fine – wasting huge chunks of time indulging in self (or should that be selfies?) is not.

That's not to say we should never open the camera function on our phones again. God has placed us in a beautiful and fascinating world. Although marred by man's sin, we can still see His fingerprints everywhere we look – both in nature and in people. God is a God of creativity and beauty, and He has placed those traits within human beings. Don't become focussed on yourself. Instead, look around you and admire the beauty you see. Enjoy it. Take photos of it, because even in your pictures you can glorify God by showcasing His magnificent creation.

35. https://www.bbc.co.uk/news/resources/idt-sh/david_hurn_photographer_swaps_magnum

MAY

As ye have... received Christ Jesus the Lord, so walk ye in Him: rooted and built up in Him, and stablished in the faith.

Colossians 2:6,7

I love to visit garden centres and wander around the plant section, marvelling at the variety of amazing colours and scents that God has created. At least one brightly coloured flowering plant will usually catch my eye and end up coming home with me. The plants are mostly small, so I relocate them to one of my ceramic pots. Occasionally, however, I'll choose something that is meant to be planted in the ground, like the lilac I bought a few years ago. I managed to transport it home in the car, and then I placed it on the patio. It was only supposed to be there for a few weeks. But we couldn't decide where in our garden to plant it, so it stayed on the patio, still in its pot.

Do you know what happens to plants which are supposed to be planted in the ground, but are still in a pot? They become what is called pot bound. The roots keep growing, but there's nowhere for them to go. So they fill the available space, and when the plant is finally lifted from the pot, there's a huge ball of roots in the shape of the pot.

My lilac was meant to be planted in the garden – in a permanent place, where it could draw water and nourishment from the ground, where the roots could grow deep and the plant would become steady and firm, able to withstand storms. Sometimes as Christians we can be pot bound. We get so caught up with temporary, earthly things, that we forget that we are part of an eternal plan. Our roots, instead of growing deeper in Bible truth and giving us stability in our Christian walk, end up in a tangle in the shape of our surroundings, with no depth. Plants in pots are often blown about when storms come.

Let's not be like my poor lilac, still in a pot, and not doing very well at all. Instead, let's live the life God intended for us to live by focussing on what is permanent and eternal – on those things above (Colossians 3:2).

> Death shall be no more, neither shall there be mourning, nor crying, nor pain any more.
>
> Revelation 21:4 ESV

MAY

2

Have you ever thought about how much pain and suffering there is in this world? What measurement would you use to calculate it, and how would you start to add it all up? All the pain inflicted by people on others, all the sickness and disease, natural disasters, and accidents. Even a quick glance at the headlines leaves us with the impression that something is not right with our world.

There are many people who, when they observe pain and suffering, either question or deny the existence of God. You've heard them, I'm sure. They come to the conclusion that either God is heartless and evil, or He doesn't exist at all. Even for a believer, the question of suffering can be a difficult one to answer. We know that God exists, that He is loving, wise, and all-powerful, yet things happen that break our hearts, and we struggle to understand why.

My husband and I have a good friend called David who has spent many years chatting to people about these very issues.[36] He knows the objections that people raise. Here's what he told me.

Our experience of suffering at a personal, physical level tells us that something is not as it should be. Pain in our bodies is a warning that something isn't right, so we make a visit to the doctor. In the same way, pain in the world makes us realise that something isn't right. This causes us to ask 'why?' Atheists, however, have no answer, and no explanation for why we think, 'It shouldn't be like this.' If this universe just happened, there's no reason to have any expectation of anything different or better. Yet within all of us is the conviction that this isn't how it ought to be.

Maybe God allows suffering here on earth to stop people from drifting through life with no thought of the much greater eternal suffering which is ahead for those who have not repented of their sin against Him. The truth is that if we never experienced any pain here, very few of us would spend much time thinking about God. Suffering is one of the ways in which God shows us how much we really need Him.

---

36. David Williamson has co-written an excellent book with Paul McCauley called *Everyday Evangelism*, published by John Ritchie Ltd in 2018. It deals with many of these issues and is well worth reading.

He Himself hath suffered.
Hebrews 2:18

W e've seen that, when it comes to pain and suffering, the vast majority of people, whether Christians, outright atheists, or those who are somewhere in between, agree that something is wrong with our world. And when we've reached this conclusion, the next question that most ask is *Why?*

We don't have to read very far through the Bible before we discover the reason for suffering. When Adam sinned in the Garden of Eden, the consequences were far greater than he could have anticipated. Not only was death introduced, but life itself would be full of challenges and difficulties. Even the natural world was cursed. All the suffering and misery we see today stems from that one act of rebellion and disobedience against the Creator.

But what is remarkable is that God did not wash His hands of this world. He loves those unworthy people He created and cares about us in our suffering. So much so, that He sent His Son to this earth. The One who is God and above suffering, came to earth to share in our suffering! He understands the pain of living in this world.

The Christian can rejoice that it won't be like this forever. Someday all pain will be removed. The Lord Jesus Christ will reign, and all will be put right. God not only cared enough about our pain to share in it, He cares enough to stop it. The miracles the Lord performed when He was here were signs of the world to come. The hungry were fed, the lame made to walk, the blind made to see, the storm was calmed, and the dead were raised.

So if God can do these things, why do we still experience suffering? Why doesn't He stop it? The problem is that people want the blessings without the Blesser. They want the pain to end, but they don't want to bow to the One who can end it. For now, God has given mankind the choice.

One day, Christ will return, and, in the words of our friend David, the promise is that ultimately sickness, starvation, natural disasters, and death itself will be driven from the universe. Unlike atheism which gives no hope of any end to suffering, there is hope in the gospel for the world.[37]

---

37. I'm indebted to David for his permission to use the information given in the devotionals today and yesterday.

Go ye into all the world, and preach the gospel.
Mark 16:15

MAY

4

What springs to mind when you hear the word 'missionary'? An elderly gentleman who tells exciting stories of life in a primitive jungle? A Christian who is on a higher spiritual level than 'ordinary' people like you or me? A doctor or nurse with limitless, selfless love and almost superhuman ability to care for desperately sick, poverty-stricken people?

Although the word isn't actually found in the Bible, a missionary is a believer who has obeyed the call of God to go and preach the gospel. God has often used people to spread the message of good news. Sometimes persecution and difficult circumstances mean that believers relocate, taking the gospel with them. Other times, He specifically and clearly impresses a Christian with His will for them – to move to a different country with the purpose of sharing the good news that Christ died for our sins.

It's pretty common to think that because God has asked these people to move to another land, they must be more spiritual than those who stay at home and live 'normal' lives. This couldn't be further from the truth. There are many godly believers who spend all their lives working, bringing up children, and attending gatherings of God's people. Although they may not be far travelled, they live for God and glorify Him in their daily lives. God's plan for each of us is different, and being a missionary isn't the top rung on some sort of spirituality ladder!

Missionaries struggle with many of the things we do. You know the way we sometimes find it hard to pray? How we struggle with our attitudes towards others? How we are often tempted to sin? They experience all these things too because they are absolutely human, the same as you and me. There may be differences – preaching and teaching responsibilities might mean that missionaries cannot get away with neglecting to read their Bible in the same way some of us might be able to, and they will also have challenges and temptations unique to their situation.

It's clear that missionaries need prayer. Not only for their physical safety (many are living and working in very dangerous places), but for their spiritual wellbeing. They need God's help every bit as much as every one of us does. Why not make a list of all the missionaries you know, and begin to pray for them today?

5

MAY

They which preach the gospel
should live of the gospel.
1 Corinthians 9:14

Yesterday, when I said that missionaries are normal people, I didn't mean that we forget about them, figuring that we have enough problems of our own to deal with. The fact that they are normal people is the very reason we *can't* forget about them! Put yourself in their shoes. They've left all they've known and loved, for as long as God asks them to. Many of them will spend their entire lives in another land. They've had to adjust to another culture, learn a new language, get used to a different range of foods, deal with new illnesses and diseases... The list goes on and on.

Many of them experience loneliness that we know nothing about. Some will always be viewed by the local people as a foreigner, no matter how well they learn the language and assimilate into the culture. And when they return to their native country for a visit, things may have changed there so that it doesn't even feel like home anymore.

Prayer for missionaries is so valuable, but there are other things you can do. You can keep in touch with missionaries. An email, or even a quick message to let them know you're thinking of them, may lift their spirits more than you'll ever know.

We also have the privilege of supporting them financially – either through our local church, or personally. You may not have much money now, but the Lord sees every sacrifice you make for Him. Don't be someone who gets agitated at how missionaries have spent 'my money'. Everything we have is given to us by the Lord, and we are *all* personally responsible for how we use it.

Another valuable way to help missionaries is to visit them. You might have to forego a relaxing beach holiday, and it takes courage to travel across the world. If you are able to go, be a help when you're there. Get involved. Help with housework, give out gospel leaflets, play with the children. You will gain many new experiences, but, more than that, you'll have been privileged to gain an insight into what God is doing in far-off places. My guess is that you'll never be the same again.

How beautiful are the feet of them that preach the gospel of peace.

Romans 10:15

MAY

6

I'm sure many of us have had at least a fleeting thought about being a missionary. I was saved only a matter of hours when I excitedly told my mother that I could now be a missionary to Japan. Her wise reply was, "Yes, if God calls you." There's something about hearing missionaries relate exciting stories of God working amongst those who've never heard the gospel before that warms our hearts and gives us a desire to be a part of it. Or maybe you have no desire to leave home. You want others to hear the gospel and be saved, but you'd rather God sent those with more courage and more desire to travel than you. We're all different.

But, as I'm sure you'll have figured out by now, God doesn't always do what we expect. Some who were desperate to burn out their lives for God in some distant land were never called to live outside their own district, while others, who had no desire to live anywhere else than where they were born, were sent to a far-off part of the world. God's plan for our lives can often be surprising. It's possible that some of you who are reading this will one day be called by God to spread His good news in another country. It will be a sacrifice. I've known a number of missionaries, and none of them ever said it was easy. But if God calls you, He will sustain you. His plan is always best, and if you are willing, He will use you as He sees fit. Be open to His leading and guiding.

In the meantime, whether you end up as a missionary or not, a good knowledge of your Bible will always stand you in good stead. Read and study it, grow closer to God, and pray. Live in such a way that you won't stain your testimony and destroy your witness for Him. And if the day comes when God calls you to leave for another land to tell others of the Saviour, go, knowing that He is faithful and able to keep you.

God is love.
1 John 4:8

Love. If any word was ever overused, yet undervalued, it's this one. We use it to speak about people, places, objects, or food, and then, when we want to express our truest, deepest sort of love, we find we need to add more words.

When God says He loves us, He means it. To Him, 'love' isn't only an expression of positivity towards something or someone. Instead, it's an all-encompassing, unconditional, and total love in its ultimate sense.

What passes for love nowadays changes frequently. One day, you might decide that you love pizza more than any other food, but after a week of eating only pizza, you'll probably change your mind. Our favourite place gets replaced by a new favourite place. We hear about couples – both celebrities and ordinary people, who declare they've fallen out of love with each other. Human love doesn't really seem to last.

As we've already learned, God is eternal, and so are His attributes. God always loved, even before He ever created mankind. But love must have an object, and it is clear that the object is none other than the Lord Jesus Christ – proof of the eternality of the Son. God will always love. But in the ages to come, He will not only love the Son, He will love those He has redeemed – you and me! God's love will never end. By the way, did you know that the love God has for His Son is the same love He has for us? Look up John 17:23.

Another awesome feature of God's love is that it is unchangeable. Our love is inconsistent. One day, we might love someone more than anything else, and the next, we could get so angry with them for saying or doing something that offended us, that we really don't care to be around them anymore. God's not like that. He knows us better than we know ourselves. Those dark, shameful corners in our minds that we'd be mortified if anyone ever peeked into, He knows all about. And yet His love for us never changes.

Love is manifested in giving and God gave the very best – His only Son – for us. Even when we are most appreciative, we still have little idea of the magnitude of this gift, and the greatness of His love. It cannot be exaggerated!

With good will doing service, as to the Lord, and not to men.

Ephesians 6:7

MAY

8

William Coltman was an ordinary man who was born in a small village in the Midlands of England. He worked as a gardener for most of his life and met regularly with fellow Christians in a local church. It was a simple life. And, if circumstances had been different, most of us would never have known that he'd even existed.

When Bill (as he was known) was twenty-three years old, he presented himself at the recruiting office and volunteered for the army. World War I had begun the previous year, and Bill felt his responsibility to his country. His conscience regarding the command 'Thou shalt not kill', didn't permit him to take anyone's life, so he became an unarmed stretcher bearer. Stretcher bearers were the first to attend to wounded soldiers – locating them, assessing and treating as they were able, and then removing them from the battlefield. It was a vital role, and Bill carried it out to the very best of his ability. In fact, he went above and beyond the call of duty many times, sacrificing his own comfort, and risking his life on numerous occasions. For his service, he was awarded twelve awards, including the Victoria Cross, Britain's highest medal for valour. The action which prompted this award was his leaving cover and risking enemy fire to tend to and rescue wounded soldiers who had been left behind on the battlefield. Three times he carried a wounded soldier to safety on his back.

When Bill returned home after the war was over, he settled back into life in Burton-on-Trent, working again as a gardener. Despite being the most decorated non-commissioned officer of World War I, he rarely spoke of the awards he'd received.

Throughout his life, Bill Coltman obeyed the commands of Scripture to work 'as to the Lord', whether as a gardener in the Midlands of England or a stretcher bearer rescuing wounded soldiers from the battlefields of France. He is an example to us all – not only because of his bravery and the value he placed on human life, but because of his faithfulness to God wherever he was found.[38]

---

38. You can read William Coltman's fascinating story in Anthony G. Tideswell's book, *William Coltman – The Story of Two Crosses*. The copy I own was published by Sovereign Bookcare in 2008.

There is a lad here...

John 6:9

"Excuse me, sir."

The disciple turned to see a boy holding a package of five loaves and two fish.

"The Master is asking for bread – He can have mine."

"Are you sure?" Andrew asked. He knew that to give up his food was a big sacrifice for a growing, hungry boy so far from home.

"Yes, take it all." The boy pressed the food into Andrew's hands, then returned to his spot on the grass, while the disciple made his way back to the Lord Jesus.

You're probably familiar with the story of the boy who gave his picnic to the Lord. We don't know what age he was, but as he seemed to have been on his own, it's unlikely that he was as small as picture books show. In fact, I have a feeling he might have been nearer your age – a teenager. He was one of a very large multitude who had come to hear the Lord Jesus speak. But now the people were hungry, and there were no supermarkets to buy food. The young man soon became aware that the Lord Jesus had sent the disciples among the multitude to look for bread. He knew he had a decision to make.

Amongst your age group there's a trait I greatly admire, if it's channelled in the right direction. It's your zeal and enthusiasm. When you believe in something, you believe wholeheartedly. When you choose to do something, you do it with your might. And, as in the case of this boy, when you willingly give, you give all you can. Did the boy know that the Lord would perform a miracle? My guess is that he knew He *could*, but he had no guarantee that He *would*. Yet he was willing to give all, to risk going hungry. And look at what the Lord did – every person, the boy included, got as many loaves and as much fish as they wanted to eat. There were even leftovers!

The boy's picnic seemed so little, but in the hands of the Lord it became enough to feed a multitude. And the same is still true today – what one young person gives to the Lord can be used to bring blessing to many.

Now Israel loved Joseph.

Genesis 37:3

The more you read through the Bible, the more you will discover links between the Old and New Testaments. Some will require a bit of digging and careful thought, others are right on the surface, clear to see. One place where you'll find plenty of this sort of treasure is in Genesis, in the story of Joseph. As you read, be on the lookout for anything that reminds you of the Lord Jesus Christ. We know that He was the only One who never sinned, yet the Bible is silent when it comes to flaws in Joseph. Surely this is one of many clear indications that Joseph is a lovely picture of the Lord Jesus. William MacDonald, in his excellent book, *Joseph Makes Me Think of Jesus*, says there are over one hundred correspondences between the life of Joseph and the Lord Jesus.[39] Over the next week, we are going to look at a few of these resemblances; there'll be plenty left for you to discover for yourself.

The first, and one of the most obvious, is the love of Jacob for his son. Although Jacob had many sons, it was Joseph whom he set his love upon in a very special way. There were a number of reasons for this – Joseph was the son of his old age, was born to his precious wife, Rachel, and no doubt Joseph's wisdom and character would have pleased Jacob and made it easy for Jacob to love him. The Lord Jesus was the precious Son of God. In everything He said and did, He perfectly pleased His Father. More than once, God proclaimed, "This is My beloved Son, in whom I am well pleased."

Love is often demonstrated by giving. Jacob showed his love to Joseph by giving to him a coat of many colours. John 3:35 says, 'The Father loveth the Son, and hath given all things into His hand.' Jacob's love for Joseph was great, but it can't compare with the love the Father had for His Son, the Lord Jesus Christ.

---

39. *Joseph Makes Me Think of Jesus* by William MacDonald was published by Gospel Folio Press in 2000.

Israel said to Joseph, "...I will
send you to them."
Genesis 37:13 NKJV

Although Jacob loved Joseph, Joseph's brothers did not. In fact, the Bible says that they hated him so much that, when his father sent him to find them, they plotted to kill him.

1 John 4:14 says 'The Father sent the Son.' The Lord Jesus Christ was also sent by His Father to seek for those who had gone their own way. But instead of welcoming Him, grateful that He had come so far for their blessing, they hated Him. 'He came unto His own, and His own received Him not' (John 1:11).

In Luke 20, the Lord Jesus told a parable concerning a man who planted a vineyard and let it out to tenants. At the time when grapes would have been produced, he sent a servant to the vineyard to bring him some fruit, but the tenants beat the servant. This happened again and again, until the owner of the vineyard decided to send his beloved son. But when they saw him coming, they said, "This is the heir: come, let us kill him."

The story struck close to home. The Lord Jesus didn't need to point out to the religious leaders that they were represented by the wicked tenants; their own consciences told them so. But how did they react? 'The chief priests and the scribes the same hour sought to lay hands on Him'!

The words of Joseph's brothers, "Come, let us kill him," when they spotted the sent one coming towards them, are identical to the words of the tenants in the Lord's parable. The hatred in their hearts boiled over into murderous rage as they watched the one who was loved by his father coming towards them. They not only hated Joseph, they hated his message. If they could kill him, they wouldn't have to listen to him any longer. So it was with the religious leaders in the Lord's day. On one occasion, after speaking in the synagogue in Nazareth, His hometown, those who heard Him were so angry that they drove Him out of the city and would have pushed Him over the cliff had He not passed through the midst of them. Of both Joseph and our Lord Jesus Christ, it could truly be said that they were 'despised and rejected of men' (Isaiah 53:3).

They took him, and cast him into a pit... and they sat down to eat bread.

Genesis 37:24,25

12

MAY

The treatment of Joseph was unjust indeed. He had done nothing to deserve his brothers' harsh words to him, never mind being taken and thrown into a pit. Likewise, the Lord Jesus had done nothing wrong. He was absolutely sinless – the only One who ever lived who didn't deserve to be punished. It should make us marvel that cruel men were allowed to treat the Lord Jesus Christ, the Creator, so roughly.

In the pit, Joseph was left alone, absolutely forsaken by his brothers. If Psalm 69 had been written when he was alive, he could have spoken the words that were prophesied concerning the Lord Jesus in verse 20 – 'I looked for some to take pity, but there was none; and for comforters, but I found none.' The Lord Jesus Christ knew what it was to be left alone, but His suffering went further than Joseph's could ever go. On the cross, He was even forsaken by God because of our sin.

While Joseph was in the pit, his callous brothers sat down, totally indifferent to his plight, and ate. Can you imagine? They had a picnic, while their younger brother was suffering in a dark, dingy pit. When the Lord Jesus Christ was suffering, nailed by hands and feet to a cross, there were also those who sat down. This time, they weren't eating. Instead, they were gambling for the clothes that He had been wearing. How callous and indifferent! The Bible doesn't say, but I wonder if the bread that Joseph's brothers ate while he was in the pit had been brought from home by Joseph himself. Certainly, the soldiers who sat down and gambled for the Lord's clothes didn't give much thought to the One who supplied everything they needed – clothes, food, and the very air they breathed. Instead, they were crucifying the Life-giver and Sustainer of all mankind.

One striking difference, though, is that while Joseph was powerless against the strength of his brothers, the Lord Jesus willingly submitted to what cruel men did to Him. He knew what Joseph likely didn't, that the suffering was for a purpose. In the Lord's case, it was so that you and I could be saved for all eternity.

13

MAY

They... sold Joseph... for twenty pieces of silver.
Genesis 37:28

Selling our brother is probably something that many of us might threaten to do at times, but, if it came to the bit, I think we'd struggle to actually follow through! Joseph's brothers, however, had no such struggle. When a group of Ishmeelites appeared on the distant horizon, Judah had a brainwave. Here was something which was even better than murder, in his eyes – selling Joseph. After all, if they murdered him, they wouldn't gain anything, but if they *sold* him, they'd actually get some money.

So sell him they did. But for what a paltry amount! Joseph, the precious son of his father, was of little value to his brothers. I'm not sure if they even watched him go. More likely, they heartlessly turned their backs, glad to be rid of the one who'd caused them so much anger and jealousy.

This is another of those resemblances that's lying on the surface. The Lord Jesus Christ was also sold for a paltry amount of silver, the price of a slave who had been gored by an ox. Just think – the One who made the universe, who knows each star by name, who owns the cattle on a thousand hills, who knows how many hairs each of us have on our heads, the One who is all-wise, all-knowing, all-powerful, righteous, holy, and just – God Himself! – valued at a handful of coins.

The betrayal in both cases was deep and must have been extremely painful. If the brothers had truly known Joseph's worth, and how in a future day their lives would be in his hand, would this have changed how they viewed him? And if Judas and the religious leaders had a glimpse of the Lord's majesty and glory, wouldn't they have bowed low in humility before Him? Thank God, we have had our eyes opened to His greatness, and ought to have a true valuation of Him. Today, let's regard Christ as He ought to be regarded, and put Him first in every decision we make.

As if being hated and sold by his brothers wasn't bad enough, when Joseph arrived in Egypt and it seemed at last as if things might actually be looking up for him, suddenly he found himself in prison. It's impossible to read the story and not feel indignation. Potiphar's wife, to cover up her own wicked desires, told a blatant lie and falsely accused Joseph. The innocent man ended up in prison – a place which the Genesis 39 account describes as 'a place where the king's prisoners were bound'.

Many years later, an even greater injustice took place. This time it wasn't in Egypt, but in Jerusalem. The Son of God, holy and perfectly sinless, was accused of crimes He never committed. His accusers were people who were desperate to turn the focus away from their own sin, which had been exposed by the blameless life of the One who stood before them. Our verse at the top of the page speaks prophetically of our Lord Jesus Christ. He was crucified with the worst criminals, as if He were one Himself. The verse holds true for Joseph as well – he was amongst the prisoners, and although they had committed crimes worthy of punishment, Joseph hadn't.

Another remarkable connection between the Lord Jesus Christ and Joseph is the mention of two specific men who were closely connected with them in their situation. In Joseph's case, we read of the chief butler and chief baker, while the Lord was crucified between two thieves. Both men spoke to the one who was blameless. In the prison, the chief butler and chief baker told their dreams to Joseph. On the cross, one thief mocked the Lord Jesus, while the other asked the Lord to remember him. I don't think it's a coincidence that in each case we read of one being exalted – the chief butler to his former position, and the forgiven thief to heaven, while the other is brought down – the chief baker lost his life, and the unrepentant thief tragically lost his soul. A meeting with the blameless one changed the course of life for each man. We can be thankful that, like the forgiven thief, our meeting with the Lord Jesus has resulted in our eternal blessing.

And Pharaoh called Joseph's
name Zaphnath-paaneah.
Genesis 41:45

I'm sure you're familiar with the story of how the chief butler finally remembered Joseph when Pharaoh had some dreams needing interpreting, and how he was brought out of the prison to stand before the ruler of the land of Egypt. Not only did Joseph interpret Pharaoh's dreams, he gave him the solution to the problem of the upcoming famine that the dreams signified. Pharaoh realised that there was something of value in this man. He asked his servants, "Can we find a man like this, in whom is the Spirit of God?" (41:38 ESV) Joseph was then exalted above all the officials in the land, only second to Pharaoh himself. As he rode through the streets in a chariot, everyone was instructed to bow down before him, even those who had put him into the prison. Later in the story, we read how Joseph's brothers, who had scoffed at his dreams and protested at the thought of him reigning over them, bowed down to him.

In Romans 14:11 we read, 'As I live, saith the Lord, every knee shall bow to Me.' One day, every knee will bow when He is viewed in His glory and majesty. This will include those who now mock and deny His deity, those who have rejected Him and His offer of grace, even those who falsely accused Him and crucified Him.

Pharaoh didn't only exalt Joseph, he gave him a new name, Zaphnath-paaneah. And before you're tempted to pity Joseph for being given such a difficult-to-pronounce name, let's think about what it means. Although there are a number of interpretations, a favourite meaning of Bible students is 'Saviour of the World'. You see, when Joseph took on his new role, he had the responsibility of gathering up all the bounty of harvests for seven years in preparation for seven years of famine. A day would come when people from outside of Egypt, including his own brothers, would travel to find food. Joseph's provision saved countless lives.

In John 4, after the Samaritan woman realised that the Lord Jesus was the Messiah, He spent two days in the city. After listening to Him, many of those Samaritans believed and declared Him to be 'indeed the Christ, the Saviour of the world.'

Joseph is a fruitful bough... whose branches run over the wall.

Genesis 49:22

MAY

16

Not only was Joseph regarded as saviour of the Egyptians, he was saviour of the world. Of course, this was the world as the Egyptians knew it – there were many undiscovered countries back then. But when it comes to the Lord Jesus Christ, we can say with total assurance that He truly is the Saviour of the world. Anyone who comes to Him for salvation is welcomed with open arms, no matter who they are, what they look like, or where they are from.

When the Lord Jesus was here on earth, His ministry was primarily to His own people, the Jews. At times, those who weren't Jews, known as Gentiles, also came into blessing, such as the Samaritans we learned about yesterday, and a Syrophenician woman, who pleaded with the Lord on behalf of her daughter, in Mark 7:26. God's plan was to bless the Gentiles through the Jews, but, in the book of Acts, when the Jews rejected the message of the gospel, the apostles turned to the Gentiles, with the result that many have been saved.

Jacob's blessing of Joseph described him as a fruitful bough – like a branch heavy-laden with the most delicious fruit – whose branches run over the garden wall. Those on the outside, who have no natural right to what is growing inside, are being blessed by the branch reaching over the wall to them. As Gentiles, we are outside the wall of blessing, with no right or claim on any of God's blessings. The Jews, those on the inside, were God's chosen earthly people. Yet, through Christ, we are blessed as the branch of salvation reaches over the wall to us.

Those in Joseph's day must have been exceedingly grateful for the provision they received from his hand, and none more so than his brothers, who not only had their every need met, but experienced his forgiveness as well. We are no less blessed. We have been brought into a place that we would never otherwise have occupied, had it not been for the One who was loved by the Father, sent by Him, rejected by men, betrayed and sold, alone and forsaken on the cross, and numbered with the transgressors, but who has now been exalted. We can truly say, "Hallelujah! What a Saviour!"[40]

---

40. If the past week's topic has whetted your appetite to read more about the resemblances between Joseph and our Lord Jesus Christ, I recommend the following books:
Joseph Makes Me Think of Jesus by William MacDonald, published by Gospel Folio Press in 2000, and *The Coat of Many Colours* by David Craig. The edition I have was published by Gospel Folio Press in 2008.

For My thoughts are not your thoughts, neither are your ways My ways, saith the Lord.

Isaiah 55:8

When I was training to be an optometrist, I spent one morning a week at a local eye clinic where an ophthalmologist examined people's eyes. Most patients were elderly, but occasionally babies attended the clinic. To be able to see the back of an eye clearly, it helps if the pupil is dilated (made bigger), and this is done by inserting drops. After the drops have taken effect, an extremely bright light is shone into the eye. It's easy to explain to older children and adults, but how do you make a six-month-old understand? Unfortunately, you can't. The parent usually has to wrap their arms around the child and hold them still. The drops sting. And the light hurts. Inevitably, the child cries – loudly. The parent too, sometimes!

To the baby, the doctor must seem like the cruellest person they've ever met. Why would someone purposely cause them so much pain? Maybe you're in a situation like the child, where things are happening in your life that you don't understand, and you're really hurting. You're wondering what God is doing and why this painful situation is happening to you. From what you know of God's character, it doesn't make sense.

The little one doesn't know what the doctor is doing. They don't realise that he or she is looking at the back of their eye to investigate and diagnose the problem, and to work out how to treat it. They don't understand that the doctor has been around for much longer than they have, that his or her knowledge is a lot greater than theirs, and that they're only doing what they're doing because they care. The motives are only good.

This is a very feeble analogy. The care that God has for us, the benefits He intends us to receive from this painful time, and His purposes for us are immeasurably superior to the doctor's for the baby. So take comfort, rest in His love, and look ahead.

I, even I only, am left.
1 Kings 19:14

"What's wrong?" Auntie Lois leaned forward, and put a slim hand on Rachel's arm. "You don't seem yourself today."

Rachel shrugged and took another sip of her caramel latte. Being 'herself' wasn't all that great anyway, but she couldn't tell Auntie Lois that. She wouldn't understand – she still lived in the very town where she'd been born and raised. She belonged here. She always would. Not like Rachel...

"I know you're probably not finding the adjustment easy. It's hard when you feel as if you don't belong."

Rachel's head shot up. "How did you know?"

Auntie Lois's smile made her warm brown eyes crinkle. "Never mind that. Old aunties often understand much more than you give them credit for."

"You're not old!" Rachel exclaimed, then sighed. "I don't feel as if I fit in. I might look like everyone else, but I never know what the right thing is to say or do. It's a totally different culture."

Auntie Lois stirred her hot chocolate thoughtfully. "Did you feel you fitted in when you lived in South America?"

Rachel hesitated. "Well... not exactly. Even though I was born there and spoke Spanish as well as everyone else, I didn't look like my friends. Oh, Auntie Lois, I hate being different! Is there nowhere on earth where I really belong?"

Her aunt smiled sympathetically. "You have a perfectly valid point, but I'm pretty sure you aren't the only teenager who feels they don't belong. I believe that everyone struggles with feeling different, to a greater or lesser extent. The thing is, Rachel," she set down her spoon, "you are different!"

Rachel groaned. "Please don't rub it in!"

Auntie Lois laughed softly. "What I mean is that everyone is unique. No matter how ordinary someone's life is, they'll never be able to find someone with exactly the same experiences. God specialises in variety. He's ordered your life like this for a reason. You're learning lessons and developing character so that He'll be able to use you for His glory. And, Rachel," her aunt leaned towards her and smiled, "I know He has a wonderful plan for you!"

This is the promise that He has
promised us – eternal life.

1 John 2:25 NKJV

Promise. There's something very special about that word. We use it often, right throughout our lives and in many situations. Little Peter could be promised a reward for behaving at Great-Aunt Edith's house, Sally might whisper some secret to her best friend, Tilly, as long as Tilly promises not to tell anyone, and Jimmy will present a gorgeous diamond ring to Jenny as a promise that he's going to marry her.

These promises, though, are nothing compared with God's promises. We can go back on our word, but God will never, ever break a promise. He is totally trustworthy, so it's impossible.

But what *has* God promised? A quick online search for 'God's promises' throws up a multiplicity of results from a wide variety of sources. We need to be careful, though, because not all of God's promises in the Bible are for believers in this day and age. Through these, we learn a lot about the unchanging, faithful character of God, and principles of how He deals with human beings. However, the way in which God dealt with His earthly people, Israel, is not how He deals with believers today. For example, many times the Israelites were told that if they would obey God's commandments and laws, He would bless them with increased flocks and herds, a good harvest, and many children. From this, we learn that God greatly values obedience, but these promises do not apply to us. Instead, as a heavenly people, our blessings are heavenly and spiritual. 'God... hath blessed us with all spiritual blessings in heavenly places in Christ' (Ephesians 1:3).

We will find promises made to us, in this age of God's grace, in the New Testament, especially in the epistles. So when you read there, look out for those promises which apply directly to you. Here are a few to start you off –

He that believeth on the Son hath everlasting life – John 3:36.

I am the resurrection, and the life: he that believeth in Me, though he were dead, yet shall he live – John 11:25.

My God shall supply all your need [not wants!] according to His riches in glory by Christ Jesus – Philippians 4:19.

I will never leave thee, nor forsake thee – Hebrews 13:5.

Redeeming the time.
Ephesians 5:16

Reaching underneath the spare room bed, I pulled out a large leather scrapbook and a box containing coloured paper, scissors, glue, photos, and memorabilia. Begun in the days well before Instagram, when scrapbooking was the fashionable way to document significant life events, this was to be my travel scrapbook. I'm afraid I only managed to complete our family holiday to Nice and the first day of a short business trip to the USA with my dad, before my creativity seemed to come to an abrupt halt. My intentions were good, but the scrapbook never even got close to being finished.

As I dumped all the various brochures into the recycling bin, I couldn't help but think about the time I'd wasted working on even those few pages. I'm not in the slightest artistic, so I can't figure out why I ever thought scrapbooking was a good idea for me! There are many other things on which I would have been much better spending my time. Fast forward a number of years, and I'm still making the same mistakes. It's so easy to fritter away precious time on things that have no real value – neither earthly, nor eternally.

That time you've spent on social media soon adds up. Those ninety minutes watching that movie can't be regained. Hours of video games can soon pass with relatively little to show for them. We need time to relax, and it's fun to have shared interests with others – but sometimes our balance can be all wrong.

At the beginning of each day, it's good to ask ourselves what we hope to achieve, and set our priorities accordingly. Would we like to get an assignment finished? To fit in some extra reading or Bible study? To spend time with people who matter? If so, we'll need to make a concentrated effort. We'll need to make choices and refuse to become distracted by things that are totally harmless in themselves but aren't the best use of our time. We should try to recognise those things, like my scrapbooking attempt, which will only fizzle out and leave a trail of wasted hours, and often resources, behind.

After all, the time that we spend doing what we know God wants us to do is never wasted. Let's get our priorities right today!

The Lord our God is holy.
Psalm 99:9

Holy. It's a word we hear so often, but try explaining what it means! Not so easy, is it? If it makes you feel any better, I had to look it up too.

Holiness has to do with being set apart, or separate, and is often translated as the word 'sanctification'. We automatically assume that this is in relation to sin, and that's true – God is absolutely and totally separate from sin. He cannot even look on iniquity (Habakkuk 1:13). But there's even more to holiness. God is separate, not only in purity, but in majesty and glory. He is greater than us in every way. His thoughts are not our thoughts, neither are our ways His ways (Isaiah 55:8). We might be tempted to try to bring God down to our level, but the truth is that He is totally separate.

God's holiness was demonstrated especially in relation to the children of Israel in the Old Testament. In the first few books of the Bible, we read the instructions God gave to protect the Israelites from approaching Him in the wrong way. In Exodus 19, when God was giving Moses the law, He gave very clear instructions to stay away from Mount Sinai. Even an animal who strayed too close was to be stoned. These people did not need to be convinced that God was holy – separated from them.

But, as we are discovering, God hasn't changed. He is still as holy as He was back then. And yet we can approach God at any time through prayer. How can this be? At Calvary, the Lord Jesus Christ was made sin for us. He was forsaken by God, because God is holy and cannot look on sin. Now, when God looks at us, He sees all the perfections of His Son, and the way has been opened up for full fellowship with a Holy God.

There's one more lesson we need to learn today, one that should affect our Christian walk. 1 Peter 1:16 says, 'Be ye holy; for I [God] am holy.' We must also be set apart and separate from sin. Our attitude to sin ought to reflect God's attitude. So in everything we do today, let's remember to ask ourselves, 'Am I being holy, as God is holy?'

Holy and reverend is His name.

Psalm 111:9

Yesterday we took a look at God's attribute of holiness and learned that He is separate from us in purity, majesty, and glory. Like His other attributes, His holiness is eternal – He is as holy now as He always was, and always will be. But we also saw that our position before Him has changed because of Christ's sacrifice for sins, so God can righteously accept us into His presence.

The blessings we've received through Christ's death and resurrection are immense. Not only have we been forgiven, we have been brought into the family of God. He is our Father, and He loves us and cares deeply for us. We can go to Him with any problem or difficulty and pour out our hearts to Him in a way we can't do to even the closest person on earth. He knows what we are feeling and thinking, and He knows the answer to every need we have.

But we should never forget that God is still holy. When we come to Him in prayer – and we should, because He loves it when we do – we are addressing the very same God we read of in the Old Testament. His character has not changed; He is still worthy of the reverence and respect that He has always deserved. It's a popular thing to try to bring God down to our level, to speak to Him in the same casual, careless way that you'd speak to someone in your group of friends, using whatever words are fashionable at that point in time. Don't adopt this mindset. You probably wouldn't dare to speak to your grandmother that way! God is still God. His name is holy and reverend. When we pray to Him, we must remember that He is our Father who loves us deeply, but He is also the Holy God, separate from us, and worthy of honour and reverence.

There is therefore now no
condemnation to them which
are in Christ Jesus.

Romans 8:1

Did you ever try to count all of your sins? It's an impossible task, isn't it? Think of all the sin we've committed every single day of our lives! All the wrong actions, wrong words, wrong thoughts. And what about everything we've done that we've totally forgotten, not to mention those sins that we didn't realise were even sins at all – those 'good' things we did with the wrong motive, those things we shared 'for prayer' which were really only gossip... It's overwhelming, isn't it?

And all of us have sins that we feel will be forever embedded in our consciences, ones which the devil loves to remind us of time and again, no matter how many times we confess them. These could either be sins that we committed before we were saved, or since we were saved. We know that God says He will not remember our sins any more, but since we can't seem to forget what we've done, we wonder how God can ever put our sins out of His mind.

That's why it's important to remember that our salvation does not, cannot, will not, nor ever did depend on our feelings, but on the sure, unshakeable, unerring word of God. And what does His Word say? 'There is therefore now *no condemnation* to them which are in Christ Jesus!' No condemnation! None at all! Not for one single sin – either 'little' sins that just about elicit a wince and are then forgotten, or 'huge' sins that loom large in our minds. Think about it for a minute. That condemnation that was upon us before we were saved is gone. I like to think of it as a big black cloud, once hanging low over my head, which has now been totally removed, leaving only clear, blue skies above.

And the reason for 'no condemnation'? Because the Lord Jesus Christ bore the condemnation for us when He suffered and died at Calvary. God punished Him in our stead. Trusting Him, we are now 'in Christ'. And for us? *No condemnation!*

What hath God wrought!
Numbers 23:23

Have you ever heard of the Morse code – you know, the series of dots and dashes for transmitting messages? You might be surprised to discover that Samuel Morse, the inventor of the Morse code and developer of the telegraph, was a Christian.

Samuel Finley Breese Morse was born away back in 1791, the eldest son of a clergyman. As time went on, he began to show promise as an artist, and went to England to study art, before returning home to the United States to work as a portrait painter. Samuel Morse obviously had a keen interest in inventions, because he helped improve the chemical processes behind portrait photography, as well as working with his brother on a water pump and a marble-cutting machine.

The telegraph, however, was where Morse focussed his efforts. Communication was terribly slow, being dependent on the mail, so Morse refined and developed the early bulky twenty-six wire telegraph into a single-wire one. It was extremely difficult to find any investors for his invention, and for eleven years Morse was very poor. However, his faith in God never wavered. He said, "I am perfectly satisfied that, mysterious as it may seem to me, it has all been ordered in view of my Heavenly Father's guiding hand."

Finally, the American government agreed to finance the telegraph and the first line was built from Washington to Baltimore. On 24th May 1844, the first official message, chosen by a daughter of one of Samuel Morse's friends in recognition of the One who had given the inspiration and help to Morse, was transmitted – 'What hath God wrought!'

In this day of internet and wireless connections, the telegraph seems antiquated and primitive, but in its day, it was a life-changing invention, one which paved the way for all the other forms of communication which followed.

Despite the fame which accompanied Samuel Morse's work, he never became proud or conceited. In fact, he described his work as 'His [God's] work', and added, 'Not unto us, but to Thy Name, O Lord, be all the praise.'[41]

---

41. https://answersingenesis.org/creation-scientists/profiles/samuel-morse-the-artist-who-invented-the-morse-code/

25

MAY

God saw everything that He had made, and, behold, it was very good.

Genesis 1:31

I'm sure you've seen video clips of chaotic messes being made – maybe a shaken bottle of fizzy juice being opened, a bag of flour bursting all over the room, or an aerosol can of squirty cream being sprayed everywhere. Or maybe a combination of all three! But sometimes, after the mess-making has been shown, the video is then reversed, and every particle of the juice, flour, or cream magically returns to their respective containers, leaving a spotlessly clean room. Why do we find videos like this so fascinating? What is it about watching disorder turn to order so effortlessly? If you've tried to tidy your room, you'll realise that it's much easier to make a mess than it is to clear it up!

You might be familiar with the word 'entropy'. This means 'disorder' or 'chaos', and it comes from the Second Law of Thermodynamics, which deals with the quality of energy and the production of useful work. Things left to themselves will result in entropy, or deterioration... maybe like your bedroom?

That's why we need to stop and think when evolutionists tell us that order has evolved from disorder. They believe that matter (where it came from, no one knows!) resulted in a big bang, and then arranged itself into a fully functioning universe, with many different forms of life. In the video, how did you know that every particle of flour didn't actually lift itself off all the surfaces it covered and make its own way back to the bag? Because that's not the way things happen. Something doesn't move from the state of disorder to the state of order all by itself. The many billions of years they talk about doesn't help their case either, as the more time there is, the greater the entropy will be.

Believing the Genesis 1 account, that, in the beginning, God created everything, makes much more sense. When man sinned, a process of deterioration began, of which we can see the effects today. But God's not finished with His creation yet – one day, there will be new heavens and a new earth. He created the laws of science, and He is the only One who can make all things new.[42]

---

42. You can read more about entropy in Robert W. Cargill's book, *Creation's Story*.

I press toward the goal.
Philippians 3:14 NKJV

I love airports! There's something exciting about being in a place where so many journeys begin. Although airports usually involve a lot of waiting – at security, in the departure lounge, or at the boarding gate – I rarely find the time long. In the bigger airports, there are more shops than in our local shopping centre and great restaurants to choose from, not to mention the fun of watching planes take off and land. Even if facilities are a bit thin, a good book and some people watching will keep me occupied. But the airport isn't my destination. I'm only there because I'm travelling somewhere else – going on holiday or to visit friends.

Sometimes the teenage years can feel a bit like being in an airport. It might be great fun, with lots of people around and plenty of things to entertain and amuse. The destination is adulthood, but you're not quite there yet. You generally don't have the responsibilities of a full-time job, or a house, or people needing cared for. In the same way that in an airport we move from security to the departure lounge to the gate, you're moving from one school to the next, through various exams, and on to further education. And in the process, it can be very tempting to think that it's not necessary to be too serious about anything because 'real life' is still ahead.

Actually, your Christian life began the moment you put your trust in Christ. This means that Day One was every bit as important as the final day of your life, and every day in between. The time to start living your life for God isn't some day years in the future when you're in a stable job, married, and with children. This may never happen. Instead, the time is right now! Putting off Bible study until you aren't so busy at school might seem tempting, and maybe even rational, but from what I've experienced and observed, you will never find the ideal time in your life for this.

So don't think of these wonderful years as waiting years – instead, press toward the goal and start living for God today!

No good thing will He withhold from them that walk uprightly.
Psalm 84:11

Reading this verse, you'd almost conclude that, as long as we are living right, God will reward us by giving us what we want. For you, that might be great exam results, a place at your chosen university, or a well-paid job. Often, God is exceedingly gracious and gives us things that we really desire. But what about those times when we don't get what we want? Even worse, what if we'd firmly believed that the school or university we'd chosen was where God wanted us to be? Or what if we wanted a job so that we could have some money to give to people in need, or to help support missionaries?

It's really hard to understand, isn't it? We're trying to walk uprightly and put our efforts into living for God. As far as we can tell, our motives are good. Don't we deserve good things? Isn't that what the verse promises? Take another look. In fact, open your own Bible and look it up. If it's like mine, you'll discover the word 'thing' is in italics. This means that the actual word isn't in the original text but was added by the translators to help people understand the passage a little better.

Let's read the verse again, only without the italicised word this time. 'No good will He withhold...' No good? But isn't what I wanted good? Of itself, it very well might be. But is it for *your* good? For the good of those around you? You see, God sees things from a different perspective. He doesn't only see the past, and this immediate point of time we call the present. Instead, He sees the whole picture. He sees

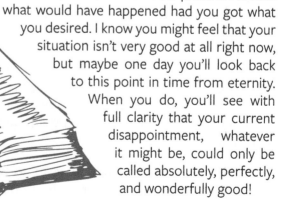

what would have happened had you got what you desired. I know you might feel that your situation isn't very good at all right now, but maybe one day you'll look back to this point in time from eternity. When you do, you'll see with full clarity that your current disappointment, whatever it might be, could only be called absolutely, perfectly, and wonderfully good!

Let not your heart turn aside to her ways.

Proverbs 7:25 ESV

Temptation has always been a huge problem for humankind, right since Adam and Eve were in the Garden of Eden. No one is excluded and, believe it or not, it'll be an ongoing battle throughout your whole life. The object may change, but we're never going to be free from temptation until we're in heaven.

In our modern world, a huge source of temptation is the internet, and being able to access it on our phones means that temptation is as close as it can get. Winning a victory over temptation is good, but there's something even better, and that's not meeting it at all. And there are ways of doing this without throwing away your phone!

Maybe you're still living at home, and your parents already have filtering apps or software installed. If they do, that's great. Don't be angry with them – this shows they care a lot about you. Barriers like these are very important, so don't try to bypass them. But if your parents haven't done this, asking them to install it would be a really good idea. Or maybe leave this book open at this page.

Another barrier is to limit your screen time, and your phone might even be able to help you with this. Make use of any helpful time-control features connected with your phone or apps.

Recognise the times when you are most vulnerable. Is it late at night when everyone else is in bed? Or when you're trying to do homework but lacking motivation? When you pinpoint your vulnerable times, you can do something about it. The best plan might be to leave the phone in another room.

Why not have an accountability partner? This is a fancy name for someone who helps you keep on track. It's best to choose a spiritual fellow believer, preferably one who is a little bit older. Whoever you choose, make sure it's someone who won't lead you astray or dismiss your sins. Tell them your goals, meet or contact them regularly, and be honest.

And finally, never forget to read your Bible and pray. We need God's help every moment of every day to live in a way that pleases Him. Cry out to Him in times of temptation and obey His voice. He has promised to help and be with us all the time.

I am God, and there is none else.
Isaiah 45:22

"She thinks she's better than everyone else!" Maddie complained.

"I know!" replied Isla. She shook her head in exasperation. "She expects us to obey her every command, as if we were her slaves or something. 'Maddie, come with me right now to my locker,' or, 'Isla, go and ask Peter if he's got the answer to Question Six.'"

"And if she doesn't need you, she'll ignore you. It's all on her terms!"

I'm not sure which of their classmates these girls are discussing, but I think we can all relate. Most of us have come across people who think they are superior to everyone else and thus deserve more attention.

One thing we need to guard against is accusing God of having the same mindset as this type of person. We'll often read in Scripture about the greatness of God, how that He is above all. He is God, and there is none else. He is to be obeyed, and He alone is to be worshipped and glorified.

But something – or someone, more likely – might whisper, "Why does God demand obedience and glory? Isn't that selfish of Him? After all, He expects you to be humble!" If those thoughts ever go through your mind, you need to expel them immediately and forcefully with the truth of God's Word, because they are from Satan, who fell from his place as an angel because of his sinful aim to be like the Most High. Since then, he has never ceased trying to rob God of His glory.

God deserves to be higher than all, because that's exactly what He is. He isn't demanding something that isn't rightfully His to receive. He is also to be obeyed. After all, He is the Creator and we are His creation, so He has every right to expect us to do what He has asked of us. His requests are not self-seeking but are made in love and in the full knowledge of what is best for us. He is also holy and righteous. Even the best people are prone to selfishness, egotism, pride, and self-centredness, but since it is impossible for God to sin, His motives are only and ever pure. He is God, and because of this, glory is His due.

I am the Lord: that is My name: and My glory will I not give to another.

Isaiah 42:8

30

MAY

Yesterday we learned that God, because He is God – sinless, holy, and the Creator – is worthy of all glory. He alone is deserving of honour and praise. We glorify God when we obey His commands, when we spend time reading His Word and praying, and when we live our lives in a Christlike way. In other words, we glorify Him when we put Him first.

Sometimes other things crowd in and take up space. We can't and shouldn't neglect our everyday work, whether that's school or university studies, a job, helping out in the family business or at home. After all, whatever we do is to be done as to the Lord; this will bring Him glory. But what about our spare time? How do we spend that? Do we look at it as *our* time, when we can do whatever takes our fancy? Maybe, without even realising it, we've assigned to God only the time we spend in our daily Bible reading. Maybe He doesn't even get that time from us, and is allocated only Sundays, or perhaps only the times spent meeting with our local church.

Did you realise that God must have first place – all day, every day? It doesn't mean spending every waking minute reading the Bible, although all of us would certainly benefit from spending more time in God's Word. Instead, it means putting God first in all our decisions, in all our interactions with people, and in all our affections. Nothing or no one should have a higher place than He.

We probably don't need anyone to analyse our lives to tell us what we might be putting before God. Is it a hobby, an addiction, a celebrity, an ambition, a reputation, a possession, or someone in our life? Remember that God's glory cannot be given to another. What is it that's taking the place that God alone should have? Who is receiving glory – honour and praise – from us that only God deserves?

Reordering our priorities and putting God first can and will be costly, but He is God, so it's no less than He deserves. God is not a despot who demands our respect and is always taking from us. Instead, He loves us with an immeasurable and giving love. Let's choose to put Him first today.

I was not rebellious, nor did I turn away.

Isaiah 50:5 NKJV

I t's fashionable to be rebellious! Even films for little children promote this message, with song lyrics such as 'No right, no wrong, no rules for me!' If you actually choose to be obedient – well, there must be something wrong with you, right?

Wrong, actually. As Christians, who should we emulate? A blonde princess in a frozen world and those who created her? Singers? Politicians? Entrepreneurs? You know the answer. As followers of the Lord Jesus Christ, we must strive to be like Him. He was obedient to His earthly parents at the age of twelve, and obedient to His Father in heaven throughout His life. It was costly. If you read the verses which follow the one above, you'll see what that obedience meant – giving His back to those who were smiting Him, and giving His cheeks to those who plucked off the hair. He didn't hide His face from shame and spitting. Did He deserve all He suffered? Absolutely not! He was the only One who was sinless.

To be obedient, there's a humility needed which often doesn't come easily to us. We want to point out all the reasons why we shouldn't be the one to do what we've been asked to do. Often, we feel that we are too good for such a menial task, that someone else could do it instead. Obedience means being submissive, and our rebellious natures don't like it.

But take a moment to consider how great the Lord Jesus Christ really is. He is God, the Creator and Sustainer of the entire universe. Those men were spitting on and hitting the One who created them, the One who kept them alive. If there was ever injustice seen in this world, it was here. And yet the Lord Jesus was not rebellious. The plan of God was that He should go to the cross and suffer and die for the sins of mankind. So He went.

I am so thankful that He didn't have the rebellious and selfish attitude promoted today. I'm sure you are too. And if He was not rebellious, as His followers, do we have any right to be either?

JUNE

1

JUNE

I can do all things through Christ which strengtheneth me.
Philippians 4:13

I've always hated exams, and I'm sure you do too. I don't know how many I've done over my lifetime – written, oral, and practical, in all sorts of subjects. They're stressful – I know all about it! No matter how hard you work, something could go wrong. The one subject you didn't have time to look at might be the one which comes up. Your mind might go totally blank. Or you might even have studied for the wrong exam! (Yes, that once happened to me.)

Teachers, lecturers, and maybe our parents often try to emphasise the importance of exams. We're pushed to our limits and made to work hard. In one sense, that's a good thing. Lots of people can do better than they think they can, especially when they put in a little bit of effort. There aren't many of us who can sail through an exam without having revised. Doing our best is what God wants too. Everything we do is to be done as for Him (Colossians 3:23).

But what happens when the pressure all gets too much? It's so easy to end up in a state of panic.

Close your eyes for a moment and pretend that your exam is a pen dot on a wall. It's not very big, is it? There's your exam in relation to your whole life. Now, imagine that the wall is so long that you can't see either end of it. The further you move back to try to view the wall, the smaller the dot becomes. And that's what your exam looks like when viewed in relation to eternity! When we're in heaven, that exam won't matter.

God has a plan for your life. Passing every exam may not be in His plan. I once failed a very important exam. I was devastated, but I learned more from that – about the topic I'd failed, about depending on God rather than on my abilities, and about God's character – than I would have, had I passed it first time.

Treat your exams as opportunities to draw closer to God. Lean on Him. Hold tight to the promises of God in the Bible. (You'll find my favourite 'exam' promise at the top of the page.) And remember that, no matter what happens, you are important to God and He cares for you.

Ask in faith.
James 1:6

JUNE

W hen Hudson Taylor set sail from England to obey the call of God to preach the gospel in China, he was embarking on a voyage that was going to take five and a half months. Back in the mid-1800s, travel wasn't as easy as it is now.

The ship on which Hudson was a passenger set sail from Liverpool on 19th September, but it hadn't gone far before it was caught in a terrible storm and was tossed about in the Irish Sea. Their situation went from bad to worse, and Hudson began to prepare for the inevitable shipwreck and his death. Miraculously, God intervened, and the ship sailed on its way to China.

But it wasn't all straightforward from there on. You'd think that the absence of wind would mean safe sailing, wouldn't you? Instead, towards the end of their journey, it caused them to drift on the current towards sunken reefs – into danger once again. What the ship desperately and urgently needed was wind, and there wasn't a breath.

As Hudson and the captain stood on the deck, the latter made the remark that they'd done all they could and could only wait. Hudson realised that there was one thing they hadn't done yet – ask God for a breeze.

So Hudson and the three other Christians on board went to their individual cabins to pray. After a time of prayer, Hudson became so sure that God had answered, that he stopped praying and went to the deck to ask the first officer to make the mainsail ready for the breeze, which God was about to send. The man began to scoff, but while he was speaking, they both noticed the corner of the topmost sail begin to move, ever so slightly, in the breeze.

"Don't you see the wind coming?" Hudson exclaimed. The man dismissed it as just a little puff of wind but consented to let the mainsail down to take full advantage of it. Within minutes, the ship was heading swiftly away on the breeze from the dangerous reefs. So before Hudson Taylor even arrived in China, God used this incident to encourage him, that no matter what needs arose in the land to which he was travelling, he could bring them to the God who cares and is able to help.[43]

---

43. This story is recounted in *The Biography of James Hudson Taylor* by F. and M. Howard Taylor, published by Rickfords Hill Publishing Limited in 2012.

As long as the cloud stayed above the tabernacle they remained encamped.

Numbers 9:18 NKJV

"**T**hey wouldn't have been able to grow rhubarb!"

I had to smile at my husband's unconventional comment. I'm not sure if the Israelites loved rhubarb as much as I do, but if they did, he was right – growing it in the wilderness would be pointless. And not only because of the growing conditions. To get transplanted rhubarb to the stage where you can eat the fruit will take over a year.

When the children of Israel left Egypt, they ended up wandering in the wilderness because of sin for forty years, until the older generation had passed on. Not until then would they be able to enter the land of promise. In the wilderness, they were guided by God. During the day, a cloud would cover the tabernacle, and by night, the appearance of fire would be over it. When God wanted the people to pack up and move on, the cloud would lift; when He wanted them to stay, the cloud remained – for two days, or a month, or even a year. When the people pitched their tents, they had no idea how long or short a time they would be there.

Imagine you're an Israelite. You arrived at the camp late yesterday afternoon after a long day's journey. You wake up, yawning, and poke your head out of the tent. The cloud is still there. Good. Maybe you'll get a few days here for a well-earned rest. You do. But a few days stretch into a week, which stretches into a fortnight... a month... two months... three... Who knows how long you'll be here? Maybe years! Why not go ahead and plant that rhubarb? After all, rhubarb would make some tasty desserts. But you never get a chance to eat it. When you've been in the same location for an entire year, and you're starting to feel at home, the cloud lifts and you have to pull up the stakes you'd put so firmly into the ground, and the rhubarb, and move again.

Sometimes the same thing happens to us. Not literally – there probably aren't many reading this who live in tents – but figuratively. Never forget that God intends us to live like pilgrims. We have something better on ahead and we aren't here to stay.

Whether it was two days, a month, or a year.
Numbers 9:22 NKJV

Yesterday we saw that it was pointless for Israelites to plant rhubarb in the wilderness because they had no idea how long they would be there. Sooner or later, the cloud over the tabernacle would lift, and they would have to move on.

Not only does transplanted rhubarb take time to reach the stage when it can be eaten, it takes work. The soil needs to be dug and cleared of stones. The rhubarb crown needs to be planted and tended. I've discovered rhubarb grows much better when the weeds are kept away, and the slugs are deterred from feasting on it before I do. Growing rhubarb takes effort.

Can you imagine the Israelite expending time and energy into planting and tending rhubarb, only to discover after a period of time that the cloud had lifted, and they would have to move on after all? All that work would have been totally wasted.

What are the rhubarb plants in your life, and how much effort do you use to tend to them? Of course, you'll know by now that I'm not talking about real rhubarb. What is it that consumes you, that you focus your energies on as if you're going to be here forever? Is it your schoolwork? It's good to work hard at school – God never intended His people to be lazy – but education shouldn't become an idol. Is there a hobby that's taking up all your spare time? How many hours do you spend on social media? What about the energy you spend on video games? Are your friends more important to you than anything else in the whole world?

In Colossians 3:2, we're told to set our affection on things above, not on things on the earth. This life is not all there is. For the Israelites, there was something better ahead – the promised land. And for the Christian, there's something even better than that – being with Christ. Like the Israelites, we're only passing through and we aren't here to stay. Some day – we have no idea when it will be, maybe two days, a month, or a year – we will be called to move on, leaving our little rhubarb plants behind.

At the command of the Lord
the children of Israel would
journey.
Numbers 9:18 NKJV

When we speak about the children of Israel wandering in the wilderness, we don't mean that they were aimlessly drifting about wherever the person in front decided to go. God had a plan and purpose for them, even when they couldn't see it. He knew when they needed to move, and when they needed to stay, and He guided them accordingly. It may not have made sense to them, but their only choice was to obey. The wilderness was a big place. If they refused, they would be in danger.

God has a purpose for your life too. He knows when you need to stay put, when you need to move, and where you need to go. Maybe things have happened that you don't understand. Maybe, like the Israelites, you've physically had to pack up and move to another house, or town, or even country. You had no choice in the matter, but that didn't mean you liked it. It didn't make sense to you. But don't forget that God *never* makes mistakes. He only ever has our good in mind, and He has a greater plan than we could ever imagine.

Many of us have a real distaste for change. We like the comfortable and the known. The longer we are in the one place, the more at home we feel. We might complain about being bored, but deep down we like things the way they are. When we become comfortable, we lose our sense of dependence on God. Isn't it true that when you find yourself in a new situation, out of your comfort zone, you turn to God for help? Oftentimes, God shakes up our comfortable little world to show us how much we really do need Him.

The Israelites really needed God. The wilderness was a hostile place. Food and water weren't easy to find; wild animals and dangerous people threatened their existence. Their only choice was to trust Him. But was their trust misplaced? Of course not! God brought the nation safely to the promised land. He'll do the same for you.

No man hath seen God at any time.

John 1:18

JUNE

6

You're at school, and the teacher is explaining to your class how something works, maybe osmosis in biology, or tectonic plate movement in geography, for instance. As he's speaking, you're building up a picture in your head. You're fairly confident you can envisage the scenario. But then he shows you a video clip, which demonstrates exactly what he has been explaining, and you realise that, good as the teacher's explanation was, what you imagined it would look like wasn't anything close to the real thing.

In the Old Testament, God spoke through men and revealed many things about His character – His love, mercy, wisdom, grace, and righteousness. But one day He sent His Son, the Lord Jesus Christ, to this earth. In sending Him, God was giving the world an opportunity to see what these attributes looked like in person. The Lord Jesus was completely human, yet completely divine. He was God.

The rest of the verse that I quoted at the top of this page tells us that while no one has seen God at any time, the Lord Jesus Christ has made Him known. We can learn about God by viewing His Son.

Take, for instance, 1 Chronicles 28:9 – 'The Lord searcheth all hearts, and understandeth all the imaginations of the thoughts.' This verse speaks of God's omniscience – His all-knowingness. Now turn to John's gospel. Chapter 2 verse 25 tells us that He knew what was in each person without needing to be told. You'll see this demonstrated in the case of Nathanael (chapter 1), Nicodemus (chapter 3), and the Samaritan lady (chapter 4). And right through this gospel you'll not only discover occasions where the Lord Jesus shows His omniscience, but you'll learn more about God as you observe Christ making Him known by what He says and does.

So read carefully through the gospels. Watch what the Lord Jesus Christ does and listen to what He says, because those things that you've read about God elsewhere in your Bible, you will see in action when you look at Christ.

What time I am afraid, I will trust in Thee.
Psalm 56:3

When I was 15, I had my appendix removed. I'd never had any surgery, and I was scared. The surgeon was going to cut right through the skin and muscle of my abdomen – wouldn't I be in agony afterwards? Or what if I didn't make it that far, but actually woke up during the operation? So many things could go wrong.

Before I was taken to theatre, my aunt called to see me. Realising that I was afraid, she quoted the verse at the top of this page. These words were what I clung to, repeating them over and over to myself as I was wheeled out of the ward, down the corridor, and into theatre. Instead of giving in to fears – both real and imaginary – I knew I could trust in the God who created me, who knew exactly what was going on inside me, and who would guide the hands of the medical team as they located and removed the ruptured appendix.

There are countless experiences we face in life that cause us to be afraid. Maybe you're even going through one of these times right now. It's good to remember that, no matter what it is, we can trust in God. There is absolutely nothing outside His control, and He has promised never, ever to leave us (Hebrews 13:5). He knows the details of each situation even more than we do, and so we must do what Peter tells us to do in chapter 5 of his first epistle, to cast our care on God, because He cares for us.

And, despite a surgery which wasn't exactly straightforward, I didn't wake up in the middle of it, nor did I experience the pain I'd imagined afterwards. What did happen, though, was that I learned a very important lesson about my fear, and a trustworthy God!

The wrath of God cometh on the children of disobedience.

Colossians 3:6

Each time we study one of God's characteristics, I hope that what we learn strengthens our trust in Him. After all, isn't it great to know that God is eternal, all-powerful, all-knowing, merciful, and loving?

So what springs to mind when you read the words 'God's wrath'? Did I just hear you take a sharp intake of breath, or maybe you're cringing a little? 'Love, no matter what' is the current sentiment of the world today, even in many religious circles, and because there is a danger that we might be influenced by popular opinion, it's even more important that we readjust our thinking to what the Bible says. After all, according to a writer called A. W. Pink, there are more mentions in the Bible about God's wrath and anger than about His love and tenderness.

It's important to remember that God's wrath is not in the least like human anger, where we lose our temper when someone annoys us. It's not a self-centred anger either, in which we often indulge when things don't go the way we want. Instead, as in everything else God does, it is absolutely perfect. All sin is against God, first and foremost – so for Him to leave sin unpunished is to go against His holy and righteous character. Even His great wrath is measured and appropriate to the circumstances.

If we want to see what God's wrath is like, there are many passages we can turn to. Genesis 7 tells the story of God's wrath poured out as a great flood on a sinful world. John 3:36 speaks of the wrath that is abiding on those who haven't accepted Christ as their Saviour. The book of Revelation will reveal to us the fearsome wrath which will be unleashed on a wicked, Christ-rejecting world. But the place where we see God's wrath at its fullest and most intense is at Calvary. There the Lord Jesus bore the full totality of God's wrath against sin. Words can never explain what He suffered so that those who only deserved God's wrath in hell forever could be forgiven. So rather than God's wrath being a necessary-but-unpleasant attribute to consider, it should turn our hearts to worship the One who willingly bore the wrath of God for us.

They were all scattered abroad.
Acts 8:1

I love summer – the longer days, warmer temperatures, trees in full leaf and the abundance of brightly coloured flowers. But summer has its downsides. The abundant growth isn't only seen in pretty plants. Weeds join the let's-grow-like-crazy party as well, including one we call robin-run-the-hedge. Its official name is *Galium aparine*, but depending on where you live, you might know it as goosegrass, cleavers, or catchweed. This weed has long, straggling stems with clusters of thin leaves... and burrs. Tiny burrs, with little hooks all over them. Perfect for working themselves into the long hair on the ears and legs of springer spaniels.

Have I mentioned that I have a springer spaniel? One who loves to go tearing through hedges, where robin-run-the-hedge usually grows? When summer comes, we end up spending a significant amount of time working burrs from her fur. But, as much of a nuisance as they are, the burrs are doing exactly what they were designed for – attaching to the fur of animals. Those burrs contain seed, and by catching a lift with the crazy spaniel, the plant is using her to help spread its seeds to areas where no robin-run-the-hedge is growing yet.

Did you know that God wants the gospel to be spread to areas where people haven't heard it? In our verse for today, we read about persecution in Jerusalem, which resulted in the dispersal of believers to many different regions where the name of Christ was unknown. And in this way, the gospel spread.

God might even be doing the same with you. Maybe in your home or at the school you previously attended there were a number of Christians, but now you've been placed in an environment where it seems as if you are the only one who loves the Lord Jesus. God has a reason for moving you – and that reason may well include the spread of the gospel to an area where He isn't known.

Another fact about robin-run-the-hedge is that it spreads. Those long stems seem to go on and on. And, amazingly, it all came from one little burr, maybe riding in the ears of an energetic spaniel. You never know how much impact your testimony will have on those around you, nor how far it will spread, maybe even onwards to another part of the world.

For no prophecy was ever
produced by the will of man,
but men spoke from God.

2 Peter 1:21 ESV

JUNE

10

One of the greatest things that can confirm our belief in the authenticity of the Bible as God's Word is prophecy – and the Bible is full of it! There are prophecies about obscure, historical nations; prophecies fulfilled by the birth and death of Christ; and those which are yet to be fulfilled. In fact, one source states that about 30 percent of the Bible is prophetic literature![44]

When I was your age, I attended a Bible class where many Old Testament books were studied. I clearly remember the Sunday that Daniel 11 was read. Have a look at it. It seems pretty confusing, and you might even be tempted to skip on to the next chapter. Don't. What you're reading is an extremely detailed prophecy written about four hundred years before it happened. That day in the Bible class, I listened in awe as the details of the chapter were explained from what is now recorded history.

Lift your Bible and look at verses 2-4. After Cyrus, the current king, four more kings would arise – from history, we learn these were Cambyses, Pseudo-Smerdis, Darius I Hystaspes, and Xerxes I Ahasuerus. The final one was indeed wealthy – he was the Ahasuerus who showed off his wealth by holding a lengthy, extravagant feast in the opening chapter of the book of Esther.

After him, another mighty king arose – a Grecian named Alexander the Great. His military skill, might, and territory were exceedingly great. But when he died at thirty-two years of age, his kingdom was divided amongst four of his generals – the four winds of heaven in verse 4.

The rest of the chapter is equally as fascinating, and I recommend that you look at it in more detail. The prophecies in this chapter are too accurate to be coincidence – so accurate that people have tried to discredit them by stating that this was written after it had happened! There are solid reasons why this can't be true – you'll find them in the book mentioned in the footnote.

Don't be afraid to believe the Bible. It needs no excuses made for it and will stand up to scrutiny. Instead, let us glorify the Author, who, after all, knows the end from the beginning.

---

44. From *Prove It: How you can know and show that the Bible is God's word* by Paul McCauley.

He had great possessions.

Matthew 19:22

Wealthy, popular, and with an exceptional talent for cricket, Charles Thomas Studd seemed to have everything going for him. He had trusted Christ when he was eighteen, but due to neglect of telling others about the Saviour, his love for the Lord grew cold, and he spent six years in a backslidden state.

His brother George's illness spoke to Charles, and he asked himself what popularity, fame, and riches were worth to George as he lay dying. In God's goodness, George recovered from his illness, and Charles was restored to the Lord at a meeting held by the famous preacher, D. L. Moody.[45]

Charles was one of seven young men, students from Cambridge University and known as the Cambridge Seven, who offered themselves for the work of the Lord in China under Hudson Taylor. While Charles was in China, he heard that he had inherited a great fortune and, unlike the rich young man in Matthew 19, promptly gave it all to the Lord, with the exception of £3400 which he kept for his future bride. It's no surprise to learn that, before they were married, she also gave this away.[46]

Over the years, Charles served the Lord in China, India, and finally Africa. He'd given up fame, a great cricket career, and a vast fortune, receiving very little of this world's goods or praises in return. Life was hard for him and his family, yet he never regretted it. He once said, "If Jesus Christ be God and died for me, then no sacrifice can be too great for me to make for Him."

He also sought to encourage others to live totally for Christ, and his well-known poem, Only One Life, has spoken to countless Christians over the years.

---

45. From https://www.wholesomewords.org/missions/bcambridge7.html
46. From https://www.wholesomewords.org/missions/biostudd.html

Two little lines I heard one day,
Travelling along life's busy way;
Bringing conviction to my heart,
And from my mind would not depart:
Only one life, 'twill soon be past,
Only what's done for Christ will last.

Only one life, yes only one,
Soon will its fleeting hours be done;
Then, in 'that day' my Lord to meet,
And stand before His Judgment seat;
Only one life, 'twill soon be past,
Only what's done for Christ will last.

Only one life, the still small voice,
Gently pleads for a better choice
Bidding me selfish aims to leave,
And to God's holy will to cleave;
Only one life, 'twill soon be past,
Only what's done for Christ will last.

Only one life, a few brief years,
Each with its burdens, hopes, and fears;
Each with its days I must fulfil,
Living for self or in His will;
Only one life, 'twill soon be past,
Only what's done for Christ will last.

When this bright world would tempt me sore,
When Satan would a victory score;
When self would seek to have its way,
Then help me, Lord, with joy to say;
Only one life, 'twill soon be past,
Only what's done for Christ will last.

Give me, Father, a purpose deep,
In joy or sorrow Thy word to keep;
Faithful and true whate'er the strife,
Pleasing Thee in my daily life;
Only one life, 'twill soon be past,
Only what's done for Christ will last.

Oh let my love with fervour burn,
And from the world now let me turn;
Living for Thee, and Thee alone,
Bringing Thee pleasure on Thy throne;
Only one life, 'twill soon be past,
Only what's done for Christ will last.

Only one life, yes only one,
Now let me say, "Thy will be done";
And when at last I hear the call,
I know I'll say, "'Twas worth it all";
Only one life, 'twill soon be past,
Only what's done for Christ will last.

Judge not, that ye be not judged.
Matthew 7:1

There are over 31,000 verses in the Bible, and out of all of them, this seems to be one of the very few that atheists and other unbelievers know and love to quote. Maybe you've had it hurled at you when you've pointed out some wrong or tried to explain your beliefs from a biblical standpoint. "You follow Jesus – He said you shouldn't judge." Isn't it strange that they seem quite happy with this verse, but they're not too keen on the rest of Jesus' commands?

Part of the problem is that many people don't understand what this verse means. Instead of a warning against being overly critical, and being careful not to judge motives, they've taken it to mean that no one can declare anything to be right or wrong. They say we can't condemn any actions as sin, and instead should happily let people choose their own idea of acceptable behaviour. Because, after all, if we let others do what *they* like, then we have full freedom to do what *we* like. If we don't judge them, we won't be judged either.

What nonsense! Anyone who reads their Bible will quickly become aware that God is very clear about right and wrong. When He states that something is wrong, we are not being 'judgmental' by agreeing with God's verdict. In fact, if we say that God condemns something, but that we can't judge, we are declaring that we somehow know better than God. The Lord Jesus said in John 7:24, 'Judge righteous judgment.' Although we don't always need to make a point of verbalising it, God expects us to judge – to be able to differentiate between right and wrong.

Escaping judgment is impossible. God has clearly stated that all will be judged – believers at the judgment seat of Christ (2 Corinthians 5:10), and unbelievers at the great white throne (Revelation 20:11-12).

So what do we do? If we read on in the passage, we find that we *must* judge – ourselves! We need to take a good hard look at ourselves in the light of Scripture and remove those glaring sins from our lives (maybe being gracious enough to receive the help of others). Then, when our own sins are confessed and dealt with, we will be able to help others with theirs.

For where two or three are
gathered together in My name,
there am I in the midst of them.

Matthew 18:20

JUNE

13

Recently, my local town had the great privilege of a visit from the Duke and Duchess of Cambridge. For those who may not be familiar with British royalty, the Duke, also known as Prince William, is Queen Elizabeth's grandson. There was great excitement, and many people flocked to catch a glimpse of the future monarch and his beautiful wife.

Did you know that Bible-based companies of believers are far more privileged than my town? At each gathering of the local church, One is present who far surpasses any member of the royal family: the Lord Jesus Christ, who will be declared King of kings! He is Creator, not only of the beautiful British Isles, but of the whole universe. Yet He left heaven, the grandeur of which we cannot begin to imagine, for lowly and poor surroundings, and for death on the cross – for us.

When we take time to stop and consider, isn't it remarkable that this One has promised to actually be among the gathered believers? I'm not sure what your thoughts are about the gatherings of the local company of Christians where you live. Maybe you don't think very much of them. Maybe they seem dull, or a bit boring, and you'd rather not go. That's certainly not what the Lord Jesus thinks about them. He has asked us to gather in His name, and He has promised to be there. Those gatherings are very important and precious to Him.

The presence of the Duke and Duchess last week gave our local town an attraction that it doesn't usually have. In a far greater way, the promised presence of the Lord Jesus Christ 'in the midst' of His gathered people will have an attraction that can never be measured. For if we love Him, it makes sense that we will desire to be where He is.

This thing is too heavy for thee; thou art not able to perform it thyself alone.
Exodus 18:18

"**N**o! I want to do it all by myself!" Does this sound familiar? You don't need to be around children often before you'll hear these words, which are usually accompanied by a shove of the interfering person's arm by a pudgy little hand. Any apology made by the parent to the unwanted helper is tempered with a gleam of pride in their offspring's independent nature.

While independence might be a healthy trait in toddlers, it has its pitfalls. Sometimes accepting help is the only way progress will be made, for example, when the child is in danger of smothering, by forcing their head down the arm of their sweatshirt in their attempt to dress.

It's not only little kids who need help at times. Some of us never really grow out of the I-can-do-it-myself mentality. We love to help *others* in whatever way we can, but *asking* for help sticks in our throat. And when someone offers to assist us, we don't even need to ponder the answer – it's an automatic 'no'. There might be others whose automatic answer is 'yes'; the book of Proverbs has plenty to say to them.

There are times when it doesn't occur to us that we need help. In Exodus 18, Moses had a huge task on his hands. Every day, from morning to night, people came to him to inquire of God. It was too much for him, but it wasn't until his father-in-law visited, expressed his concern and made suggestions, that things changed. It's good to listen when others tell us that we need help with something.

Maybe our biggest problem with accepting help is plain old pride. We like to think of ourselves as clever and capable. Letting someone else help us is an admission that we're deficient in some way.

Accepting help because we need it is a really good idea! Another reason why it can be good to accept help is because it blesses the other person. You see, God has commanded that we do good works, and that's kind of difficult if no one wants anything done for them. So let's not, by our stubborn pride and independence, rob another believer of the opportunity to help others.

It is not good that the man should be alone.

Genesis 2:18

JUNE

15

As humans, we seem to be obsessed with love and romance! That desire for companionship isn't by chance. When God made Adam, the first man, and placed him in the Garden of Eden, He declared that it wasn't good for man to be alone, and gave him a wife, Eve. Marriage was instituted by God and it's a picture of Christ and the church. It is often His will for a man and woman to be united together in this way. Marriage is good and right. Of course, there are those for whom marriage isn't God's plan. If, in the future, you realise that this includes you, you can rest in the knowledge that, despite the heartache this may sometimes bring, God's will is always best. He won't see your life as unfulfilled, and you will be able to bring Him much glory.

But right now, you're likely scratching your head and wondering what on earth I'm writing about marriage for when some of you aren't even legally old enough to get married. What I want to look at over the next few days is what old folks might call courting, or dating – simply put, having a boyfriend or girlfriend.

There are many reasons for desiring a boyfriend or girlfriend. Perhaps you're lonely or want to feel valued and special. Maybe everyone else is pairing up, and you're feeling the pressure to be one half of a couple too. Or, maybe by having a boyfriend or girlfriend, you think people will give you more respect. Perhaps you're desperately in love with someone and you long that your dreams would be realised!

Whatever the reason, the desire to be part of a couple is perfectly natural, placed within us by God. However, it should not be indulged in as merely an enjoyable activity. Like most of our natural desires, there needs to be balance and control. Take food, for instance. We desire food. We need food. And yet that desire must be regulated for the sake of our health. Tomorrow we will think about why control in the area of dating is so important.

All things are lawful for me, but all things are not helpful.
1 Corinthians 6:12 NKJV

Yesterday we saw that the desire for companionship is natural, placed in us by God, but needs to be regulated. The first question we should ask is, does the Bible have anything to say about dating? Not specifically. There's plenty about marriage, though, and maybe that tells us something – when two people attach themselves to each other, marriage should always be the goal. You won't find any mention of people going together for a little while, breaking it off, finding someone new, then repeating the process until they are ready to settle down.

Why would that be? Let's look at it from a human standpoint. You may have been around those who've just suffered a breakup. Maybe it's happened to you. It hurts, doesn't it? Even if you discovered you weren't that keen on the person, or you know you're better off without them, it still makes you wonder if there's something wrong with you, some deficiency or flaw. Breakups leave scars which can affect future relationships. Who hasn't seen symptoms of this – insecurity, a need to prove oneself, or fear of becoming too attached? Having boyfriend after boyfriend, or girlfriend after girlfriend, can lead to unfair comparisons and unreasonable expectations. God doesn't need to spell it out in His Word – it can all get messy.

Waiting for God's will and timing is never wrong. Others may think you strange and slander you, but trust Him. If having a boyfriend or a girlfriend should be with marriage in mind, then it is a choice to be made carefully. There's no rush. In fact, your future husband or wife may not even be a believer yet.

These years of your life are so valuable. This is the time when you will form your own convictions and learn how to make good choices. Use the time wisely – grow spiritually, develop a godly personality, and make use of the education you may be receiving. It is during these years that you're laying the foundation for the rest of your life: concentrate on that. If marriage is God's will for you, building a special person into your life can come later, when the foundation is solid.

We've learned that having a boyfriend or girlfriend should be with a view to marriage. For many, marriage will still be a long way off. It takes money, and an ability to budget, to run a household, so an income will be necessary. Having your own home will bring with it many decisions that, up until now, your parents have always taken. Men should also be the spiritual guide of the home – are you mature enough for this?

Maybe you believe that it's now time to find that special someone to share your future. Or perhaps you weren't looking, but someone has unexpectedly come into your life, and you're wondering if this is the person God has for you. Many relationships leading to wonderful marriages today can be traced back to teenage years – mine included.

What or who should you be looking for? Firstly, it is imperative that the person is saved. Read the verse at the top of the page again. The Bible is totally clear about this. No matter how you may choose to justify it, being 'yoked together' with someone who isn't a Christian is against God's Word. This is an agriculture term. Imagine two animals harnessed together, pulling a plough. One is a donkey, the other an ox. They are different heights, have different gaits. It's not comfortable for them, and I'm sure you can imagine how the furrows are going to look! Finding a partner in life who loves the Lord and has the same priorities and convictions is so important. Not only will this couple get on well together, they may even be more profitable to the Lord as a couple than they were as single people.

I'm sure we've all met those who make us want to be better people. That's the sort of person you're looking for, not one who drags you down and leads you to sin. Choose someone you can see yourself with in years to come. Physical attraction is important, but remember that looks will eventually fade.

Finally, pray! And pray some more. Pray until you're as sure as you can be that it's God's will. For His will is always best.

That in all things He might have the preeminence.
Colossians 1:18

You're sure of God's will and have made your choice, but how should you use the time between finding a suitable companion and getting married?

A common symptom of new couples is a tendency to think only of themselves. For some, you'd almost think that the whole world could disappear overnight, and they'd never even notice! Close friends, maybe those they've been pouring out their hearts to in recent days, are suddenly discarded. Please, young couples, don't do that to your friends! I understand that life is different now, that your boyfriend or girlfriend is your 'someone special', but your friends are still very necessary. It's sad when a couple finally lifts their gaze from each other's eyes to discover that their friends are no longer around.

The greatest challenge that most unmarried couples will face, however, is that of purity. It's something that's not valued in this world but has been commanded by God for our blessing. Be very, very careful. Keep away from situations where you know purity will be difficult to maintain. Consider asking an older believer to keep you accountable. And pray for God's help to honour Him in everything you do as a couple.

Having a boyfriend or girlfriend is an exciting time, but don't forget that 'real life' doesn't begin when you get married. You can grow now and focus on becoming the person God wants you to be, so that you will be a good husband or wife. It's also the time to get to know the person you hope to spend the rest of your life with, to lay a strong foundation for a future marriage. And always remember to keep Christ at the centre, so that, even in your relationship, He might have the pre-eminence.

A final word – maybe the readings over the past few days have been difficult for you. Perhaps you've been conscious of mistakes you've made, or of failed relationships. Maybe you're hurt and broken. Take heart. God understands your pain, and He longs to comfort you. If you've sinned, He is faithful to forgive. Turn to Him, in repentance, or for comfort. Sometimes we believe we are in His will, yet things don't work out; God alone knows why. Rest in His love and cling to Him. Keep trusting Him for wisdom. He has promised to guide you and will never lead you astray.

I sat where they sat.

Ezekiel 3:15

zekiel may not be an easy book to understand, but that doesn't mean we shouldn't read it. In fact, the last time I read Ezekiel, I learned an unexpected lesson from the verse at the top of this page. In the chapter, Ezekiel was given instructions regarding the nation of Israel who were in bondage in Babylon. Afterwards, he was lifted by the Spirit of God and taken to a place where the captives were. He sat where they sat, feeling their pain and burden.

We also ought to be willing to sit with those going through tough times. We need to feel their pain, and weep with those who weep. Sitting with people is a very effective way of associating ourselves with them. Did you ever see someone approach a homeless person on the street and take a seat on the pavement beside them? People who sit are on the same level. As I considered this, I realised that there are a number of times in the gospels when we read of the Lord Jesus Christ sitting with people. It's striking that the One whom Isaiah saw sitting on the throne, high and lifted up, in Isaiah 6, came to this earth and sat with those who were captive to sin and Satan.

At twelve years of age, the Lord Jesus sat in the midst of the teachers. Did they catch a glimpse in Him of the One Daniel called the Ancient of Days? In the synagogue in Nazareth, He read from the book of Isaiah and sat down to teach those He had grown up amongst. The result? They wondered, but then were filled with wrath and sought to kill Him. He sat with publicans and sinners at a feast, but also sat to eat in the house of a Pharisee, a religious leader. And the night He was betrayed, He sat down for the last time before His crucifixion, to eat the Passover with His disciples.

The Lord Jesus Christ was made in the likeness of men, and He associated Himself with mankind in sitting with them. He also sat where we sit – He feels and knows our burden and pain. But He is able to do more than even Ezekiel could: He is able to deliver the captives – us – from bondage.

If we confess our sins, He is faithful and just to forgive us our sins.

1 John 1:9

Jack snapped his Bible shut. He might as well have been reading his older brother's university textbook for all it meant this evening. Praying hadn't gone well either. When he'd tried to speak to God, the words would hardly come, and those that had didn't seem to make it past the bedroom ceiling. He flopped onto the bed, hands behind his head. What was wrong? Surely it wasn't anything to do with how he'd acted in geography earlier? Everyone talked in class and made fun of Miss Clarkson behind her back. But no matter how much he tried to make excuses, the nagging feeling was still there. Was what he'd done really wrong? The teacher was such a strange lady, and wasn't it basically her fault that she couldn't control her class? Maybe he was actually doing her a favour!

Jack winced. He knew that he was only making excuses. The words he'd just tried to read in Colossians 4 suddenly struck him with clarity – 'Let your speech always be gracious…' His words earlier certainly hadn't been gracious. With a groan, he slid to his knees. He knew what was wrong, and what he needed to do. His sin had put a big, black cloud between him and God, and the only thing that would remove it would be confession to God of what he had done wrong. Of course, Jack knew that his salvation wasn't at stake. Even if he'd died in the middle of making fun of Miss Clarkson, he'd have gone to heaven, because when Jack had trusted Christ, he was saved for all eternity. But now communion with God was broken, and it needed to be put right. Like the time he kicked Dad in a temper when he was four. He hadn't wanted to look Dad in the eye, but when Jack apologised, Dad forgave him, gave him a hug, and they were the best of friends again.

Jack took a deep breath, addressed His heavenly Father, and told Him about his sin, calling it exactly what it was. He rejoiced that God had forgiven him because of Christ's death at Calvary. As he stood up, he smiled. Communion with God was restored; the black cloud was gone.

There shall be no night there.

Revelation 22:5

JUNE 21

D o you know where I'd like to be on this date? Somewhere like a Scandinavian country, or perhaps Shetland, those islands north of mainland Scotland. You see, it's summer solstice in the Northern hemisphere, when the North Pole is at its greatest tilt towards the sun. Here, the hours of daylight are at their maximum, with the sun rising early and setting late. For those in the Arctic Circle, there is continual daylight. Even in Shetland it never gets properly dark.

Doesn't that sound amazing? Many people (and I'm probably at the top of the list!) aren't fans of the dark nights of winter, so to experience a night without darkness must be wonderful.

The great thing is that when we get to heaven, we *will* get to experience not having any darkness. In fact, it's going to be even better than that – there won't even be night at all! Did you ever have a really wonderful day, one that you wished would go on forever? That's what it's going to be like – one long, wonderful, continuous day that will never, ever end. It would be great to experience twenty-four hours of daylight in the Arctic, but eventually darkness would begin to return, and by the time we reached winter solstice, there would be twenty-four hours of darkness. No matter how much time passes in heaven, there will never be any darkness because the Lord God will give us light. He has no end, so the light will never come to an end. All will be forever bright and radiant.

Whether we ever get to experience the brightness of a northern summer solstice or not, we can be assured that one day we're going to live in a place where it is always light, because the Lamb Himself is the light thereof (Revelation 21:23).

The Lord our God is righteous in all His works which He doeth.
Daniel 9:14

Recently an elderly lady was telling me that she'd been left badly shaken after having been robbed of a fairly substantial sum of money by two men who tricked her into letting them enter her house. I'm not sure if the police caught the criminals – I really hope they did – but let's imagine that the men are brought to court to stand trial before a judge who is well-known for his kindness and generosity. On this particular day, he decides to show kindness to the burglars and give them the shortest sentence possible. Can you imagine the uproar? Is that kind of the judge? Is it fair?

Of course, it depends from whose perspective you view the sentence. If it's from the criminals' side, the judge's decision is kind. They might even believe that his judgment is fair. But from the lady's side, it's certainly not kind or fair. Those men deserve a proper punishment, and a short sentence only makes light of the trauma she suffered. The judge might be kind, but he certainly isn't righteous.

What is righteousness? The clue is in the name – the quality of being right or just. And, unlike the judge in our hypothetical story, God is entirely righteous. Of all God's attributes, His righteousness seems to be the one on which most doubt is cast. People see wickedness in the world and ask how a righteous God can let it go unpunished, yet don't see themselves as deserving of punishment for their own sins. Our widely differing views as to what righteousness is do not count, because it is *God* who sets the standard of righteousness, not us.

Righteousness doesn't only have implications for judgment, but for blessing. Because Christ has taken our place, God can righteously bless us. Another reassuring fact of God's righteousness is found in 1 John 1:9 – when we confess our sins, He is faithful and righteous to forgive us. It would actually be unrighteous of God if He didn't forgive us!

Although we may not comprehend many aspects of God's righteousness yet, in a future day it will be seen in all its fullness. In the meantime, though, we can hold firmly to the truth found in Genesis 18:25 – 'Shall not the Judge of all the earth do right?'

Isaac walked alongside his father, carrying a burden of wood. They had left the other young men behind; now it was only he and his father. Their destination was ahead somewhere, a place God had told his father about. It was clear that the purpose of their journey was to offer a burnt offering to God, but they had no animal to sacrifice, so Isaac turned to his father and asked, "Where is the lamb for a burnt offering?" His father didn't have to ponder before he answered. Instead, he replied, "My son, God will provide for Himself the lamb for a burnt offering."

I can't help but see Christ each time I read this story. Abraham's answer to Isaac was deeper and much more prophetic than he likely realised. In John 1, when John the Baptist saw the Lord Jesus Christ coming toward him, he proclaimed, "Behold! The Lamb of God who takes away the sin of the world!" (John 1:29 NKJV)

Isaac himself is a very clear picture of Christ – another beloved Son who carried a wooden burden – a cross – on His way to *the place* of sacrifice. 'And when they had come to *the place* called Calvary, there they crucified Him' (Luke 23:33 NKJV). The Lord Jesus Christ was not only bound to the wood, but nailed by His hands and feet. Like Isaac, He did not struggle or resist, but was obedient and willing to be the sacrifice. Abraham received Isaac back alive, a picture of the resurrection of our Lord Jesus (see Hebrews 11:19).

Towards the end of the chapter, we learn that obedience produced far-reaching outcomes – a multitude of people would result, and all nations of the earth would be blessed. Isn't this what's happening today because of Christ's obedience unto death? A great multitude, of which we are a part, will be in heaven through His sacrifice and death, from all nations of the earth.

In Isaac's willing submission to his father, he was foretelling the most important event that would ever happen in the history of the world – the sacrifice of the Lord Jesus Christ for the redemption of mankind.

Children, obey your parents in the Lord: for this is right.

Ephesians 6:1

Don't let the first word put you off – the word 'teenager' is relatively new, and certainly wasn't around when Paul was writing to the Ephesian Christians. In any case, if you're under eighteen and living at home, this applies to you.

You don't need me to tell you that it isn't easy! None of us like being told what to do, and it's especially hard in those years when you've left childhood behind but haven't reached full adulthood yet. You're becoming your own person – learning who you are, locating your boundaries, figuring out your place in the world and what's important to you. Friction between you and your parents is often a normal part of the process.

What you have to remember though, is that, providing it doesn't go against God's Word, you are still to obey them. You may not want to, and you might not understand why they're asking you to do, or not do, certain things, but God commands obedience. That should be enough of a reason to submit to their wishes.

Most parents will have good reasons behind their requests. I know they probably seem old to you, and you're certain that they have no idea what it's like to be a teenager right now. But don't forget that they also thought exactly the same thing when they were your age, and they also faced things that *their* parents hadn't experienced. Why not ask them to explain the reason why they're asking you to do, or not do, something (respectfully, of course). And don't be afraid to talk to them and tell them what you are facing. Most likely, they love you more than you realise and want to help you through these eventful years.

Now take a look at the last four words of the verse. No matter how difficult obeying your parents might be, God has declared that it is right. It might not seem a very important thing, or a very worthy task, but when you obey your parents, it pleases God.

What type of problems are you facing today? Maybe trouble with schoolwork, problems at home, issues with people, or concerns with your health. So many different things can happen to cause us anxiety and make life really tough.

Joni Eareckson was only seventeen when she faced something that few of us have ever had to deal with. One day, while out swimming with her sister, Joni dived into shallow water, severing her spinal cord. Although her sister managed to save her life, Joni was diagnosed with quadriplegia, having lost the use of her arms and legs. The energetic, active teenager was going to spend the rest of her life in a wheelchair. Can you imagine what it must have been like for Joni to hear that news? To never walk again! To be dependent on others for the most basic tasks!

A few years ago, Joni wrote an article on the fiftieth anniversary of her diving accident. In it, she says, "It sounds incredible, but I really would rather be in a wheelchair knowing Jesus as I do than be on my feet without Him."[47] You see, when Joni was fourteen, she trusted Christ as her Saviour. He would never leave her nor forsake her. But as time went on, Joni became more interested in living for herself. She knew this wasn't the way God would want her to live, so she prayed, "Lord, do something in my life to jerk it right side up, because I'm really living this life wrong."[48]

Things didn't change overnight after Joni's accident. She went through a time of anger, depression, and doubts. Life has never been easy for her – not only has she suffered with all that goes with quadriplegia, including chronic pain, but she has had cancer twice. And yet she has seen the blessings in her sufferings. In the article, she quotes the verse at the top of the page.

Joni has been used greatly by God. These days, we're faced with the growing belief that it's better not to live at all than to live with a disability. Yet Joni has already proved this wrong. She has shown that, no matter what our situations might be, God can take our lives and turn them into something beautiful – for Him and for His glory.

47. As told in https://www.thegospelcoalition.org/article/reflections-on-50th-anniversary-of-my-diving-accident/
48. As told in https://www.youtube.com/watch?v=VVXJ8GyLgto

Therefore with joy shall ye draw water out of the wells of salvation.

Isaiah 12:3

How long is it since you trusted Christ? Maybe it was only a few weeks or months ago – or maybe you've been saved for a number of years. No matter how long ago it was, I'm sure you remember the joy you had when you realised that you were now a child of God.

But maybe that joy has dimmed a bit. You've realised that your surroundings haven't changed – bad things still happen in your life, you're still tempted to sin, and you're still living amongst people who, truth be told, maybe like you less now that you're a Christian. The shininess has worn off your salvation and, with it, much of the joy.

It doesn't have to be like this. In fact, it *shouldn't* be like this! Being saved is wonderful. It is the only thing worth having in this life and is absolutely vital for eternity. Just think – we have been delivered! As sinners, condemnation was all we deserved, but God – the One against whom we had sinned – provided the remedy through the death of His Son, our Lord Jesus Christ. Now we've been forgiven. All those sins that troubled us are removed – as far as the east is from the west (Psalm 103:12). We'll never face them again.

Forgiveness of sins is only one of the blessings we've received. Think about the new relationship we have with our Father – brought near to God, with access into His presence at any time of the day or night. We have the Holy Spirit indwelling us. We have the Lord Jesus as our Advocate when we sin. No matter what we face, we will never be alone, but will always have One with us to help and guide us. And then there are the numerous heavenly blessings of which we have glimpsed only the faintest sight, things which we can hardly even begin to imagine.

It's a marvellous thing to be saved! God wants us to revel in it, to drink deeply from the wells of salvation – to take time to think about and enjoy the many blessings which are ours – and experience the limitless joy that it brings.

Beauty is vain.
Proverbs 31:30

Searching for admiration isn't a new phenomenon, but my guess is that it's never been so popular as it is today. Before social media, the only way people could show off their new hair, clothes, or physique, was by going somewhere crowded in search of admiring glances and possibly a sprinkling of compliments. Nowadays we don't even need to leave our own bedroom.

Let's imagine a thirteen-year-old girl. We'll call her Katie. Katie brushes her hair, applies her makeup, and changes into her cutest top. She takes the perfect selfie, filters it, then posts it, and waits for the comments. She doesn't have long to wait. One after another appears, liberally sprinkled with heart, flame, or princess emojis, from friends and complete strangers alike.

Look at you – you beauty!

Stunning!

I LOVE your hair... #goals

The comments make Katie smile with pleasure. She loves to be told she's a beauty. Deep inside, she figured she was pretty, but it's nice to know that everyone else thinks so too. Katie has fallen into the trap of vanity.

What is vanity? Online dictionaries are agreed that it is excessive pride in oneself, not only in appearance, but in ability as well. And the Bible goes further when it speaks of vanity; the thought is of emptiness. Vanity is totally worthless. Proverbs 31 is a fascinating chapter – it's advice from a mother to her son on qualities he should look for in a potential wife. Would you believe that beauty isn't even mentioned until the very end? And when she does get around to it, she tells him that beauty is vain – empty!

That sure doesn't tie in with the selfie culture of today, does it? So if focussing on our outward appearance is worthless, what *is* important in God's eyes? (Because while it was Lemuel's mother who spoke these words, it's part of Scripture – God's Word.) 'A woman that feareth the Lord, she shall be praised.' God wants all of us – both male and female – to be focussed on Him and our inward attitude towards Him.

Outward appearance fades. We won't be here forever. Our time on earth is a tiny dot on the great scale of forever, so let's not use it on the emptiness of vanity, but on what really counts.

A flattering mouth works ruin.
Proverbs 26:28 NKJV

Yesterday we met Katie and watched as she posted a selfie, then waited for the compliments to come rolling in. It didn't take long. Someone called her stunning, another person admired her hair, and another commented *Look at you – you beauty!* Katie was thrilled – how could she not be with such flattering comments?

Flattering... Hm! Remember yesterday we looked up the meaning of 'vanity'? Here's a summary of what many online dictionaries say about flattery – it is excessive and insincere praise, usually with a self-serving motive. Those positive comments might not be so great after all! But maybe they come under the category of 'praise' instead. Let's look it up. Words that appear in relation to praise include 'approval', 'respect', and 'commendation'. Can you see the difference? Praise is merited and genuinely given with no thought of getting anything in return. Flattery is insincere, unconcerned with the truth, prone to exaggeration, and has an ulterior motive.

It's possible that some of the comments on Katie's post are praise. But others seem a bit forced, a little fake. Maybe someone fishing for a return compliment – *Says you, you pretty thing!* Or another is hoping for some attention from the beautiful Katie.

Sometimes it's obvious what is flattery and what is praise; other times it's impossible to tell. If we keep vanity under control, we won't get too concerned with trying to tell the difference. What we must try to do, however, is guard against being a flatterer. God says that flattering is a very serious matter – just look at the verse at the top of the page.

How do we know when and how to compliment someone? First of all, why do we want to compliment them? Is it to ingratiate ourselves with them, to make them think of us in a positive light? Or is it for some other self-serving reason – answers to the maths homework, perhaps? When we compliment, is it honest – or excessive, gushing, and exaggerated? Has the person done something worthy of praise? If so, say it! It shouldn't matter who the person is and whether we like them or not. Praise can often be harder to give than flattery. But next time you're tempted to compliment someone, check your motives. Praise can build up, but a flattering mouth works ruin.

Back when I was in school, I learned about George de Mestral being inspired to create Velcro when he noticed how burdock seeds clung to his dog's fur. Since then, I've been fascinated with how mankind invents and improves technology by observing nature. This is called biomimicry.

One area that I find especially fascinating is aviation. There's something about watching a bird soaring through the air that has always captured the hearts and imaginations of earthbound humans, but it wasn't until the beginning of last century that flying actually became a reality. Since those early days, many different aircraft have been invented and fine-tuned.

For all man's wisdom, however, there will always be room for improvement. Each new model of plane comes with new features designed to make it more energy-efficient. And many of those features are taken from nature.

Take the idea of winglets, for example – those little curved ends on many planes' wings. The reason why a plane is able to stay in the air is to do with air flow. As the engines move the plane forward, air flow is generated around the wings to produce lift. Air pressure is reduced above the wing and increased beneath it. But what happens at the tips of the wings where these areas meet? A vortex is created, which results in lowered efficiency.

Enter the eagle! This large bird is capable of flying long distances but spends very little of its time in the air actually flapping its wings. Instead, it soars and glides. One feature of this majestic bird is that the tips of its wings turn up during flight, to reduce drag and increase efficiency. The vortex is weaker and some of the energy which would have been wasted is converted to an apparent thrust. Aircraft manufacturers have now incorporated this into many of their planes, and wing design continues to be an area of research and development.[49] The wings of future planes may resemble birds' wings even more than they already do!

Humans love to boast about their great achievements in the world of technology – and they are great, no question about it. But instead we should give the glory to the Creator – the One who designed the energy-efficient eagle in the very beginning.

49. https://www.hydro.aero/en/newsletter-details/what-you-should-know-aboutwinglets-and-wingtips.html

When I consider... the work of
Thy fingers.
Psalm 8:3

When was the last time you stood outside on a clear night and gazed up at the numerous stars? Or sat and watched a glorious sunset, the sky painted in a vibrant riot of purples, pinks, and reds? Or lay on your back on the soft green grass, watching fluffy clouds floating overhead against a blue backdrop? What about watching the activities of the insect creation – scurrying ants, busy bees, capable spiders? Listening to the birds singing and twittering beside a gurgling brook? Or, my favourite, leaning your arms on the top bar of a gate, watching a field of peacefully grazing cattle?

One of the fallouts of living in an increasingly atheistic society is that any view that we have of creation is usually accompanied by some thought or other regarding the undeniability of the existence of God. And while that's all well and good – after all, creation does proclaim His existence – it does no harm at all to just enjoy the beauties and wonders of the world around us. We don't always have to consciously remind ourselves every time we look around us of the folly of those who deny His existence.

Each detail in creation – both large and small – has been placed there to declare God's glory. We see His might and majesty in the vastness of the universe, the magnificence of snow-capped mountain peaks, and the roaring ocean waves. We see His wisdom and care in the activities of tiny creatures and insects. We see His liberality and bounty in the variegated shades of plants and flowers during a walk in a garden or forest. We learn lessons from creation about the awesome God we have.

Today, take time to pause and observe nature, because God has given us His creation to enjoy. And when you do, reflect on what it reveals about God, then bring Him glory by praising Him for His abounding greatness.

JULY

And Rebekah spake unto Jacob her son.

Genesis 27:6

Hands up who struggles with being patient! There likely aren't too many of us whose hand isn't in the air right now. Mine certainly is. The problem with impatience is that we sometimes jump ahead and take matters into our own hands, often with disastrous consequences.

I'm sure you've read the beautiful story of Rebekah, who travelled a long distance to marry Isaac, a man she'd never seen. It's a romantic tale, isn't it? But here we see her, twin boys and a good number of years later, and she's got a really big problem.

You see, in those days, the oldest son was entitled to what was called the birthright. This came with great privileges and blessings and was extremely valuable. But Esau, the older of the boys, didn't value it the way he should have, and sold it to his brother, Jacob. It had actually been God's will all along that the younger brother should have the birthright, but how that would have come about, we aren't told. Now it was time for old Isaac to bless the son who had the birthright. As he gave instruction to Esau in preparation for blessing him, Rebekah's eyes must have widened in horror. The birthright belonged to her favourite, the younger son, Jacob. She couldn't let Esau have the blessing!

So Rebekah set to work. After explaining her plan to Jacob, they executed it to perfection. Isaac was deceived. When Esau returned some time later, it was too late. The blessing had already been given to Jacob.

On the surface, it all looked good. After all, it had been God's will all along that Jacob should have been blessed. But Rebekah's hasty actions were to have terrible consequences. Esau was angry. Really angry. So angry, in fact, that Jacob had to flee for his life. Rebekah never saw her favourite son again. By the time he was able to return, she had died.

I often wonder how God would have worked out His will in this situation. I'm sure His plan was marvellous. But because of Rebekah's actions, we'll never know. It's the same when we take matters into our hands. God has a plan for us, but we need to wait for Him to work. His plan is always best!

> They received the word... and searched the Scriptures daily to find out whether these things were so.
>
> Acts 17:11 NKJV

JULY

2

There are certain things each of us believe and practice, both in our local church and in our personal lives. But if someone asked you, "Why do you do such-and-such?" could you answer them? By now, you'll have met Christians who meet differently to you, or who don't share your convictions. Maybe you're beginning to wonder if what you do is biblical at all, or only tradition. It's good and right to obey your parents in the Lord, but there must come a time when you develop your own convictions. Doing something just because your mum or dad do it is commendable, but not enough. What happens when you leave home, or when your parents are no longer with you? What will determine then what you deem important?

The Bereans left us a good example. These new believers accepted the word spoken by Paul and Silas, then followed it up by searching the Scriptures for themselves. Asking for help from others in our genuine search for truth is good, and listening to sound teaching is a wise thing to do, but it's even more important to check everything we're told, or that we read, against God's Word. You don't need me to tell you that in your search for answers, the Bible is the final authority. Our feelings and preferences, man-made rules, and even family traditions must be set aside. You need to discover for yourself what the Bible says.

Of course, tradition isn't always bad, and just because we can't find some direct instruction relating to it in Scripture, either for or against, doesn't mean it's wrong. There are customs of the local church which are good and helpful, and which are purely for practical convenience; for example, the use of hymnbooks. Principles found throughout Scripture can also guide us, even when there is no direct instruction. Our conscience shouldn't be overlooked either – God has given it to us for a reason.

These are probably the most formative years of your life. It's what you learn now that will influence the rest of your days. Take the time to search the Scriptures and develop your own convictions, which will stand you in good stead as you live each day for God's glory.

You are of more value than many sparrows.
Matthew 10:31 ESV

My husband once visited a small village in the mountains of Mexico. It was a rustic place, and he was enjoying watching the many hens and chicks wander about, until he looked around and saw a little girl trying to prop a poor half-squashed chick back onto its feet. The tiny ball of fluff didn't make it, and my husband watched as its life quickly ebbed away.

Time and again, I'm reminded of how fragile birds are. Not only are they easily trampled on, they often try to fly through windows, get hit by cars, are caught by cats, or succumb to disease. All the little bones and feathers are part of an intricate design to help them fly, but they certainly aren't very robust. Compared with other birds, sparrows are not only delicate, but one of the plainest little birds you can find. So invaluable that in Bible times two were sold for a penny, and five for two pennies – one extra thrown in free. Yet God notices each sparrow which falls, and not indifferently, either. He has a care for each tiny bird.

If He cares for frail little birds, He will care for you too. You are of more value than a whole flock of sparrows, and nothing will happen to you that God doesn't know or care about. He knows how you feel, whether you're happy, sad, or something in between. Every situation you face, whether it's good or bad, He sees. He watches over you with immaculate care. He will never lose sight of you. And when tough times come, He will be right there with you. Often we feel fragile, very small, and forgotten by other people, but none of this changes our Father's care for us. We have the assurance that He sees us, and values us much more than many little sparrows.

Whilst we are at home in the body, we are absent from the Lord.

2 Corinthians 5:6

4

JULY

Away back in the days when people laboured hard from morning to night, and it was difficult to make a living, many left the shores of the British Isles and sailed across the ocean to America to make their fortune. One of these was a man called John Macduff, from Scotland. He took his new wife and, after spending some time in New York, headed west. Unlike many poor people who made the arduous journey to the new world and ended up in a situation little better than the one they left, John Macduff became very successful. But he had one problem. His wife was so homesick that her health began to fail, so they sold up and moved to the east coast where she could see the ocean and watch the ships departing for Scotland.

Being closer to her homeland wasn't enough to recover her health, so, valuing his wife more than any earthly possession, John Macduff abandoned his American dream and they returned home in an attempt to save her life. It worked. At the sight of all that she had longed for during those years across the ocean, she revived.[50]

Just as Mrs Macduff wasn't at home in America, neither are believers at home here on this earth. We have been saved and prepared for something more – an eternity in heaven with our Saviour. Down here, we are only strangers and pilgrims passing through.

Although we often aren't very good at remembering that this isn't our home, there will usually be some desire in the hearts of Christians to be with Christ. At times, however, we go through periods of difficulty and deep crisis. It is then that we see more fully the emptiness and sadness of all that is around us. Our eyes are drawn to a distant shore, and we long to leave and head for home.

If this is you right now, keep holding on. God has promised to take us to heaven, and He always keeps His word. The Saviour, who loved us so much that He came from heaven to earth to die for us, desires that we be with Him. Someday, maybe sooner than we imagine, we will finally be home!

50. As recorded in http://www.hymntime.com/tch/htm/m/y/a/i/myaincou.htm

Let us offer the sacrifice of praise to God continually... giving thanks to His name.

Hebrews 13:15

Recently, my youngest brother trusted Christ. It was a time of great joy in our family because he'd been the only one who wasn't saved, and we had been praying for his salvation for many years. Of course, when God answers prayer, our natural inclination is to thank Him. But have you ever noticed that the time and effort we spend pleading with God is typically much greater than the time and effort we spend thanking Him when He answers our prayers? We're great at asking, and not very good at saying thanks!

Prayer takes effort. You know that, right? But did you know that giving thanks can take effort too? When we thank God, we praise Him. God is worthy of all praise and honour. But what the devil doesn't want is for God to get praise, and he's not going to make it easy for us. Neither is our own sinful flesh; we'd rather indulge ourselves. To offer to God the praise that He rightly deserves will take effort. And sacrifice. Isn't that what our verse says at the top of the page? Giving thanks is a sacrifice of praise.

Maybe you feel that there isn't very much you can sacrifice for the Lord. After all, sacrifices often involve money, and when you're young you probably don't have a lot to spare. But here is something you can do. You can sacrifice time you usually spend on yourself and your interests to praise God. You can sacrifice energy – prayer doesn't always flow easily, and it can take effort. Knowing verses and passages of Scripture can help us praise God. Building up a store of them in our minds will mean sacrificing other activities you might want to do. Prayer can also take courage. If you are part of a local church, God expects males to pray audibly to Him in church gatherings. Standing up and praying in public is a sacrifice for many young men.

Whatever you may sacrifice to give thanks to God, let's not forget that He is worthy. We are to praise Him continually, giving thanks in everything – not only in big things, like the salvation of a sibling, but in little things as well.

The sandy cove nestled at the base of tall, sandstone cliffs. Sheltered from sea breezes, with caves to explore and water of azure blue, it was the perfect beach on which to spend the day. But there was something which stood out in stark contrast to the peaceful scene, not seeming to realise that the whole setting was supposed to be one of tranquillity and relaxation: the sound of raging waves, amplified by the tall cliffs. Wave after wave after wave rose up, tall and powerful, before crashing with great force onto the sandy shore. Swimming was out of the question. Even standing in the rolling surf was challenging, as I quickly discovered after being knocked off my feet.

There are a lot of loud, boisterous voices in the world today. Voices which roar against the existence of God, proclaiming that science has shown us that the world came into existence without Him, declaring that religion is out of date and that Christians are prejudiced and intolerant. They proudly assert that man does not need God. Rising up, they appear so tall and powerful, keen to knock us off our feet and throw us into the crashing surf.

Yet, on that beach, I couldn't help but notice that each of those boisterous waves, so loud, fierce, and full of energy, soon petered out, and ended up as flimsy froth on the shore. Someday, perhaps very soon, those atheistic voices will be silent. Their power and might cannot and will not last.

Waves may seem mighty, but if even a sandy shore can halt their power and cause them to fizzle out, how much more futile is it for feeble man to rage at our mighty God, the One whom the Bible describes as the Rock? So when you face the crashing waves of our modern anti-God society, stand firm, and plant your feet on the solid Rock. He will last. The waves won't.

O give thanks unto the Lord,
for He is good.
Psalm 107:1

I s God good? I can't imagine that there are any true believers who
would answer in the negative! But maybe there are times, when
everything seems to be going wrong, that deep down inside you
wonder if God really is always good.

First of all, let's be clear that everything that the Bible says is true.
It is God's Word, and He cannot lie. So all those verses about God's
goodness, and there are quite a number of them, are absolutely
accurate. It doesn't matter how we feel about it. *God is good!*

He is good, not only in what He does, but in who He is. He cannot *be*
anything else but good; He cannot *do* anything else but good. All the
evil in this world is a result of the fall of mankind in the Garden of Eden,
which affected the whole of creation. God gave people free will, but He
did not create evil.

Unsaved people often question God's goodness, instead of looking
around and seeing all that God has done for them. Sometimes believers
do the same. While we can't yet see things from a heavenly perspective,
there is enough of the goodness of God on display that should cause
all, both saved and unsaved, to bow our hearts in repentance (Romans
2:4).

But maybe you're wondering how we are to make sense of a good God
who lets bad things happen to His children? Remember Joseph? I'm
sure he could have asked the same question. Through no fault of his
own, his brothers hated him so much that they sold him as a slave. He
ended up in Egypt as a servant, then he was falsely accused and put
in prison. When he finally had hope that he might be set free, he was
again forgotten. What was going on? Where was God's goodness here?

You know how the story goes. Using his God-given wisdom, Joseph was
instrumental in saving the lives of countless people from starvation
and was used to bring about his brothers' repentance. By the end of
the book of Genesis, we see that Joseph understood what God had
been doing all those years. 'You meant evil against me; but God meant
it for good.' God's goodness had not failed. God was good then, and
God is good now.

He giveth His beloved sleep.

Psalm 127:2

JULY

8

Unlike the animal world, we human beings have a very complicated relationship with sleep! Some people need lots of sleep, others seem to be able to do with less. Many of us don't want to go to bed when we should, but we don't like getting up either. Scientists freely admit that there's a lot about sleep they don't understand, and they become baffled when they look at it through the lens of evolution. One thing they all agree on, however, is the importance of sleep. Sleep is vital for our energy and concentration levels, immune system, general health, and mental wellbeing, including the lowering of stress levels.

As Christians, the concept of sleep makes perfect sense. Our Creator knew we would need to spend about a third of our lives in recovery and rejuvenation. Rest is vitally important and is God-given.

But sometimes actually going to bed and availing of that restoring sleep isn't very appealing. Did you know that what scientists call your circadian rhythm shifts in your teens, and melatonin (sleep hormone) is produced later at night, which makes you want to stay up late? Unfortunately for you, you can't use this as an excuse to put off going to bed! Growing bodies need more sleep, and when you must get up early for school or work, you won't have the opportunity to catch up in the morning.

So what do you do? As you get older, you'll realise that you need to be in charge of your own health and wellbeing. Your parents might think you are sleeping, but you could be scrolling through social media or watching videos under the duvet. Maybe you aren't sleepy – but did you know that screens emit the same wavelength of light as the morning sun, meaning that looking at a screen before you go to bed actually has the effect of waking you up? No wonder you don't feel ready to sleep!

Or sometimes we don't go to bed because we're too lazy to pull ourselves off the sofa, get changed, and brush our teeth. Eventually we realise that the longer we slouch there, the harder it's going to be.

In the verse quoted above, the earlier part reads that it is vain to sit up late, but that God has given us sleep. We should wholeheartedly embrace His precious refreshing gift to us.[51]

---

51. Information from *The 4 Pillar Plan* by Dr Rangan Chatterjee, published by Penguin Life, 2017; and *Sleep* by Nick Littlehales, also published by Penguin Life, 2016.

Do not love sleep, lest you come
to poverty.
Proverbs 20:13 NKJV

Iended yesterday's reading by saying that we should embrace
God's gift of sleep. But, as with most physical blessings, it is to
be enjoyed in moderation. In Ecclesiastes, Solomon speaks of the
sweetness of sleep for those who labour. When you've spent a day
working hard, there's nothing more satisfying than drifting off to sleep
in a comfortable bed. But that's not all that Solomon says. In Proverbs,
we find warnings about excessive sleep. He asks in chapter 6 verse 9
NKJV, 'How long will you slumber, O sluggard? When will you rise from
your sleep?' The picture is of a lazy person who is so intent on sleeping
that he doesn't realise that poverty is about to attack. It seems that
the onslaught will be sudden. Instead of being watchful, taking steps
to ward off the strike, he is unprepared and at great risk of becoming
destitute.

I tend to picture the sluggard as a grubby, overweight, middle-aged
man, loud snores emanating from the great pile of quilts on his bed,
but what if the sluggard is actually more like someone closer to home?
Like me – a chronic snooze-hitter. Or like someone in their summer
holidays who has got into a pattern of staying up too late at night,
then sleeping half the day away. There are times when everyone, for
whatever reason, needs to catch up on sleep, but this is not what the
wise man is speaking about. Instead, he is warning that laziness will not
lead to a productive life. Choosing sleep over activity won't benefit us
or others. When we habitually sleep late, we're not only messing up
our body clocks, we're wasting precious time that God has given us, as
stewards, to use for His glory.

Don't forget, as well, that the roots of the habits you form in your
teenage years are the ones which will go deepest. To change these
habits at a later date can prove to be difficult. On the other hand, a
habit of self-discipline will always be invaluable, no matter what sphere
and phase of life you are in. So the next time we're tempted to stay in
bed, let's remember what happens to sluggards. It won't be long before
our feet hit the floor!

I will both lay me down in peace, and sleep: for Thou, Lord, only makest me dwell in safety.

Psalm 4:8

We've seen that sleep is good, but in moderation. So what happens when, no matter what you try, you can't drop off? You never really realise how long a night is until you're tossing and turning, rearranging your pillow, counting sheep, or whatever it is you do to try to find your way to the land of nod.

It can be hard to switch off, especially after a busy day, so trying to wind down before bedtime is a good idea. If we have identified anything that triggers anxiety, whether it be social media or stressful studies, we should deal with it earlier in the day or, if possible, avoid it altogether. And, as we've already learned, the light emitted from screens can hinder our ability to drop off to sleep, so technology is best avoided before bedtime.

Sometimes people struggle to sleep because of a physical reason. Nothing will chase sleep away like pain and discomfort, or it could be something as simple as a head cold with a tickly cough. The reason for many people's sleepless nights, however, is their thoughts – thoughts of the past, thoughts of the future, thoughts about what they did that day, thoughts about what they need to do the next day, even thoughts about how long they've been lying awake! Often, the thoughts which keep people awake aren't merely thoughts, but worries. In this situation, the very best thing we can do is to turn to the One who gives sleep, to the One who knows the end from the beginning. He wouldn't have us to worry. As our verse for today says, He makes us dwell in safety. We are safely sheltered by Him – nothing is out of His control, and nothing will happen to us that He hasn't allowed. For that reason, we can commit it all to Him, and lie down in peace... and sleep![52]

52. Information taken from *The 4 Pillar Plan* by Dr Rangan Chatterjee.

He was in the hinder part of the ship, asleep on a pillow.
Mark 4:38

Over the past few days, we've been thinking a lot about sleep, but today I want to look at the Lord Jesus Christ's attitude to sleep. When we fall asleep, we're pretty much unconscious, unaware of what's going on around us and totally oblivious to the passage of time. When we sleep, we're vulnerable, so it's vitally important that those who protect others must not fall asleep while they are on their watch. That's why Psalm 121:3 NJKV says 'He who keeps you will not slumber.' God is always watching over His people, day and night.

Yet, look at the verse at the top of the page. The Lord Jesus, who is truly God, slept on a pillow in the midst of the storm. The truth that God became man, taking on the weakness and frailty of a human body, is something that makes us wonder and worship. He was still God, even while sleeping, and could still watch over His people. The disciples were in no danger whatsoever, especially with the Lord in the boat.

The Lord wasn't having a nap because there was nothing better to do. If you look at His schedule over the previous days, you will understand why He took the time to catch up on sleep. He'd been busy! In Mark 1:35, we even read that He rose up a great while before day and went to a solitary place to pray. Getting up early to pray is something that doesn't come naturally to us, but if the Lord Jesus felt the need to forego sleep to commune with His Father, how much more should we feel the need to do the same? There's nothing so comfy as our beds first thing in the morning, but rather than rolling out of bed late and racing off to begin our day without praying, we should follow the Lord's example. We surely won't regret spending a little extra time on our knees. If the sinless Lord Jesus Christ made time in the morning to pray, why do we, with our propensity to sin, think we can head off into the world, with all its attractions and temptations, without committing the day to God and asking for His help to live like His Son?

If any man be in Christ, he is a new creature.

2 Corinthians 5:17

If you'd seen Rodger Luke coming down the street towards you, you'd have ducked into the nearest shop. In fact, if it was market day, you'd have heard him before you'd have seen him, because he was often heard roaring like a bull on his way home. Rodger Luke was born in 1813 and was brought up by an aunt, but became a wild man who was very fond of alcohol. He was so violent that the police had even inserted a special ring into the wall of the police station to tie him to. Rodger himself said that he'd been the devil's honest servant.

I'm not sure that very many of us would have held out much hope that such a sinner would come to trust the Lord Jesus Christ – yet Rodger did! After hearing the gospel preached, he became concerned about his soul, but thought that there was no salvation available for a sinner like him. Finally, he came to realise that he could be forgiven through Christ's death for him on the cross.

The change in Rodger's life after he trusted Christ must have been reminiscent of the change in the man of Gadara in Mark 5. The old habits and sins were gone. He told the police that they could remove the ring in the police station because he'd met the 'subduer'. Rodger began to read and pray with his children, spread the gospel to friends and neighbours, and visit the sick and poor. In 1897, as an elderly man in his mid-eighties, he left this earth for heaven.

Never underestimate what God can do! The same power that transformed the man of Gadara and Rodger Luke, is exactly the same today. No matter how wicked the sinner, God is still able to save that person and change them, setting their feet on the path of living for Him.

13

JULY

Neither is there salvation in any other.

Acts 4:12

I n reading through the Bible, you'll come across a number of fairly long words ending in 'ion'. They're the sort of words that people may not find easy to pronounce, let alone know what they mean, but they are very important. These words are the names of doctrines – teachings – which relate to us as believers. Doctrine isn't something dry and only for elderly, spiritual men. It's for all of us. Knowing our position *in* Christ will affect how we live *for* Christ each day. Over the next week, we're going to look at seven doctrines and discover what they mean to us.

We've got a well-known one to start with – salvation. You don't need to be a Christian to understand that salvation has to do with deliverance and rescue from danger. From a biblical point of view, we understand the danger to be the consequences of sin – hell and the lake of fire.

While being saved from hell is an immeasurable blessing – much more than we ever deserved – there's more to salvation than that. The word actually includes many other doctrines and Bible themes under its umbrella. In fact, not all mentions of salvation in the Bible are discussing the same event. Some verses may be discussing salvation in the *past*, when we trusted Christ and were saved from the *penalty* of sin. Others speak about our *present* salvation – we can be saved from the *power* of sin. And yet others mention our *future* salvation, when we will be in heaven, saved from even the *presence* of sin. But no matter which of the time periods we think about, the basis of salvation is only through the death of the Son of God, the Lord Jesus Christ. There is no other way we can obtain salvation. It is only found in Him, not in ourselves or in anyone else.

Maybe you've scanned this page, thinking, 'I'm saved – I already know all this!' Even so, it's important that we never forget these great truths. We understand that, now we are saved, God expects us to live a godly life, but sometimes the thought creeps into some believers' minds that we are partly responsible for our own salvation. This isn't true! The work Christ accomplished is finished – forever. We couldn't add to our salvation when we trusted Christ, nor will we ever be able to add to it.

Therefore being justified by faith, we have peace with God through our Lord Jesus Christ.

Romans 5:1

JULY

14

Justification. One of those words I talked about yesterday that can make us scratch our heads! Yet it's a really great doctrine to learn about. Here's why.

We are all sinners, and just like someone who has been convicted and charged of a crime, we stand before God, with nothing to say in our defence. All the evidence is against us; to try to argue that we are innocent is absolute folly. We know, and God knows, that we're guilty. And as guilty sinners, we're condemned already.

It sounds hopeless, doesn't it? But listen to this – God can justify the guilty! He can take a condemned sinner and declare him to be absolutely righteous. Imagine if a judge today did such a thing. The country would be in an uproar, and rightly so. "That wicked criminal has actually been *declared righteous*!" So how can God declare sinners righteous? In Romans, we read of three aspects of justification.

1 – By grace (3:24). We deserved nothing less than eternal punishment, but God is a gracious God, One who freely gives and bestows grace on people who do not merit anything.

2 – By blood (5:9). No matter how gracious God is, He must deal righteously with sin. He cannot ignore it. Here we learn that justification is by the blood of our Lord Jesus Christ. He paid the penalty for us, so that when God declares us righteous, He does so lawfully. Christ took on Himself the condemnation that was ours.

3 – By faith (5:1). The provision for our justification has been supplied, but for us to be declared righteous, we must accept by faith the sacrifice of our Lord Jesus Christ on our behalf. It is only then that we can say that we are justified.

Justification is a wonderful doctrine! We have been acquitted and cleared of every single charge. Our record is wiped totally clean, and we will never, ever face the punishment for even one sin. We can stand before God without fear of condemnation, because of Christ's finished work.

In whom we have redemption through His blood, the forgiveness of sins.

Ephesians 1:7

The theme of redemption is one which runs through the whole Bible. In Exodus 6, God told Moses that He would redeem the children of Israel from bondage in Egypt. You'll find in chapter 13 that a newborn donkey could only live if it was redeemed by the death of a lamb. And when you read the book of Ruth, you'll discover that Boaz redeemed the land which had belonged to Elimelech and, in doing so, redeemed Ruth as well. But when we come to the New Testament, we learn that *we* are the recipients of redemption.

Different words are used for redemption in the Bible. They have the same basic meaning, but each one has its own emphasis. One word has the thought of buying something, another 'buying out', and yet another has the idea of deliverance on payment of a ransom. In the days of slavery, both in Roman times and, more recently, in the American South before the Civil War, slaves could have been bought to be set free. When we were saved, we were bought with a price (1 Corinthians 6:20), bought out from the curse of the law (Galatians 3:13), and set free from the bondage of sin (Ephesians 1:7).

The price paid for our redemption was the precious blood of Christ (1 Peter 1:18,19). All other redemption prices ever paid in Scripture pale into insignificance in light of the vast and exceedingly costly sum which was paid for us.

Redemption is a great truth, one that causes us to rejoice, but it should have a practical effect on our lives. Paul says, 'You are not your own, for you were bought with a price' (1 Corinthians 6:19,20 ESV). Presenting our bodies to God is only, as it says in Romans 12:1, our reasonable service. Like the slave who was set free in Exodus 21, our only appropriate response to such a price paid for us is to love our Master and serve Him forever.

God... loved us, and sent His Son to be the propitiation for our sins.

1 John 4:10

JULY

16

Propitiation. Of all the words we're learning about this week, this is probably the one which is most difficult to pronounce, spell, and maybe even to understand. It's not mentioned very often in the Bible and some translations use different words to convey its truth. So why should we know about it? Because behind the complicated name, you'll find essential truth. There's much, much more to propitiation than what we can cover in one page, but we'll have missed out if we don't understand even the basics of what it means.

So what does it mean? The clearest explanation I've come across is in The Wiersbe Bible Commentary. In his comments on Romans 3, Warren Wiersbe says, "'Propitiation' means the satisfying of God's holy law, the meeting of its just demands, so that God can freely forgive those who come to Christ.'[53] In other words, when it comes to our forgiveness, propitiation is closely linked with the satisfaction of God. We've already seen how we stood guilty before God, but that God was able to justify us – declare us righteous. The reason that God can declare us righteous is because He is satisfied with the shed blood of Christ. This can and will never change. The death of Christ on the cross satisfied God's righteousness forever, in a way that the shed blood of Old Testament sacrifices could never do, even though they pointed to the cross. The sacrifice of Christ, which perfectly satisfied the demands of the throne of God, is the basis for our salvation – not only in the past, but in the present and future.

The satisfaction of God also has implications for those times when we sin. The Lord Jesus Christ is our Advocate – One who pleads and intercedes for us to the Father. He can do this because it was His death which satisfied God. And because it fully satisfied God, no charge can be laid against us. God must show mercy. Communion with the Father can be restored because Christ is the propitiation for our sins.

So we see that this word, complicated as it may seem, is one that can give us great assurance and peace. If Christ's death totally satisfied God, there's not one single reason why we oughtn't to be satisfied too.

---

53. *The Wiersbe Bible Commentary.*

According to His mercy He saved us, by the washing of regeneration.

Titus 3:5

In the short letter that the apostle Paul wrote to Titus, he emphasised over and over that Christians ought to be diligent in good works. But in the section where our word for today – regeneration – is found, we read that good works had nothing to do with our salvation! Instead, it was according to God's mercy that He saved us. That's fairly easy to understand, isn't it?

But then we come to a phrase that might bewilder us – 'by the washing of regeneration'. What does this phrase mean? Is it, as some think, a reference to baptism? Let's look at the word 'regeneration' first. Regeneration has to do with being made new. When you trusted Christ, things changed. You were made a new person; you are in a new state.

Now what about the word 'washing'? Do you remember that, in the upper room in John 13, the Lord washed the disciples' feet? When He came to Peter, Peter protested, first telling the Lord that He'd never wash his feet, and then doing a 180-degree shift and asking that his head and hands be washed as well. In verse 10 NKJV, the Lord replies, "He who is bathed needs only to wash his feet, but is completely clean." In other words, those who are saved don't need to be saved again, but only need cleansing from the day-to-day defilement that they pick up going through this world. The washing of regeneration is speaking about salvation, and not baptism. We know from other passages that baptism, while commanded by God, does not and cannot save. If it did, the thief on the cross could never have been in heaven.

So how should regeneration – being made new – affect us every day? Although our regeneration wasn't produced by our righteous deeds, God now expects us, as believers, to do good works. Right at the end of the section containing the teaching about regeneration, we read this phrase in the NKJV – 'These things I want you to affirm constantly, that those who have believed in God should be careful to maintain good works.' Being regenerated makes a change in a person's life.

We have been sanctified through the offering of the body of Jesus Christ once for all.

Hebrews 10:10 NKJV

JULY 18

anctify, sanctified, and sanctification are words you'll come across fairly frequently as you read your Bible. While sanctification may be a rather long word, the meaning behind 'to sanctify' is 'to set apart' or 'to be set apart'. It's also sometimes translated 'holiness'. We all know what it means to be set apart in an everyday sense, but in a biblical context it involves being set apart for a purpose.

Sanctification is a big topic, so we're only going to take a quick look at different aspects of it.

Positional sanctification – Our position in Christ is what's in view in the verse at the top of the page. The very moment we were saved, we were set apart through the work of Christ. We're different now – no longer like those who are still on the way to judgment – but separated to God.

Practical sanctification – Because we are set apart through the work of Christ, we must live set-apart lives. What we are positionally, we must live out practically. We can no longer live like those in the world – we are distinct. A number of the references to practical sanctification speak about morality (1 Thessalonians 4:3). We don't need anyone to tell us that this world is a terribly immoral place. Christians should be different. There are movies that unbelievers might watch, places they may go, games they could play, and music they might listen to, which are not for those who have been saved and set apart. And while self-control is very necessary for practical sanctification, we need more than that, which is why the Lord Jesus prayed in John 17:17, "Sanctify them through Thy truth: Thy word is truth." Spending time in the Word of God, the Bible, will help us remember our set-apart position, and give us the strength and desire to live accordingly. God uses those who are set apart for Him.

Perfected sanctification – A day is coming when we will be sanctified completely (1 Thessalonians 5:23 NKJV). We will see Christ and shall be like Him – holy and without one trace of sin.

Whom He justified, them He also glorified.
Romans 8:30

We're now at the end of our mini-series on biblical doctrines! It hasn't always been light reading, but I hope you understand some of these teachings and why they are so important.

We've one more to go. Today, we're looking at the word glorification. While the doctrines we've considered contain truth which is more than our minds can really comprehend, they also give us cause to be immensely thankful. Glorification is no different. In fact, when we look at this doctrine, I think we'll begin to appreciate, in our limited way, that God is multiplying blessings to us that we could never, in our wildest dreams, have anticipated.

The definition of glorification is 'to do honour to, or to make glorious'[54] (W. E. Vine). We know that the Lord Jesus Christ deserves glory and that we should live in a way that brings glory to Him. Equally true is the fact that we, sinners who only deserved judgment, are to share in His glory! Future glory is often linked to past suffering – Romans 8:17 NET says, 'We suffer with Him so we may also be glorified with Him.' Suffering now leads to glory in the future, in heaven.

But if you look at our verse for today, you'll see that 'glorified' is actually past tense. The Lord Jesus Christ in His prayer in John 17:22 also uses the past tense when speaking of giving glory to believers. In other words, we have already been glorified in Christ. Just think of that – as we go to school or work, as we're sleeping, or eating our meals, we're actually glorified! This glorification is ours 'as a present possession and it is only a short step ahead for full realisation.'[55] While we haven't experienced the full revelation of this glory yet, it doesn't change the reality of it.

And, as always, this truth should affect our lives. Someone who is glorified in Christ won't be wasting time on earthly, trivial matters, on things that don't matter and won't last. Their main aim and goal in life will be to live for Christ, the One through whom we receive all the wonderful spiritual blessings we've been learning about over the past few days.

---

54. *Vine's Dictionary.*
55. From *Romans*, by F. E. Stallan, What the Bible Teaches series, published by John Ritchie Ltd in 1998.

Which of you by worrying can add one cubit to his stature?

Matthew 6:27 NKJV

20

JULY

One year, when we were on holiday, new friends invited us to their home for a delicious barbecue. We had a wonderful evening, but before we left, something happened that I'd never experienced at anyone's home before. One by one, we stood against a wall and our heights were recorded. We then signed the appropriate pencil mark and added the date. We certainly weren't the first visitors to be added to this unusual chronicle; the wall had dozens of similar marks and signatures. Some were so high, I needed to stand on tiptoe to read the signature; others, I had to stoop down. All heights of people were represented.

Recorded on that wall are probably those who would love to be a little bit taller. Maybe most of their classmates seem to tower over them, or they're at a disadvantage in various sports. They might look at that wall, and see names up near the top, and really, really wish they were there too.

Did you know that the Bible has something to say about worrying about our height? Read our verse for today again. Maybe you don't find it very satisfying, because what it's saying is that no matter how much you worry, you can't change your height. That makes sense, doesn't it? Our height is generally determined by our genes, with a bit of input from external factors. Worrying about it will not add to your height one fraction of a centimetre!

What is the Lord trying to teach us? Is it really that we shouldn't worry about height? That's certainly included, but it's more than that. You see, the Lord knows our hearts. He knows how prone we are to worry, especially about things that we can't do anything about. He's pointing out how ridiculous it is to believe that worrying can help the situation. We could spend a week worrying about our height, and at the end of that week, will that worrying have made us grow? Of course not! We'll only have given ourselves a lot of worry and distress for nothing. So let's listen to and obey the Lord's words, and not waste time worrying over situations we can't do anything about.

Let brotherly love continue.
Hebrews 13:1

Do you have brothers or sisters? How do you get on with them? I have two younger brothers who, growing up, seemed to believe that the sole reason for their existence was to annoy their big sister at each and every opportunity... and they worked hard at it! Our house was pretty noisy when we were young.

I have to admit that I struggled with verses like the one at the top of this page, verses that expected that there would be love and kindness between siblings. We generally had more insults flying about than kind words of love. I was the bossy big sister, and they were having none of it. Fights were commonplace. I often wished that I'd had sisters instead of brothers, little realising that, from what I've been told, sisters fight too.

But one day at school, I overheard someone say something about one of my brothers. I can't remember what it was, but it wasn't very complimentary. Almost before I knew what I was doing, I'd turned around and given that person a sizeable and very firm piece of my mind. He was so shocked by my uncharacteristic outburst that he sat, stunned, unable to say another word. I guess I actually did love my brother after all! My suspicion is that if someone said the same about your sibling, you'd likely do the same.

Hard as it might be to believe, your siblings won't always be so annoying. But what do you do in the meantime? It's not easy, but try to be patient. You know those verses in the Bible about how to treat people – with love, kindness, respect, and good works? This doesn't only apply to those you meet when you're out and about, but to your family too. You'll never find a better opportunity to put into practice some Christlikeness than in your own home. Will you fail? Most likely! But keep going. God knows how hard you find it, and He sees your efforts.

As time has passed, I've come to realise what brotherly love is. Those two annoying rascals have turned into generous, helpful, caring men, who would do pretty much anything for that bossy big sister of theirs! Brotherly love is actually a real thing.

O the depth of the riches both
of the wisdom and knowledge
of God!

Romans 11:33

JULY

22

If you had to personify wisdom, what sort of a person would you pick? I'm guessing you'd choose the same as I did – someone really old, with white hair, and a grave, wrinkled face, denoting many years of experience. When we say that God is wise, we need to remember that His wisdom is much greater than that of the wisest person on earth – so much higher, in fact, that we can't even begin to comprehend it, let alone compare it with human wisdom. We've already looked at God's knowledge – His omniscience. The difference between knowledge and wisdom is that knowledge refers to the information known, while wisdom is *the ability to rightly use this information*.

Creation shows God's wisdom. I'm an optometrist, and I've yet to come across anyone who, despite their great knowledge, knows absolutely everything about the human eye. It's the same in every branch of science, yet God knows it all! What's even more remarkable is that, in His wisdom, He uses that knowledge to control and manage every aspect of His creation, both great things, like the solar system, and tiny, almost-invisible particles. Many things about this creation don't make sense to us, but God has a purpose in it all.

God's wisdom is also displayed in His dealings with people and nations. We often wonder why certain rulers are raised up – but God has the insight, which characterises wisdom, into the consequences of different courses of action. Don't forget, God is *always* good!

Best of all, God's wisdom is seen in salvation. Could humans ever have devised such a marvellous plan? To take guilty sinners and make them into children of God, because of the sacrifice of Christ? In fact, it is this thought that causes Paul, in wonder, to burst into the doxology at the top of this page. Why not take a few minutes to read it, and rejoice in the wisdom of God?

The Father sent the Son to be the Saviour of the world.
1 John 4:14

When I was about your age, I had to study a poem in English class called 'The Charge of the Light Brigade' by Lord Tennyson, which was set in 1854, in the Crimean War. In one particular battle, over six hundred British light cavalrymen were wrongly ordered to attack Russian gun emplacements. It was a doomed mission, right from the start. The Light Brigade weren't suited to the task, and they knew it. But rather than disobey orders, they rode on, straight into the 'valley of Death' as Tennyson calls it.

The lines of the poem that struck me most, and that I still remember, are in the second verse:

> Theirs not to make reply
> Theirs not to reason why
> Theirs but to do and die...

About 110 men were killed that day. They were obedient, right to death.

Rewind time back further, to AD 33. On a Roman cross, a man is hanging, nailed by His hands and feet, wounded and bruised. He cries, "It is finished!" and dies. He, too, was given an instruction to go. He, too, knew He would die. Yet, as a writer wrote of Him – 'He became obedient unto death.'

Who sent Him? Not some inexperienced officer with incorrect instructions, as happened in the Crimean War. Instead, it was God, His Father. Sending the Lord Jesus Christ wasn't a senseless act. He didn't die a vain death, but, instead, that death brought life to us.

What made the charge of the Light Brigade so tragic is that it made no difference to the war. Over 110 men lost their lives for nothing. But the death of the Lord Jesus has made all the difference – not only then, but now, and for all eternity.

We all know what waiting is like. Maybe you're nervously waiting for exam results, or to find out whether you've got into a certain school or college. You know what it's like to wait for an exciting parcel to arrive. And when you're in a triple period of maths, the wait for the bell to signal that it's lunchtime seems interminable! On most occasions, we know that waiting will, sooner or later, come to an end. But there are other times when we don't know if what we're waiting for will ever come to pass. Maybe you, or someone close to you, has a chronic illness. You pray regularly for recovery, but nothing happens. Or maybe you have no Christian friends, and every day you plead with God to send someone in your direction. You don't understand the delay. Wouldn't what you're praying for help you to live a better life for God?

Did you know that the Lord waits? Look at the verse at the top of the page. The chapter that it's taken from is an address to Israel, who are called here 'rebellious children'. Instead of trusting the Lord, they had trusted in Egypt, and had listened to false prophets who led them astray. Now God calls them to repent, but they refuse. God will now stand back and let them be pursued by their enemies, until they are like a beacon on a hill – a clear target for the enemy. He hadn't abandoned them, though. He was waiting. Waiting for them to return to Him, so He could bless them.

Sometimes the problems that we get into are of our own making. Maybe we've been disobedient, and we realise that we're suffering the consequences. Often, we begin to blame God, thinking that He ought to have kept us from messing up, or stepped in before things became desperate.

We need to examine our hearts. Is God waiting because our attitude isn't right? God is a gracious God and many times gives us what we don't deserve, but often by waiting and letting us hit rock bottom He brings us to a point where we turn back to Him.

Tomorrow we'll look at another example of divine waiting and discover a further reason why God often waits.

This sickness is not unto death, but for the glory of God.

John 11:4

" **L**ord, if Thou hadst been here, my brother had not died," was the heart-wrenching cry from both Martha and Mary. They loved their brother so much, and the pain caused by his death was very real. The sisters knew that if the Lord Jesus Christ had arrived in time, Lazarus would not have died, for how could death have claimed anyone in the presence of the Prince of Life? And yet, He had delayed.

When you read the passage, it's clear how precious Lazarus and his sisters were to the Lord Jesus, but instead of leaving straight away when He got the message, and travelling as fast as He could to Bethany, he waited two days. The journey may have taken at least two days as well, so by the time the Lord arrived, Lazarus was already dead. Why did He wait? Here was certainly a delay which didn't seem to add up.

Divine delays, whether in the case of our disobedience, or – as in the death of Lazarus – seemingly for no reason at all, are for the same purpose. The glory of God. When the Lord is gracious to us and we turn back to Him for forgiveness, in humble repentance, glory is brought to Him. And here in John 11, the Lord mentions twice that the situation concerning the death of Lazarus will bring glory to God.

You will often find that, despite living for Him, He delays, so that in a future day, when the situation seems most hopeless, He will step in and work a miracle of great magnitude so that His glory will be displayed. In that day, He will receive more praise than He would have, had our prayers been answered at the beginning.

So when your delay is getting you down, look up, and remember that He may be choosing to use you and your situation to bring glory to Him, the awesome and eternal God. Wouldn't that make it all worthwhile?

I went by the field of the lazy man... and there it was, all overgrown with thorns.

Proverbs 24:30,31 NKJV

26

JULY

For a number of years, I've had a little vegetable plot in my garden. I'm not a great gardener, but every year we enjoy homegrown peas, carrots, parsnips, and rhubarb. That's if the weeds don't take over first! Very often, it feels as if I'm fighting a losing battle when it comes to keeping the plot weed free. Hours of back-breaking work only lasts a few days before another relentless army of weeds begin to show their little green faces.

Weeds are tenacious. Vegetables need a lot of nurture and care, and even then, they might not survive. Weeds get no attention whatsoever, but before you know it, they're taking over the whole plot.

There's a lesson in this. Your life is like a vegetable plot with great potential for spiritual growth, but it will take work. You'll need to spend time digging the soil, taking out the stones – those things that weigh us down – and planting only seeds of Christlike qualities that God wants to see growing in our lives. Things like love, joy, self-control, wisdom, and good works. Time spent reading and studying the Bible and in prayer, will help to nurture those seeds so they will grow.

But we must be aware of the weeds – those things that effortlessly take up the space and energy that the seedlings ought to have. It's easy to lift our phones and scroll through social media, play games, or text friends. Before we know it, a couple of hours have passed – time that we could have used to help the seeds grow. There is so much choice in what to watch these days. Maybe you've realised that some of it removes your desire for the Word of God. Or the messages contained in the music you listen to might be dulling the sharpness of your conviction in God's commands.

Weeds need removed or it won't be long until the garden is overgrown and next to useless. It's much harder to clear the whole plot of thick, deep-rooted weeds than it is to pluck out little ones on a regular basis. Make sure you take control of the weeds in your life – inspect your life regularly and work consistently in pulling up anything that will hinder your growth for God.

My son, eat honey because it is good, and the honeycomb which is sweet to your taste.

Proverbs 24:13 NKJV

Isn't honey a remarkable substance? Not only is it beautiful to look at, it's naturally sweet, and even has healing properties. But how much do you know about the busy little insects which go to such lengths to produce it?

There are a number of types of bees, but the one which produces the honey that we use is the honey bee. Honey bees live in hives, each of which has a queen bee, sterile female workers, and male drones. The queen is bigger than the others and is the only one to lay eggs, which have been fertilised by the male drones, who then die. The queen can live up to five years, after which the bees choose a freshly hatched larva to be their new queen.

The bees responsible for the production of honey are the worker bees. These are the busy ones, which fly from flower to flower, feeding on nectar. In the process, pollen sticks to their fuzzy legs – this is important in the pollination of plants. After the bees have gathered the nectar, they fly back to the hive and it is transferred to other worker bees, which add an enzyme to break it down to simple sugars. It is then placed into the hexagonal cavities of the honeycomb. At this point, there is still a high moisture content, so the bees fan it with their wings to reduce moisture and thicken it. The honey is used to feed the larvae, but we benefit from it too because they make more than they need.[56]

One of the most fascinating things about honey bees is that when the worker bees arrive back at the hive, they perform a 'waggle dance' which tells the others where food can be found. The bees fly in a short, fat, figure-of-eight pattern. The orientation of the middle section, which contains the 'waggle', gives the direction where food is to be found, and the time spent 'waggling' communicates the distance to the food source.[57]

Honey bees have many other abilities – making honeycomb, housekeeping, and caring for the queen by helping to keep her warm in winter. They are tiny little insects with God-given instincts and a purpose, not least of which is to proclaim the glory of the Creator.

56. As seen on https://www.youtube.com/watch?v=KPKg43uUUtA and https://www.youtube.com/watch?v=YFXamn5cia4
57. As seen on https://www.youtube.com/watch?v=bFDGPgXtK-U and explained in *Creation Considered (Ants, Bees and Other Insects)* article by Robert Cargill in Believer's Magazine, January 2020.

Now unto God and our Father
be glory for ever and ever.
Philippians 4:20

28

JULY

I know very little about art, but when I'm on holiday I can never resist popping into art galleries to admire the paintings. My favourites are those which, up close, look like a mass of small, thickly applied brushstrokes with no pattern at all. You wonder how all those random blobs could ever create a picture. But to see it clearly, you need to stand back and observe it from a distance. When you do, all the brushstrokes will combine to form a richly textured, beautiful landscape or seascape.

Oftentimes, in life, we forget to stand back, and instead, focus on the tiny daubs of paint which don't seem to make sense. The humdrum, everyday activities, like going to school, working on assignments, or doing household chores, all seem so small and unimportant. We want to do big things for God, not these mundane duties. And sometimes when we do things for God, we get discouraged because things don't work out the way we hoped. Maybe no one seems to see or appreciate our hard work. Something we started with great gusto fizzles out. We ask ourselves what it's all about anyway, and soon we're inspecting the brushstrokes!

I once heard someone say something that caused me to step away from my inspection and view the whole painting. It was this – "We are contributing to the progression of God's ultimate goal. When we see the glory, it'll be worth it."

Do you see those mundane tasks? Those unseen things you do for God? They are actually really important. God places a high value on obedience and faithfulness. Those brushstrokes, small as they might seem, are actually adding to the greatest masterpiece that will ever be created. When the picture is finished, do you know what all our brushstrokes will have contributed to? The ultimate goal of the glory of God!

I count everything as loss because of the surpassing worth of knowing Christ Jesus my Lord.

Philippians 3:8 ESV

When I was at school, everyone was issued with a fancy burgundy folder which bore the title of *National Record of Achievement*. Into this gold-cornered binder went swimming or music awards, exam certificates, Duke of Edinburgh awards, and anything else we could think of that might make us look valuable to future employers. National Record of Achievement folders are now a thing of the past, but I'm sure many of you have a little stash of awards and certificates. You might also be proud of achievements that will never be recorded on paper – your family's wealth and status, your popularity amongst your friends, the number of likes you get on social media, or knowing the name of every player in every team in the Premier League. You might even be proud of your volunteer work, your achievements in memorising Scripture, or your extensive Bible knowledge.

The apostle Paul had a long list of achievements in relation to his nationality and lineage, his religion, his character and good deeds. No Jew could boast of more than Paul. His Record of Achievement folder would have been stuffed full! But take a look again at what he says. All those achievements, counted as loss. Why? Because there was something infinitely and incomparably greater than any achievement he could hope to gain here on earth – knowing Christ.

How important to us is knowing Christ? None of us would dream of arguing that it is unimportant, and yet where do we place it in relation to all the other things we hope to achieve? Are we involved in pursuits and pastimes that are taking up time that could be spent reading the Bible? At school, you're probably encouraged to get involved in all the extracurricular activities you can, but before you agree to anything, evaluate whether it will help or hinder your knowledge of Christ. Even in spiritual things, be careful that a desire for achievement doesn't prevent you from actually knowing Christ. Achievements may have their place in this life, but when compared with the surpassing worth and joy of knowing Christ, even the greatest achievement will pale into utter insignificance.

Others were tortured, not accepting deliverance; that they might obtain a better resurrection.
Hebrews 11:35

30
JULY

The finely built, red-haired, sixteen-year-old girl knelt on the straw, tied a blindfold over her eyes, and laid her head on the executioner's block. Within seconds, her head was severed from her body, her short life over.

Lady Jane Grey, born during the tumultuous reign of King Henry VIII, had accepted the monarchy after the death of Henry's son, Edward. It was not a position she desired or sought, and she made attempts to reject it, but was overruled. Deposed from the throne after nine days and viewed as a traitor and a threat to the reign of Queen Mary, Lady Jane was sentenced to death.

Executions were commonplace in Tudor England. Any sign of disloyalty was met with imprisonment and often beheading, so Jane's sentence was not entirely surprising. Her death seemed inevitable.

A few days before the scheduled execution, Queen Mary sent a startling message to the young prisoner. If Jane would recant and accept Mary's religion, she would be given a full reprieve! Her life would be saved, and she would be free to leave the confines of her prison at the Tower of London.

Jane refused. She didn't even consider the suggestion. This teenager firmly believed that 'faith only in Christ's blood saves us.' It was a vital truth for which she was willing to die. To her, God's word was of utmost importance. She said, "I ground my faith upon God's word, and not upon the church." To accept the religion of the state would have been a denial of everything she believed. She wouldn't do it.

Lady Jane Grey's entrance to heaven was immediate. Before her head rolled into the straw, her soul had taken its flight from Tower Green in London and arrived in mansions of glory unlike any she'd ever occupied on earth, right into the presence of the One who is greater than any monarch this world has ever seen.[58]

---

58. The full story is told in *Lady Jane Grey – Nine Day Queen of England* by Faith Cook, published by Evangelical Press in 2004. It's a book which is well worth reading.

31

JULY

Josiah was eight years old when he began to reign... and he did that which was right in the sight of the Lord.
2 Kings 22:1,2

What were you doing when you were eight? Probably not being crowned king! If you were Josiah, by this stage you would already have been king for a number of years.

When we read about the kings of Israel and Judah, we often come across phrases such as, 'He did that which was evil in the sight of the Lord, according to all that his father had done.' Often, son followed father in doing evil and displeasing the Lord – one after the other after the other. But now and again a light shone through the darkness, and King Josiah was one of those lights.

Josiah didn't come from a very good family. His grandfather, Manasseh, didn't follow in the path of his own God-fearing father, Hezekiah, instead reinstituting the evil practices of idolatry and murdering innocent people. Josiah's father, Amon, also did evil in the sight of the Lord, following in the ways of Manasseh.

Maybe you're a bit like Josiah. You don't come from a family of Christians; perhaps no one else in your entire family is saved. Maybe you feel inferior and, deep inside, you believe that you'll never reach the same spiritual heights as other people who have a great lineage of Christian testimony.

Josiah might have been young, and from a wicked family, but he didn't let that stop him purposefully living for God. When he was eighteen, the high priest brought the book of the law to Josiah. As it was read before him, Josiah was convicted by the message, and later put into practice what he'd learned. It took a lot of courage to choose a course that couldn't have been any more diverse than the path which his father and grandfather had walked.

Whatever our background happens to be, each of us, as an individual, can make the choice to put God first. Like Josiah, we can be a light shining in the darkness. As his story teaches us, not one of us is at a disadvantage when it comes to living for Him.

AUGUST

There shall no man see Me,
and live.

Exodus 33:20

Earlier in the year, we learned about the holiness of God – how He is set apart from us in righteousness, majesty, and glory. When He gave the law to the nation of Israel at Mount Sinai, His holiness was especially evident. Over the next few days, we are going to look at three different aspects of God's holiness and compare them with the account of the life of the Lord Jesus Christ in the gospels, remembering that He is God, and therefore no less holy.

When Moses was given the job of leading the children of Israel through the wilderness, he wasn't given an easy task. The people were rebellious and often complaining, and Moses spent much time with God interceding for them. In the chapter that this verse is taken from, the Lord has been speaking to Moses as a friend. Moses asks God to show him His glory, and he is given a partial glimpse of it.

But it's what God said to Moses that we want to think about today – that no man can see God, and live. Sinful man can never stand in the presence of a holy, righteous God. The Lord Jesus Christ is God. Isn't it remarkable that He came to earth and walked among sinners, and yet they weren't destroyed?

In Exodus 19:21, when God came to Mount Sinai to meet with Moses, a command is given to the people to stay back 'lest they break through unto the Lord to gaze, and many of them perish.' Gazing on the Lord had serious consequences.

With that in mind, think for a moment of Matthew 27:36 – 'Sitting down they watched Him there,' and Psalm 22:17 – 'They look and stare upon Me.' These weren't looks of love, such as His mother or His followers would have given Him. Instead, scornful gazes of cruel Roman soldiers and those who hated and despised the Lord Jesus were directed towards Him. Why were these men not instantly destroyed? To look upon God meant instant death, yet He showed these men mercy. We have also received mercy, which was provided for us through His death on the cross. That mercy, which we have received, means that one day, forgiven and cleansed, we will stand in the very presence of a holy and righteous God.

Let not God speak with us, lest we die.

Exodus 20:19

AUGUST

2

When the law was given to the nation of Israel, the people experienced thunder and lightning, heard the noise of a trumpet, and saw the mountain smoking. It terrified them, so much so that they pled with Moses to convey to them what God wanted them to know. They believed that to hear the words from God Himself would mean certain death. It was more than they could bear.

God's words to the nation were words of law and instruction, commandments that the nation would end up breaking time after time. The standards were high, and disobedience and rebellion would have consequences, including being taken as captives to other lands. The small glimpse the people got of His holiness reinforced this aspect of His character in their minds. No wonder the people were fearful of God's words to them. We would have been the same.

When the Lord Jesus Christ came to earth, He, true to His character as God manifest in flesh, spoke words of truth. He did not reduce the holy standard that God demands. But He also spoke words of grace (Luke 4:22). Mankind had fallen short of God's standard, but the Lord's death on the cross was going to make provision for all who realise that they can never be right by their own efforts. Salvation was being provided by grace!

Reading through references in the gospels to the Saviour speaking makes an interesting study. On two such occasions, He revealed to two very different people who He was. In John 4, He spoke to the Samaritan woman, and revealed that He was the Messiah. In John 9, while speaking to the healed blind man, He revealed that He was the Son of God. Think about it – the Messiah, the One sent from God, God Himself, speaking with a sinful Samaritan woman at a well! The Son of God, God incarnate, talking with one who, a short time before, had been a blind beggar! His words to them were words of grace, not of judgment. Of life, and not of death.

He speaks the same words to us. The officers of the Pharisees in John 7:46 ESV never spoke truer words when they said, 'No one ever spoke like this man!'

Whoever touches the mountain shall surely be put to death.
Exodus 19:12 NKJV

We've been learning about the holiness of God from the story of the giving of the law at Sinai, then comparing what we've learned with the account of the life of the Lord Jesus Christ in the gospels. It's been amazing, hasn't it? To read that One who is God was seen by people and talked with them.

We've dealt with sight, hearing, and speech, but there's another sense that we haven't looked at yet. Touch. There were many who felt the touch of the Lord Jesus – those who were ill, blind, deaf, lame, and even those who had died. There were others who touched Him – Simeon lifted Him in his arms when He was eight days old, the woman with the issue of blood dared to reach out and touch the hem of His garment, and Mary wiped His feet with her hair.

Let's pause for a moment and go back to Mount Sinai where God gave the law to Moses. You'll remember that God put very specific directions in place for the people's protection. They were to stay back in case they broke through to gaze at the Lord. And more than that – they weren't to climb the mountain or even to touch its base. If any person, or even any animal, touched the mountain, they were to be killed, so great was the holiness of God.

Isn't it astonishing that the Israelites were forbidden to even touch the mountain where God's presence was, yet the Lord Jesus Christ, who is God, touched people, and allowed them to touch Him? Even more so, when we consider that not everyone who touched Him did it out of love and respect. 'Then did they spit in His face, and buffeted Him; and others smote Him with the palms of their hands' (Matthew 26:67). 'One of the officers which stood by struck Jesus with the palm of his hand... Then Pilate therefore took Jesus, and scourged Him' (John 18:22; 19:1). Angels must have watched in wonder and amazement as the Son of God was treated so, without swift and severe retribution being administered to those who dared lift their hands against Him.

Again, we can only bow in worship at His mercy that led Him to endure all the sufferings of Calvary – for us.

The moment we were saved, something very wonderful happened. Actually, many great things happened – we were redeemed and forgiven, our eternal destiny was changed, and we were given new life. But something happened that we probably didn't think very much about at the time – the Holy Spirit began to dwell in us.

The Holy Spirit has many functions – to guide us, to make intercession for us, and for our assurance that we belong to God. But this morning I was reading about another astonishing purpose. In the early chapters of 1 Corinthians, Paul is talking about wisdom – the world's wisdom versus God's wisdom. He explains how that God's wisdom is vastly superior to man's wisdom, so the worldly man cannot understand or comprehend God's thoughts. He tells us that the only one who can understand someone's thoughts is the spirit of that person. In the same way, the Holy Spirit alone is able to comprehend God's thoughts, as He is God.

But here's the amazing part – we were given that very same Holy Spirit the moment we trusted Christ! The One who comprehends God's thoughts, who is God, dwells in us. Think of what this means for us. Obviously, it doesn't mean that we are able to comprehend all that God is and does – God is infinite and we are limited. But it means that we are actually able to know God! We have an insight into His character. It also means that when we read and make the effort to study the Bible, the Holy Spirit is able to illuminate our minds to understand what we're reading. Understanding the Word of God is less about intelligence and worldly wisdom, and more about the Holy Spirit helping us to comprehend the great truths of Scripture.

So next time you come across a difficult section in your Bible, or you hear a complicated passage being explained, don't flip across to an easier section, or shrug your shoulders and switch off. You have the same Spirit as every other believer, so you are at no disadvantage. In fact, you have every advantage – you have the Holy Spirit dwelling in you. That's something to rejoice about!

We know that all things work together for good to them that love God.
Romans 8:28

Forest fires can cause huge devastation. Recently, on holiday, we stayed in an area that had suffered a severe wildfire ten months previously. On the mountainous landscape, blackened tree trunks dotted the charred and barren earth where eucalyptus forest and lush vegetation used to grow. The damage was extensive... but not permanent. New growth was beginning to appear. Out of the blackened, barren earth, new trees and shrubs were beginning to shoot up. Even a few trees touched by the fire were showing signs of life.

Did you know that fires, dreadful as they are, are actually very important to the ecosystem? Dead and decaying matter is burned, and this releases nutrients into the soil. Fire also helps to remove diseased plants and harmful insects from the forest. And the removal of undergrowth makes way for new seedlings to absorb the sun's rays and grow.

Have you ever gone through a fire in your life? Not the sort with actual flames and smoke, but a time when you had a great difficulty or problem. Sometimes we might feel that we're not going to survive because things are so tough. But, as in the case of forest fires, God often uses difficult situations to clear away the clutter in our lives so we can experience the light of God's truth, and the warmth of God's love and care for us. Maybe His purpose is to remove harmful influences from our lives, things that are stunting our spiritual growth. Or it might be that, through this experience, we are going to learn lessons about God and His Word that will nourish us and help us grow as Christians. The verse at the top of the page reminds us that God never lets anything happen to us, no matter how terrible, without it having a purpose for our good. But remember that it's our response to the difficulty which will determine how much we benefit.

Noah went... into the ark, because of the waters of the flood.

Genesis 7:7

6

AUGUST

One of the most-ridiculed Bible stories is the account of Noah's ark, which tends to get relegated to the 'fable' section, or amongst children's stories. But not only is it in the Bible, which is totally reliable, there are many other non-biblical sources which point to the flood being a real, global event.

Every few years, my husband and I visit Mexico. It's an interesting place with a fascinating history. When the Spanish arrived in 1519, ancient civilisations had been living in areas of what is now called Mexico for thousands of years.

But what has ancient Mexico got to do with Noah? Quite a lot, actually! In Mexico, and right across the world, many civilisations had tales of a flood. In fact, one geologist states that there could be at least *five hundred* flood stories! In every habitable continent of the world, varying versions of a story of a global flood have been found.

Of course, these stories aren't exactly what we find in the Bible, and some of them have very little resemblance to the biblical account, apart from the mention of a flood. Others have details that are anything but a coincidence. For example, Aztecs have a legend about two people surviving in a boat which came to rest on a mountain. Another story from Mexico says that a man escaped the flood in a closed chest – probably more like the actual ark than what we often see depicted today. This one even mentions the building of a high tower, and the confusion of languages which resulted. Yet another tale tells of a raven being sent out which never returned, followed by a dove which came back with an olive leaf.

A worldwide flood, sent as a judgment because of man's wickedness, a boat which ultimately ended up on top of a mountain being the means of survival of a certain family and many animals, and the sending out of birds are common features in many of the stories.

Could it be a coincidence that so many people, scattered right across the world, would somehow make up a story with so many similarities to the biblical account? Impossible! As one writer has said, 'These traditions agree in too many vital points not to have originated from the same factual event.'[59]

---

59. From https://apologeticspress.org/apcontent.aspx?category=9&article=64

Great is Thy faithfulness.
Lamentations 3:23

This world is full of broken promises. From cancelled business contracts and broken marriage vows, to the divulging of secrets and sheer neglect of following through on what was promised, every age group and social situation is affected. There isn't a single person on this earth who is incapable of letting us down. We've all been hurt by others' unfaithfulness, and we've caused hurt to others by our lack of reliability too.

This makes the faithfulness of God even more precious. He is absolutely faithful, trustworthy, and reliable. Every single promise, big or small, that He has ever made, He will fulfil. He will always act in complete accordance with His character – in goodness, in love, in righteousness. God will never forget to do what He has promised. When we place our confidence in Him, He will always be worthy of that trust. He will never cancel or break any promise He has made. He will never change His mind.

When we read in the Bible about promises God has made to us, we can stand firmly on them. When we read in 1 John 1:9 that when we confess our sins, He is faithful to forgive us our sins, we can confess them and go on our way, knowing without a doubt we've been forgiven. In 2 Thessalonians 3:3 we can hold fast to the promise that the faithful God will establish us and keep us from evil. When we are in trial and temptation, God's faithfulness assures us that we will not be tempted beyond our ability (1 Corinthians 10:13). And best of all, God's faithfulness doesn't depend on us – even when we are faithless, God is so trustworthy that He cannot be anything but faithful (2 Timothy 2:13).

> Bodily exercise profits a little, but godliness is profitable for all things.
>
> 1 Timothy 4:8 NKJV

AUGUST

8

Jack bounces out of bed at six o'clock every morning, changes into his workout gear and heads out for a ten-mile run. He arrives back as his twin, Jill, is dragging herself out of bed, having snoozed her alarm far too many times. After school, Jack makes his way to the gym to lift weights, while Jill goes home and flops onto the sofa. The heaviest weights she's lifting are a chocolate bar and her phone.

Which twin are you most like? Are you fitness obsessed, or have you an aversion to anything that resembles physical activity?

At school, for a number of reasons, I hated PE! Since then, I've come to realise that exercise is a very necessary part of being a good steward of what God has given me – my body. Exercise is profitable, as the Bible tells us. It cuts our risk of certain diseases, increases our energy levels, keeps our minds alert, and even plays a huge part in improving and maintaining good mental health. We all need to incorporate some form of exercise into our routines, if at all possible.

But, as with anything, there is danger in becoming over-obsessed. If exercise is what you're living for, if it's taking up more time than you can really afford, or if the positive reaction of other people is your main motivation, then you need to pull back.

Have a look at our verse at the top of the page. Even better, look it up in your Bible and read the rest of it. The writer is comparing bodily exercise to the exercise of godliness. He tells us that bodily exercise is good, but godliness is even better. Why? Because bodily exercise only has temporal benefits, but the benefits of living a godly life will last forever. We need to be balanced. Physical activity is good and important, but never let it squeeze out time spent developing a godly character – reading and studying the Bible, prayer, attending the gatherings of your local church, and doing those things we know God wants us to do.

Turn my eyes from looking at worthless things.
Psalm 119:37 ESV

Have you ever been tempted to think that even though the Bible is important, it's not terribly relevant to life in this very modern world? Take a look at the verse at the top of the page. I can only guess what sort of worthless things the people back in the psalmist's day would have been tempted to look at, but I'm sure you'll agree that there are many things today that we could certainly call 'worthless things'. In fact, with our ease of access to the internet, this verse almost seems to be more relevant to our day than to any other!

Take, for instance, social media. We might not be viewing anything particularly bad, but haven't we all sat and scrolled through an endless feed, oblivious to the passage of time? Or maybe we've been glued to a stream of mind-numbing videos, maybe harmless in themselves, but which eat up the hours.

Time wasting is one thing, but much of what's online has a more sinister side. 'Worthless' in the Bible is often linked with the name 'Belial' – the personification of evil. Are you making a choice to look at things that you know to be wrong? Please remember that what you view now can have long-term consequences and could very well affect you for the remainder of your life.

But if we turn *from* worthless things, what do we turn *to*? The psalmist asks for life in God's ways. Life. We often have the mistaken belief that we never fully live through an experience unless we've documented it on social media. What if Daniel had taken a selfie in the lion's den? And Jonah, inside the whale? The pictures would have been great, but we would have missed out on the valuable lessons they learned about God through these never-to-be-forgotten experiences. These men, instead of thinking about 'likes', were probably in earnest, sincere prayer.

Wouldn't you like experiences like that? Times when we are totally focussed on God, when we learn more about Him and His magnificent attributes, so we can live more fully for Him? If so, then let's lift our eyes from worthless things and live in God's ways.

Be strong and of good courage...
the Lord your God, He is the
One who goes with you.
Deuteronomy 31:6 NKJV

10

AUGUST

No one likes to think of the end of the summer, but sooner or later it will be time for many to go back to school. The obligatory 'first day' photo will have been taken, the bag packed with new stationery, and a stack of new notebooks and textbooks given out. For some, there will be a new school with new subjects, new teachers, new friends, as well as new challenges, and most likely new fears. Will I be able to do the work? What if no one likes me? Or maybe you're starting a new college, work placement, or job. I know from experience that it doesn't get any easier as you get older. The fears are still there.

Thankfully, we have One who has promised to be with us. When we go somewhere new, having someone there whom we know makes it so much easier. And who better to have with you than the Lord your God. A friend from your previous school might not be in all your classes, but God will be right beside you all day.

Knowing that God is with us is good to remember when situations arise where we will need to be strong and of good courage. Living for God at school can be difficult – I certainly found it so. When we got saved, God could have taken us straight to heaven. Instead, He left us here to live for Him, and to bring Him glory. When we do what we know He wants us to do – things like being kind and caring to someone who really needs a friend, being honest and trustworthy, working hard, not succumbing to gossip or saying nasty things behind people's backs... I'm sure you can add to the list – all these things bring glory to God. Maybe some of the people in your class have never even heard about the Lord Jesus Christ. You might find opportunities to share the good news with them.

So, as you begin this new school year, and maybe even attend a new school or college, make it your priority to live for God, knowing He is with you and will help you. Be strong and of good courage!

11
AUGUST

He was wounded for our transgressions.
Isaiah 53:5

Peter Orasuk was a heroin addict who lived in Prince Edward Island, Canada. His life was a mess. He'd sold everything he could, even his wife's wedding ring, to fund his habit. What's more, he was heavily involved in dealing drugs, becoming one of the main drug dealers in Prince Edward Island.

One day, two men shared the gospel with Peter. He knew little about their message, but as he argued with them, one of the men opened his Bible and read Isaiah 53:5,6. Peter had never heard these words before, and as the man read, a glimmer of hope shone into the dark tunnel of his life. Peter was touched by the words, but to cover this up, he said, "Anybody could have written about Jesus. I've heard Christmas carols. I know the story." The man who read the verses turned to him and replied, "How do you know it's talking about Jesus? It was written seven hundred years before Christ came into the world!"

In Peter's own words – "Here was something written about Christ, seven hundred years before He was born, and a drug addict from the gutters of Charlottetown could see what it was talking about. That's how clear the prophecy is. This is not an ordinary book – it's the Word of God!"[60]

Isn't that so true? People try to discount the Bible as only a book written by men, one that can't be trusted and is irrelevant in today's society, but nothing could be further from the truth. It is the Word of God, and it contains all the truth this world needs for salvation and satisfaction.

Shortly after, Peter trusted Christ and his life was miraculously transformed. For the rest of his days, he bore testimony to the changing power of God's salvation.

---

60. You can listen to Peter Orasuk's story at https://www.heaven4sure.com/2006/12/21/peter-orasuk-from-drugs-to-christ/

Moses said unto Joshua... go out, fight with Amalek.

Exodus 17:9

AUGUST 12

Are you prepared to be a Joshua – one who dares to do great things for God and who stands out from all the rest?

We first read of Joshua in Exodus 17. God blessed the Israelites by giving them water from the rock, and as they were enjoying this blessing, we read three very ominous words. 'Then came Amalek...' Who are these people? If we turn to Genesis 36:12, we learn that Amalek was the son of Esau by a concubine. Amalek can be considered a picture of the flesh. Isn't it true that, so often, while we are enjoying the Lord's blessing, 'then comes Amalek' – those fleshly, sinful lusts and desires?

We need to read Deuteronomy 25:18 to discover that not only did Amalek attack Israel, they attacked from behind – the weakest part of the company. Often our weakest point is most susceptible to attack from the flesh, so we need to be constantly on our guard.

Moses, an older man, instructed Joshua, a younger man, to fight. Joshua listened to Moses and did as he said (verse 10). Sometimes young people feel that older people don't really know what it's like to be their age. It's easy to make excuses and disregard their advice, and it's tempting to think that the battle is either too unimportant or too difficult to fight. Often, we need older people to remind us to fight against those sinful desires, and to fight with all our might.

But, on its own, fighting is not enough. Joshua needed the intercession of Moses, and the help of Aaron and Hur. He was not alone in the battle. You are not alone either. It's an amazing thought that you have the intercession of the Lord Jesus Christ for you as you fight. Not only that, you have older believers who are spending much time and energy praying for you. Moses, Aaron, and Hur were on the hillside. They probably had a clearer view of what was happening in the battle than those in the middle of it would have had. The same is often true of those who are praying for you.

So as you fight the battle of the flesh, be thankful and appreciate older believers' prayers. Listen to their instruction. They know how vitally important it is to fight this battle.

Moses arose with his assistant Joshua, and Moses went up to the mountain of God.

Exodus 24:13 NKJV

Yesterday, we met Joshua fighting against Amalek, and today we will learn more about this courageous younger man. In Exodus 24, God has called Moses to come up the mountain to receive the two tables of the law. Before he leaves, he tells the people what God expects of them, and they answer confidently and unhesitatingly, "All that the Lord hath said will we do, and be obedient."

So Moses sets off with Joshua. It's here we read that Joshua is Moses' assistant, or attendant – a common role for younger men in the Bible, especially ones who would eventually take over from the older man. One day, Moses would die, and someone would need to take his place. It's the same in our day – the older generation will pass on, and others will need to step up and take their place. Are you willing? When we spend time with older, wiser people, we will learn lessons that will stand us in good stead when the time comes to fill their shoes.

There came a point when Moses went further, leaving Joshua completely on his own. The time of testing had come. Would he be faithful? Or would he turn and make his way back down the mountain? Sometimes God removes those people we are depending on, in order to test us. Will we be proved faithful? Or will we turn back?

After forty days, Moses returned and together they made their way back down the mountain. As they got nearer to the camp, Joshua's ears picked up a concerning sound. Was it war? Moses, the older man, knew better. It was singing and revelry. While Moses was being given the tables of the law, and Joshua was faithfully waiting, the people had disobeyed and broken their promise. How disappointing this must have been to Joshua! Often, when we are young, we have high expectations – not only of ourselves, but of others. There's nothing wrong with that, but when the Lord's people sin, especially those we have regarded as more spiritual than ourselves, we are devastated. God was teaching Joshua the valuable lesson that even when people promise to obey, they are still prone to failure. The important thing is that, no matter what others do, we must remain faithful.

His servant Joshua, the son of Nun, a young man, departed not out of the tabernacle.

Exodus 33:11

14

AUGUST

One of the consequences of the sin of the children of Israel was that the tabernacle – the tent used at that time as a meeting place with God – was to be moved outside the camp. They would no longer enjoy God's presence in their midst. Instead, if they wanted to seek God, they would have to make their way to the tabernacle as individuals.

It's in this context that we read another interesting little fact about Joshua. In case we mix him up with any other Joshua, we're told that this is the same one who was Moses' assistant, the son of Nun, and a young man. This same Joshua departed not out of the tabernacle. He had made the effort to spend time with God. There were undoubtedly many young men in the camp of Israel at this time, but Joshua stood out.

Do you stand out amongst all the other young people? Are you spending time in God's presence? It will take effort. It will often mean turning your back on all that occupies the world and taking a different path. Those activities that absorb so much of your friends' attention, whether they are legitimate or not, may have to be relinquished if you're going to be like Joshua. Reading and studying God's Word and taking time to pray are all vitally important for a believer.

Today, unlike in Joshua's day, God doesn't dwell in buildings or manmade structures, so there's nothing sacred about the actual *place* where we meet with other believers. We will find His presence, however, in the *gatherings* of His people, so a Christian who wants to be in God's presence will not only spend time with Him in private but will make attending the meetings of their local church one of their top priorities.

Joshua's choices in his earlier life affected not only the person he would become in later years, but the entire nation. God is still looking for Joshuas – those who fight against the flesh, who are faithful, and who make spending time in His presence their priority. Will you be a Joshua?

Moses sent them to spy out the land of Canaan.
Numbers 13:17

When Moses sent twelve handpicked men to spy out the land of Canaan – the land God had promised that the children of Israel would possess – is it any surprise that Joshua was one of the number? The instructions were specific. Survey what the land was like, observe what the people were like, and assess the cities they lived in. Take note of the fruitfulness of the land, bring a sample back, and, above all, be courageous! The information they would glean would be invaluable in their preparation for possessing the land. And the foretaste of the fruit would encourage the people, buoying them up through the inevitable days of war.

It all seemed to be going so well. A single branch of grapes was so luscious and fruitful that it had to be carried by two men. When they gave their report, they unanimously agreed that the land was good, 'flowing with milk and honey'.

But...! The inhabitants were strong, the cities were walled, and there were even giants! The people began to murmur. *Giants! How awful!* The encouragement of Caleb, Joshua's godly companion, made no difference. It would be too much, the other ten argued. They would be defeated, and everyone would die. Discouragement is contagious, so mass panic set in. Someone suggested they return to Egypt – surely it would be better to die there! Another attempt in the morning by Joshua and Caleb to turn the people's eyes to God's goodness, presence, and preservation was in vain. They wouldn't listen. So for forty years they wandered in the wilderness, until all those who refused to go into the land perished.

What was the difference between Joshua and Caleb, and the other ten spies? Only this – that they had faith in God, and the others didn't. They knew that God had promised them the land, and He would fulfil that promise, no matter how difficult it looked.

It's a good lesson for us today – God is still faithful. Often, we face situations that seem impossible. Never forget that nothing is impossible with God. If we know His will, we can step out in full confidence, knowing He will give us the strength to deal with whatever giants we have to face. And, as Joshua and Caleb realised, the blessings of God will be worth it all.

Take thee Joshua the son of Nun... and lay thine hand upon him.

Numbers 27:18

16

AUGUST

I was utterly hopeless when it came to many of the sports we played at school, eliciting groans rather than cheers from my assigned team. But while sport wasn't my forte, I learned a few good lessons from it. An obvious one is that when someone has the ball, the other players in the team do all in their power to keep the opposing side away and to aid the person in their pursuit of the goal. And if the person who has the ball detects that their time with it is coming to an end, they look around before passing it to someone else who can speed it closer to the target. The intended recipient needs to be ready, however. If they aren't, or no one on their team is close enough, it may be costly.

Moses' time as leader of the nation of Israel was coming to an end. It was time for him to relinquish the ball and pass it on to someone else. As he looked around, there was one younger man who stood out, who for many years had stayed near Moses, helping him, and fighting against the opposing forces – Joshua, God's man to take over and lead the nation into the promised land.

Someday, God willing, you may be called upon to take over from some older Christian. Leaders and shepherds – those who guide, feed, and protect God's people – are always needed. Believers who care for others are an essential part of Christian life, whether in a local church capacity, or in a quiet, personal way. If this is what God has for you to do in the future, He will guide you, and equip you for the task. We've been learning that Joshua's whole way of life from his youth was God-centred. Preparation for responsibility began years before – and it still does. Never forget that the way you live in your teens can have a huge impact on the rest of your life. Keep focussed on the ball, so that if you, like Joshua, are called upon to take over in years to come, you'll be found ready and willing.

Arise, go over this Jordan, thou, and all this people, unto the land which I do give to them.
Joshua 1:2

The time had come for Joshua to act. Moses was dead, and the responsibility of leadership had been passed on. It wasn't going to be easy, but he would have the greatest resource known to mankind – God's unfailing help and presence. There were going to be new challenges – instead of leading people through a wilderness like Moses had done, it was time to possess the land, but the same God who was with Moses had promised to be with Joshua.

Joshua's first conquest was the city of Jericho. The spies he sent brought a report of the feared reputation the children of Israel had amongst the citizens of that land. The city would be an easy one to take. In fact, they were so sure of victory that they declared that the Lord had delivered all the land into their hand. So they set forth. Joshua had experience in war – remember how he fought with Amalek when we were first introduced to him? A terrified enemy and an experienced leader – an ideal situation.

But read Joshua 6. Instead of Joshua using his military prowess, God asks him to do a very strange thing. The army was to march around the walls once every day for six days, blowing trumpets, then return to the camp. On the seventh day, they were to march around seven times, and give a great shout. The walls would fall, and they would march straight into the city. Simple? Yes, but I'm sure many of the soldiers would rather have carried out a surprise attack on Jericho, rather than announcing their presence every day for almost a week! What God asked them to do probably seemed illogical.

There are times when God asks us to do things that seem illogical to us, and situations where all we want to do is use our own efforts. Waiting on God's timing and His plan often goes against every natural instinct and requires faith in our all-wise and all-powerful God. But if we obey His command, we will discover, as Joshua and his army discovered, that God's timing and God's plans are always best.

> Choose you this day whom ye will serve... As for me and my house, we will serve the Lord.
>
> Joshua 24:15

18

AUGUST

We have now come to the end of Joshua's life. I've enjoyed our little study, and I hope you have too. There are many more lessons we could have learned, but you'll have to read about this godly man and look for those yourself. Before we go, we'll visit him one last time. He's speaking. Let's tiptoe a little closer to hear his last words to the leaders of Israel. I'm sure we will learn something important that will help us as we live for God.

Joshua begins by recounting all that the Lord had done for the children of Israel throughout the generations. He had remarkably delivered them from Egypt and brought them safely to the promised land, giving them every blessing. Isn't that like us? We've been delivered from the bonds of sin, and have been blessed with every spiritual blessing in Christ.

'Now therefore...' In light of these blessings, it was the duty and privilege of the children of Israel to fear God. They were to put away the false gods and idols and serve only the Lord. This is our duty and privilege too. The idols which rob God of what He is due in our day may be different from those which tempted the Israelites, but they are no less attractive. Possessions, importance, appearance, entertainment, and many more things besides, can be a snare to God's people. To which of these are we going to devote our time, money, and effort?

Or are we going to be like Joshua, with a firm and steady conviction? "We will serve the Lord!" Joshua's sincere and honest declaration rings out, setting an example and encouraging others to live for the God who had so generously blessed the nation. Our choices can powerfully affect others, for good or bad. Are we living a life that influences other Christians to live for God as well?

So Joshua passes away. Sooner or later, life will come to an end for each of us. Let's get our priorities right and live as this great man did, making God the focus and goal of life. He certainly didn't regret it, and, if we live for God, neither will we.

Their sins and their iniquities will I remember no more.
Hebrews 8:12

How's your memory? Like most of us, at some stage or another you've probably forgotten to do a homework, pass on an important message, or bring that item from the shop for your mum or dad. I think we've all discovered that it isn't only people your grandparents' age who struggle to remember things!

Sometimes, despite our best intentions, things genuinely slip our minds. Other times, we don't make much effort to remember, maybe because we think that what we were told isn't very important, or because it doesn't matter to us. You'd have to agree that, whether we could have tried harder or not, forgetting is a human failing.

Our verse for today talks about God no longer remembering our sins, but it's not that God thinks they are unimportant or that they don't matter. God is holy, and sin is obnoxious to Him. Before we were saved, it was a huge barrier between us and God. It took the death of His Son to pay the price and remove the barrier. Could our sins slip His mind? Absolutely not! God has no such failings.

Did you notice it doesn't say that God will *forget* our sins? "What's the difference?" you might argue. "Isn't 'forgetting' and 'not remembering' the same thing?" It's not. God actually *chooses* to remember our sins no more. We aren't very good at putting something out of our minds. Inevitably, it will creep back in again if we're not careful. But God is omnipotent – all powerful – and when we are forgiven, He removes our sins from His memory.

Did you ever wrong someone, and later ask for their forgiveness? Maybe the other person told you they'd forgiven you and forgotten what you did. But one day they got angry and brought up again what you'd done. God will *never* do that. Notice those little words at the end of the verse – 'no more'!

Isn't it wonderful to know that all your sins are forgiven, and God will never remember them ever again?

I packed my school bag, stuffed my tiny alarm clock in my coat pocket, and off I set. Out the door, across the patio, and down the steps into the garden. Then I tripped and fell, skinning my knee. Figuring that running away wasn't really worth it after all, I turned and came back into the house. Where would I have slept and what would I have eaten anyway?

I'm sure I wasn't the only child or young person ever to decide to run away. In fact, some young people can't wait to leave home, to break the restraints that their parents have set, and go and do their own thing. Some head away for work or go off to university. I've even heard stories of those who decided to travel to the other side of the world, in an attempt to get away from their Christian background and upbringing.

Sometimes Christians run away too. They might be like Jonah – instead of going and doing what God has asked, they try to flee from God's presence. Or they might be trying to escape from themselves, maybe thinking that if they were in a different location, around different people, that they themselves would be different, better, without the problems and difficulties that haunt them at home.

The truth is that when we run away – whether it's to the far side of the world, or only down the road – we cannot escape God, and we cannot escape ourselves. God is omnipresent. He's everywhere, as Jonah and many others have found. And when we run away, we take ourselves with us. Those character traits and failings that we're blaming on our circumstances will still be with us, even if our location and environment changes. We bring the whole flawed package, no matter where we go.

So what do we do? Instead of running away from God, let's run to Him. He is the One in whom we find shelter and safety. He is the One who can change us and make us more like Christ. And, as the old hymn rightly says, 'There's no other way to be happy in Jesus, but to trust and obey.'

Flee from sexual immorality.
1 Corinthians 6:18 ESV

Sexual immorality. It's everywhere – in films, song lyrics, books, and everyday life. To speak out and say it's wrong is to invite laughter and scorn. You'd be called all sorts of names – *old-fashioned* probably being the kindest.

But does that make it right? Is it, as they say, that the Bible is outdated and not relevant for today? That those rules belonged to the dark ages, but it's different now?

God never gives instruction for the fun of denying us something we want. Behind every command is a reason. Did you ever buy something that needed set up or constructed, and you thought you knew exactly what to do? Then something went wrong, and you discovered that you really should have read the instructions in the first place. The manufacturer knew something that you didn't! God knows far more about His creation – us – than we could ever know.

The physical relationship between a married couple is part of God's perfect design, but sexual immorality comes with a price. There may be physical consequences – sexually transmitted diseases are more prevalent amongst unmarried people. There are emotional consequences – it's so easy to get hurt at a time when you are vulnerable. There are future consequences – previous experiences may leave people with psychological scars which can affect their marriage many years later. Awakened desires lead to further temptation. And, not least, there are spiritual consequences – communion with God is broken, and moral failure now may disqualify you from future service for God.

Even if we can see no reason why we should do as God says, it doesn't alter the fact that we must obey Him. Wrong doesn't become right because the world says so. You may be unpopular, laughed at, pressurised to cave in. But stand firm, pray for God's help, and hold on. And if this warning has come too late for you, confess your sin to God who is faithful to forgive, take steps to prevent it happening again, and pray. God is faithful and will not allow us to be tempted beyond what we're able (1 Corinthians 10:13).

The Lord... is longsuffering to usward, not willing that any should perish.

2 Peter 3:9

AUGUST

22

I'm sure most of us have had at least one teacher who for a few minutes was just about able to tolerate the antics of some troublemakers in the class, and then *boom!* He or she seemed to explode! The mischief-makers were stunned into silence, and everyone else kept their heads down in case any eye contact would reignite the outburst.

Being longsuffering may not be very common in this world, but thankfully it's one of the characteristics of God. He will never become irritated and lose self-control because of the continual wickedness of human beings, the way a teacher does with naughty pupils. My Bible dictionary explains longsuffering as 'self-restraint in the face of provocation which does not hastily retaliate or promptly punish.'[61]

Can you imagine all the sin and rebellion against God, repeated day after day after day? Most of us are well aware of the modern attitude to God – the scoffing words, the sinful actions, the outright denial of His existence. And we're only seeing a tiny portion of all of the wickedness and debauchery. Why doesn't He sweep the whole world away in deserved judgment?

The answer – because He is longsuffering, not willing that any should perish, but that all should come to repentance. Ezekiel 33:11 tells us that God doesn't take pleasure in the death of the wicked but desires their repentance. The reason that God waits is to give them opportunity to repent. His longsuffering has already been at work in our lives too. What a merciful and gracious God we have!

A day will come, however, when God's longsuffering will end, not in an outburst of uncontrolled anger, but in righteous judgment against those who don't know God and have refused His free offer of salvation.

---

61. *Vine's Dictionary.*

A man's heart plans his way,
but the Lord directs his steps.
Proverbs 16:9 NKJV

From our altitude, the mountainous scenery was spectacular – deep gorges and valleys, with clusters of tiny houses clinging to steep, thickly foliaged slopes. The only problem was that our flight was supposed to land near the coast. Beautiful as this area was, it was certainly not the coast, and the little airport we landed at was not our expected destination.

Sometimes we set out in life with a goal. We plan, we work towards it, and yet, for whatever reason, we end up miles from where we intended to be. Maybe we didn't get the grades we needed in a certain subject. Despite hours of practice, nerves took over and we failed the driving test. The perfect summer job didn't work out and we had to settle for less – or worse, no job at all!

In a foreign country, with only a rudimentary knowledge of the language, we had no idea what was going on. Why had the pilot decided to take us here, three hundred miles from where we were supposed to be?

It's good to plan, but we must remember that God is in control. We need to trust Him, even when things go awry. A change in plans may not make sense to us, but He knows something we don't.

Our diversion was due to fog. Had we carried on and attempted to land, visibility was so poor that it would have been dangerous. We didn't know – we could only trust the pilot... and wait! A few hours later, we arrived safely, in glorious sunshine, at our destination.

God may be asking you to wait. If He does, there will be a very good reason. You might not know what it is, but you can be confident that His plans are for your good.

In the Lord Jesus' day, poverty was a very real thing. People lived hand to mouth, and often they didn't even know where their next meal would come from. The Lord Jesus Christ was assuring them that God would provide for their every need, including clothing. For most of us, though, obtaining clothing isn't an issue. Our biggest clothes-related problem is deciding which items to select from our overstuffed wardrobes!

Fashion changes rapidly. What was on trend last year is out this year, and this year's fashion will be a thing of the past next year. Keeping up can be an expensive business, especially with the pressure to conform.

While there's certainly no need to closely follow the latest trends, there's nothing inherently wrong with wearing fashionable clothes. Choosing to dress in out-of-date or worn-out clothes in an attempt to display frugality or self-denial may not be a good testimony before unbelievers. As long as your clothes don't violate any scriptural commands or principles, you can wear whatever you like. But it's always good before you put on, or even better, before you buy any item of clothing, to look at it through the lens of the Bible.

Firstly – is buying this top or these jeans good stewardship? I might be able to afford them, and we need to wear clothes, but I already have several similar items. Is this the best way to spend my money? Then – what's my motive for buying this item? Is it because I actually need it, or am I looking for admiration from others? Is it pride? And what about the item itself? Will wearing it honour God? Many clothes, both for male and female, are designed to display your bodily shape. Other items expose large areas of skin. We aren't commanded to wear long, baggy clothes, but please take modesty into consideration when you're choosing what to wear. Listen to your conscience, check your motives, and if you aren't sure, ask the opinion of other believers, although not necessarily your own peer group. They may be able to give you a different perspective on whether an item of clothing will honour God or not.

Clothes can say a lot about someone – what are yours saying about you?

Behold who hath created these things.
Isaiah 40:26

It was Trudi, my English springer spaniel, who first alerted me to the mouse under the hens' drinker. I had no idea it was there until I lifted the drinker and the furry little creature darted out. Trudi isn't too good at catching mice, so it got away – that time, at least! What she is good at, though, is sniffing them out – along with other varieties of wildlife. She loves nothing better than to zigzag through a wide-open space, sometimes for hours, tracing a scent, finally returning thirsty, filthy, and exhausted.

It's no wonder that smells fascinate Trudi so much. After all, a dog's sense of smell can be around ten thousand times better than ours, they have around 220 million olfactory receptors compared with our 5-6 million, and the part of their brain which interprets odours is forty times the size of the part which carries out the same function in ours. A dog would be able to smell just one drop of blood diluted into a quantity of water which would fill two Olympic-sized swimming pools!

This amazing ability of dogs has been harnessed by humans. We're all familiar with police dogs which sniff out missing people, drugs, or money. Army dogs can find explosives and weapons. Both we and our luggage have experienced the excited scrutiny of security dogs at airports. There are other roles – detecting cancer, or, the most unusual one that I've read about, finding bedbugs in hotels!

So how do these animals smell so well? One of the reasons is that dogs have an organ we don't have, called Jacobson's organ, which is important in the detection of pheromones, or body scents. Dogs also breathe differently – we both smell and breathe as we inhale, whereas a fold of tissue separates the smelling and breathing functions of their noses. When dogs exhale, the air is expelled through slits at the side, and this helps to bring new smells into a dog's nose. They can also use each nostril independently to determine which direction a scent is coming from!

It's fascinating, isn't it? But these aren't only interesting facts. Instead, they are something to make us marvel and prompt us to worship our amazing and all-wise Creator, who gave one of our favourite animals this remarkable ability.[62]

---

62. Information taken from the following websites - https://www.pbs.org/wgbh/nova/article/dogs-sense-of-smell/
https://answersingenesis.org/mammals/souped-sniffers/
https://answersingenesis.org/creation-science/baraminology/what-a-dogs-nose-knows/
https://www.purina.com.au/dogs/behaviour/sniffing#.XoSyIGnTWdM

I press toward the goal for the prize of the upward call of God in Christ Jesus.

Philippians 3:14 NKJV

AUGUST

26

When I was fifteen, a friend and I set our imaginations loose. The result was a piece of writing called *Ten Years' Time*. To be clear, this wasn't a school assignment – I'm not sure we'd have spent so much time on it if it had been. Instead, it contained our predictions of what we and all our friends would be doing in ten years. Most of it was wildly outrageous, so it wasn't a surprise that when we reached the year in question, not one of us had done what my friend and I had envisaged!

Where do you think you will be in ten years? No one knows if we'll still be on this earth. But if you are, where do you see yourself? Do you have goals for the future? Maybe you plan to go to university and focus on your career. Maybe you're dying to leave school so you that can spend more time on the farm. Maybe what you want more than anything is to marry and have children. Or maybe your dream is to travel and see the world. Everyone's ambition is different.

But what about your spiritual goals? Where do you see yourself as a Christian in ten years? I'm sure you'd want to know more about your Bible, to be more like Christ. Maybe you wonder if God might call you to serve Him in another part of the world.

When we strive towards a goal, it involves sacrifice and discipline. This isn't only true in the secular sphere, but in the spiritual as well. You know you'll never get that coveted place on the university course unless you work hard. If you don't watch your spending, it'll take a long time to save up for flights to that country you'd love to explore. And to reach spiritual goals, it also takes sacrifice and discipline – maybe choosing to stay at home for an evening to study your Bible rather than always being out with your friends. It might involve getting up earlier in the morning to take time to pray.

In ten years' time you might have regrets about some choices you've made. But you will never regret spending time working towards your spiritual goals.

27

The peace of God, which surpasses all understanding, will guard your hearts and your minds.

AUGUST

Philippians 4:7 ESV

Compared with your parents, who may have worked in the same place doing the same job for years, you will be encountering many changes in a relatively short space of time. You'll come across different teachers and lecturers, find yourself in different classes or places of education, and maybe have a changing group of friends. Even within subjects and modules, new topics will be introduced one after the other. Each day will be different from the previous one. If you're anything like me, you might not like that very much. Change can often be scary. Once I fretted all summer long because of a certain stern teacher I knew I would have when I went back to school. The truth is that it changed nothing, and I ruined my summer by worrying about it.

Maybe peace is something you struggle to enjoy too. Maybe you're dreading a specific subject which you know isn't your strength, or being around another student who isn't very nice to you. Or maybe it's the unknown which scares you. But whether you're dreading something actual or not, God has a solution to your problem. His peace. You see, it isn't just an absence of stress. Instead, it's the peace of God, something active and real right in the middle of our stress. Our verse says that it surpasses all understanding – beyond what we can imagine – and it guards our hearts and minds. Often, when we lack peace, we begin to worry and to think thoughts that aren't true, but this peace will protect our minds and our hearts, like tough and well-armed soldiers guarding a very important castle.

How do we avail of this peace? You'll find the secret in verse 6 – prayer. We will never know peace until we tell God everything, thank Him for what He has already done and what He will do, and leave it all with Him. Don't be anxious about anything! His supreme peace is available and able to guard your heart and your mind from worry.

Who is the first person to spring to mind when you're asked to name a famous female missionary? For me, it's always Amy Carmichael. I'd heard stories about Amy when I was quite young, and finding out that she'd been born and brought up only forty-five miles from where I grew up (although well over one hundred years before) only increased my interest in her life story.

When Amy was three years old, she asked God to give her blue eyes, and was bewildered and disappointed when she woke up the next morning with the same brown eyes as she'd had the day before.

At fifteen years old, Amy trusted Christ for salvation and, rather than concentrating on temporary amusements and pleasures, chose to live for what is eternal. She worked hard in reaching children, young people, and factory and mill girls for God, but the thought of people dying without ever hearing of Christ burdened her greatly, and eventually she heard the call, 'Go ye.'

After a time in Japan, then in China and Ceylon (modern Sri Lanka), Amy ended up in India, where she was to spend the rest of her life. It was while there that she understood the reason that God had answered her prayer for blue eyes with 'no'. Amy discovered that little girls were being used as Hindu temple prostitutes and, while rescuing them, she realised that her brown eyes helped her blend in with the Indian people in a way that blue eyes never could.

Amy was a gifted writer and poet, and her poems give us a glimpse into her deep commitment and love for God, no matter what. Here is my favourite:

> And shall I pray Thee change Thy will, my Father,
> Until it be according unto mine?
> But, no, Lord, no, that never shall be, rather
> I pray Thee blend my human will with Thine.

Amy Carmichael, the girl from Millisle, departed for heaven in January 1951, aged eighty-three. The greatest portion of her life had been spent for her Lord; she'd sacrificed much for Him. Do you think she has any regrets? I think I know what she would say![63]

---

63. Elisabeth Elliot tells Amy Carmichael's story in *A Chance to Die – the Life and Legacy of Amy Carmichael*, published by Revell in 1987.

Jesus wept.
John 11:35

At Sunday school, one of the most common questions we were asked was, "What's the shortest verse in the Bible?" Well, that's easy – "Jesus wept!" Even the tiny children knew the answer to that one! In this chapter, Lazarus, the brother of Mary and Martha, had died, and the Lord arrived four days afterwards. When He asked where they had laid him, Mary and Martha, accompanied by a group of mourners, took Him to the grave.

The whole scene is one of great sadness and weeping. The sisters had lost a very precious brother, probably at a younger age than they had anticipated. Mary's words to the Lord Jesus Christ were an echo of what Martha had said to Him earlier – that if He had been there, Lazarus wouldn't have died. So why did Jesus weep? Was it regret – because He had made a mistake? Absolutely not! Elsewhere in this devotional we learned that He had a very good reason for the delay.

We aren't told exactly why He wept, so we draw our own conclusions. One clue is in the words in verse 33 – He was deeply moved (which can also be translated 'indignant') and troubled. If you've ever experienced losing someone close to you, you'll agree that death is difficult. It's hard and cold. Every fibre of our beings wants to cry out that this isn't how it ought to be. And it's not – it was man's sin that brought death into the world, and the consequences of that sin have been with us ever since. The plight of dying humanity touched the Lord Jesus so that He wept.

The Lord is also full of compassion – why wouldn't the sight of Mary, broken and crying at His feet, have moved our caring Lord to tears?

And, finally, the Lord's tears spelled out to the Jews the love He had for the one who had passed away. The siblings were very dear to Him, and the death of Lazarus caused His tears to flow.

'Jesus wept' might be the shortest verse in our English Bible, but behind those two simple words are truths that can comfort and help us when we find ourselves grieving like the two sisters in the chapter.

Thou saidst, I will surely do thee good.

Genesis 32:12

J acob was scared, and no wonder. The last time he'd seen his brother, Esau, he'd cheated him out of his birthright – a most serious matter. Now Esau was coming to meet him with four hundred men. Poor Jacob could only conclude that he was coming to take revenge. Maybe, despite the difficulties in Haran, he was wishing that he'd never left.

Yet, in leaving Haran, he was doing exactly what God had told him to do – to 'get out from this land, and return unto the land of thy kindred.' Jacob was in the centre of God's will.

Have you ever been obedient to God, sure that you were exactly where God wanted you to be, yet things weren't working out the way you expected? It's not an easy place, and all we can do – in fact, the best thing we can do – is to tell God about it. This is exactly what Jacob did. He reminded God of what He'd told him to do. In effect, Jacob said, "God, You told me to leave Haran, and I did. I've been obedient to Your command."

Jacob was very aware that he hadn't always been in the centre of God's will. He hadn't always pleased God. He told God that he wasn't worthy of the least of all His mercies. Isn't that true for all of us?

He then told God all about the problem. He knew that no one on earth could possibly help him – any deliverance would come solely from God. While it's good to talk to others about problems we are facing, no one really understands or cares like God does. He is the only One who can truly help us.

And finally, Jacob turned to the promises of God. He knew that if Esau killed them all, the promises that God had given to Jacob (and to Abraham and Isaac) wouldn't be fulfilled. God had to help him. We also have promises from God – that He will never leave us, that He cares for us, and many more beside. God doesn't need to be reminded of His promises, but we do. However, when we bring these promises to Him, we are making prayers that carry weight.

Did Esau kill Jacob? No, he didn't! In fact, God's promises to Jacob were fulfilled beyond what he could have imagined. And our God is still faithful today.

31

AUGUST

They all forsook Him, and fled.

Mark 14:50

Idon't think there are many of us who know what it is to be totally and utterly forsaken. Maybe you've been treated like an outcast at school – and that's extremely difficult – but you know your parents still love you. Or maybe you're in the tragic position of having parents who truly don't care about you, but you know you have someone, maybe a grandparent or teacher, who's got your back. And even if every single person on earth forsakes us, we know that God has said that He will never leave us nor forsake us (Hebrews 13:5).

There was One, however, who knew what it was to be totally and utterly forsaken. The Lord Jesus Christ was betrayed by one of His disciples, and not to people who were demanding only a fine, or that He stay a few weeks in prison. They actually wanted to kill Him! If that wasn't bad enough, the rest of the disciples then forsook Him and fled. Soon Peter, who had promised to die with Him, denied that he even knew Him. Psalm 69:20 gives the thoughts of the Lord's heart when it says, 'I looked for some to take pity, but there was none; and for comforters, but I found none.'

But on the cross the Lord Jesus Christ suffered the greatest forsaking – by God Himself. He cried, "My God, My God, why hast Thou forsaken Me?" The only One who always had perfect and complete fellowship with God, who never sinned, either in thought, word, or action, was forsaken by God while He suffered the horrors of judgment. We cannot begin to comprehend what He faced as He bore our sins. And to realise that He suffered all alone is staggering.

What makes it even more incomprehensible is that Psalm 37:25 NKJV says, 'I have not seen the righteous forsaken,' yet here was One, who was the personification of righteousness, forsaken by God Himself. Can you understand it? Neither can I. We can only bow our heads and thank Him for being forsaken for us, so that we will never, ever know what it is to be forsaken.

SEPTEMBER

Well done, good and faithful servant.

Matthew 25:23

In June 2018, Wee Nancy took ill and died. She was a tiny old lady, with a weather-beaten face from years of hard work in the house, her garden, and the farm. Never travelling far from home, she lived a quiet, simple country life. Her circle of acquaintances was mostly made up of family, neighbours, and the Christians she met with each week.

It's a common misconception that the best way to please God is to do some 'big thing', like becoming a missionary, or using some natural talent to reach thousands of people and bring glory to God. If that's what God has for you, live that life to the best of your ability. But what about people like Wee Nancy, who never venture far from their country cottage and don't have the means, let alone the desire, to become what we might call 'great'?

That's the good part! God doesn't make any distinction between living in the public eye, or up a quiet country lane. What He values above everything else is just the same – faithfulness.

But what does faithfulness actually look like? It's simply getting up every morning and doing what's been put in front of you to do that day, whether that's going to school or work, writing an essay, cleaning the house, visiting those who are sick, or heading out to reach people with the gospel. It's being a reliable person, someone others know they can depend on. It's obeying God's commands, which are found in the Bible. It's being a good steward of money and time, and whatever else God has given to you.

Faithfulness isn't actually very exciting. It's being steady and dependable, plodding on, day after day, month after month, year after year, even when it's tough. It's often tempting to look for something more exciting to do or to be involved in, but faithfulness doesn't quit when it knows it's doing exactly what God wants.

And that's the crux of the matter. God really values faithfulness. Blazes of glory are all well and good, but it will be the faithful, including those like Wee Nancy, who will receive the 'well done' from Him in a future day.

The sea is His, and He made it.
Psalm 95:5

SEPTEMBER

2

One of the features of the theory of evolution is its insistence on a universe which is billions of years old. It seems to be that the proponents understand that the likelihood of the many complex systems in nature developing by their own accord is so impossible that, if they could only provide them with enough time, it might just give them the chance to succeed against all the other odds... and blow our minds in the process! When we get into numbers that large, it's easy to shrug and say that anything could happen in such a vast amount of time.

Did you know that the ocean might have some clues about the age of the earth? Let's go deep-sea diving, right to the ocean floor. Do you see all the sediment – twenty-five billion tons of dirt and rock being washed into the sea *per year*? The only way any of it can be removed is when one tectonic plate slides beneath another, taking sediment with it. But this only removes about one billion tons each year, leaving a lot behind with nowhere to go. The evolutionists claim that the seas are three billion years old, but if that were the case, they would be choked up with many kilometres' depth of sediment.

By measuring the amount of sediment and calculating backwards, the maximum number of years from the point when sediment would have commenced being deposited until now is twelve million – much less than what the evolutionists claim for the age of the seas. And this doesn't even take into account the massive deposits that the global flood would have laid down in a very short space of time, meaning the world is very likely many years younger again.

It's the same for sodium in the sea – there just isn't enough at the current rates of input (450 million tons) and output (121.5 million tons) for the seas to be three billion years old.

So when you're bombarded with the theory of evolution and its talk of billions of years, don't blindly accept it. We are certain from Scripture that God created the universe, and evidence points to the fact that we live on a much younger earth.[64]

64. Material based on presentation notes from the Apologetics Conference (2019) at Hebron Gospel Hall, Bicester, by David Vallance. The powerpoint presentation can be accessed at https://hebrongospelhall.org/sermons/fossils-dinosaurs-apemen-58-min/

Man shall not live by bread alone,
but by every word that proceedeth
out of the mouth of God.

Matthew 4:4

During a visit to Mexico, our friends took us to an all-you-can-eat buffet. Every type of food imaginable for each course was on offer. In fact, there were so many options that my husband and I ended up wandering around the restaurant, wide-eyed at the selection, with no idea what to try first.

When we pick up our Bibles, we can often feel like we are at a large buffet with numerous options. But instead of choosing between starter and main course, we're faced with the choice of law, history, poetry, prophecy, or letters. Once we've picked a category, we still have to narrow it down to a particular book and chapter.

The danger of buffets, and the reason why eating at one should be reserved for a special treat, is that we generally take only what we fancy. *You don't want vegetables? That's fine – don't put them on your plate. You'd like ten desserts? Sure, go ahead! Eat as many as you want!* You don't need me to tell you that this isn't what you'd call a balanced diet. We need to eat foods that we don't have much enthusiasm for, so that we don't become deficient in vital nutrients.

Bible reading is the same. We all have those passages that we love to turn to – chapters or verses that encourage us, that tell us of God's love for us. And those passages are important. There's no such thing as junk food or empty calories when it comes to God's Word. But equally important are those parts that instruct us, and even the ones which can seem a bit bland, full of names we struggle to pronounce or measurements that we can't relate to. If God says that all Scripture is profitable, then it's profitable! And never forget that if we really look, we will find glimpses of Christ.

So make sure you are reading all the Word of God. There will be pages of your Bible which will be crinklier and more worn than others, and I'll explain tomorrow why that should be the case, but there definitely shouldn't be any untouched pages. After all, the Bible is a feast, but it's not a buffet!

That the man of God may be
complete, thoroughly equipped
for every good work.
2 Timothy 3:17 NKJV

SEPTEMBER

4

Reading the Bible is vitally important for a Christian. It's the Word of God, so it almost goes without saying that we need to be spending time in it. If we ignore it, we will be starved, and our growth stunted.

I've emphasised the importance of reading all of the Bible, but there are certain key passages on which we need to focus so that we get a really good knowledge of them. Many of these are found in the gospels and epistles and are chock-full of vital truth for a believer.

Take John 1:1-18 for instance. In this section, we read of One who was the Word, who was there in the beginning. We're then told that He was both *with* God and that He *was* God. When we get to verse 14, we discover that this Word, who was God, actually became flesh and lived with people here on earth. I'm sure you don't need anyone to tell you that this is speaking of Christ. But what is so vital about this passage is that it makes it clear that our Lord Jesus Christ was perfectly God from all eternity, and perfectly man. His deity and humanity are vital doctrines that every believer depends on. And this is only one precious truth from that amazing passage.

Another portion that we need to get to know is Philippians 2:5-11. This passage tells us of the Lord's journey from heaven, to the shame and humiliation of the death of the cross, and back to heaven in glorious exaltation. It's one of those sections that we can look at time and time again and never fail to get lost in the wonder of it.

There are many other passages like these, but rather than list them here, you'll find some of them at the back of the book under 'Key Passages'. Take time to look at them. Read them over and over. Study them in detail. Check the context – read what comes before the passages and what follows them. Find out what others have to say about them. And stand firm upon them, because they contain basic, fundamental truths which every believer needs to know.

Do not be deceived: "Evil company corrupts good habits."
1 Corinthians 15:33 NKJV

There are probably many types of people at your school. Loud ones, quiet ones, fun-loving ones, sensible ones, sporty ones, studious ones. Such a variety! We really don't have much choice as to who is in our class, but there are other occasions, both at school and outside of school, when we *can* choose the people with whom we spend time. I'm sure there are certain individuals you always want to be around. Maybe they're funny, popular, or good-looking, or maybe you share a common interest.

But are those people good for you? They might be friendly, have a great sense of humour, or make you feel valued, but do they have habits that could rub off on you? Maybe their language isn't good; or their conversation isn't very clean. Have they a lack of respect for authority? Or are they involved in things that are bordering on, or actually are, illegal?

The Bible warns us about our company. We cannot and should not cut ourselves off from unbelievers. The Lord Jesus often spent time with sinners, and as His followers, sharing the gospel often involves getting to know people first. But choosing to be friends and spending time with those who aren't helpful to us as Christians is very different. Friends are people we often turn to for support, reassurance, or advice, so bad company can be harmful to a believer. Sinful habits desensitise us to sin and may even rub off on us. Sometimes those 'friends' can encourage us to do things that we know aren't right, things that we could very well regret for a lifetime and, more importantly, that will grieve God.

So, in choosing your friends, choose wisely. Choose those who won't pull you down, 'corrupt' you, or lead you away from the Lord. And, if possible, choose those who will even encourage you and help you as a Christian to live a life that pleases God.

The very first topic that I studied in history class at secondary school was 'The History of Medicine'. It wasn't a great appetiser to a school subject that I could have enjoyed. I mean, what twelve-year-old wants to look at ancient medical diagrams, or learn about doctors treating people by drilling holes in their skulls? One picture from the grubby textbook that stands out in my mind is that of three men, looking a bit worse for wear. One is out cold on the floor, another is asleep at the table, and the other is coming to, with what appears to be a severe headache. Rather than an example of the effects of alcohol, it's actually supposed to be a depiction of Sir James Young Simpson and colleagues during the discovery of the anaesthetic possibilities of chloroform.

James Simpson, born in 1811, was a pioneer in anaesthesia, Senior President of the Royal Medical Society of Edinburgh at twenty-four years old, professor of Midwifery at Edinburgh University, and Queen Victoria's favourite doctor. But when asked by a journalist what his greatest discovery was, he didn't even mention chloroform or any of his achievements. Instead he replied, "That I am a sinner and that Jesus is a great Saviour!"

Despite being brought up attending church, as time went on, James Simpson had become increasingly troubled by the state of his soul, and after having been witnessed to by one of his patients, he trusted Christ when he was about fifty years old. It is recorded that he later said when recounting his testimony, "I looked and saw Jesus, my substitute, scourged in my stead and dying on the cross for me. I looked and cried and was forgiven."[65]

Atheists would have us believe that great scientific minds could not possibly believe that God exists. Yet here was one of the greatest doctors of his time, one to whom we owe a great debt (because who would like to have surgery without anaesthesia?), who not only believed that there is a God, but had trusted in His Son for his eternal salvation and sought to win others for the Saviour as well.

---

65. Quoted in https://www.christianheritageedinburgh.org.uk/2018/12/07/a-scientists-testimony-sir-james-young-simpson-pioneer-of-anaesthetics/

This God is our God for ever and ever.

Psalm 48:14

Every couple of weeks, since the beginning of the year, we've learned about a different attribute, or characteristic, of God. We've learned that He is eternal and unchanging, omnipotent, omnipresent, and omniscient. We've seen His grace, mercy, love, and goodness; His holiness, righteousness, and wrath; and His wisdom, faithfulness, and longsuffering. We haven't by any means exhausted all that God is – there's much more to be discovered. Keep reading your Bible and learning about God. Don't forget that, because He is God, all these attributes are found in the Lord Jesus Christ. Look for them when you read about Christ in the gospels.

Take a moment to think over all you have learned about God. We will have to agree with the psalmist who said that 'great is the Lord, and greatly to be praised; and His greatness is unsearchable' (Psalm 145:3). Dwelling on and thinking about God's attributes should cause us to praise and worship Him, to bow humbly before Him. He is worthy of our deepest reverence.

But take another look at our verse for today. This God – the One who has all knowledge and wisdom, who is all-powerful, the righteous and holy One – is our God! *Ours!* What an immense privilege. He is not, as some think, a far-off, distant God, too lofty to be interested in us. Instead, He is our Creator, and our Father. He has redeemed us; we are His purchased possession. He is intensely interested in every detail of our lives. He has plans for us, and He is using circumstances and difficulties to bring those plans to fruition, to develop us, and mould us into the people He wants us to be. Every aspect of His character – each attribute – has a bearing on our lives – either for comfort and encouragement, or for challenge. But He is not only our God down here on earth – He is our God for ever and ever. Throughout the ages of eternity, the very same all-powerful, all-knowing, righteous, holy God, will be our God forever.

He that abideth in Me, and I in Him, the same bringeth forth much fruit.

John 15:5

There's something very special about eating fruit and vegetables from your own garden. They seem to taste better, somehow! This year, we are looking forward to eating the fruit that has been growing on our young fruit trees.

There is one tree in my mini-orchard that doesn't bring me as much joy as the others do. It's a tall, leafy tree – much taller and leafier than the others. It looks good. Really impressive, actually. It's a pear tree, but the problem is that I've searched in vain for one single tiny pear amongst its abundant foliage.

The Lord Jesus Christ is looking for fruit from our lives – those qualities mentioned in Galatians 5:22-23, which we looked at earlier in the year. He has a plan for each of us, and when we obey Him, it pleases Him greatly. We can only bring forth fruit after we have been saved (Romans 8:8); however, Christians can sometimes live unfruitful lives. All of my trees had the same amount of daylight and water, but unlike the others, which used the resources to produce fruit, the pear tree put all its energy into becoming tall and impressive.

We can be tempted to do the same. It's too easy to concentrate all our energy and resources on our appearance, our education, or our entertainment. The problem is that we then have nothing left with which to serve Christ and to do what He wants us to do.

In my garden, some of the other trees aren't much to look at. They aren't very tall, and some of the branches don't have very many leaves. But when the cherries turn red and juicy, and when the apples have grown and ripened, that won't matter at all.

At the end of the day, it's the fruit that counts.

Filthiness, nor foolish talking, nor coarse jesting... are not fitting.
Ephesians 5:4 NKJV

Hands up who is exposed to bad language on a regular basis? Pretty much everyone, then! You'll hear it at school, at work, or even walking down the street. The entertainment industry is full of it – films, books, music, and social media are all permeated with it. But why is bad language so wrong?

Many people are taught from a young age that there are certain words we aren't allowed to say. As children, some of us may have inadvertently heard and repeated a word that caused our parents to gasp and issue a stern warning to 'never, ever say that word again!' I often wondered who got to decide which words were 'bad', but as time went on, I realised that many of the popular words I heard, particularly at school, have meanings which are actually vulgar and immoral.

God has addressed the issue of using words like these in the passage from which I've quoted a small part at the top of the page. He tells us plainly that these words are not fitting for one who has been redeemed by the death of Christ.

Maybe you can't recall ever using unsavoury language. That's great! But how many times this past week have you been exposed to bad language voluntarily? Take social media, for instance. Did any of those memes from that account you follow contain words you know displease God? You might not use them yourself, but are you comfortable with others using them? Maybe you even enjoy their use. After all, that meme wouldn't be quite as funny if a tame word was used instead.

Did you ever realise that to take pleasure in others' sins is the same as if *you* were committing those sins (Romans 1:32)? That makes it pretty serious, doesn't it? It's as if those words had come out of your own mouth!

So the next time that you are about to follow someone who uses bad language, or when filthy words pop up in your social media feed, remember what God says – that filthiness is not fitting. Making the right choice doesn't take long – you can unfollow someone in a matter of seconds – and in doing so, you'll be walking as God would have you walk – as children of light (Ephesians 5:8).

Put on the whole armour of God, that ye may be able to stand.

Ephesians 6:11

SEPTEMBER

10

When I was a child, my favourite type of children's meeting was one where the speaker brought an object with him to illustrate his message. Did you know that the apostle Paul used objects to illustrate spiritual truth in his letters? He wrote about farming, athletics, and construction, but in this passage his object lesson involved a typical Roman soldier, like the one he was chained to during his imprisonment. I'm sure the man was taken aback the day Paul dictated the letter to the Ephesian believers, instructing them to put on their armour, and listing each item in turn! The soldier must have wondered what sort of enemies the people to whom his prisoner was writing were going to face. It certainly didn't sound like any battle that the Roman army had ever fought in!

The soldier would have been right. The enemy that a believer faces is greater than 'flesh and blood' – people. It is a spiritual battle, against Satan and his forces. We often forget that there is more happening around us than we realise. Satan's goal has ever been to rob God of His glory. He will try to do this by hindering the salvation of souls. If he can't do that, he will attempt to destroy the lives and testimonies of the Christians. Satan has his agents everywhere and the battle we are in is much bigger than we imagine.

Yet 1 John 4:4 says, 'Greater is He that is in you, than he that is in the world.' The devil is no match for our great God. Satan will ultimately lose, and he knows it. We will never be lost, but the devil will try his best to impede our efforts to fully live for God. The good news is that we haven't been left defenceless. We have God's salvation and the Holy Spirit indwelling us, and God has given us all the armour we need to stand against the attacks of the wicked one. Over the next few days we will inspect each piece of armour, learn what it's for, and how to put it on.

Stand therefore, having
fastened on the belt of truth.
Ephesians 6:14 ESV

Have you ever heard the saying 'A picture is worth a thousand words'? It's going to be especially true this week as we look at each piece of armour worn by a Roman soldier, which Paul used as an example of the armour of God that we're to put on every day. There are plenty of pictures of Roman soldiers online, and at some stage (though not necessarily right now) you'll find it useful to look at some of these and identify the various pieces of armour.

Paul starts off with the soldier's belt. The belt that the Roman soldiers wore was a little different from the belts we are familiar with, because it had a number of purposes – not only did they tuck the excess fabric of their clothes into it to help them move more easily in battle, it also held other parts of the armour together. The truth should have a firm hold on our lives. All those things which waste our time and energy will be gathered up and moved out of the way if we are focussing on the truth.

The devil is the father of lies (John 8:44) – the very opposite of the One who is the truth. He has always sought to cast doubt on what God has said. The only way to combat Satan in this battle we face every day is by standing firm on the truth.

What is the truth and where is it to be found? The Lord Jesus said, "I am... the truth" (John 14:6). Just before His arrest and crucifixion, He prayed to God, "Thy Word is truth" (John 17:17). With that in mind, we understand that truth is found in the Bible and in Christ. Spending time reading the Word of God and thinking about Christ is vital in a believer's life.

So, today, let's make sure we put on our belt of truth – spending time in God's Word, allowing it to saturate our minds, and focussing on what is true.

Having put on the breastplate of righteousness.
Ephesians 6:14 ESV

SEPTEMBER **12**

I've just made a quick online search for chest protectors, and it looks like big business! From bulletproof and stab-proof vests, to chest protectors for activities like motorsports, snowmobiling, and horse riding, it's pretty clear that our upper torso is worth protecting. The Roman soldiers evidently realised the same thing, and wore breastplates made of leather or metal.

We all know that inside our chests are the vital organs of the heart and lungs. These organs work together for the purpose of taking in and distributing essential oxygen around the body and getting rid of the waste product of carbon dioxide. Damage to these organs could ultimately cause death, so it's crucial for a soldier in battle to have chest protection.

We need to protect these vital organs too. In the Bible, the heart often speaks of the part of us which rules and determines everything we do. Satan loves to attack our heart, accusing us of being worthless, guilty sinners. When we listen to what he says about us and our shameful past, he rejoices, because it hinders our ability to live – really live! – for God. It's very important, therefore, that we put on the protective breastplate of righteousness – putting away our crippling guilt and shame, and being confident in the truth that, when we trusted Christ, we were given a righteous standing in Him (2 Corinthians 5:21). God has declared us righteous, and nothing Satan can do or say changes that fact.

We must also live in a way that shows that we believe this to be true. If we believe that we have been declared righteous, we will live as someone who is righteous. We will guard our hearts against wrong desires and feelings – sin, doubt, despair – things which damage our ability to live our lives for God. Instead, we will focus on those things – reading the Word of God, thinking about Christ, and praying – which are like oxygen to a believer, and which will help protect our hearts by reminding us that we are righteous before God.

As shoes for your feet, having put on the readiness given by the gospel of peace.

Ephesians 6:15 ESV

I don't think I've ever seen a soldier, Roman or otherwise, in bare feet. It's obvious that footwear is vitally important when it comes to fighting battles. And when it comes to the armour of God, He has provided shoes for us too – gospel shoes!

In this verse, the gospel is called the 'gospel of peace'. Do you remember the peace that first flooded your soul when you trusted Christ? You realised that your sins were forgiven, and all was well for eternity. The peace that comes from knowing Christ as Saviour is far greater than anything that unbelievers might call peace. But Satan, as always, wants to disturb it. He knows that if we aren't at peace, we won't be bringing God the glory that He rightfully deserves. That's why we must strap on the shoes of the gospel of peace and focus our minds on the great facts of the gospel.

But shoes were made for walking, and the gospel shoes will also affect our walk – our behaviour – as we make our way through this world. Those around us should notice that we are different. We will have different interests, speak different words, take part in different activities. They'll also notice that we have a peace that they are still searching for. As well as living out the gospel, we ought to be ready to share it. Many people today are desperate for peace but are looking in the wrong places. Sharing the gospel doesn't mean standing up on a chair in the lunch room and loudly preaching a sermon. Instead, it may be answering a question from a curious friend, telling others how we came to know Christ as our Saviour, asking them to come and hear the gospel preached, posting verses on social media, or passing on a gospel leaflet. If we keep our eyes open, we will find little opportunities here and there to help spread the gospel.

So today, let's put on our gospel shoes – rejoicing in the peace that the gospel brings us, walking in a way that pleases God, and ready to share the good news with others.

Take up the shield of faith, with which you can extinguish all the flaming darts.

Ephesians 6:16 ESV

SEPTEMBER

14

An essential piece of the Roman soldier's armour was his shield – a large, rectangular piece of wood, covered with strong leather. During battle, as if shooting pointed arrows wasn't bad enough, the enemy first dipped them in a flammable substance and set them alight. Satan likewise loves to shoot flaming arrows at us. Warren Wiersbe says these could include 'lies, blasphemous thoughts, hateful thoughts about others, doubts, and burning desires for sin.'[66] We have all been and, until we reach heaven, will continue to be a target for the enemy.

That's why the shield is so very important, but merely holding it at our side is no good. When the arrows come, we need to direct the shield towards them. Arrows can come from any direction – in front, behind, from either side, and even from above, and we won't know where to hold the shield unless we are vigilant and look out for them. We don't have very long to wait after we are saved to realise that we are under attack, and it soon becomes clear to us which arrows the devil uses to affect us most. Maybe for you it is the arrow of doubt about your salvation, or perhaps the arrow of temptation for self-glory.

So how do we practically use the shield of faith in order to extinguish these darts? Warren Wiersbe also says that the faith mentioned here is a trust in the promises and the power of God. We know from the Bible that God is greater than Satan. He is able to keep us, and He will be with us right throughout life. Holding these, and many other truths, is more than enough to extinguish any arrows Satan might shoot at us.

However, the Roman soldiers didn't always fight solitary battles. When fighting together, their shields interlocked in such a way that they could form a wall. Some Christians think that they don't need to meet or spend time with other Christians. But while God has made provision for each believer individually, the truth is that we all need each other. When we have others standing beside us, reminding us of God's promises and power, we will gain even more protection.

---

66. *The Wiersbe Bible Commentary.*

Take the helmet of salvation.
Ephesians 6:17 ESV

If you told a Roman soldier that he had to leave one piece of armour at home, I wonder what he would leave behind. I think he would have a very hard time trying to decide, and most likely it wouldn't be his helmet. Head injuries can be extremely serious, even fatal, and protection for the head is vital in many circumstances.

But did you know that Christians also need head protection? Our minds are in great danger from the enemy. The values and thoughts of this world are very dangerous to the believer, and Satan would love nothing better than for us to be affected by them. If we imbibe the world's twisted values, we will be spiritually useless. That's why Paul told the Romans not to be conformed to the world, but to be transformed by the renewal of their minds (Romans 12:2 ESV). We're sometimes made to feel out of date and old-fashioned for holding to the truth of Scripture, but we must remember that while this world changes, God never does and neither do His standards.

We put on our helmets by focussing on what God declares in His Word. The word 'salvation' doesn't only mean our salvation from sin, but every aspect of it – past, present, and future. Thinking and meditating on the whole scope of salvation will have a guarding effect on our minds and our lives. Bryan Joyce says, 'As we continue to bring our thoughts into line with Christ's thoughts, we have greater control over our sinful tendencies.'[67]

Putting on our helmets requires work on our part. You often expend a bit of effort in wrapping your heads around some complicated system in biology, or in remembering a maths formula. Sitting down to look at a theme or subject in the Bible is an even better use of brain power.

Our minds also need trained. When we begin to sense the attacks of the enemy on our minds, we can do nothing better than think of the cross and the work of our Lord Jesus Christ for us there. Satan knows that the cross means defeat for him, and no enemy wants to be reminded of defeat. So let's put on our helmets and focus on our salvation from the penalty, power, and presence of sin.

---

67. Quote from *Spiritual Warfare (7): The Helmet of Salvation* by Brian Joyce in Truth and Tidings magazine, December 2018.

Did you notice that all of the items we've been examining over the past few days are solely for the soldier's protection? Not this one! The sword is used for fighting and not for defence. Roman soldiers carried a short, sharp, double-edged sword – just like the Word of God (Hebrews 4:12). The enemy is no longer shooting fiery arrows from a distance but is close – within arm's length – so it's vital for the soldier to have an effective weapon and the ability to use it.

Thankfully, we have an effective weapon to use against the enemy. God's Word is powerful, more powerful than any weapon that Satan might try to use against us. It belongs to those who are saved, those who have the Holy Spirit dwelling in them. The original word used in the verse for 'word' is described in a Bible dictionary as meaning 'not the whole Bible as such, but... the individual scripture which the Spirit brings to our remembrance in time of need.'[68] In other words, to use the sword of the Spirit is to recall an appropriate Bible verse or passage, which directly fits the need we're facing at that moment in time. When we are tempted to worry, Matthew 6:25-34 will deliver a stabbing blow – 'Your heavenly Father knoweth... take therefore no thought for the morrow.' When our finger hovers over the screen, ready to press 'Play', 'Turn my eyes from looking at worthless things' (Psalm 119:37 ESV) will do damage to the desire which could cause us to waste precious time, or worse. And when it seems that everyone is against us and the thought slithers into our minds that even God doesn't care anymore, directing a well-aimed thrust by recalling God's words, 'I have loved you with an everlasting love' (Jeremiah 31:3 ESV), will silence the whispers of the enemy.

The sword needs to be close by. It would be a disaster if the soldier was faced with an enemy, only to discover that he'd left his sword back in the barracks. We need to have our sword, the Word, nearby too – in our mouths and hearts (Romans 10:8), and this will only happen if we read and memorise Scripture. Let's spend time polishing our swords today!

---

68. *Vine's Dictionary.*

Praying at all times in the Spirit.

Ephesians 6:18 ESV

After putting on every piece of armour, one vital action is left – to cover everything we do with prayer. To attempt to defend ourselves and fight against the enemy in our own strength is utterly pointless – we need the power of God. Prayer not only involves asking God for His help in the battle but is vital to align our minds and hearts with God's will.

We are to pray at all times. Obviously, this doesn't mean going about our day with our eyes shut, lips moving as we speak to God. Instead, it's living in such a way that prayer is our natural response to each situation we face. A simple, "Help me, Father," before and during a test at school or college, a plea for wisdom when faced with a tricky situation with a friend, an exclamation of worship when we see a glorious sunset, or a whisper of gratitude when we have won a victory over temptation are all examples of how we can pray at all times. Of course, it's essential to spend time on our knees at the beginning and end and maybe throughout each day as well.

In this battle, it is important to keep alert. A guard who sleeps on duty instead of watching out for danger will deservedly lose his job. We are in a fierce battle and we can't relax, not even for one moment. Perseverance is also vitally important.

Maybe, as you're reading this, you're feeling less than enthusiastic about the thought of spending time in prayer. Maybe your mind wanders, or you struggle to express your thoughts the way you think you should. Maybe you even wonder if God hears you at all, or if you're speaking to the ceiling. Firstly, be assured that God does hear. And secondly, no one ever said prayer was easy! Why do you think Paul uses the word 'perseverance' later in the verse? Do you think the devil wants Christians to pray? Prayer is so vital to a believer that he is going to do all in his power to hinder you from spending time with God.

Let's make prayer a priority in our lives, praying specifically about every need and detail of our day, keeping alert, and persevering in prayer in this fierce battle that rages about us.

Prayer is vital; we saw that yesterday. But not only should we take our own needs to God, we must learn to pray for others. You probably already pray for those who are closest to you, and that's good. After all, praying for someone is the greatest thing you can do for them. We're also instructed to pray for our enemies (Matthew 5:44). Praying for that person in your class who hurt you, or the teacher who picks on you isn't so easy, is it? Yet God asks us to, and we must obey. I hasten to add that it doesn't mean to pray that they'll get what they deserve!

But, while it's important and expected of us that we pray for those who don't know the Lord Jesus Christ, especially for their salvation, this passage is talking about praying for our fellow Christians. We're all in a battle with the same enemy, and we need to pray for one another. No one is safe from attack or able by their own strength to withstand the onslaught of the wicked one. We each need the power of God to resist the forces of darkness.

Have a little look at the verse at the top of the page. Who is asking for prayer? It's the great apostle Paul – the one who saw many people saved, who wrote letters which were divinely inspired, and who was even caught up to the third heaven! You'd wonder why this great man needed the Ephesian believers to pray for him, wouldn't you? Yet he's asking them to pray that words would be given to him so that he could boldly proclaim the gospel.

When I was younger, I used to think that older believers, missionaries, Bible teachers, and elders were so spiritual that they didn't really need prayer. I've come to discover that I was *so* wrong! The apostle Paul needed prayer, and so does every believer, irrespective of age or situation. Everyone faces battles and has needs that we may not even imagine. So, whether you have a list of names in a notebook to pray through, or you use your own memory, make sure not to neglect any category or age group. We all need prayer.

Take now thy son... and offer him.

Genesis 22:2

What do you have that is precious to you, that you would hate to be without? Maybe it's a possession, like your phone. Maybe you're always first in your class in Maths, and you'd hate to lose that top spot. Or you don't think you could survive if you didn't have your group of friends.

Abraham's greatest treasure was his son Isaac. He was a long-awaited son, the fulfilment of God's promise to Abraham, the one through whom God would make of Abraham a great nation, but God asked Abraham to offer him up! Can you believe it? How would you feel if God asked you to give up your most precious possession?

And yet we read that Abraham rose up. Early. If that were me, I think I might have procrastinated, put off the inevitable. But Abraham didn't delay in his obedience to God. Imagine if Abraham had refused. What if he had reasoned that there was no way that God would give him something and then ask him to release it? That if he carried out this request, the promise of the great nation would never come to pass? Abraham might have lived out the rest of his life with his precious son Isaac by his side. But he would have missed out. Not only was Isaac spared, but in verses 16-18, God tells Abraham that because he obeyed His voice, in blessing he would be blessed, in multiplying he would be multiplied, and that even all nations of the earth would be blessed.

Sometimes we must let go of something we are clinging to. In itself, it may be good, but God has something better for us. We never release something to God without Him giving us greater blessings in return. Very often, in fact, most of the time, these blessings are not physical blessings. Instead, God may be teaching us valuable lessons about Himself, showing us His character, and teaching us lessons for the future. These difficult experiences can strengthen our confidence in God, and lead to greater joy in Him. One thing we can be sure of – if God removes or asks us to give up something precious, we can be sure that He will only give us the very best in return.

> You shall stand up before the grey head and honour the face of an old man.
>
> Leviticus 19:32 ESV

SEPTEMBER 20

Each year, on the third Monday of September, Japan has a national holiday called Keiro no Hi, or Respect for the Aged Day. On this day, elderly people are celebrated and honoured, with many people using the long weekend to visit the older people in their families. If that's not possible, cards are sent or phone calls made, and gifts may also be given. Respect for elderly people isn't something that happens only on one day of the year in Japan, as it is a country with great respect for older people.

As Christians, we should also have great respect for the elderly. It's easy to look at an older person and see only a frail, helpless little old lady or man, and forget that they were once as young and full of life as you are. One day, if we are spared, that will be you and me with the walking frame, hearing aid, and boxes of pills.

When dealing with elderly people, bountiful patience may be required. Most of them don't hear as well as they did, and sometimes they struggle to understand what we're talking about even when they do hear us. Because of poor mobility, it can often take a long time for them to move a short distance. But despite their worn bodies, they are still valuable because they are human beings, made in the image of God. Those who try to tell us that elderly people have no worth because they can no longer positively contribute to society refuse to believe this very important fact.

Another reason we ought to respect elderly people is because of their experience and wisdom. They have lived through every stage of life, and while their teenage years were probably very different in many ways to yours, some things stay the same in every era. They have learned much over the decades of their lives. Don't discount their wisdom just because they grew up without the internet!

And if these reasons weren't enough, we're to respect the elderly because God says we should. Old people are to be honoured, not only in Japan on the third Monday of September, but across the world, every single day of the year.

A great multitude... from every nation, from all tribes and peoples and languages.

Revelation 7:9 ESV

A number of years ago, my husband and I attended a Bible conference in Malaysia. The conference was held in a hotel on the coast, and most of those who were attending stayed in the hotel and had their meals together. Malaysia isn't far from the equator. It's very hot and humid there, so one afternoon, between meetings, we decided to go for a swim in the hotel pool to cool down. Presently, we were joined by two young men, also believers attending the conference. As we chatted, we discovered that they were from another part of the country – East Malaysia, which shares the island of Borneo with Indonesia and Brunei. The attendees at the conference were mostly Malaysians of Chinese descent, but these young men were of a different ethnic background altogether. Their first language wasn't English or even Malay, but a language of their own people. They were from the Iban tribe, a fearsome group of headhunters who live in the jungles of Borneo... and we were sharing a swimming pool with them! Probably noticing our looks of shock, they were quick to reassure us that, while many still live in longhouses, headhunting – taking and preserving the head of a victim after they are killed – is not something their people practise nowadays.

As we chatted, I couldn't help but think of the verse at the top of the page. Rather than heaven being heavily populated by people from the western world, as we might sometimes imagine, I think we will discover that the majority are from parts of the world where we never knew there were Christians at all. After all, God is saving people from every nation, all people groups, languages, and tribes, including the fierce, headhunting Iban tribe of Borneo!

The Lord is my helper.

Hebrews 13:6

We all have an idea of what helping is. We've watched the child 'help' his mother with some household task, usually undoing her hard work in the process. You might have been called to help with some DIY task around the home. And we've maybe held out an arm to help a grandparent or another older person move from the living area to the dining table.

But none of these examples adequately illustrate what this verse actually means. The Lord is not someone we only call for when we need assistance. He is always there – the previous verse tells us that He will never leave us nor forsake us. Neither does He help in the sense of giving a hand with some task. Instead, He is all-powerful, and able to come to our aid. Hebrews 13:6 is a quotation from Psalm 118:6 – there it says, 'The Lord is on my side.'

Think of it in this way. Imagine you are walking down a dark, narrow side street. The buildings are close together and ominous doorways loom on each side. Your flitting eyes can't see far ahead, but the shadows seem to be moving and shifting. The hair on the back of your neck rises and every nerve is on edge. Then someone steps beside you, someone tall and strong. He is armed and has experience of dangerous situations, well able to protect you. He is there to help you. He is on your side.

The verse continues, 'I will not fear what man shall do unto me.' There are many scary situations in which believers may find themselves. Hudson Taylor, the famous missionary to China, was often in danger from others – men who wanted to rob and kill him. There could come a time when you or I may be in danger of our lives. Or maybe we won't face physical danger, but we might encounter hatred and scorn from others. Very often, the Lord will deliver His child, as He did for Hudson Taylor, but on occasions when He permits the danger, He will still be right there, helping and aiding in a way that only He can. So no matter in what situation in life we find ourselves, it's vital and comforting to remember that the Lord is *my* helper.

I... am as a sparrow alone upon the house top.

Psalm 102:7

As Alice walked into the lunchroom, she could see her friends all huddled together, deep in conversation. She knew what they were discussing – she'd overheard whispers that morning. Suddenly, one of them looked up, and, glancing in Alice's direction, hushed the small group. Alice could see the guilty faces as she approached, noticed the way that no one would look her in the eye. The faint hope that her invitation to Emmy's party was still to be given melted like ice cream on a warm summer's day, and in its place a cold reality struck – she was being left out.

Have you ever known what it is to be left out of something? It's not a nice feeling. Thoughts and questions go through your mind – *What's wrong with me? Why don't they want me around? I mustn't be good enough/pretty enough/funny enough for them.*

Whether this is a normal occurrence for you, or you've suddenly become unpopular for some unfathomable reason, being shunned is really tough. However, there are some things to remember. One is that those people are not the only people in your life. This group may have excluded you, but there are likely other people, probably in your family, who wouldn't dream of doing this to you. Another is that life moves on, and the people whose opinions you so value will become a distant memory. It might be tough right now, but hold on – it won't be like this forever. And maybe it's a good opportunity to look around and see if there are others being excluded that you could get to know. You might make a really good friend that you wouldn't have made otherwise.

And, lastly, even if you feel that there isn't one single person on this earth who likes you, don't forget that the Lord Jesus Christ is always with you. He will never exclude you or shun you, and He has experienced what you're going through. His disciples were the closest people He had on earth – one betrayed Him, and the others deserted Him at the very time they should have been standing with Him. He understands, and He loves you. Lean on Him, for He will never let you down.

I seek not Mine own will, but the will of the Father which hath sent Me.

John 5:30

A little ambition can be a good thing. There's nothing wrong with working hard so we can make progress. We may be able to give more to the Lord if we have a better salary someday. And God can use believers in various situations for His glory. But there are many people in this world whose chief aim in life is to be great. As well as having a large salary, their goal is to be Somebody. Some people are always trying to climb the ladder of promotion, their eyes on the top position in the company. Some want to see their name at the top of the charts. And others are seeking greatness through social media, using every possible means to increase followers and likes.

That's why it's all the more remarkable that the One who could go no higher – who was greater than the angels and co-equal with God – could say that He did not seek His own will. Instead, He left His rightful place of honour and glory and came to this earth, to a small, despised village. He knew what it was to be poor. The religious leaders of the day hated Him. Many people who followed Him proved to be fickle, only out for what He could give them. Instead of mixing with those who were in power, He associated with the outcasts.

But, greatest of all, He did not spare Himself the agony of Calvary. His death was no overpowering of a mere man. Instead, He willingly submitted Himself to the hands of wicked men, who beat Him, spat on Him, mocked Him, and crucified Him. He suffered the wrath of God against sin. And He willingly laid down His life for us.

Greatness in this life is often all there is for the poor souls who have focussed their ambition on this world, to the exclusion of any preparation for the next. How much better would it be if we were like our Lord and Saviour, refusing to make earthly greatness our focus, but instead living for the greatness of a 'well done, good and faithful servant' from the Master Himself.

Do not swear at all... Let your
'Yes' be 'Yes,' and your 'No,' 'No.'
Matthew 5:34,37 NKJV

When I was at school, people were very fond of prefacing their sentences with 'I swear'. In many instances, it was used as a verbal exclamation mark, and the more emphasis they wanted the sentence to have, the greater the enthusiasm they put into those two words. Other times, it was used to try to convince the listener of some fact, usually that the speaker really didn't commit whatever misdeed they were being accused of. And sometimes the phrase 'I swear' wasn't even enough on its own, so they added an object or even someone's life to it, in an attempt to give their sentence even more authority. What I often observed was that the greater the attempts to deny something, and the more they swore on whatever object they might choose (their granny's grave, for instance), the less likely they were to be telling the truth!

The Bible has some great instruction about using these words. Look at the top of the page. 'Do not swear at all.' There's absolutely no need for us to begin or end our sentences with 'I swear'. But why not? Doesn't it add more clout to our claims? No, actually. As Christians, we should be like our Lord and Saviour – absolutely truthful. If we are, then stating the truth is enough.

But that is dependent on our word being dependable. If someone only speaks the truth when they say, 'I swear', that means that everything else they say is untrue. As Christians, everything we say should be true, so that no one has any doubt that when we speak, we are speaking the truth. When we say 'yes', we should mean 'yes', and when we say 'no', we should mean 'no'. Of course, we're very much aware that it's often not as easy as it sounds, but we have the Holy Spirit to help us in our daily life. He will help us to become like the One who is the Truth.

I once watched a documentary series on penguins, which used footage from camouflaged spycams that had been placed around the breeding sites of three different species – Emperors, Rockhoppers, and Humboldt penguins. It was truly fascinating!

My favourite of the three is the little Rockhopper. They are the smallest of the crested penguins, only around half a metre high, and found throughout the Subantarctic. And, as their name suggests, they hop! Once they arrive at the shoreline nearest to their breeding site, they bellyflop out of the sea onto the rocks, and then use their strong legs and claws to climb and hop up the steep cliff-face. Often, a wave will wash them back into the sea and they'll need to start from scratch. But, finally, they make it to the top.

They then face a new challenge. These tiny penguins mate for life and now have to find their chosen mate amongst hundreds of thousands of other birds. It's fascinating to watch. How amazing of our God to put into these little creatures, who have spent the last few months hundreds or even thousands of kilometres apart, the instinct to return to the same spot, and be able to find the same mate.

Once the eggs are laid (usually two), the parents take turns to protect them from predators, using their sharp beaks. After a month, the chicks hatch, and when they are one month old, they join a creche with other babies, where they are taught how to swim and hunt, while their parents head back to the hunting ground for more food. At two to three months old, it's time for them to leave the nest. But before they can leave the colony to make their own way in the sea, they must learn to hop. And again, God-given instinct comes into its own. With practice, and many topples, they soon master the art of hopping, living up to their name. Off they all set, down the cliff face and into the sea. One day, they will return to the same site, and the cycle will begin all over again.

Tell them what great things the Lord has done for you, and how He has had compassion on you.
Mark 5:19 NKJV

The man was wild! He was fierce and uncontrollable, living in a cemetery and wearing no clothes. Then he met the Lord Jesus Christ who cast out the many demons that possessed him. Now things were different. You'd hardly have known it was the same man. Yet, instead of being thankful that the dangerous man from the graveyard had been transformed, the local people pleaded with the Lord Jesus to leave. Understandably, the healed man wanted to go with Him. Is there anyone who has been delivered from Satan's bondage who wouldn't want to be with the Lord?

But the Lord Jesus had something specific for this man to do. He was to go home and tell his friends what had happened. They knew, better than anyone, what he had been like. The change would be obvious to them, and they must have wondered what had caused it to take place. By recounting the kindness and dealings of the Lord with him, his testimony would bring glory to God.

Have you been saved recently? Do people notice a change in your life? Or maybe you've been saved for a while, but people have come to discover you're different. Salvation will make a change, after all. We should be different from those who don't know Christ and who are seeking their satisfaction from earthly enjoyments. If we are living as we should be, people will notice. What do you answer on a Monday morning when your classmates ask what you did at the weekend? Are you ever asked why you don't go to certain places or do certain things? Do they wonder at the peaceful way you cope during hard times? Many of these questions can provide an opportunity to tell others what the Lord has done for you.

And what *has* the Lord done for you? Why not take a couple of minutes and write down as many different spiritual blessings as you can, beginning with your salvation. When we have a grateful heart, the words will spill over. You never know, others you meet may be craving those blessings you possess.

When you do good and suffer,
if you take it patiently, this is
commendable before God.

1 Peter 2:20 NKJV

SEPTEMBER

28

The story of Darlene Deibler isn't easy to read. In fact, it's downright difficult in places. Darlene was an American missionary in the late 1930s to what was then known as the Dutch East Indies. She was saved at nine years old, and when she was ten, she heard and willingly accepted the call of God to serve Him, no matter the cost. And what that cost was, no one could have envisaged.

As the Japanese invaded the islands and countries in the Far East, the opportunity arose for Darlene and her husband, Russell, to leave. They were each convinced that they should stay. Three days later, they heard that the ship they would have been on had been torpedoed and sunk, with no survivors.

Then one day, Russell was taken by the Japanese. Darlene never saw him again. Prison camp followed for Darlene, but her situation was to become even worse. She was taken to a prison, accused of spying for the Americans. The punishment for such a crime? Beheading. As well as the knowledge of her fate, this dear servant of Christ suffered in many other ways. Basic necessities, such as water to wash, were denied her. The 'porridge' came with small stones, chaff, and worms floating in it. Insects were rife. Dysentery, cerebral malaria, and beriberi all took their toll on Darlene's body. Interrogation and torture were regular, and the distress of only being able to guess what was happening to the others in the prison added to her suffering.

Yet through it all, God never left her. Sometimes He showed His care for her in practical ways – a large bunch of bananas that she had longed for, or memories of hymns and verses of Scripture when she needed them most. Once, Darlene realised that she could no longer sense God's presence. In that time, she placed her trust in the unfailing Word of God. If God said He'd never leave her or forsake her, He meant it. She did not need to feel Him near. It was enough that He had said it.

Darlene Deibler survived. Years after the war, she wrote these words – 'I can thank God for every storm that has wrecked me upon the Rock, Christ Jesus!'[69]

---

69. *Evidence Not Seen*, by Darlene Deibler Rose, was published by Authentic in 1998.

Ye are all one in Christ Jesus.
Galatians 3:28

Racism has almost always been a problem in our world. Despite greater ease of world travel, and the vast increase in our knowledge of other countries and cultures due to the internet, racism is as rife as ever, if not more so.

When we look around us at nature, we realise that God is a God of variety, and this divine creativity is also displayed in mankind. We are all made in the image of God, yet no two people are exactly alike – even identical twins have subtle differences. Skin tone, eye and hair colour, height, build, and facial features all differ – and that's only what we see on the outside! But, as human beings, although we may look different, we will always have more similarities than differences. Acts 17:26 reminds us that God 'made of one blood all nations of men for to dwell on all the face of the earth.' We have all descended from the same family.

It's vital to remember no group of people is superior to another. God saves those from 'every tribe and language and people and nation' (Revelation 5:9 ESV). He recognises differences but holds no bias or partiality. For Christians, those who are His children and who should reflect Him in their lives, it's obvious that racism is not an option. In fact, to entertain thoughts that you are superior in some way to another ethnic group, or to disrespect someone, or worse, because they are different to you, is sin.

This is even more apparent when we read Galatians 3:28 – 'There is neither Jew nor Greek... for ye are all one in Christ Jesus.' In Christ, all racial barriers are removed, and we are united in Him. Each believer, irrespective of skin colour, language, or culture, is a child of God, and therefore our precious brother or sister in Christ. It's a bond which is closer than the physical, natural bond of family!

So, as we live in this discordant world, let's be a testimony by displaying the love of God to each of our fellow human beings, and by living in unity with our spiritual family.

I have perceived among the youths, a young man lacking sense.

Proverbs 7:7 ESV

SEPTEMBER

30

Did you ever watch a film where the character, totally unaware, was heading straight towards danger? You could see the peril, you knew who or what was lurking around the corner and maybe you even yelled at them to turn and run!

Proverbs 7 is like that. In the scene is a young man. As darkness falls, he makes his way to an area of the city where he encounters great temptation. In horror, we watch as he becomes ensnared in the clutches of an immoral, evil woman. The final glimpse we get is of him following her as an animal does when it goes to the slaughter. The ending of this tale is anything but happy – 'he does not know that it will cost him his life.'

When we look deeper at this tragic tale, we see that his actions had a deliberateness about them. Did you notice that he didn't set out in broad daylight? Instead, he waited until it was twilight. By the time he arrived, it was a 'black and dark night'. He seemed to have a destination in mind – this was no random wandering where he happened to bump into this woman. He flirted with danger – first walking nearby, then walking right to her house.

Maybe he thought he could change his mind. After all, he wasn't there yet. But temptation met him before he was ready, and he'd bargained without her persuasive speech. She made sin sound so appealing, so inviting. It would all be hidden – no one would ever know.

You may never meet a person who tempts you in this manner (although it is possible), but you have great temptation much nearer than in the streets of the city. It may be in your very hand! A few taps of the screen, and you could be in the clutches of great danger that you will struggle to extricate yourself from, and which will scar you for life and could destroy your future. You need to recognise the danger. Do battle against it. Don't reason your conscience away. Close your ears to the appealing words. Don't even go down those streets in the first place! Instead, put preventative measures in place, pray, and turn to the light of the Word of God.

Remember, you are fighting for your life!

OCTOBER

The God of all comfort; who comforteth us... that we may be able to comfort them...

2 Corinthians 1:3,4

Has something bad ever happened to you, and no matter how you looked at it you couldn't figure out any way it could ever be used for good? In fact, maybe you felt that God might even be harming His own interests in letting this trial happen!

We often can't come up with any explanation for difficulties, but the truth is that God will always have reasons for permitting such things in our lives, even if we don't understand. One simple reason could be that we will be able to help others who, in the future, will also face what we're going through right now. You see, when we're struggling through a tough time, sooner or later we'll realise that we can't deal with it on our own, and turn to God. When we do that, we'll discover words of comfort and help in the Bible. We'll learn more about God. We'll remember that He cares for us, that He helps us, and has promised that He will always be with us. We are comforted. The reasons for our trial might not be obvious, but we are content to lean on God and let Him work it all out in His time.

Then, down the line, you come across someone who, believe it or not, is going through the same difficulty you went through! They confide in you, telling you how difficult things are for them, and how they feel so alone. You know exactly what they're talking about, because you've walked in those shoes yourself. And because of this, you can assure them that you really do understand. You can tell them what you learned about God, and how He helped you through the difficulty. You can comfort them by sharing what you've learned.

So never feel that problems and difficulties are pointless. You never know how and when God may use you, and your experiences, to comfort others in the future.

All the rivers run into the sea; yet the sea is not full.

Ecclesiastes 1:7

Evaporation, condensation, precipitation, collection. You probably learned about the water cycle a long time ago. The basic facts are pretty straightforward, aren't they? Yet the water cycle wasn't 'discovered' until about 1580 by a man called Bernard Palissy, and it was only in the early 1800s that his views were finally accepted in mainstream science.

But 2500 years before Palissy worked on his theories, the water cycle had already been revealed by God. In writing about the cyclical aspect to human life in Ecclesiastes, Solomon illustrated this by the water cycle – water is collected in the seas, yet they don't overflow because it returns to where the rivers begin (evaporation, condensation, and precipitation). Amos 9:6 talks about God calling for the waters of the sea (evaporation) and pouring them out on the face of the earth (precipitation). And listen to Elihu's words recorded in the ancient book of Job – 'He draws up drops of water (evaporation), which distil as rain from the mist (condensation), which the clouds drop down and pour abundantly on man (precipitation)' (Job 36:27,28 NKJV).

We're often given the impression that science and the Bible have nothing in common, yet there are numerous examples, like this one, of scientific 'discoveries' which were in the Bible all along. Did you know that at one time many scientists strongly denied that the universe ever had a beginning? And while they still don't accept the account of creation, 'In the beginning...' is now an accepted scientific fact. So let's not be ashamed of believing the Bible. God knows more than all the scientists who ever lived – He is the Creator of the universe after all – and His Word is totally dependable. I'm excited to see what they 'discover' next, which God has already revealed in Scripture!

Before I formed you in the womb I knew you.
Jeremiah 1:5 NKJV

Sarah looked at herself in the mirror and grimaced. What she wouldn't give to have a nice, straight nose, instead of this little one that turned up at the end. Such pale skin too. And as for those freckles...!

David sat at the end of the table and pretended to inspect the contents of his lunchbox. Why did he have to be so shy and awkward? Everyone had their eyes fixed on Mark, laughing at his latest joke. Mark was so popular, so much fun to be around. While David? Well, people barely noticed him.

Grace pushed her bedroom door closed behind her and sank onto the bed. Pulling out her phone, she found her favourite playlist and hit play. At least here she could listen to whatever she wanted, no matter how strange her taste in music might seem to her friends.

You may not be Sarah, David, or Grace, but I'm pretty sure you have something you often wish that you could change. When I was your age, I often asked why God made me the way He did.

Perhaps God decided to make us all different for variety, the same way there are countless species of plants? It's possible, but there's a bigger reason – He had a plan for you. Look at the verse. He knew us before we were even formed! He knew what you would look like, and what your character traits and interests would be. Those things are not a mistake. Remember Amy Carmichael's prayer for blue eyes? God has a plan for your life, and your unique characteristics are a part of that plan. We might not understand how certain features or traits could ever be used by Him, but rest assured that He can and will use each believer in the way He sees best.

They shall... put Him to death.

Luke 18:33

OCTOBER

4

Are you the type of person who would love to see into the future? Or would you prefer to take life as it comes? Either way, if you were able to see what was going to happen, I'm sure you'd make some changes. Most of us have said at one time or another, "If I'd known then what I know now, I'd have..."

The Lord Jesus Christ knew what was ahead. He knew how people would respond to His teaching, how some would accept Him, and others would reject Him. He even knew that He would be betrayed, arrested, and put to death. His knowledge didn't change His actions. He didn't avoid going to Jerusalem at the time of Passover. He didn't avoid the Garden of Gethsemane that dark evening. He didn't hide from Judas and those sent to arrest Him. He knew they were coming. He knew what they would do to Him.

We don't know what our death may be like. If we did, we would probably take all the measures we could in order to avoid it.

The Lord Jesus knew every detail of His suffering and death. He knew exactly what men would do to Him, and how much pain He would suffer. He knew how all the disciples would forsake Him. And He knew that He would bear the full and dreadful weight of sin upon His sinless soul. Even from our standpoint, after the event, we can't begin to comprehend how much He suffered underneath the load of judgment.

But He knew and yet He went on. He did not use His foreknowledge to escape the suffering. Why? You know the answer. In the words of the hymn – 'It was for me, yes, all for me'! It was His knowledge of what is ahead for those whose sins are unforgiven that drove Him on. The dreadfulness of hell must be very great, for the Lord Jesus to have suffered all that He did in order to save sinners. Let us never take for granted all that He did for us.

Seek ye first the kingdom of God,
and His righteousness; and all these
things shall be added unto you.
Matthew 6:33

When I was your age, my mum often quoted this verse to me. She loved to remind me that if I put God first, I'd never lose out. As a teenager, there are many decisions to be made – some minor, some major, and all shades in between. But, as a Christian, in many of the situations you face, you will need to make a choice that unsaved people never consider – whether or not to put God first.

Maybe you'd love to learn how to play the guitar, but the only available lesson is Wednesday at eight o'clock – and that's Bible study night. Or maybe you've been given some money for your birthday, and you're dying to get to the nearest shopping centre. Just as you head off on your shopping trip, you remember that when you heard the missionary speak last month about the poverty in his country, you wished you had something to give. Now you do, but it will cost you that new top.

What are you going to do? Sometimes we have Scripture to guide us – Hebrews 10:25 says we should not forsake the gatherings of the local church. Other times, there are no verses in the Bible to tell us exactly what to do. In either case, the verse my mum quoted will help us make the decision – when we choose to obey God or make choices that please Him, we are seeking first the kingdom of God. And putting God first is always the right thing to do.

There's a promise attached to this instruction. Today, our blessings are spiritual and heavenly, although I've discovered that our loving God often graciously gives us earthly things as well – guitar lessons on a different night with a better teacher, perhaps, or a surprise gift from a grandparent. Even if He doesn't, we will still be 'added to'. You may not get those guitar lessons at all, but you'll have had the immeasurable blessing of learning from God's Word. You might have to make do with the clothes you have, but God has noticed your willing heart, and will reward you in heaven for your sacrifice. It's true – when we put God first, we will not lose out.

Let this mind be in you, which
was also in Christ Jesus.
Philippians 2:5

OCTOBER

6

Have you ever seen a pig wallow? It'll make its way to a wet, mucky area, and sink deep down into the mud, grunting with contentment. The word 'wallowing' even sounds a bit like a large animal indulgently rolling around in a thick, gloopy substance!

Humans often like to have a good wallow as well, but instead of mud, we choose to wallow in self-pity, misery, envy, and even self-indulgence. If I wallow, it is to serve one person, and one person only – me! How easy it is to make our way to the puddle, to sink down into the mud – the self-pity, self-indulgence, self-righteousness – and thoroughly coat ourselves, until we're totally absorbed with ourselves and our problems. The more we wallow, the more we feel justified in wallowing, and the harder it is to pull ourselves from the sticky mud.

We all have something that we use as our mud puddle. Life isn't always fair, and others seem to have it easier. People can hurt us, both intentionally and unintentionally. Maybe we look around and feel we don't measure up. Or maybe we're smug and proud of our accomplishments or appearance. The media likes to tell us we're worth it and that indulgence is our right.

But should we wallow? Let's look at the first few verses of Philippians 2. In the New King James Version, part of the passage reads – 'Let nothing be done through selfish ambition or conceit...' Do you think wallowing might fall into this category? If so, are there any instructions for what we should do instead?

Listen to this – 'Let this mind be in you, which was also in Christ Jesus...' The passage goes on to tell us about the Lord Jesus Christ, who was equal with God, yet who willingly humbled Himself. He didn't look only on His own interests, but came to die for us, so that we can have salvation through trusting in Him.

This is the mindset that we are to have. Instead of focussing on ourselves and on our circumstances, we are to be like Christ, focussing on the interests of others. If we were to do that, I have a feeling that our mud puddles could dry up completely.

The Lord is my portion.
Lamentations 3:24

When we hear the word 'portion', we tend to think that it means a small piece or section of a much bigger whole, like a birthday cake which has been cut into twelve slices. Of course, everybody wants the biggest portion, especially if it's chocolate... or is that just me?

In the Bible, the word 'portion' often refers to an inheritance. You remember the prodigal son in Luke 15 who asked his father for the portion of goods that would fall to him? In other words, he wanted his inheritance. As we read through the Bible, we don't get very far before we discover that inheritances were really important. They're still pretty important today, but back then there was a certain protocol in dividing the inheritance – in the Old Testament, the oldest son would be given a double portion. At the other end of the scale were the daughters, who usually didn't feature too highly unless they had no brothers. If you weren't the oldest son, you might feel that things weren't quite fair.

While receiving a share of a legacy can often be useful, earthly inheritances really won't matter in the long run. Money is only for time, and the only bearing it has on eternity is whether we used it for God while we were down here. Instead, Jeremiah could say, 'The *Lord* is my portion.' No earthly inheritance could ever compare to having the Lord, and all the immeasurable blessings we've been given. This inheritance is not some tiny sum left over after being divided out amongst too many people. Everyone will receive a large portion – including the younger sons and the daughters. There is no limit to the riches we have received and will continue to receive in Christ. Sometimes people receive their inheritance and it still falls short of meeting a need, but our inheritance will supply every need, and much more. Everything we have and will be given is according to the riches of His grace – bountiful and unlimited. We will forever be discovering new treasures in Christ, who is our portion.

More to be desired are they than gold, yea, than much fine gold.

Psalm 19:10

OCTOBER

8

The fifteen-year-old girl waded through the stream, then paused at the far bank to wipe her legs dry with some moss. Looking back, she could see the steep slopes she'd just climbed, and the rugged Welsh valley spread out beneath her. God's creation truly was beautiful, but she couldn't stop to admire it for long. She had many, many miles to travel.

As she set out once more on the rocky path, her bare feet sped along. For almost six long years, she had saved up, penny by penny, until finally she had enough to purchase the only thing in the world she really wanted. No longer would she need to walk two miles to her neighbours' house any time she wanted to read God's precious Word. Soon she would hold in her hands her greatest treasure – a Bible of her very own.

How many Bibles do you own? If you're like me, you've probably lost count. For us, owning a copy of God's Word is a small thing. Bibles are easily accessible and relatively inexpensive. And if, for some reason, you can't get a copy, you'll find it online. We're privileged. So privileged that we now take the availability of Bibles for granted.

That's why Mary Jones' story is so important. We can hardly imagine someone saving up for so long, and walking so far – twenty-five miles, and without shoes – to buy a Bible. I'm sure Mary could hardly wait to get home, and when she did, she probably couldn't wait to read it. Maybe she read into the wee hours of the night, and when she awoke the next morning, she probably couldn't wait to read more.

How much do you value the Word of God? Is reading it something you look forward to, or is it a task you feel obliged to do? Or have you begun to neglect it altogether? Many things have changed since Mary Jones was your age, but one thing hasn't changed at all, and that's the importance of God's Word. It's as relevant today as it ever was, and if we neglect it, we are losing out.

So next time we lift one of our Bibles, let's remember Mary Jones and thank God for such a precious possession.

The law of Thy mouth is better unto me than thousands of gold and silver.

Psalm 119:72

Yesterday we thought about Mary Jones and how she valued God's Word so much that she saved up for six years and then walked twenty-five miles barefoot to buy a Bible. She must have felt that it was a dream come true when the precious Book was placed in her hands and she made her way back across the Welsh mountains to her little home. When she got back, I wonder where she kept the Bible. I imagine it was likely placed on a shelf or on a bureau, somewhere out of harm's way, where feet wouldn't stand on it, and food couldn't stain it. She probably took great pains to make sure her hands were clean before she touched it; she would be careful not to crease the pages or destroy the binding. It had been worth a great deal of sacrifice to her, and if something happened, she couldn't order another Bible online with express delivery or pop into the nearest Christian book shop.

How do you treat your Bible? Do you look after it, handling it with care? Or do you carelessly drop it on the floor, where it is stepped on and gets dirty and damaged? Is it looking bedraggled and uncared for? In comparison, how do you treat your phone? Which gets the better treatment? Accidents happen, and a well-read Bible will understandably show signs of usage, but should your Bible look like a book that an unsupervised toddler or your family pet has attacked, rather than something that is a treasure? Obviously, there is nothing sacred about the leather, paper, and ink, and we worship God, not a book, but we must remember that the Bible is the Word of God, so it should be treated with respect. How will you look after your Bible today?

> We which are alive and remain shall be caught up... in the clouds, to meet the Lord in the air.
>
> 1 Thessalonians 4:17

OCTOBER 10

Where I live, buzzards are a common sight. High in the sky they circle, keeping their eye firmly fixed on some small creature down below. Then they swoop to the ground, and, in an instant, snatch their victim away. Because of this method of hunting, buzzards, along with other birds of prey such as hawks and eagles, belong to a family called *raptors*. And it's from this word that another word is derived – *rapture*.

While the word isn't actually mentioned in the Bible, 1 Thessalonians 4 speaks about the rapture of believers. The Thessalonians were concerned that their fellow believers who had already died were going to miss out in some way if the Lord returned, so the apostle Paul wrote to them to assure them that they wouldn't miss out. In doing so, he explained a very important biblical truth.

One day, maybe today, the Lord will return, not to the earth just yet, but to the air. He will come 'with a shout, with the voice of an archangel, and with the trumpet of God' (NKJV). Bodies of believers who have already died will rise from the graves and from the sea. Those which have been cremated will come together again.

Then those of us who are alive on earth will be caught up together with them in an instant, even quicker than a buzzard catching its prey, and we will all meet the Lord in the air. One moment, we will be at school or work, eating dinner, sleeping, travelling in the car or on the bus, and the next, we will be with the Lord! If you've never really thought about this passage before, or understood what it means, it may be hard to take in. Planes need a lot of fuel and a great deal of engineering to be able to make their way up into the clouds, and yet we're going to be there in an instant. And what about gravity?

Don't forget who created the laws of gravity. The One who created them is perfectly entitled to overrule any force that holds us to the earth – and He will overrule it! We will experience this event – a greater miracle than this world has ever seen. And then we will 'always be with the Lord.'

Therefore let us not sleep.
1 Thessalonians 5:6

Yesterday we learned about the rapture – the return of the Lord to the air to take the Christians to heaven. One moment we'll be here, the next we'll be in the air. It's going to be sudden – we won't have any warning, and this leads us to today's subject – how the rapture should affect our everyday life.

Paul didn't only write one letter to the Thessalonians. Right after the first letter, we'll find another one he wrote – 2 Thessalonians. But because we only have one side of the conversation, we have to read between the lines to figure out what happened or what was said to prompt Paul to write what he did. It seems that some of the Thessalonians were taking seriously what Paul had said about the Lord returning at any moment. So seriously, in fact, that they had quit their jobs and were sitting around, waiting for the rapture. Because they had nothing to occupy their time, they were beginning to indulge in gossip and were poking their noses into others' business.

This was not God's intention at all. It still isn't. Although the Lord may come before school tomorrow, it doesn't mean that you don't need to do your homework! It doesn't mean that you don't need to study for your exams, or think about a career, or make any sort of plans for the future.

On the other hand, there's a very real danger that we might forget, or not really believe, that He is coming soon, and so we put down our roots too deeply. We can get very earthbound, and instead of living for the next world, we focus too much on this one.

We need to live a balanced life. It's possible (and looking at the state of the world, probable) that the Lord will come very soon. God is merciful – He has waited around two thousand years in mercy on a perishing world, but we don't know of any reason why He wouldn't come today. There is not one single prophecy in the Bible to be fulfilled before He comes. The rapture should be kept at the forefront of our minds. In the meantime, we ought to keep busy, and have God-focussed goals and plans for whatever time we have left here. 'Therefore, let us not sleep!'

> Blessed is that servant, whom his lord when he cometh shall find so doing.
>
> Matthew 24:46

OCTOBER 12

While the Lord has waited in mercy, He could come at any moment. What would you like to be doing when He comes? I'm sure you're probably answering 'praying', or 'reading the Bible', or 'at church'. While it's probable that there will be many believers doing these very things when they're caught up, the reality is that not all believers will. Because of different time zones, it will be night in certain parts of the world, and many in these countries will be sleeping. In the countries where it is daytime, others will be doing normal things like homework, grocery shopping, or cutting the lawn.

While it's vital to read, pray, and attend the gatherings of the local church, we also glorify God in our daily lives – when washing the car, or practising for our Spanish oral, for example. Those things are perfectly legitimate and right. But what if He comes when we're doing something that we know doesn't please Him? If we have trusted Christ, we are saved forever. We can't lose our salvation, and the Lord Jesus won't leave any of His redeemed ones behind – He died for us, after all. We are forgiven, and that will never change, but wouldn't it be so sad to meet Christ when we know that what we've been doing hasn't pleased Him?

Or what about baptism? I remember having a conversation with my cousin about baptism, when we were teenagers. Sitting on the stairs leading up to her little attic bedroom, we both agreed that we wanted to be baptised before the Lord came. If we weren't baptised, we would still be in heaven, but would have lost the opportunity to have obeyed God.

The any-moment return of the Lord Jesus to the air isn't some wonderful-but-fanciful story. It's a reality, and because it is real, it should affect how we live. We may have things to put right in our lives. There may be certain habits we need to change. We might need to do some things a little differently. Let's live today as if we'll be with Him by bedtime – because we could be!

The God of hope fill you with all joy and peace in believing, that ye may abound in hope.

Romans 15:13

"Christians have so much to be happy about – they should be a joyful people!" I'm sure you've heard this statement before, but maybe you rolled your eyes and muttered to yourself that it's much easier to say than to put into practice. It's a fact that life is hard, even for Christians. God never promised that we would be saved from the everyday struggles and hardships that human beings face. So how can we be joyful?

Earlier in the year, we learned that joy and happiness aren't the same thing. Happiness depends on our external surroundings. Reading a good book in the sunshine whilst eating a bar of chocolate would make me happy. But when the rain comes on, and I drop the book in a puddle in my hurry to get indoors, my happiness is spoiled. Joy, on the other hand, is independent of what is going on around us.

Lately, I've been pondering where joy comes from, and I've discovered that it is closely linked with peace. In our verse for today, the apostle Paul links the two words together. If we have peace, it will produce joy, but if we have no peace, it will be very difficult to have joy.

So how do we have peace? Well, we're told in Romans 5:1 that, 'being justified by faith, we have peace with God through our Lord Jesus Christ'. Peace with God is one of the indisputable blessings of salvation. We can't argue against it; we can't deny it. It's a fact. To be saved and not have peace with God is an impossibility. Once we were at enmity with God, but we've been reconciled to Him. If that's not something that will give us joy – deep and settled, irrespective of external circumstances – I don't know what will!

There's another word that's often linked with peace and joy, and that's hope. We have the sure and certain hope of a great prospect ahead. We have peace because of what happened in the past, because of that we can have joy in the present, and we rejoice in our hope for the future. Christians really should be a joyful people after all!

And we know that all things work together for good to them that love God.

Romans 8:28

OCTOBER 14

When I was seven years old, my granda had a stroke. He was so ill that the doctors weren't sure if he'd survive. He did, but spent the remaining almost seventeen years in a wheelchair, unable to walk without assistance. Although he lost his ability to sing, he was still able to speak, and his mental capacity wasn't diminished in the slightest. We loved Granda. He was wise, down-to-earth, and godly, with a huge repertoire of funny stories that he loved to tell – usually while laughing so hard himself that we could hardly work out what he was saying! Amongst his grandchildren, he had no favourites, yet he made each of us feel special and took a great interest in our lives.

One year, I got a birthday card, written by Granny as usual, but with a little note, from Granda, paper-clipped to the inside. It read,

Romans 8:28 – We know that <u>all</u> things work together for good to them that love God.

<u>All</u> things for good
There is not one exception
For He who promised also will fulfil,
His hand controls
His word all things obeying,
Work out the purpose of His perfect will.

As for God, His way is perfect – Psalm 18:30.

I can't remember what was going on in my life that prompted this personal message, but Granda must have discerned that I needed this assurance. For him, Romans 8:28 wasn't a verse to be glibly quoted when others are finding things hard. He'd lived it out. For such an active and independent man to be confined to a wheelchair, depending on others to do the most basic tasks for him, must have been humiliating and desperately frustrating, yet I never once remember him complaining. I think the secret of his acceptance is in the words on the page, and especially the little word he underlined. <u>All</u> things – strokes included! Granda knew that God was in control and that He assuredly would use the difficulties for good. After all, God's way is *perfect*!

The Lord hath called by name Bezaleel... and He hath filled him...
Exodus 35:30,31

A few thousand years ago, there was a very important job to be done. It required someone with the right skills and abilities. Natural talent, although important, wouldn't be enough. Mistakes weren't an option; there would only be one chance to get it right. This task was going to need very special workers to carry it out, but no job advertisements went online. There was no need, because God had already chosen His workmen – Bezaleel of the tribe of Judah, and Aholiab of the tribe of Dan.

Not only had God chosen these men, He had fitted them for the task. He knew what they would need – firstly, the Spirit of God, followed by skill, intelligence, knowledge, and all craftsmanship. They would need to teach others, so God gave them this desire and ability too. All their efforts would be for God alone, and for His glory. They were to build and furnish the tabernacle – the dwelling place of God in the camp of Israel.

God has something for each of us to do too. He doesn't require a house on earth now, but He does require people who are committed to living and working for Him. God fits each of us with the skills we require to do the tasks He has for us. That knowledge you are gaining, and those interests and talents you have, may be an indication of God's choice of career or occupation for you. Choosing to study subjects that you know you struggle with, rather than ones you're good at, isn't a very wise move unless you have a really solid reason.

Maybe Bezaleel and Aholiab wondered why they had been given skills in craftmanship when they were living in tents in the desert. After all, their skills weren't being put to use. But God had a better plan than mere housebuilding. He had given and would continue to give these men the skills they needed to do the task *He* had for them to do.

And He will do the same for you. Wherever you will bring God most glory, He will fit you perfectly for that spot – not only in natural ability, but in God-given skill, intelligence, and knowledge, and with the Holy Spirit's power and help.

If you have anything against anyone, forgive him.

Mark 11:25 NKJV

Daniel shrugged his schoolbag higher on his shoulder and kicked at a stone on the road. It shot down the tarmac before bouncing three times and landing in the grass verge. If only the memory of what Kelly had done could be dispensed with so easily! Instead, it kept gnawing at him, the way a rat had chewed through a plastic water pipe on the farm. Every morning, his first waking thought was of Kelly's betrayal. As he brushed his teeth and dressed for school, he formulated and rehearsed a cutting response to her spiteful deed. But when he arrived, his speech dissolved in a fresh renewal of speechless anger at the humiliation she had caused him. His friend Leah assured him that everyone else, including Kelly, had forgotten the incident. Maybe they had, but he hadn't. How could he? Leah also told him he should forgive Kelly. After all, Christ had forgiven Daniel, so how could he do less than forgive Kelly? But there was a difference, wasn't there? Kelly had never asked for forgiveness.

Daniel sighed and turned into the lane leading to his house. He hadn't done well in his latest round of tests. Teachers would soon be asking questions. It was hard to concentrate. Even helping out on the farm didn't hold the same satisfaction as before. He couldn't go on like this: if he did, the rat of resentment would chew right through, and rather than a slow leak, there would be an explosion.

"Let go!" The words that Leah had spoken to him earlier in the day whispered through the rustling beech trees. "Forgetting can be really difficult, but you can at least let it go." Daniel stopped to lean his arms on the top bar of a gate and watch the sheep. Leah was right. His resentment was binding him, strangling him. By holding the memory of what Kelly had done, he had thought to punish her, but instead he was the one who was suffering.

It was time. Time to confess his grudge-holding and his lack of forgiveness. Time to give it to God and to let it go. He might need to release it on more than one occasion, but in time he would be able to truthfully say he had forgiven her. After all, he owed God no less.

Out of the abundance of the heart the mouth speaketh.
Matthew 12:34

Do you know what happens when you open a fizzy drink just after it's been given a vigorous shake? The second the can is opened, or the bottle top is removed, the release of the built-up pressure causes the drink to spray everywhere.

Isn't that a bit like our words? Stressful situations can cause our emotions to build up inside us, and the release can be very messy! Whatever is in our heart overflows into our speech, and it's so easy to let loose with words that can't be recaptured and returned.

So how do we prevent the outpouring of angry, hurtful, and unwise words? The glaringly obvious fact, which we hate to admit, is that our words are a reflection of what is in our hearts. When we speak hurtful words, it's because we have entertained hurtful thoughts.

Let's take a look for a moment at One whose words were always pure and holy. Every single word that He spoke was perfect and totally appropriate to the situation. He spoke words of comfort to the bereaved, words of grace to sinners, and words of rebuke to the hypocritical Pharisees. He never had to apologise, for He could never do or say anything wrong. From His heart overflowed words that displayed His perfect character.

The desire of every believer is to be like Christ. Thank God, in a future day we will be like Him, with all sin removed. But our goal today is that we should strive to reflect Him so that others will see Christ in us. What's the secret to speaking Christlike words? It's a Christlike heart. The more we read and learn of Him, the more like Him we will be, and the more our words will reflect the heart of Christ.

My words shall not pass away.

Matthew 24:35

OCTOBER

18

It often seems as if the world is full of rules and guidelines. You probably have rules at your school, some of which you might think are totally unnecessary. And no matter what job you end up with in life, there will be some form of guidelines, either verbal or written, that you will have to follow.

But the more guidelines we seem to be given in the professional world, the more people talk about freedom and tolerance in their personal lives. Freedom to believe what we want, say what we want, and do what we want. If it feels right, do it. In some cases, even if it doesn't feel right, if we want to do it, nothing or no one should stop us. Beliefs that were accepted in the past seem to be no longer welcome in our society. The whole world is changing rapidly, and it makes our heads spin. What is right? What is wrong? How do we even know anymore? And wouldn't it be good if we had some guidelines to keep us right?

Thankfully, we do! No matter how much the world changes, this guidebook is always valid. Professional guidelines are always being updated, but God's Word never needs to be amended. It was up-to-date when it was written, and it is still perfectly up-to-date today. Even if the world keeps changing, which it will, the Bible will still stand as sure as ever. When God calls something sin, it is still sin. When He states a fact, He still means it.

When guidelines are given, they are meant to be followed to ensure the safety and comfort of everyone – not only of those who are following the guidelines, but of people around them. It's the same with God's guidebook. He made us, He knows us. He has a reason for the guidelines; they were given out of love and care for us. To ditch them for the world's wisdom is a very dangerous thing to do. Put your trust in your Father's wisdom, and follow His Word.

God created... every living creature... which the waters brought forth... and every winged fowl.

Genesis 1:21

F or most people, there's something about home that we love. But blindfold us, take us hundreds of miles away (or far less in many cases!), and tell us to find our way back on foot without our phones, signposts, or the help of others, and we'll probably still be wandering around in a few years' time. We really don't have a good homing instinct.

Many animals do, however. Numerous species of birds make journeys of up to twenty thousand miles each spring and autumn, moving between their summer and winter homes. Man has made use of the amazing ability of homing pigeons to carry messages in times of war. But the ability to travel long distances without GPS isn't only limited to birds. Last autumn, my husband was awed at the sight of thousands of butterflies making their way south to an overwintering site in Mexico. Various mammals also migrate, including wildebeest in the Serengeti in Africa, and the saiga antelope in Kazakhstan. Salmon make a journey upriver of up to four thousand miles, choosing the best routes and leaping up waterfalls, in order to find the same section of stream in which they were born! What makes this even more remarkable is that when they left this spot as young fish, they spent several years feeding in the open sea before returning to lay their own eggs.[70] How do they do it?

It seems difficult to say for sure, but the in-built instinct for returning creatures may be to do with one, or a combination, of the following factors – the earth's magnetic field, cues from the position of the sun, infrasound data, sense of smell, and temperature and saline information about the water in the case of fish.

While many instincts of animals have puzzled scientists and caused them to delve deeper into research, we love to remember that these creatures were designed and created by God. It was He who placed the homing instinct into so many of them. No matter how much time, effort, and resources are expended, mankind will always be learning, never able to exhaust the depths of God's knowledge and wisdom. Best of all, this God is *our* God, who is our helper, our keeper, and our preserver (Psalm 121).

---

70. Information from https://www.scientificamerican.com/article/how-do-spawning-fish-navigate-back/ and *Creation's Story* by Robert W. Cargill.

If you confess with your mouth that Jesus is Lord and believe in your heart that God raised Him from the dead, you will be saved.

Romans 10:9 ESV

OCTOBER 20

As Christians, one of our greatest joys is knowing that others have also trusted Christ for salvation. We love to hear about people being saved from their sins and becoming new creatures in Christ Jesus, living to bring glory to God. It's especially joyful when a friend or relative gets saved – they are now our brother or sister in Christ, and we have so much more in common than we ever had before. It's important to remember, though, that salvation is between a person and God. Because of this, our desire to see people come to know the Lord Jesus Christ as Saviour needs to be mixed with wisdom.

There have been many cases over the years of people being talked into a profession of salvation, maybe by a well-meaning friend or religious leader. We can see from our verse today that a statement of confession doesn't save unless it is accompanied by belief. Salvation is 'repentance toward God, and faith toward our Lord Jesus Christ', as Acts 20:21 says. And that's not something that we can talk a person into, no matter how much we might like to. Of course, that doesn't mean we never speak to others about their souls. People often have questions that we may well be able to answer from the Word of God, and many, maybe including you, have been helped by a chat with someone who is already on their way to heaven.

The danger is when we give people a formula – maybe a prayer, or a few rote phrases, or signing their name somewhere – and when they have dutifully carried out what they've been asked to do, we tell them they are now on their way to heaven. Salvation is not found in completing an external act, but in trusting in Christ alone. We don't know what is going on in that person's heart before God, so we can't declare that they are now saved. Often the best thing to do is to focus their attention on Christ as revealed in the Scriptures, then retreat to pray for them. After all, the Lord Jesus said, "Him that cometh to Me I will in no wise cast out" (John 6:37).

Christ Jesus: who, being in the
form of God... made Himself of
no reputation.
Philippians 2:5-7

The Human Rights Act was passed in the United Kingdom in 1998. It protects various human rights by law – the right to life, liberty, privacy, education, freedom of thought, religion and belief, and free speech. Everyone is equal and should be treated as such – God doesn't discriminate, and neither should we.

The danger with focussing on human rights, however, especially in the developed world, is that we can begin to feel entitled. Instead of making sure everyone else has their rights, we concentrate on ourselves. *Freedom of speech...* for us, not for the person who has the opposite viewpoint. *The right to life...* as long as it's our life and not the life of the unborn child we're responsible for.

The truth is that if God had given us our rights, we would all have been under His judgment for eternity. We don't deserve a shred of mercy.

The only One who lived on this earth who ever truly merited any rights was the Lord Jesus Christ. He dwelled in the splendour of glory, worshipped and adored by angels. Praise and honour were His true and unquestionable rights. He left it all. Just think – the One who was equal with God – who *was* God – leaving the grandeur of glory for the poverty of a tiny village in ancient Israel. Even to come as royalty would have been an unimaginable condescension, but to stoop even lower, and finally to submit to the hands of wicked men who crucified Him, is extraordinary. The reason is even more astounding. The One who deserved everything gave it up for those who deserved nothing but punishment for eternity. In love, He was willing to forego His rights in order that we, whose only right was judgment, would be given blessings that we never could have anticipated.

While we rejoice in this, it should have a practical effect on our lives. The point of the passage in Philippians 2 is not only to create gratitude in our hearts, but to teach us to hold others in higher regard than ourselves – to follow the example of the Lord Jesus Christ. When we do this, our rights, which previously seemed so important, won't even come into it.

I will say of the Lord, He is my refuge and my fortress.

Psalm 91:2

OCTOBER

22

I love visiting castles, learning about the past, and wondering who walked across the well-worn, cold, stone floors before me. As I look out over the walls, I sometimes like to imagine that I'm watching for signs of an approaching enemy. Of course, there aren't likely to be any enemies marching towards a British castle nowadays, but if there were, well, it is definitely a safe place to be, with its thick, impenetrable walls, towers, and gates. Even the positions of the castles were chosen with defence in mind. Many, like Edinburgh Castle, are set on a high, steep hill. Others use water as their main defence – Elizabeth Castle in Jersey can only be accessed by foot at low tide. Slits in the walls were designed for shooting arrows through, with some castles later being adapted for guns. To attack a castle would have meant risking being shot, or having a heavy, spiked portcullis dropped on your head as you went through the gateway. Of course, castles, often known as fortresses, haven't always been failsafe refuges, but back then they were the safest places to be.

In the same way as those medieval fortresses provided refuge and safety to those sheltered inside, so the Lord will keep those who have put their trust in Him. The forces of evil cannot penetrate the solid walls of God's protection. When the sky is ablaze with the hail of fiery darts, the fortress will prove to be impenetrable. Not one arrow will find its target. The battering ram can make no impact on the solid gates of God's safeguarding of the believer. The enemy may attack again and again, but the fortress will stand sure, safely sheltering those inside.

Often the biggest risk to ancient fortresses was that of siege, with a lack of supplies causing the inhabitants to starve. This needn't be a worry for Christians, because our God not only protects us, but provides for us as well.

The devil may – and often will – attack, but the Word of God assures us that we are sheltered and safe within a fortress which is far mightier than any which exist on earth.

Why are ye so fearful?
Mark 4:40

One of my favourite stories in the gospels is of the storm on the Sea of Galilee in Mark 4. When the Lord Jesus and His disciples had set off from the shore, all was calm, but now a great storm has arisen – so great that waves fill the ship. The disciples awake the Lord, who is asleep in the back of the boat. In their panic and distress, the words explode from them – "Do You not care that we are perishing?"

Did He care? Of course He did! We know without a doubt that the Lord Jesus has nothing but the greatest care for His children. What's more, there's no way the boat could have gone down with Him on board. He would tell them later on, "I am the life." He could not die, until He would lay down His life Himself as a sacrifice for sinners.

He had also promised that they would safely reach their destination – "Let us pass over unto the other side." As Creator and God, He did not have to add 'weather permitting' or 'God willing'. If He said they would pass over, they would pass over.

We all face storms in our lives, but no matter how wild the winds, or how great the waves, we have the Lord Jesus Christ with us. He has given us the promise 'I am with you always' (Matthew 28:20). He doesn't need to add any qualifying clauses. His word is totally sure and certain. He will not let us sink.

The Lord Jesus knew the storm was on its way. He could have prevented it or calmed it sooner. Why didn't He? There were lessons about Him the disciples needed to learn. Maybe He wanted them to recognise their need of Him, and to learn to trust Him in the storm. The storms we go through are no different. Sometimes the Lord waits for us to acknowledge our need of Him. Other times He wants us to trust Him while the storm is raging. One thing is sure – it cannot last forever. Sooner or later, the wind will cease, and the waves will be calm. In the meantime, we must trust Him. After all, He has promised to be with us in the waters (Isaiah 43:2).

Not I, but Christ.

Galatians 2:20

'There was nothing in the world to be done but to fall down on one's knees and, accepting this Saviour and His salvation, praise Him for evermore.' So said Hudson Taylor, recounting the moment he was saved at seventeen years old. This marked a turning point in his life, with new desires to read the Bible, pray, and work for God. He had a real awareness that he was not his own, and this led to a deep longing to see others won for Christ.

A few months after he was saved, Hudson emerged from a crisis experience in his Christian life, with the settled consciousness that God was calling him to serve Him in China, and for the next few years he worked towards that purpose. Not only did he choose a medical career with missionary work in mind, he made it his goal to live by faith, never asking anyone for money, even in the direst of circumstances. Only one object threatened to turn him from God's will, and that was a young woman. When Hudson learned that she was not prepared to go to China, effectively ending their relationship, the devil tempted him to give up the idea of missionary work. In Hudson's distress, he turned to God, and emerged with a greater sense of the call of God on his life. Afterwards, he wrote to his mother, 'I cannot describe how I long... to carry the Glad Tidings to poor, perishing sinners... I feel as if I could not live if something is not done for China.' His love and earnest desire for the salvation of the Chinese people never wavered throughout his long life, nor did his wholehearted trust in the faithfulness of God.

When he was twenty-one years old, Hudson finally set sail for China. After a long and perilous sea voyage halfway across the world, the boat sailed up the estuary of a river, and Hudson saw, for the first time, men from that great nation for whose salvation he had long prayed.

Hudson Taylor may have arrived in China, but he had many years of deep trials to face. Through them all, he proved God to be faithful, and God used him in the salvation of countless Chinese and in the spreading of the gospel through that vast land.[71]

---

71. From *The Biography of James Hudson Taylor* by F. and M. Howard Taylor.

Abel... brought of the firstlings of his flock.
Genesis 4:4

Where I grew up, amongst the hills and valleys of rural Northern Ireland, sheep and lambs were a common sight, so I didn't think it unusual to have so many references to sheep in the Bible. Those living in the land of Israel probably felt the same way. Maybe you live somewhere where sheep aren't very common, and you wonder why they feature highly in the Scriptures. Interestingly, sheep can be used as a picture of a sinner (Isaiah 53:6), Christians (John 10:27-28), and of the Lord Jesus Christ (Isaiah 53:7).

Many times, the Lord Jesus Christ is represented in the lamb. Over the next week we'll be discovering a number of mentions of the lamb throughout the Bible. We'll learn the story of redemption and view how it builds to a climax in the book of Revelation. It will be a fascinating study!

Today, we turn to the first mention of 'sheep' and 'flock' in the Bible. Although the word 'lamb' isn't actually mentioned, I think it is implied in the wording used. But, before we get ahead of ourselves, let's get the background to the story.

Adam and Eve, after they sinned and were put out of the Garden of Eden, had two sons called Cain and Abel. Genesis 4 tells us that Abel kept sheep, but Cain worked the ground. We don't know what the occasion was, but one day Cain brought an offering of what he had grown to the Lord, while Abel brought of the firstborn of his flock. Young sheep are known as lambs until they are one year old, and my guess is that the animals that Abel brought were probably young.

While there is debate as to whether Cain's sacrifice was rejected because of his attitude, or because it didn't involve the shedding of blood, the truth remains that Abel's sacrifice pleased the Lord. When their parents had sinned, God had clothed them with coats of skin. An animal had had to die for them. Abel likely realised that shedding of blood was necessary. What he didn't understand was that one day, about four thousand years down the line, God's own Son would shed His blood and become a sacrifice for sin, bringing fulfilment to the type first introduced in this story.

God will provide Himself a lamb for a burnt offering.

Genesis 22:8

OCTOBER **26**

O f all the stories in the Bible, this is one of my favourites. I love to read of the obedience of Abraham and the submission of Isaac. There are so many practical lessons we can learn from it, but I especially love to see Christ in this Old Testament passage.

We likely all know the story. If it's been a while since you've read it, take a few minutes to read the chapter. Abraham is being tested by God and has been told to take his precious son Isaac, go to a certain mountain, and offer him for a burnt offering. Abraham arises and goes, taking everything that he needs for the sacrifice. But Isaac has noticed one glaring omission. They have the wood, the fire, even a knife, but there's no lamb for a sacrifice. I'm sure he must have wondered as they made the long trek to the land of Moriah. Everything is here – except for the lamb. But it's not until they leave the servants behind and begin to climb the mountain – just the two of them – that he asks his father the question that's on his heart. "Where is the lamb for a burnt offering?"

If you'd been Abraham, how would you have answered? "Well, Isaac, you see, it's like this – *you're* actually going to be the sacrifice"? Or, "Let's talk about that when we get there"? Instead, Abraham's answer, which on first glance might seem to a casual reader like false reassurance to a hapless Isaac, reverberates down through the ages of time, arriving at Calvary, when the innocent Lamb of God's providing was sacrificed for a world of lost sinners. Abraham was given a glimpse of God's redemption plan.

Isn't it interesting that God provided a *ram* for the sacrifice when Abraham had said that God would provide for Himself a *lamb*? The word 'lamb' had significance and reached far beyond the present situation to a future day when One would come who would be known as the Lamb of God.

Your lamb shall be without blemish.
Exodus 12:5

The Passover is a major theme throughout the Bible, and central to the Passover is the lamb. I urge you to take the time to read the first twelve chapters of Exodus, especially if you're unfamiliar with the story of the exodus of the children of Israel from Egypt. When you come to chapter 12, you'll be introduced to God's plan for their redemption – the lamb. This lamb is a very beautiful picture of our Lord Jesus Christ, as we can see from various instructions given and a number of things that are said about it.

First of all, we see in verse 4 that while the household might be too small for the lamb, the lamb was never too small for the household. Here we learn that Christ is fully sufficient for every believer. We will never come to an end of wonderful things to learn about Christ and on which we can meditate.

The lamb was to be without blemish, kept from the tenth to the fourteenth day of the month, presumably for observation to prove that no flaw was found in it. Our Lord Jesus Christ is truly spotless and sinless – 'in Him is no sin' (1 John 3:5). He spent three and a half years in the public eye, and no one could point a finger of accusation at Him.

The lamb's blood was to be shed. In the upper room, while Judas was betraying Him, the Lord Jesus talked about His blood which would be shed (Matthew 26:28). Moreover, no bone of the Passover lamb was to be broken (Exodus 12:46) and this was fulfilled at the cross when not one bone of the Lord Jesus Christ was broken. Instead, the lamb was to be roast with fire. Our Saviour bore the fire of the wrath of God.

There was a set time for the lamb to be killed. Originally, the religious leaders didn't want to put the Lord Jesus to death at Passover time, so was it a coincidence that He died at the time that the Passover lambs were likely being slain?

The Israelites in the book of Exodus had no idea of the importance of the commands regarding the Passover, yet each detail was essential as it foreshadowed the Lamb of God, whose blood would be shed for an entire world.

Reading through the Bible from Genesis to Revelation is a great idea! But how many of us get stuck partway through Exodus? We love the stories in Genesis, and Exodus starts off with great excitement, with the Passover, the parting of the Red Sea, and the happenings in the wilderness. Then, as if we've suddenly reached the base of a mountain, it gets a bit steep. The chapters don't seem as interesting. Things get confusing. And when we get to Leviticus, we can barely sort one offering from another. What were the offerings all about anyway? And why do they even matter to us today?

The reason they matter is because, within them, we will see Christ. Hebrews 10:1 says that the law was a shadow of good things to come. The sacrifices were pointing forward to the greatest sacrifice of all – our Lord Jesus Christ. You see, God can only be approached on the basis of sacrifice. The difference between those sacrifices in the Old Testament and the death of Christ is that the sacrifices which were offered couldn't take away sin in the way that it is forever removed by the blood of Christ. Continual offerings needed to be made.

Often, the lamb was used as a sacrifice in various offerings. A lamb is docile and meek, illustrating the submission of our Lord Jesus Christ as He was crucified for us. It had to be without blemish – the Lord Jesus was absolutely and perfectly sinless. Each day, two lambs were offered for a continual burnt offering – one in the morning, one in the evening. The burnt offering had to do with the people's approach to God, and it is precious to remember that the burnt offering caused a pleasing aroma to rise to God. Everything about Christ pleased the Father. The lamb was also used in the peace offering, which was an offering of praise and thanksgiving (Leviticus 3:6,7), and in the offering for sin (Leviticus 5:6).

I've only pulled back the curtain the tiniest bit and given you the smallest of glimpses into the rich symbolism in the offerings. There's so much more, and it will be well worth your time to study this part of your Bible and view Christ as the Lamb.[72]

---

72. *Looking Through the Shadows* by Adam D. Thropay, published by Scripture Teaching Library Ltd in 2016, is only one of a number of good books and commentaries about the subject which you can use to help you with your study.

He is brought as a lamb to the slaughter.
Isaiah 53:7

The slaughter of animals is not a pleasant subject to consider, and even less so when it involves a lamb. UK law dictates that, except for specific reasons, an animal to be slaughtered is stunned first so their death is humane. But in the slaughter of lambs in Bible times no stunning would take place. The meek, gentle, innocent creature would be led away to a harsh and painful death with a knife. It's hard to think about, isn't it? Yet this is the reaction that God wants us to have, because if we recoil at the thought of an innocent lamb being slain, we get the faintest of pictures of the injustice of the death of the Lord Jesus Christ.

He was meek (Matthew 11:29), and sinless (1 John 3:5). When they came to arrest Him, He went willingly. When they accused Him, He was silent. He gave His back to the smiters, and His cheeks to those who plucked off the hair: He hid not His face from shame and spitting (Isaiah 50:6). He could have called thousands of angels (Matthew 26:53) who would have swiftly and gladly moved to do His bidding, yet He stayed silent. He let cruel Roman soldiers nail His hands and His feet to a rough, wooden cross. He was led as a lamb to the slaughter.

But there was more. If all that the cross had involved had been what man did to the Lord Jesus, that would have been terrible, but the Lord suffered more than we could ever begin to comprehend. Isaiah 53:10 says, 'Yet it pleased the Lord to bruise Him; He hath put Him to grief: when Thou shalt make His soul an offering for sin...' On the cross, the Lord Jesus was made an offering. All the blood of all the lambs that had been slain in all the sacrifices could never take away sin, but here was One – a perfect sacrifice – who would bear sin in all its totality. How could you begin to imagine the full weight of it on His holy, sinless soul? The Lamb's blood was shed, and the fire was spent on the sacrifice, bringing a pleasant aroma to God, and providing the way for us to be fully forgiven.

Behold the Lamb of God, which taketh away the sin of the world.

John 1:29

One of the many things I love about the Bible is that no matter how deep we want to dig, we'll never exhaust all the treasures within it, yet there is enough lying on the surface for the newest believer to enjoy. The topic of the lamb falls into both categories. There are references to the lamb that require a bit of digging to discover precious things, and then there are references like this one, which are so obvious that no one could miss it.

A few days ago, we watched Abraham and Isaac making their way to the mountain of sacrifice. En route, Isaac turns to his father and asks a valid question – "Where is the lamb?" At this point, let's hit pause and skip through almost two thousand years, before landing in the AD 30s. We see two men – John the Baptist and the Lord Jesus Christ. John the Baptist is about to speak, so let's turn up the volume and listen carefully. "Behold the Lamb of God!" Here is the ultimate answer to Isaac's question all those years before. The Lamb is here, on this earth, sent by God Himself! And in case there was any doubt as to why the Lamb of God was here on earth, John finishes, "which taketh away the sin of the world."

I often wonder if those who heard John speak realised for the first time that all those sacrifices which had been offered throughout the ages were pointing forward to One who would come. Over the millennia, men had been bringing sacrifices, but now God had sent the perfect sacrifice, the One who could remove sin forever. No longer was the Jewish nation the only people God would make provision for – it would be for the whole world.[73]

God's chosen earthly people were the Jews – the Jewish nation were redeemed from Egypt by the blood of the lamb, and the instructions for sacrifice were given to the Jewish people, yet we have been brought into blessing. 1 Corinthians 5:7, written to Gentiles, says, 'Christ *our* passover is sacrificed for us.' Let's thank God today for His love and mercy to us!

---

73. *The Wiersbe Bible Commentary.*

Worthy is the Lamb that was slain.

Revelation 5:12

When we begin to study a book of the Bible, we're told that it's a good idea to read through it a number of times and look out for key words – words that are mentioned often. If we look up these words in a concordance (either online or a hard copy), we'll usually find that they are used much more frequently in certain books of the Bible than in others. Judging by the number of references to *Lamb* in the book of Revelation, I think we can safely conclude that it is one of the key words.

The first mention of the Lamb in Revelation is in chapter 5. John is weeping because no one is found worthy to open the book (usually thought to be the title deeds of earth). One of the elders instructs him not to weep because the Lion of the tribe of Judah is able and worthy to open the book. The lion is a majestic animal and signifies kingship, courage, and victory, and so typifies the Lord Jesus Christ in all His majesty and might. But when John looks, he doesn't behold a lion. Instead, he sees a Lamb as it had been slain! There couldn't be any greater contrast than a slain lamb and a mighty lion, yet Christ fulfils both types perfectly. We've discovered this week that the lamb is an important theme throughout our Bible, firstly as it pointed forward to the perfect sacrifice who was to come, and then as a title of the Lord Jesus in the New Testament, because He fulfilled the sacrifices in the Old by His suffering and death at Calvary.

The very fact that the Lord Jesus is called the slain Lamb in Revelation shows that His sacrificial death will forever be remembered. It isn't something that will be relegated to the past and forgotten about. Instead, it will be at the forefront of our minds for all eternity. We will worship Him and praise Him forever for redeeming us to God by His blood, out of every kindred, and tongue, and people, and nation (Revelation 5:9). In that day, we will proclaim with a loud voice, "Worthy is the Lamb!"

NOVEMBER

For to me to live is Christ,
and to die is gain.
Philippians 1:21

The young woman set down her baby and followed her husband from the room where they had been held captive. Bound with ropes, they were led through the streets of the town to a hill, where the woman watched as her husband was ordered to kneel and was then beheaded. Moments later, suffering the same fate, she was reunited with him in glory.

John and Betty Stam were American missionaries to China in the 1930s. From their teenage years, both were determined to live for God. As time passed, John began to be greatly burdened for the Chinese people and became increasingly convinced that God would have him go to China to tell people of the Lord Jesus Christ.

Betty, although born in America, was brought up in China by missionary parents. When she left to go to America for her education, she had a great desire to return to China as a missionary herself to win others to the Saviour. She was a plain and unassuming girl, but a very gifted poet, and many of her poems and writings show the depth of her spiritual experience and desires. While still at college, she wrote, 'I don't know what God has in store for me... It's as clear as daylight to me that the only worthwhile life is one of unconditional surrender to God's will, and of living in His way, trusting His love and guidance.'[74] Less than a decade later, she and her husband would give their lives for their Saviour.

None of us knows what is ahead. In terms of the earthly and temporal, following Christ is certain to be costly. The Stams left home and family. They turned away from a comfortable lifestyle, and ultimately gave their lives. They knew when they left their baby in that room, they'd never see her again on this earth. For them to live was Christ. But in following Him unto death, John and Betty Stam found their greatest gain.

---

74. The Stams' story is told in *The Triumph of John and Betty Stam* by Mrs Howard Taylor, published by Overseas Missionary Fellowship in 1935.

> Now the serpent... said
> to the woman, 'Has God
> indeed said...?'
>
> Genesis 3:1 NKJV

NOVEMBER

2

Y ou are in the most wonderful garden. Everywhere you look, there is nothing but beauty. And not only is this garden stunning, growing on the trees are the tastiest fruits you could imagine, all free for the taking. That is, apart from the fruit from one tree in the middle. It isn't to be eaten. Everything else, however, is freely given to be enjoyed.

You recognise this garden, don't you? It's the Garden of Eden. And you know what comes next. Take another look and you'll see the serpent, maybe lounging against one of the trees near the centre (because it is thought that in those days snakes were upright). He's waiting for someone. Eve. And when she comes, he's going to sow a seed. Not into the fertile ground, but into her ear.

Closer she strolls, admiring the beauty around her, maybe selecting a shiny, purple plum. Then her eyes light on the tree in the middle of the garden. At that point, the devil (for that's who the serpent is in disguise) sows his seed. "Has God indeed said, 'You shall not eat of every tree?'" Do you notice what the devil is doing? He's sowing a seed of **doubt**.

What is doubt? One definition is 'a feeling of uncertainty or lack of conviction.' The devil loves to make people doubt God's Word. Think about it – if we are uncertain about God's Word, or lack conviction in what God says, we're less likely to obey. We'll hesitate to praise and glorify God. Satan has always wanted to rob God of His glory, and by making us doubt, that's exactly what he's doing.

But did you notice in the definition of the word that doubt is a *feeling*? Feelings originate from within and aren't necessarily based on truth. In some instances in our lives, feelings of uncertainty might turn out to be well-founded, but never when it comes to the Word of God. God is truth, and everything He says is totally dependable.

So when the devil whispers to us, 'Has God said?' we can turn to the Bible, point to the Scripture, and say a firm and resounding 'Yes!'

Then the serpent said to
the woman, "You will not
surely die."

Genesis 3:4 NKJV

"The Bible is only a book of made-up stories written by men."

"The Bible is out of date and irrelevant to our modern day."

"I know God said that, but does it really matter? It's the twenty-first century, after all!"

Do any of these statements sound familiar to you? I'm sure you've heard them, maybe numerous times. After all, the Bible isn't a very popular book in our society nowadays. Not because *it* has changed in any way, but because our *society* has changed. People want to do their own thing. They don't like being told what they should or shouldn't do, so the easy solution is to dismiss instruction.

Yesterday we saw that the devil caused Eve to doubt God's Word. The next thing he does is to flat-out contradict what God told Adam and Eve. Just like the devil is still doing today, he **dismisses** the Word of God. In effect, he's saying, "God's wrong. He told you you'd die, but you won't. The Word of God that you heard? It's unreliable – don't live by those standards. Do your own thing!" Sound familiar?

So is the Bible reliable, or is it a 'bunch of made-up stories'? There is actually far more evidence for its reliability than we have space for here! Take a look at prophecy, for instance – in the book of Daniel, many events which were future when the book was written have now been fulfilled in remarkably accurate detail. Think about the number of human writers – around forty of them, of different ages, and from various backgrounds and locations, whose accounts and writings all fit together beautifully, yet without being identical, proving that they weren't copying from each other. And what about the life-changing effects of God's Word on people's lives, arguably the biggest piece of evidence for the Bible's reliability?

If the Bible is real – and it is! – then its instructions and truths are still relevant. Never forget that while mankind's morals and goals may change, God never changes. He is the same now as He was in Genesis 1:1, and even the same as He was from all eternity.

'For ever, O Lord, Thy Word is settled in heaven' (Psalm 119:89).

The serpent said... "For God knows that in the day you eat of it... you will be like God."

Genesis 3:4,5 NKJV

NOVEMBER

4

Over the past couple of days, we've been overhearing what the devil is saying to Eve – planting a seed of doubt and dismissing God's Word. He has another ploy up his sleeve. But before we learn what that is, let's take another look around us.

This garden is truly beautiful, a feast for the eyes, with majestic trees, brightly coloured flowers, lush grass, and a river running through it all. It's a feast for the taste as well. In it, you'll discover the largest selection of fresh, ripe, pick-your-own fruit. It's the best fruit you could ever find – perfect, juicy, and full of flavour, fit for a queen or a president. And, apart from the fruit from that one tree in the middle of the garden, all free for the taking.

Now the devil sows another seed. This one is called **discontent**. Wouldn't you think that with all the trees that they were allowed to eat from, Eve would be perfectly content? And she was, until Satan sowed that seed. Now, instead of focussing on everything God had given them, Eve's attention was turned to the only tree that God had said they *weren't* to eat from. Eve began to think that God was withholding something from her. Something good. Something much more desirable than all the bountiful blessings that they had richly received.

You know what happens next. Eve took, ate, gave to Adam, and the consequences were immediate and disastrous. As sinners, we know all about that choice. God was not trying to withhold something better from them. Instead, He was preserving them.

The devil is still trying to make us believe that God is withholding something wonderful from us. When things go wrong, or we don't get what we want, it's tempting to think that God is being unkind. We couldn't be farther from the truth! Everything that God does and commands is done out of love and care for us. So when – or even better, before – Satan tries to make you doubt, dismisses the Word of God, or sows a seed of discontent, turn to the Scriptures. God's Word is the source and substance of truth.

Jesus Christ... gave Himself
for us... to purify for Himself a
people... zealous for good works.

Titus 2:13,14 ESV

How do you know what's important to someone? Maybe there's a person in your class you haven't known very long, and you've never been to their house, but every time you talk, certain things – fashion, sport, pets, or music – keep cropping up in conversation. You begin to realise that these things are important to this person. Others likely draw conclusions about you from what you often talk about as well.

We can apply the same rule to Bible study. When you begin to look at a passage or study a book of the Bible, it's a good idea to look for words and phrases which appear often, and highlight them. Titus is a short epistle with only three chapters, but there are a number of words and phrases which you'll find repeated. One of these is 'good works'.

There are religions in the world which state that to get to heaven we must do good works, but how would someone ever know how many good works were needed? Titus 3:5 ESV says that 'He saved us, not because of works done by us in righteousness, but according to His own mercy.'

As believers, though – 'His own special people' (Titus 2:14 NKJV) – God expects us to be zealous ('filled with intense enthusiasm' as one online dictionary explains the word[75]) for good works. It's obviously extremely important... but why? One reason is that we will be like the Lord Jesus Christ. It says of Him in Acts 10:38 that while here on earth He 'went about doing good'. We can and should do good works for everyone – strangers and family members, enemies and friends, believers and unbelievers. In fact, by making unbelievers the focus of our good works, we may draw them to our Saviour for salvation. But, best of all, doing good works will bring glory to God. Have a look around – what good works can you do today?

---

75. https://www.thefreedictionary.com/zealous

Man looketh on the outward appearance, but the Lord looketh on the heart.

1 Samuel 16:7

6

NOVEMBER

I rummaged through the bananas in the Spanish supermarket, trying to find one that wasn't so short and stumpy and didn't have black marks all over the skin. Finally, I had to give up – the perfect banana wasn't to be found. But, later, when I peeled back the skin and took a bite, I realised that my assessment was all wrong. Inside there wasn't a blemish, and the perfectly ripe fruit was full of flavour.

It got me thinking. I had judged the banana from what I could see on the outside... and isn't that what happens with people so often today? In this age of social media, appearance seems to be more important than it ever was before. We see pictures of people with perfect bodies, fashionable clothes, and flawless faces and hair, and we're made to feel that the exterior is all important.

In 1 Samuel 16, the prophet Samuel was given the task of identifying the next king of Israel. Jesse's sons began to pass by him one by one. Eliab was tall and handsome. "Surely," thought Samuel, "this is the one God has chosen to be king."

But what did the Lord say? "Do not look at his appearance or at his physical stature, because I have refused him. For the Lord does not see as man sees; for man looks at the outward appearance, but the Lord looks at the heart" (1 Samuel 16:7 NKJV).

The Bible has a lot to say about what's outside and what's inside. For example, in 1 Peter 3:3-4 NKJV, as well as being instructed on their outward adornment, the women are told not to let their adornment be merely outward, but rather 'the hidden person of the heart, with the incorruptible beauty of a gentle and quiet spirit, which is *very precious in the sight of God.*'

Although these verses are about women, the principle applies to men too. Everyone is under extreme pressure to look good, but we need to be reminded that it's what's inside that counts. What God finds very precious is that believers live a godly life – a life that pleases Him.

After all, He sees the heart, and this is the only part that truly matters.

7

NOVEMBER

The Lord is my strength and song.
Exodus 15:2

I n Exodus 15, the children of Israel have just crossed the Red Sea and are praising God for their deliverance. Not too long before this, the mood was very different. A large company of people of all ages were trapped, with the sea before them and the army of Egypt behind them. If they'd ever felt their weakness, it had to have been then. There was nothing they could do to help themselves. It was up to God to deliver them – but how, they weren't quite sure.

God proved Himself well able to help. With His mighty strength, He opened up the Red Sea and the vast company of people walked through on dry land. That wasn't all. When all the Israelites were safely across, God caused the path through the sea to close, and all the armies of Egypt were drowned. The Israelites' links with Egypt were severed – they needn't fear anything from them anymore.

Do you ever feel as if you are standing on the shores of the Red Sea? Maybe feeling trapped in a situation that you know you are not able for? No matter which way you turn, you can't see any way out. You lack the strength for the way ahead, and as time passes, you become more and more conscious of your inability and your weakness.

Never forget that we have a great God! As the hymn says, 'I am weak, but Thou art strong.'[76] We are not expected to do anything in our own strength, because we don't have enough. Even the apostle Paul felt his own weakness – he recounted how the Lord told him that His strength was made perfect in weakness, and then Paul finished by saying, 'When I am weak, then am I strong' (2 Corinthians 12:10).

So when we are weak, we must rest on God. We have the promise of His strength. He will work for us, and through us. And when we find He is our strength, as He promised, He will also be our song as we praise and worship Him.

---

76. *Just a Closer Walk with Thee*, author unknown.

Live peaceably with all men.

Romans 12:18

I'm writing this three and a half hours into a ten-hour flight, and, let me tell you, 'living peaceably' certainly isn't happening amongst some of my fellow passengers! Cramped conditions, along with a patch of bumpy turbulence, doesn't make for a calm mindset. And when nerves are frayed, it's easy to fall out with people. One person demanding their rights (in this case, not allowing the person in front to recline their seat), leads to another demanding theirs, until the whole thing blows up in an argument.

It doesn't only happen in the air. It can be hard to stay calm when we feel someone has overstepped the mark. Getting our toes trampled on makes us lash out. And then there are some people you meet who are out to pick a fight. Ever come across someone who seems to make it their life's goal to be awkward? No matter what you do, how much you bend over backwards to try to keep them happy, they get angry with you. Living peaceably with people like that is barely possible, through no fault of yours. I think that's why the verse quoted is prefaced with 'as much as lieth in you'. To the best of our ability, we're to live at peace with others.

The best example is the Lord Jesus Christ. Many, many times He was provoked by the religious leaders, yet He always displayed the utmost patience and peace. 'When He was reviled, [He] reviled not again; when He suffered, He threatened not' (1 Peter 2:23). At a time when our fear and self-centredness would have got the better of us, the Lord remained as calm as He ever was. He was the only One who could have justly demanded His rights, yet He gave them up for you and me.

So when you are next confronted with an argument, take a moment to consider whether it is a battle worth fighting. In most cases, we'll likely find that foregoing those two or three extra inches of aeroplane seat space aren't really that important, especially in light of what Christ sacrificed for us.

Thou art of purer eyes than to behold evil, and canst not look on iniquity.

Habakkuk 1:13

Amongst the little books towards the end of the Old Testament, you will find nuggets such as the verse above. From it, we learn the lesson that God is absolutely holy, and we see how utterly obnoxious sin is to Him – He cannot look with approval upon it.

Now, keep that in mind while we think of the Lord Jesus Christ, who was God incarnate, coming to this earth to live amongst sinful people. Can you imagine how it must have grieved His heart to witness the sinful words and deeds that were all around Him? Even their very thoughts grieved Him. He knew what was in man; no one needed to tell Him what they were thinking.

Let's go further. On Calvary, the Lord Jesus – the holy One who was God, of purer eyes than to behold evil – was actually made sin for us (2 Corinthians 5:21)! While on the cross, God dealt with the Lord Jesus Christ as if He were sin itself. He laid on Him the iniquity of us all (Isaiah 53:6). And while He was bearing the wrath of God that sin deserved, He was bearing it alone. God could not look on iniquity. "My God, My God, why hast Thou forsaken Me? Why art Thou so far from helping Me, and from the words of My roaring?" (Psalm 22:1) was His cry.

It is at the cross that we see the utter vileness and seriousness of sin against a righteous, holy God. We will never fully understand what our Lord Jesus Christ went through to cleanse us and bring us to God, but let's stand a little longer today at the cross and consider, thanking Him from the depths of our souls for saving us.

Now the sons of Eli... knew not the Lord.

1 Samuel 2:12

NOVEMBER

10

A few years ago, circumstances led to us taking a thirteen-hour road trip across the southern part of Mexico. We'd been driving all day, and we were tired, but we needed to reach a certain city by bedtime. The sun set in a magnificent glow of pinks and oranges over the Gulf of Mexico, then darkness gradually fell. As we drove, we left all streetlights behind. Surrounding us was a thick, black darkness. It was then we noticed the stars. They were far more numerous and much brighter than I'd ever seen them before, even in rural Northern Ireland, where the skies are unpolluted by light. I couldn't help but think of the old saying – stars shine brightest when the night is darkest.

In the Bible, Hannah illustrates this truth in a remarkable way. Things were really dark in the days when she lived. The sons of the priest were behaving abominably, taking for themselves that which belonged to God. And Eli, their father, seemed to have lost control for he wasn't doing anything about it. And if this was how things were in the temple, God's dwelling place, how much worse was it in the rest of the land? These were the days when every man did that which was right in his own eyes.

Enter Hannah. This lady had the spiritual vision to see that things weren't as they ought to be. She knew that if anything was going to change, a man of God would be needed to serve Him, so she began to pray to that end. Her deep exercise and honour for God stands out like the brightest star against the black night of wickedness.

Maybe you feel that your surroundings are like those in which Hannah found herself. Evil and wickedness are rife on every side. Few have any desire to live for God or even have any thought of God.

Don't let the world dull your sparkle and zeal for God. He sees how you stand out against the black backdrop of your surroundings. It pleases Him greatly. Not long after these events, God said, 'Them that honour Me I will honour.' God hasn't changed. He still honours those who honour Him. Shine on!

This do in remembrance of Me.
Luke 22:19

At 11 o'clock in the morning of 11th November 1918, World War I officially ended. It brought to a close more than four years of fighting and bloodshed which left millions dead and wounded. But despite being called the War to End All Wars, in little over twenty years' time another war would erupt, lasting six years and killing tens of millions in the deadliest conflict in history. In the years since, other wars have taken place in which men and women have given their lives for their countries.

We owe a lot to those courageous people. Had they not boldly gone into conflict, life might have looked very different for most of us today. Because they gave up so much for us, it is dishonourable to discount their sacrifice and deem it irrelevant. That's why taking time to remember them is so important.

There is another sacrifice we ought to remember – a vastly superior one with much greater significance. The Lord Jesus Christ came to this earth to die for those who were at enmity with Him! His life wasn't taken from Him – instead, He laid it down of Himself. He didn't come to protect our freedom and inheritance – He came to give us perfect freedom and a far richer inheritance.

And He has asked us to remember Him. Before He died, He introduced the disciples to the Lord's Supper, which is now an occasion when believers in a local church regularly gather to take bread and a cup of wine in order to remember the Lord Jesus. To willingly neglect to do this when we have the opportunity is to discount His sacrifice, especially since He Himself has asked us to remember Him. If those from the battlefields of earth deserve our remembrance and respect, how much more does our Lord Jesus Christ, who loved us and gave Himself for us as an offering and a sacrifice to God (Ephesians 5:2)?

The waters stood above the mountains.

Psalm 104:6

NOVEMBER

12

Did you know that fossils of shellfish have been found in the Himalayas, the highest mountain range in the world? Isn't there something strange about fossils of sea fish being discovered thousands of feet above sea level? How did they manage to get there?

There's a very simple answer to that question – a global flood. Some argue that there couldn't have been enough water on the planet to have covered Mount Everest, but we must remember that the topography of the earth was totally devastated and re-landscaped by the force of water, and by the fountains of the deep being broken up. With all the rearrangement of the earth's surface, mountains appeared, including the Himalayas, complete with sea creatures buried in layers of mud.

There are other evidences for the flood in geography. Two layers of rock can be traced right from North America across the Atlantic, one ending in Israel and the other in England. It would have taken a global flood to have laid down so much sediment over so vast a distance. If the layers had been laid down slowly over time, weathering would have occurred. Instead, there is no evidence of erosion within the layers.

Mass graveyards of animals buried together have also been found, and fossils have been discovered of creatures having died mid-bite, or while giving birth – all signalling that something sudden had occurred. We all know that rapid decay takes place from the moment of death, yet the detail in fossils is remarkable, even in creatures like jellyfish. There's no way these creatures would still have the detail they do, if they had been buried for the length of time that some scientists propose.

There's something that scientists have never been able to find – transitional forms of life. If evolution had occurred, and fossils had been formed slowly over time as some scientists believe, the huge variety of fossils should have had previous forms buried in layers beneath them. Yet, for all the searching, no rock layers are missing, and no transitional forms have ever been found.

Contrary to popular opinion, creation and a global flood do not contradict the findings of science. When we open our eyes, we see how everything in our world fits into the account of Scripture, in exactly the way that God planned.[77]

---

77. Material is based on presentation notes from the Apologetics Conference (2019) at Hebron Gospel Hall, Bicester, by David Vallance. The powerpoint presentation can be accessed at https://hebrongospelhall.org/sermons/fossils-dinosaurs-apemen-58-min/

Thy word have I hid in mine
heart, that I might not sin
against Thee.

Psalm 119:11

August Van Ryn was a Dutchman who was saved at twenty years of age. Four years later, he was told that he might lose his eyesight, so he began to memorise Scripture. He learned the whole of the New Testament and large portions of the Old Testament, including the entire book of Psalms. Although his eyesight was restored, the time spent learning Scripture wasn't wasted, because he became a highly respected Bible teacher with great biblical knowledge.

Do you learn Scripture? Maybe you've been given verses to learn in Sunday school or Bible class, but you don't see the point. After all, the Bible is online, and doesn't everyone carry a phone with them? Why would you actually need the verses in your mind?

For one – in case, like August Van Ryn, you lose your sight! Eyes are fragile, and it's not impossible that one day you or I may no longer be able to read. Or have you considered that the tide of popularity is turning against Christians? The day could come when reading a Bible will be illegal. If that happens, you'll be glad for any Scripture stored in your heart.

There are other reasons – ones that will benefit us right now. When we learn verses, we are letting the Word of God dwell in us. Knowing the passage off by heart gives us a better understanding of it than merely reading does, and when we learn verses about Christ, we can meditate on Him no matter where we are or what we're doing. Knowing Scripture also helps us express our praise and supplications to God in prayer.

Another very important reason to learn Scripture is found in our verse for today. The Word of God in our hearts has a preserving effect when we're faced with temptation to sin. Not only will we know God's commands, we will have God's wisdom on how to handle various trying situations.

Knowing God's Word is also invaluable when it comes to speaking to others, either encouraging believers, or telling unbelievers about the Saviour. Pulling out your phone and searching for a relevant verse mid-conversation isn't always appropriate.

Let's all make a point of learning more of God's Word. Rather than wasting our time, we will discover that it has eternal benefits.

I have blotted out, as a thick cloud, thy transgressions, and, as a cloud, thy sins.

Isaiah 44:22

The plane moves down the runway, faster and faster, finally rising into the air. The airport recedes, and cars shrink until they resemble small dots. Buildings and roads begin to look like toys for very tiny children. Maybe, like me, you try to identify familiar landmarks as the plane banks – a mountain, or a town, or lake. You crane your neck for one last glimpse as wisps of white begin to obscure your view. Before long, the entire aircraft is enveloped in a thick cloud and you struggle to even see the tips of the wings. Everything that you had been viewing from the window has been blotted out.

God uses the image of a thick cloud to describe His view of sins which have been forgiven by Him. Isn't it remarkable that He, the all-powerful God, actually chooses to blot them out of sight?

Clouds aren't always high in the sky – instead we may experience them closer to earth as fog. Fog shuts runways, slows traffic to a crawl, and severely hampers people's ability to navigate. And there is not one thing we can do about it! Snow can be cleared, ice can be melted, but humans are helpless when it comes to removing fog.

So it is with the cloud covering our sins. We can't see through it; we can't remove it. We know, from driving in thick fog at night, that light shining on fog will reflect and make it even more difficult to see through. The light of God's Word will show us how thoroughly God has dealt with our sins and give us the complete assurance that God has forever blotted them out.

Before they call, I will answer.
Isaiah 65:24

Helen Roseveare was a missionary doctor in what is now known as the Democratic Republic of Congo. One night, in spite of her best efforts, a mother died, leaving her premature baby and a two-year-old girl. Although they were on the equator, nights could be very chilly, and the baby needed a hot water bottle to keep her warm throughout the cold night. The nurse went to fetch one but returned with the news that their last hot water bottle had burst. Dr Roseveare gave the nurse instructions on how to keep the baby warm that night, but somehow they would need to find a new water bottle soon. If the baby got chilled, the little one could easily die.

The next morning, Dr Roseveare visited the orphanage. While there, she told the children about the little baby and the need for a hot water bottle. As they prayed about the problem, one little girl not only asked God for a hot water bottle to arrive that very afternoon, but added a request for a doll for the baby's older sister, 'so she'll know You really love her.' Dr Roseveare admired her faith but doubted it could happen. The only way that a doll and a hot water bottle could arrive that day would be from home, and no one had sent a parcel in four years! And why would anyone think of sending a hot water bottle to the equator?

That very afternoon a large parcel arrived. The children from the orphanage gathered around in excitement as Dr Roseveare opened it. In it were knitted jerseys, bandages, raisins... and then a hot water bottle! The little girl who had prayed rushed forward. "If God has sent the bottle, He must have sent the doll!" she said. And sure enough, right at the bottom, was a small, beautifully dressed doll!

The parcel had been packaged and sent five months earlier by Dr Roseveare's former Sunday school class. Not only had it arrived right when they needed it most, but with exactly what they'd asked God for.[78]

What a wonderful illustration of the care and sovereignty of God, who can guide people and order situations to meet a need that may as yet be unknown.

---

78. As told in https://pastorhistorian.com/2018/05/06/prayer-a-water-bottle-and-a-baby-doll/

They recognized that they had been with Jesus.

Acts 4:13 ESV

NOVEMBER 16

Wildly swinging his sword and lopping off a man's ear (was he aiming for his head?), taking to his heels and fleeing when things didn't go as he expected, and later persistently denying the very One he had promised to die with; this was not Peter's finest hour. All his great claims and boasts had dissolved, and he was left miserable and weeping in the knowledge that what he had said and done could not be recalled.

Another scene, only a few months later – this time two men are arrested and put in prison overnight. In the morning, the authorities bring them out to question them. These men are confident; the sight of the large crowd doesn't bother them. As the interrogation begins, one of them takes the lead. Boldly, he proclaims the name of Jesus Christ as the only way of salvation.

Do you know who this man is? It's Peter, the one who at least three times denied that he knew the Lord! The audience included the high priest – the owner of the palace where Peter vehemently denied the Lord Jesus, and the master of Malchus, the man whose ear had been cut off by Peter and healed by the Lord Jesus.

The rulers, elders, and scribes don't seem to have comprehended who they had arrested until Peter began to speak. At this point, they realised that these men were 'uneducated, common men' who spoke with a Galilean accent, and they recognised them as those who had been with Jesus.

How many present in that room had heard Peter's strong denial only weeks before? Surely they were astounded at the about-turn. In all likelihood, Peter was now proclaiming the name of the Lord before some of the very people to whom he had previously denied it.

If Peter's story had ended with the gospels, we wouldn't have been surprised. After all, God might have restored Peter, but how could He use someone who had failed so spectacularly? That isn't how God works. Instead, He gave him another opportunity to stand for Christ.

God hasn't changed. Like Peter, we fail the Lord Jesus Christ, denying Him by words and deeds, and often by what we *don't* say! But God is gracious. God wasn't finished with Peter, and He isn't finished with us either!

This is the will of God, even your sanctification.
1 Thessalonians 4:3

The period of life that you're currently in will probably bring the greatest concentration of life-altering choices you'll ever have to make. Choosing to continue or drop certain subjects will affect the courses open to you, and ultimately your choice of a career. It may even be in these years that you will make a decision about choosing a boyfriend or girlfriend who could turn out to be your husband or wife! So with all these decisions to make, you're probably doing what most young Christians do when faced with a choice – praying... a lot! But how do you know God's will for your life?

Over the next three days I want to look at some ways we can know God's will. I've discovered that while it may not be easy to find at times, it's absolutely worthwhile to search for.

The best thing you can do is read God's Word. There are certain things that God wants us to do, which are made very plain in the Scriptures. For example, the verse at the top of the page is clear that His will for us is purity. It's something we don't even need to pray about. Other things like this include baptism, gathering with a company of believers, love for others, kindness etc. Neither do we need to spend time determining whether God's will for us is to have an unsaved boyfriend or girlfriend – 2 Corinthians 6:14 makes it crystal clear that it never can be His will.

When we are searching the Scriptures to find God's will, there is a danger of which we need to be aware. This danger is taking verses out of context – applying something to ourselves that was meant for someone else, or that was speaking about a different situation entirely. It's easy to make up our minds what we want to do and then pluck out a verse to fit that desire, but that's not finding God's will!

Instead, your first step is to look for clear commands pertaining to your situation. The more you read your Bible, the more familiar you will be with God's instructions, so don't neglect the Word of God.

The heart of man plans his way, but the Lord establishes his steps.

Proverbs 16:9 ESV

NOVEMBER 18

We learned yesterday that the first thing we must do when searching for God's will is to see if the Bible has anything to say about our situation. When it does, we generally need to look no further. But sometimes there are decisions to make that aren't so clear, where there is nothing wrong with either choice, and where we won't be committing any sin by choosing one option over the other.

God can lead us in whatever way He chooses, and sometimes that leading will be in a direction we never anticipated. The majority of the time, though, the right choice will often be the most logical one. Take choosing subjects at school, for instance. If history drives you crazy, it's probably not the subject you should choose. Or if, like me, your drawing skills don't stretch far beyond stick men, why would you pick art?

I've heard of people who believed that God was leading them to become a missionary doctor, so they ordered their education towards that goal. God has a plan for each of us, and if that is His plan for you, He will help you each step of the way. But if you faint at the sight of blood, or can't understand biology, then maybe you'd best not set your sights on a medical career, no matter how much you'd love to serve God as a medical missionary.

It's good to be balanced too – in things that have no bearing for good or evil, and without long-term ramifications, we are free to choose as we deem best. You don't need to specifically pray about whether to eat cornflakes or porridge in the morning, or whether to buy a red t-shirt or a blue one. We can go to God with anything – no problem is too tiny for Him to listen to, but to feel duty-bound to pray over every minute detail of everyday life is not how God would have us live. After all, He created us with a thinking mind, and He expects us to use it!

That ye might be filled with the knowledge of His will.

Colossians 1:9

Are you ever asked to choose something for someone from a coffee shop? How easy do you find it to make that choice? Do they prefer a latte with a shot of caramel, or are they more a hot-chocolate-with-whipped-cream-and-marshmallows type of person? I'm sure you'll agree that the more time you spend with someone, the easier it is to know their preference.

Quite often, when we are looking for guidance in certain situations, we feel as if we come to a fork in the road. There are no clear commands in Scripture to guide us, and it's not at all obvious which road we should choose. How do we figure out what path God would have us take? After all, the young Christian who loves God will want to please Him and walk in the way of His choosing.

How well do you know God? Have you ever considered that the more time you spend in God's Word, getting to know Him, the easier it will be to know what pleases Him? You'll learn more of His character, of how He has guided others and of what is truly important.

And God certainly guides through His Word in a very special way. There were times when I'd been praying about a decision, and during my everyday reading a verse or phrase that I'd never really noticed before, yet which was so very relevant to my situation, almost seemed to stand out from the page. God was clearly leading me. Sometimes we'll hear something said at a meeting or service, or read something based on Scripture that we know is a word from God for us.

It's natural to fear making a mistake, but my experience of determining God's will has been that, while it may take longer than we'd like, He is able to reassure us in many ways that we are walking in His will. And once you have peace about your decision, move forward in confidence, always leaning on Him.

Hate evil, and love good, and establish justice in the gate.

Amos 5:15 ESV

NOVEMBER

20

Atheists love to imply that Christians are weak people who feel the need to cling to something. And while there isn't one of us who would deny that we desperately need Christ, many believers are anything but the delicate, fragile creatures that atheists purport us to be.

One such man was Sir Robert Anderson, who was born in Dublin in 1841. After studying in France and at Trinity College, Dublin, he became a barrister, and later was made Irish Agent at the Home Office, with responsibility for dealing with the terrorist threat of Irish republicans. In 1888, Sir Robert was promoted to Assistant Commissioner at Scotland Yard and Head of the Criminal Investigation Department (CID). This was at the height of the Jack-the-Ripper scare, when a number of women were brutally murdered in the East End of London. Although no one was ever charged with the crimes, due to a lack of witnesses willing to testify, Anderson's legacy was a dramatic decrease in crime rates during the years he was in office. He was appointed Companion of the Order of Bath in 1896, and on his retirement in 1901 became Knight Commander of the Order of Bath.

The most important happening in Sir Robert Anderson's life occurred years before he rose to prominence. Despite being brought up in a religious home, he had never accepted Christ as his Saviour. After hearing John Hall proclaiming 'forgiveness of sins, and eternal life as God's gift in grace, unreserved and unconditional,' Robert tackled him about what he considered to be heresies. Before the preacher left him, he asked Robert if he was going to accept Christ or reject Him. 'After a pause – I know not how prolonged – I exclaimed, "In God's Name I will accept Christ." I turned homewards with the peace of God filling my heart.' Sir Robert Anderson went on to write many books on biblical topics, some of which are still in print and are often recommended for Bible study today.

Sir Robert Anderson left a good testimony behind. He was spoken of in the House of Commons as having 'discharged his duties with great faithfulness to the public,' and described by a writer as 'one of the men, to whom the country, without knowing it, owes a great debt.'[79]

79. From https://www.spink.com/lot/18003000318 and https://www.brethrenarchive.org/people/sir-robert-anderson/

His feet shall stand in that day upon the mount of Olives.
Zechariah 14:4

I have a bad habit. When I'm reading a book, I can't seem to read from Chapter One, to Chapter Two, to Chapter Three, and so on, until I reach the last chapter. Instead, I read the first few chapters... and then, because I'm dying to know what happens, I begin to flick through the pages. Before I know it, *I've read the end of the book!* I've spoiled the surprise. The story has lost its excitement.

There is a book where skipping through to see what happens doesn't take away from the excitement. Instead, it adds to it! In this book, we find out who is going to win, and we discover what will happen to the enemies. I'm sure you've guessed – it's the Bible.

One of my favourite future scenes from this book is found in the final chapters of Zechariah. This world is in a sad and sorry state, but one of these days the Lord Jesus Christ will return to the air and call the believers home to heaven (1 Thessalonians 4:13-17). After that, there will be terrible times for those who are left on this earth (read the book of Revelation). This awful period, known as the great tribulation, will culminate in a huge battle scene. The nations of the world will gather against Israel, and it will look as if all hope is lost. But then something amazing will happen – the Lord Jesus will return to the very same place where He left when He ascended up to heaven, the Mount of Olives. It says in Revelation 1:7 that 'every eye shall see Him, and they also which pierced Him.' The last time the Lord Jesus Christ was on earth, He was rejected, despised, and crucified. This time, He will return in glory. Israel will acknowledge the Lord Jesus as her rightful Messiah who was wounded for her transgressions. 'And the Lord shall be king over all the earth' (Zechariah 14:9). Isn't that wonderful?

The great thing about the Bible is that, instead of spoiling the surprise, the more we read it, the more we enjoy it, and the more we look forward to that day when our Saviour will be exalted over all the earth.

The Lord is my rock.
Psalm 18:2

From the stunning stretches of golden sand of the north coast, to the high cliffs and sheltered coves of the east, in Northern Ireland we love our beaches! Although the Atlantic Ocean is usually too cold to swim in unless it's a warm day, paddling in the shallow water is refreshing. It's mesmerising to stand at the water's edge where the foaming, broken waves race around your ankles. As the water is drawn back to the sea, ready for the next big wave, the sand underfoot shifts and moves, burying your feet and making you feel a bit dizzy. Sometimes you hardly know if you're standing upright or not!

A rocky beach is different. There, huge boulders rise up out of the water. You clamber up and stand on one of these, watching the waves crash against the rock. You might get splashed, but you know there's no chance of the water shifting the boulder – it's too big, too solid. No matter how many waves crash against it, the rock won't move. It is stable and sure.

I think this is the picture that the psalmist David had in mind when he said, 'The Lord is my rock' – an illustration of something unchanging and immovable. Sand is always shifting, easily washed along. How like the opinions and beliefs of the world around us which change swiftly with every tide. This world is always fluctuating, always changing, and will continue to do so. Keeping our balance will be impossible if we try to rest on one of the world's beliefs or even in our own strength.

But in this unstable world, Christians have a sure foundation. God will never change; we have a firm foundation for our feet. The sands of earth tumble along, toppling those who try to use them as their basis for life, but the person who plants his feet on the solid rock will be able to stand secure.

If any man will come after Me, let him deny himself, and take up his cross daily, and follow Me.

Luke 9:23

When I was at school, I caught the bus home at the station in the town. Our bus was pretty rowdy! There was no orderly queueing to get on. Instead, everyone pushed for all they were worth towards the doors, and when they opened, the passengers at the front were forced through. Occasionally, a poor, unsuspecting person, who had no intention of travelling into the hills and valleys of County Antrim, found themselves caught in the middle of the crowd and shoved onto the bus. Their only option was to wait at the front until all the unruly passengers had boarded, and then get off, hoping that in the meantime their own bus hadn't left the station.

This world is a bit like my old bus. We're all being pushed and shoved along by those who despise God and His Word, and to turn around and go in the opposite direction is more difficult than we can handle in our own strength. But even amongst believers, we may feel like the innocent bystander who ended up being propelled through the doors of the bus. There are many Christians who are happy to go with the flow. A little bit of Bible reading, a little bit of prayer when it's needed, no need to make any sacrifices or deny ourselves any of the entertainment and fun that's out there. "Why attend *all* of the church gatherings? Surely once a week is plenty... that is, if you feel like it. We're saved and going to heaven. No need to be so *extreme* about it!"

Look at the top of the page and read again what the Lord Jesus Christ said. Doesn't it sound as if 'extreme' is exactly what is expected for those who are His followers? Following Christ is not an easy road. It involves sacrifice, it involves self-denial, it involves a daily commitment, and may even involve suffering. It will mean pushing against and going in the opposite direction to not only the world, but many Christians as well. Are you willing to turn around and strain against the pressure all around you in order to lose your life for His sake but gain eternal reward?

In our world of social media, image is all-important. Whether we want to gain compliments or make people laugh, great care is taken in choosing the appropriate picture and fine-tuning it until it fits the image we want to present. Before we post another picture, let's ask ourselves a few questions.

1 – Why am I sharing this picture? Answer honestly! Within all of us lies the desire to be liked and admired, and social media plays dangerously into these desires. How else could we have so many people telling us, either by words, or by little heart symbols, that we have something praiseworthy about us? Some may even share things that aren't so happy to gain sympathy and attention. Either way, we like to be the centre of our universe. But is this right? Philippians 2:3 NKJV has the answer. 'Let nothing be done through selfish ambition or conceit...'

2 – Do you really want everyone to view this picture? You might think that it's only going to be your friends who will see it, but take a moment to consider the other ways this photo could spread. Also, does this picture reflect who you really are? Is it only an image of who you are pretending to be? And is it how you want to be remembered?

3 – Finally, is someone forcing you to share something, either publicly or privately? Maybe one of your friends is encouraging you to post something you don't feel comfortable sharing. Or, even more seriously, is someone blackmailing or bribing you? Do not post anything you don't want to, no matter how much you are urged to do so. It's *your* reputation and testimony that's on the line, not the other person's, not to mention the fact that blackmail is illegal. You must find someone reliable – maybe an older person in your family or local church – to talk to who will give you wise advice and help to support you through the situation.

While social media may have some benefit, it often seems to be all about image. Did you know that God is concerned with our image too? If you follow His will for Christians – to be conformed to the image of His Son – you'll have no regrets.

The eagle... seeketh the prey, and her eyes behold afar off.

Job 39:27, 29

The eagle is famous for its amazing ability to catch prey, but did you know exactly what causes it to be so successful? One of the main reasons is its incredible eyesight – estimated to be about four to eight times stronger than that of humans. Eagles can see a rabbit two miles away!

Eagles' eyes have been specially designed for their purpose. Despite eagles being much smaller and lighter, their eyes are roughly the same size as the eyes of human beings. Our eyes are wonderfully complex, but the eyes of eagles have even more remarkable features. As the eagle descends towards its prey, the curvature of its corneae, the clear windows at the front of each eye, changes to maintain sharp focus. Eagles even have an elite version of retina. In human eyes, the fovea is the part of the retina which is used for central vision. It has the highest concentration of cells – approximately 147,000 per mm². The eagle, however, has not only one fovea, but two, and these have as many as one million cells per mm². No wonder its vision is razor sharp! Colour vision is also exceptional, which is another reason why these birds can locate and catch their prey so well.

Their eyelids have also been specially designed – they have three of these, one of which acts like a windscreen wiper. A special chemical in the tears helps prevent eye infections.[80]

It's no wonder that when God created everything, He said it was very good. Each of His creations, whether in the animal or plant world, was specially designed for a purpose. And the same Designer who intricately formed the eye of the eagle to fit into His purpose for creation has a plan for your life too.

---

80. From https://www.nationaleaglecenter.org/eagle-eyes/

Put on the Lord Jesus Christ, and make no provision for the flesh, to gratify its desires.
Romans 13:14 ESV

NOVEMBER

26

In your bedroom are two outfits. One is hanging in the wardrobe, brand new, neatly pressed, and very formal – a smart suit, or a beautiful dress, perhaps. The other has been tossed over a chair, or onto the floor. It's seen better days, frankly. The dull fabric is faded and worn, a few holes have begun to appear here and there, and it could do with a good wash.

Today you are going to attend a wedding. And not just any wedding. The photos will be all over social media. Your picture will, without a doubt, be seen by thousands of people. After showering and fixing your hair, you reach for your clothes. As you slip the old, worn fabric over your head, you sigh with pleasure. These old garments are so comfy! They smell like your pillow – safe and cosy. You'll be so snug all day. No stiff formalwear for you.

Woah! Hold on! Didn't you get the memo? You're going to a wedding! You don't wear scruffy clothes to a wedding, no matter how cosy they are! Put on your formal outfit – don't you realise your garments should be appropriate to the occasion?

You give me an incredulous look and put your arms into the worn sleeves. This is what you've chosen to wear.

Seems ridiculous, doesn't it? But how often in our Christian lives do we slip into the old clothes of fleshly desire, instead of putting on the Lord Jesus Christ? His provision for us is eminently suitable for our standing as sons of God. Yet so often we are tempted by those old familiar habits within arm's reach – that phone with all that is accessible on it, that temper that flares so close to the surface, the pride that rises up so easily.

You know, if those worn clothes hadn't been so handy, you wouldn't have been as tempted to slip them on. It would have been much easier to have lifted the formal outfit from the wardrobe.

So let's put on the Lord Jesus Christ, and take all those habits and dump them outside in the bin, where they belong – making no provision for the flesh.

We shall all stand before the judgment seat of Christ.
Romans 14:10

The judgment seat of Christ isn't a topic I often hear discussed. Preachers might mention it, but it generally doesn't come up in conversation with friends. Maybe you find the same.

The judgment seat of Christ is mentioned by name twice in the Bible – in the verse quoted above and in 2 Corinthians 5:10. It's also alluded to in 1 Corinthians 3:13-15 and 4:5. It's different from the Great White Throne judgment in Revelation 20:11, which is for sinners who never trusted Christ for salvation. The judgment seat of Christ is for believers – those who have been saved. One very important thing to remember is that it is *not* to judge sin – this was once and forever dealt with at Calvary when Christ bore God's judgment for us.

So, what then is the purpose of the judgment seat? 2 Corinthians 5:10 tells us it is to receive what is due for what was done in the body, either good or evil. In other words, it is to do with receiving reward for our works here on earth. We will have to give account to God for what we have done. Everything will be reviewed, and those deeds that merit reward will be rewarded. In 1 Corinthians 3, Paul speaks about natural materials – gold, silver, precious stones, wood, hay, and straw – and their values. Only half of these can withstand fire. The others, big and bulky though they are, burn up, leaving only a little pile of ash behind. At the judgment seat, our deeds will be tried in the same way as fire tries these materials. Only what is of value will remain. There, our works will be revealed for what they were. No one can assess our motives, not even ourselves at times, but there it will all be made clear.

It's great to know that, in each believer, God will find something to praise and reward (1 Corinthians 4:5), but wouldn't it be so sad to see our huge pile of works burned up to reveal only a few pieces of silver, and to lose out on potential reward? Let's live today so that we won't wish that we had put greater effort into what really counts for eternity.

The Lord disciplines the one He loves.

Hebrews 12:6 ESV

Everything was going wrong. Lucy had mixed up the date for handing in her coursework and now it was going to be late. She'd forgotten to bring lunch. Her best friend was spending all her time with her new boyfriend and wasn't even speaking to Lucy anymore. Mum's new job and longer commute meant that Lucy was now in charge of supervising her annoying little brother, Benny, until Mum got home, as well as starting dinner. How was she to find the time to do her homework? Lucy couldn't take any more. As she walked up the path to the front door, she felt as if she was about to explode. She reached to open the door, and her phone slipped from her hand. Bending down to pick it up, she noticed that the screen had shattered. Lucy couldn't hold back the sobs as she sank to the doorstep. "Why, God? Why is everything going wrong?"

Lucy didn't know how much time passed before she gathered herself up and walked into the house. All she knew was that, on the front doorstep, she had poured out all her problems to God, told Him how much she was struggling to cope, and how that she couldn't do this all by herself. How foolish and wrong she was for thinking she could! She'd recalled the promises of God that He would never leave her nor forsake her, and that He was her help in trouble.

As she prepared a snack for herself and Benny, she promised that she would try never to drift away from God again. She needed Him. Each and every day, hour, minute, and second. With every breath and heartbeat. The problems might not disappear, but God would help her through them. Her heart bubbled over in gratitude as she thanked God for His faithfulness in bringing her back to Himself.

Lord, and what shall this man do?
John 21:21

There's something about this story that always makes me smile! The Lord has told Peter what He wants him to do, given him a summary of what lies ahead for him, and finished up by saying, "Follow Me." What happens next? Peter is silent, pondering all the Lord has told him? No! Instead, Peter turns around, spots John, and asks what *he's* going to do! Isn't that so typical of human nature?

God has given clear instructions in the Scriptures, which every believer ought to obey, but there are also special tasks for each person to carry out. Different believers have different spiritual gifts and natural abilities. Sometimes we have individual God-given burdens. Figuring out what God means us to do for Him can take exercise and prayer; usually it is doing what's right in front of you.

In a local church, there is never any shortage of work to be done. Maybe it's something simple, like cleaning the building, gathering up the hymnbooks, or arranging seats. Maybe you've a special talent with young children – the overactive toddler's frazzled mum is more grateful than you'll ever know for your ability to distract the little one from making a bolt mid-service for the platform. Maybe you have a gift for sharing the gospel, or a way of making worn-down older people smile. Keep your eyes open, and you'll soon see ways you can help out.

Did you ever try to follow someone while looking over your shoulder at something else? You'll have discovered that you quickly veer off in the wrong direction! The Lord Jesus had to remind Peter to follow Him, rather than looking over his shoulder at John. It's the same for us. Too much time spent observing others, watching what they're working at (and often criticising them), does not make for useful God-focussed service on our part. There's plenty for us to do. So next time we're tempted to look over our shoulder at others, remember the Lord's words – Follow *Me!*

Every couple of years, our local church hosts a Bible exhibition for ten- and eleven-year-olds. As the children are guided through the exhibition, they look for answers to a list of questions. One is, 'How do we speak to God?' and the next, 'How does God speak to us?' We all know the answers – that we speak to God through prayer, and He speaks to us through the Bible, but isn't it amazing that we often spend so little time on each?! I know you're busy, but reading the Word of God is absolutely vital for your growth and preservation as a believer. I can't stress enough how important it is to take even a little bit of time each morning before you leave the house to read and pray. But maybe... hopefully... you'd like to read more of God's Word than what you can squeeze in before you leave the house.

With that in mind, here are a few suggestions as to how you can increase your daily intake of the Word of God.

- Work your way consecutively through the Bible or follow a reading plan. This means that you don't end up in a situation where you use most of your reading time deciding on a passage.

- There are numerous free Bible apps available to download. You'll always have the Bible with you, and you can make use of any spare time you have available.

- Listening to the Bible is also a great way to take in more of the Word of God. This can also be done via various Bible apps and is a great idea when you're out for a walk or run, or maybe working on a mundane task like cleaning your room.

- Make a conscious decision to say no to things that you know are timewasters. It's so easy to while away a few hours with precious little to show for it, when we could have spent the time finding out what God has to say to us.

- Finally, keep your goal of reading more of the Scriptures at the front of your mind. That way, you will be looking out for suitable times to read. Even a few minutes in God's Word will bring immeasurable blessing.

DECEMBER

1

DECEMBER

When you walk through the
fire, you shall not be burned,
nor shall the flame scorch you.

Isaiah 43:2 NKJV

We all love the story of how Shadrach, Meshach, and Abednego refused to bow down to King Nebuchadnezzar's golden image and were thrown into the fiery furnace. Those who threw them in were consumed by the heat, but these three men were safe. The fire had no power over them. It was exactly as God had said in Isaiah 43 – they were not burned, and the flame didn't scorch them. When they stepped out of the fire, there wasn't even the smell of smoke about them! And, best of all, they'd had the presence of the Lord with them in their fiery trial (Daniel 3:25).

In the Bible, we read about God's wrath against sin being like fire. Fire is all-consuming and powerful. Every year we hear of areas across the world where uncontrollable wildfires break out. It requires all of man's strength and intelligence, coupled with the latest technology and resources, to make any impact. But no efforts of man can ever make any impact on God's punishment for sin. The only way that we can be free from the fire of God's wrath is if One has already taken the punishment, and has been the sacrifice and borne the fire of His judgment.

Think of the contrast between the three friends in Babylon and the Lord Jesus Christ. Neither deserved to be in a place of punishment, yet the three men were delivered, without a single hair of their heads singed. In the words of Lamentations 1:13, which we can apply to the Lord Jesus, it says, 'From above hath He sent fire into my bones, and it prevaileth against them.' He fully experienced the fire of God's wrath against sin. While the three friends had the comfort of His presence in the fire, the Lord Jesus Christ suffered alone.

In those places where the fire has consumed all, it cannot turn around and burn again. We stand on the ground where God's judgment has already been. Christ bore the wrath of God for us, so we will never experience it ourselves.

Mary has chosen the best part.

Luke 10:42 NET

DECEMBER

2

One day, Martha invited the Lord Jesus Christ into her home. Can you imagine the great commotion that would take place in your house if word arrived that the Lord was coming to visit? The living room would need to be tidied, the house cleaned from top to bottom, and the ideal menu planned. I think Martha wanted everything to be picture-perfect. But that was the problem. Somewhere along the line, her desire to serve the Lord with the best of what she had, turned into fussing and fretting over little unimportant details.

The Lord never said her choice was bad. In fact, we'd all have to agree that going to such effort to serve the Lord was a good thing. But there was something better, and that was what her sister, Mary, had chosen to do – to sit at the Lord's feet.

Sitting at someone's feet suggests two things – firstly, humility, with the admission that the one at whose feet you're sitting is greater than you. Secondly, that you are learning something from that person. Both were true in Mary's case. She recognised the greatness of the Lord and worshipped Him, listening to everything He had to say and learning from Him.

Sometimes in our busy lives we forget that it's not just our good works that God wants, although they are really important and expected of Christians. We need to spend time like Mary at the feet of the Saviour, worshipping Him, reading God's Word, and learning from Him. Often, we need to make choices between what's good and what's better – the best part, which is what Mary chose. Sometimes, like Mary, those choices won't look so good in the eyes of other people, and harsh words might be spoken about us, but the Lord will notice that we have chosen Him above all else.

By the time the Lord was about to be betrayed and crucified, Mary had gained an insight and perception that even the disciples were lacking. It was then that she was able to move forward into action, to good works – sacrificing a very costly container of ointment to anoint the Lord – which was seen by all, and, more importantly, deeply appreciated by Him.

Lord, what wilt Thou have me to do?
Acts 9:6

When Saul of Tarsus set off on his journey to Damascus, he was intent on the murder and persecution of Christians, but by the time he arrived, he was a Christian himself. Wouldn't you have thought that his conversion would cause him to avoid Damascus? After all, he no longer had any reason to be there. And what would people think of this fiery Pharisee now being led, blind and helpless, into the city? So why was he there? It was because the Lord had told him to go. A desire to obey God and do His will is one of the marks of a true believer.

I wonder what sort of answer Saul was expecting to his question, which is quoted at the top of this page. Did he think that God was going to give him a detailed plan for his life? Sometimes I would love it if God gave me such a plan, especially when difficult decisions need to be made. But instead, God gives Saul only one instruction – go into the city. That's all! I'm sure Saul had questions. What was he to do in the city? How long was he to stay there? But that wasn't all God told Saul. He also gave him a promise – "It will be told you what you must do." All Saul could do was obey, and wait.

Often, that's all God asks of us. To obey, then wait. Saul had no idea how long he was to wait. Hours, days, or weeks? Maybe even years? For most of us, the waiting is often the hard part. We've done what God has asked, but things don't seem to move on. Sometimes we wonder if we've heard God right, or if He could possibly have forgotten about us.

But sooner or later, in God's time, the answer will come. In Saul's case, after three days Ananias arrived with further instructions. Saul was probably given more details than most about his future, but even he wasn't permitted to see around every corner. In the same way, God won't give you all the details of your life, but step by step He will lead and guide until you're safely home.

The tongue of the wise uses
knowledge rightly.
Proverbs 15:2 NKJV

DECEMBER

4

If you study physics at school, you'll have heard of the unit of temperature measurement called the kelvin. But do you know anything about Lord Kelvin, the man after whom this measurement was named?

Lord Kelvin was born William Thomson in 1824 in Belfast, the son of a mathematics and engineering teacher at Royal Belfast Academical Institution. When he was nine, the family moved to Glasgow, and William began studying at the university at the age of ten. He had a brilliant mind and later attended Cambridge University, before becoming a professor at the University of Glasgow at the age of twenty-two.

Lord Kelvin wasn't only known for establishing the scale of absolute temperature. Amongst many other achievements, he also worked on the First and Second Laws of Thermodynamics, developed a mariner's compass, and was heavily involved in laying the first transatlantic cable. As far as the world's honours go, he was a great man, having been given no less than twenty-one honorary doctorates and numerous awards.

But in all his achievements and greatness, Lord Kelvin never lost sight of the Creator. He was never swayed by the popular atheistic opinion of his day. Instead, he was thoroughly convinced that rather than science disproving the existence of God, it would do the opposite. He is quoted in statements such as, 'If you think strongly enough you will be forced by science to the belief in God.'[81] 'With regard to the origin of life, science... positively affirms creative power.'[82] 'Overwhelmingly strong proofs of intelligent and benevolent design lie around us... the atheistic idea is so nonsensical that I cannot put it into words.'[83]

Lord Kelvin often argued against Charles Darwin's position that the earth did not have a beginning, a belief that modern-day scientists (including atheists) no longer hold. But this great man had learned the greatest truth of all. He said, 'Christianity without the cross is nothing.'[84] He recognised that at the root of man's desire to disprove the existence of God was a desire to reject Christ. Lord Kelvin stood firm against the onslaught of atheism. He truly was a wise man who used his knowledge rightly.

81. https://www.christianheritageedinburgh.org.uk/2016/08/23/sir-william-thomson-lord-kelvin-1824-1907/
82. http://creationsciencehalloffame.org/inductees/deceased/lord-kelvin/
83. https://crev.info/scientists/william-thomson-lord-kelvin/
84. Ibid.

As the heavens are higher
than the earth, so are My ways
higher than your ways.
Isaiah 55:9

"What do you want to be when you grow up?" is a question that likely all of us were asked as children. Maybe you're one of the few who sets their course early on and sticks to it. Or perhaps you're like me – always changing your mind! When we are little, the possibilities are limitless. A child has no concept of the skills or abilities required for various occupations. The little one who wants to be an electrician might be unaware that they have a colour deficiency which will close that door to them. Others who wish to enter the medical field may discover that they are much more skilled in languages than in biology and chemistry. It's in our teenage years that we begin to understand which doors might open, and which are most definitely shut.

Often, though, we believe that when we have settled the big question of our career, everything in life will follow along nicely. We look at our parents and expect that one day we will get married and have children too. Or maybe we look at our parents and promise ourselves that we will go farther and do more than they ever did. We will travel the world, aim for the top, seek experiences that previous generations could hardly even dream about. We hope to stay healthy and grief-free. We reason that when we begin to earn money, we will be able to afford nice cars, good holidays, and all the bits and pieces that contribute to a comfortable lifestyle.

But remember – God's ways are higher than ours! There's nothing wrong with many of our ambitions, but God may well have – and likely has – a different plan for you, in some way or another. There is no such thing as a standard life, so don't be surprised when God shakes up your expectations. Even though His plan for you may be different than what you would have chosen, you can be assured it will be better! He has a higher purpose and everything He does is absolutely perfect.

Temptation is something that all of us have experienced, probably on a daily basis. As Christians, we know that we are supposed to resist the temptation to sin. We have the Holy Spirit indwelling us to help us, and the Word of God to guide us. And yet, because our old nature has not been removed, we often fail.

Sometimes it's no wonder we fail. There's an old story about a monarch who needed a new coach driver. During the interview, each applicant was asked how close they could drive to the edge of a precipice. Most of them boasted of their skill – a metre, half a metre, ten centimetres – but the one who got the job was the one who said that, with such an important person on board, he would stay as far from the edge as he could.

Which attitude do you have to temptation? There are occasions when we find ourselves facing temptation in unavoidable situations. In times like these, we need to pray that God will help and preserve us, and then we need to escape as soon as we can, as Joseph did.

But I want to talk about those times when you choose to make it your goal to go as close to the edge of the precipice as you can without falling over. What about picking up your phone when you're behind your locked bedroom door, knowing you won't be disturbed if you delve into things online that you know without a doubt are wrong? What about agreeing to spend time with those classmates who love to indulge in gossip and backbiting and draw you in to doing the same? What about making plans to head off somewhere private with your boyfriend or girlfriend when you know very well it will lead to moral temptation?

The advice at the top of the page is found in Proverbs and concerns the path of the wicked. The writer leaves us in no doubt what our attitude and action towards it should be. When we see the precipice of temptation ahead, we should avoid it with everything in us. We shouldn't take a single step towards it, but instead turn away and pass on, leaving it behind us.

The Lord is my shepherd.
Psalm 23:1

Across the hills and valleys where I grew up, sheep are a common sight. If there's one thing about them, it's that they're great at getting themselves into scrapes! Sometimes they squeeze themselves through a hole in the hedge and wander into another field or along the road. And they're not too good at getting back to where they belong. Other times they manage to get hopelessly tangled up in thorns, or even get stuck on their backs, their heavy wool coats leaving them helpless and unable to roll onto their feet again. Sheep need a lot of care.

Just like us! We're equally good at getting into scrapes – prone to wander, get tangled up, and even land in situations we can't possibly extricate ourselves from. It's no wonder that, in the Bible, we are often likened to sheep. Sheep who desperately need a shepherd.

There are many different types of shepherds – from ones who barely look at their sheep from one week to the next, to those who know each sheep individually, even when the flock numbers well into the hundreds. But even the best shepherd cannot give each sheep perfect care. There will be times, maybe during unexpected flooding, when the shepherd cannot get to the sheep to feed them. Sometimes they need to dig the sheep out of deep snowdrifts. They can't be with them 24/7.

We have a Shepherd who is greater than any shepherd in this world. The rest of the verse says, 'I shall not want'. He is with us all the time. And with such a Shepherd, every one of our needs has been supplied. We are protected and cared for with impeccable attention. We're fed, watered, and given rest. We're guided when to move and which is the best path to take. When the path leads our feet through dangerous and perilous ways, we need not fear because He will protect us from thieves and predators. There isn't one moment in which we are out of our Shepherd's care.

But there's another way in which our Shepherd differs from all the shepherds in this world, no matter how good they are – our Shepherd actually died for His sheep. That's how precious we are to Him, so we should never doubt the care of our shepherd for us.

The host of heaven cannot be numbered.

Jeremiah 33:22

When I was a little girl, I used to try to count all the stars that I could see from my bedroom window. I don't think I ever managed it, and I'm pretty sure I lost count on many occasions!

I wasn't the first person who tried to count the stars, nor will I be the last. But one thing is sure – we're all doomed to fail. God has told us that it is not possible for human beings to number the stars. It would be a difficult enough task to count all the visible stars with the naked eye – there aren't too many of us who can accurately count up to six thousand! But use telescopes and modern technology, and mankind gets lost in the vast number.

Years ago, people had a very simplistic view of their surroundings. They had little idea what the earth, solar system, and universe were really like. It wasn't until Galileo invented the first telescope in 1610 that scientists began to understand that there were many more stars than they'd previously believed. But, as in many other instances, they were learning what God had told them in His Word all along – the stars cannot be numbered.

Who hasn't looked up into the night sky and marvelled at the sight? God has placed stars where we can see them, and many more where we cannot. There are probably stars that mankind will never discover. If there's one thing that declares God's glory, it's the night sky. It's awesome to think that out there in the vast reaches of space, there is an innumerable company of stars that humans will never lay eyes on, shining in glory to the Creator.

And what makes the thought even more thrilling is that, as Psalm 48:14 says, 'This God is our God for ever and ever.' This God – the One who created, numbered, and knows each star by name – is the One who loves you, cares for you, and will be with you to the end.

Let no one despise your youth,
but be an example to the
believers.

1 Timothy 4:12 NKJV

"No one takes me seriously!" Jamie grumbled. "No matter what opinions or great ideas I have, they laugh. I can't wait until I'm older and people finally listen to me."

Does this sound familiar? I think we've all been there at some point, even Timothy, the recipient of two letters from the apostle Paul, which we find in the New Testament. Paul, who was a spiritual father figure to Timothy, had left him in Ephesus to help the local church. He knew, however, that there were those who would think Timothy was too young to be taken seriously. Of course, he was probably older than you, but still young compared to the people he would be trying to teach and correct, so Paul told him not to let anyone despise his youth. It sounds like good advice, doesn't it? But how would you go about it? Catch the people by the fronts of their shirts and snarl into their faces? Or complain about it to Paul so he can come and sort them out?

That wasn't what Paul advised. Instead of being confrontational about the issue, he instructed Timothy to be an example. Well, that's a bit of an anti-climax! I'm sure if you're like me, you'd have liked to have seen these people put in their places. But God has a different approach – and a much more effective one. You see, someone who is living quietly in such a way that they can be an example to other believers, is someone who is worth listening to. We've all known people who say foolish things, those whose behaviour is less than commendable, and some who maybe don't show love to others. Are you as inclined to take these people as seriously as you do those whose lives remind you of Christ?

If we want to be people who are listened to and taken seriously, why don't we let our lives do the talking first, and live in a way that we can be examples to others in word, in conduct, in love, in spirit, in faith, and in purity?

EXAMPLE

Practise these things, immerse
yourself in them, so that all
may see your progress.

1 Timothy 4:15 ESV

DECEMBER

10

Remember yesterday we met Jamie and sympathised with him in his frustration over not being taken seriously? We then listened to some really great advice the apostle Paul gave Timothy about what to do when older people despised his youth. But that wasn't the only instruction from God that Paul gave to his son in the faith. Over the next few days, we'll look at some more advice that Paul, an older man, gave to Timothy, a younger man, and learn from it too.

Imagine you are standing at the edge of an inviting swimming pool. The warm sun is glinting off the still, blue water, making you squint against the brightness. You stretch out a foot and dip your toe into the water. The temperature is perfect – refreshing enough for such a hot day, but not so cold as to make you flinch. You jump in, letting the water pass over your head, surrounding you, cool and refreshing. You are immersed – totally wet all over!

In this passage, Paul is telling Timothy to immerse himself. Not in water, but in spiritual things – godly behaviour, the reading and study of the Bible, using his spiritual gift. He wasn't only to dip a toe in here and there, he was to let these things permeate every part of him and his life.

It's all too easy to dip in and out of living for God. Maybe we hear a message, or read something in a book, perhaps have a conversation with someone who is living an 'immersed' life, and for a while we attempt to do better. But then something else catches our attention and away we run, barely wet at all. Being immersed takes time and effort. It means forming new habits, sacrificing our own desires, going against the flow. It will take more than a quick scan of a few verses while we fix our hair or wolf down our breakfast. Instead, it will mean living in the Word of God to such an extent that, without ever saying a word about what we are doing, others will begin to notice. After all, someone who has been immersed will stand out in a crowd!

Younger men as brothers, older women as mothers, younger women as sisters, with all purity.

1 Timothy 5:1,2 NKJV

"No, that's not how you do it! This wire goes here, and the battery goes there, and-" Holly tutted impatiently. "Here, give it to me. I'll fix it for you. Miss Cartwright asked me to make sure you know what you're doing, and it looks like you don't!"

Is anyone else wincing at Holly's condescending, know-it-all attitude to her poor fellow pupil? Isn't it good that Timothy didn't treat the Ephesian believers like this? The first letter that Paul wrote to Timothy was packed full of important teachings for him to pass on to the believers. It may have been a temptation to develop a condescending attitude, especially since he'd been instructed not to let anyone despise his youth. When older men needed correction, it was to be done in a respectful way, with plenty of encouragement.

You see, the family of God is exactly that – a family, especially in the local church. The older men are like fathers to us, the older women like mothers. Respect for parents is extremely important to God, and this is equally true in His family. You might think that the older people are behind the times, knowing nothing about life nowadays, but they are often the ones you need to thank for praying for you each day, as you face temptations and difficulties that they might not understand, but which God does.

The younger people are also deserving of your respect. The young men are your brothers in Christ, and the young women are your sisters in Christ. Can you imagine how you would feel if some girl strung your brother along, then dumped him for his best friend, or if some boy took physical liberties with your sister, leaving her with deep emotional scars? You'd be furious, as well as deeply hurt. In the family of God, it's important to remember that we ought to treat other young people the way we would expect someone to treat our siblings, especially when we begin to think about building a special relationship with a fellow believer – with all purity.

So let's appreciate each member of our spiritual family – both old and young – and treat them as valued and precious family members.

When is enough money enough? If you conducted a survey with this question, I'm sure you'd get a variety of answers. But if you asked a second question – do you consider yourself to have enough money? – what do you think the most common answer would be? You see, despite having more money and possessions than our ancestors ever had, contentment isn't very common nowadays. We always want a little bit more.

At this point in your life, you probably don't have very much money. Some of you may have part-time jobs, others might receive pocket money. Whatever your income is, or isn't, you probably feel you could do with more – to buy those shoes you've had your eye on for ages, or to upgrade to the latest model of phone, or to splurge on your favourite hobby. We need to be very careful that the desire for money doesn't lead us into temptation and a snare. Working for a salary is an honest way to earn money, but how many people have found themselves on the perilous path of gambling or criminal activity? The internet only feeds the addictions that people have – rather than having to leave the house to visit the bookmakers, people can now gamble twenty-four hours a day from the privacy of their own homes. Others try to earn money online by compromising their purity. Both are extremely dangerous paths to set foot on and should be avoided at all costs.

Even someone working in a legitimate job isn't always free from covetousness. How many people climb the promotion ladder by stomping on others on their way to the top? What about those who put their job before their family, spending all their time at work so they can live a lavish lifestyle? Or even those whose desire to earn extra money causes them to neglect things like reading their Bible and attending church gatherings?

What does Paul say to Timothy? "Flee these things!" Run as fast as you can, and as far as you can, from covetousness, which will only lead to sorrow and destruction. Instead of following earthly riches, we are to follow after true spiritual riches – righteousness, godliness, faith, love, patience, and gentleness. We might have to get by with a little less, but in God's eyes, we will be the richer for it.

God hath not given us the spirit of fear; but of power, and of love, and of a sound mind.

2 Timothy 1:7

Did you ever believe that God wanted you to do something for Him, but you were so *scared*? Courage doesn't come naturally to everyone, and, if you're like me, doing something which involves stepping out of your comfort zone will likely be accompanied by a pounding heart, sweaty palms, and maybe even a sensation of terror. But we timid people can take heart – reading between the lines, it seems that Timothy experienced the same. How else can we account for Paul's words to him at the top of this page?

Timothy had an important job to do. In the church at Ephesus there were people who were teaching wrong things. It was his responsibility to confront them and teach the truth instead. He had some pretty hard things to say, and don't forget that people had a tendency to despise his youth. It would have been much easier for him to have waited for Paul to come back and put things right.

But that wasn't what God wanted. His plan involved Timothy and He would give him the necessary help. He will help us too. A fearful spirit isn't from God. Instead, He has given us His Holy Spirit to indwell us. Because of this, we can experience power – the power of God! No situation is too difficult for Him.

We are also given love. 'Perfect love casts out fear' (1 John 4:18 NKJV). Many times, those occasions which cause us the most fear involve other people. If we focus on our love for them, it will give us a motive to act, which is greater than the fear which holds us back. If that fails, then surely our love for God should be enough of a motivator for us.

A sound mind, or self-control, is also given to us. Fear can be crippling, and we must often do battle with ourselves to take that first step and move forward in obedience to God. We have been given the self-control required to make that happen.

God has a plan for each of us. He sees our fear but wants us to obey Him. He has given us the necessary resources, because it is in obedience that we'll receive the greatest blessing.

> Flee also youthful lusts; but pursue righteousness, faith, love, peace.
>
> 2 Timothy 2:22 NKJV

When I was growing up, Granny had a valuable crystal jug. It wasn't a jug for everyday use but was brought out especially for visitors. I remember her lament when someone inadvertently placed it in the dishwasher where it was in danger of being damaged. It wasn't like the other jugs in the house – this one was special.

In 2 Timothy 2, Paul is using the example of an honoured vessel in a house, like Granny's crystal jug, to illustrate to Timothy how God is looking for believers who are set apart and different from the others. It's easy to be the same as everyone else, to keep our spiritual ambitions manageable. But God is looking for those who are prepared to put in extra effort, for those who are clean and ready for use – young people like Timothy.

Paul gives Timothy some advice on how to be a vessel of honour. He tells him to flee youthful lusts. I always thought this only meant sexual lusts until my husband pointed out that, while this is definitely included, it takes in much more. It can include childish attitudes – that of wanting our own way, throwing temper tantrums, and being selfish. For many of us, no matter what age we are, it's past time to grow up and live in a more God-honouring way.

It also includes our interests. Think back to when you were little. When you weren't at school, what took up most of your time? Kids' video games? Playing with dolls or cars? Riding your bike around the yard? Probably many of the things you were interested in then don't interest you so much now. That's normal – they were childish interests. 1 Corinthians 13:11 says, 'When I became a man, I put away childish things.' But what about now? What do you spend most of your free time doing? I don't mean that we should give up every hobby, but we certainly shouldn't let our interests take over our lives, no matter what age we are. Is there something you're playing at or spending far too much time on, when you know you should put it in its proper place and focus more on those things that Paul advised Timothy to pursue? Things like righteousness, faith, love, and peace, which are developed through spending time in God's Word.

You must continue in the things which you have learned and been assured of.

2 Timothy 3:14 NKJV

Imagine that someone very special wrote a letter to you, but not any letter – this letter was going to be the last one you'd ever receive from them. In the Bible, the second letter to Timothy was the very last one he would ever receive from his father in the faith, the apostle Paul. Soon, Paul would be slain by Nero, the wicked Roman emperor, and Timothy would no longer have the help, advice, and support of the older man.

We often depend on others to keep us going, especially when we're younger. Maybe an older Christian who frequently asks us when we last read the Bible, or a friend who encourages us to turn to God when our problems get us down. But sometimes God takes away those helps, and we must stand on our own two feet. It's the choices we make for ourselves, without any coercion from or accountability to others that reveal what we're really like at the core.

Standing on our own will take work. We can become discouraged so easily and we may often feel alone, but Paul's word to Timothy stands regardless – "*You* must continue!" No matter what others do, even if they decide to throw overboard all they once thought regarding the Scriptures, *you* must continue! Even if this world attacks and batters your confidence in our great God, *you* must continue! Don't waver. You didn't merely swallow what men told you. Instead, you searched the Scriptures and learned the truth for yourself. You've been assured of it – you were convinced by it – and God's Word is always relevant and can never change.

A little later in the letter, Paul explains to Timothy that the Word of God has value in every sphere of life and is given so that people who live for God will be complete and thoroughly equipped for every good work. If we want to be men and women of God, people who are able to live for Him no matter what happens around us, we will need to spend time with the Bible. Read it often, live in it, and let it hold you with its life and power, because it is an ever-living and powerful Word.

Some things are easy to give thanks for – like food, friends and family, pleasant teachers, and good exam results. Others (you'll know what these things are in your own life) aren't so easy!

In the Second World War, two Dutch sisters called Corrie and Betsie were sent to a concentration camp for sheltering Jews in their home. Conditions were terrible. The work was hard, the guards were cruel, and the prisoners hadn't enough to eat or to wear. All their belongings had been taken from them when they arrived, and the sisters were packed into barracks with dozens of other women. The place was smelly and very dirty and there were even fleas in the filthy straw on which the prisoners slept. Could you thank God for fleas? Betsie did! Corrie could give God thanks that she and her sister were together. She could even thank Him for the cramped conditions because others would hear them read from the little Bible they had miraculously managed to smuggle into the camp. But she struggled to thank God for the fleas. What possible use could there be for fleas?

As time went on, more and more women began listening to them reading the Bible, many of them hearing of Christ, yet the guards never disturbed them. Everywhere the prisoners went in the camp, they were under intense supervision, but not in the barracks. They couldn't understand it.

One day, Betsie asked her supervisor to come to the barracks where they were working as there had been confusion about sock sizes in their knitting group. She wouldn't. The supervisor's answer? "That place is crawling with fleas!"

When Corrie heard, she remembered how that Betsie had thanked God for the fleas and learned a lesson that we all should learn – that God can use even the worst of circumstances for His glory. We can truly give thanks in everything.

Wine is a mocker, strong drink is a brawler, and whoever is led astray by it is not wise.

Proverbs 20:1 NKJV

I'm sure many of you will have overheard the conversations of classmates, fellow students or work colleagues after a night out. Accompanied by much laughter, their chat will include tales of those who had a drink or two too many and lost control of their actions, saying and doing all sorts of dubious and outrageous things. Maybe the person in question has no recollection of what they did, and is sitting there, trying to laugh, but secretly terrified of what will be revealed.

The Bible is exceptionally clear when it comes to the subject of excess drinking. God has nothing good to say about it. To be drunk is to lose self-control – something which is extremely important for Christians to maintain. We can't argue with Scripture – one who has trusted Christ for salvation should not find themselves in this condition.

Some will argue that the Bible doesn't forbid alcohol consumption, and point to Paul's advice to Timothy (1 Timothy 5:23). If you look at the verse, however, you'll see that Paul is not telling Timothy to *drink* wine, but rather to *use* it, as a medicine.

But let us imagine, for a moment, that there's nothing wrong with drinking alcohol, providing you don't get drunk. How much alcohol would it take before you lose control? And without getting drunk, how would you find out? How drunk is drunk? Just one glass of wine has a relaxing effect on the body and can even impair judgment.

More seriously still, how do you know that you don't have a propensity to alcohol addiction? When an alcoholic was asked which drink caused the problem, he replied, "The first one." I have heard some tragic stories of those whose lives were utterly ruined by alcohol addiction.

Those who make the choice to drink alcohol will affect others. Even if you could handle one drink, you may lead other believers astray. As far as unbelievers are concerned, alcohol is often connected with enjoyment, so saying 'no' is a great testimony to the joy and satisfaction found in Christ.

There are many reasons why a believer should avoid alcohol. Rather than being controlled by wine, let us be filled with the Spirit (Ephesians 5:18).

Blessed are they that have not seen, and yet have believed.

John 20:29

DECEMBER 18

I'm sure most of us, at one time or another, have wished that we had been alive when our Lord Jesus Christ was on earth. Wouldn't it have been amazing to have looked into His kind face, to have heard His gracious voice, and to have watched Him perform miracles – maybe on us or on some of our family members? Maybe we can see ourselves standing beside those faithful women at Calvary, our hearts broken by the suffering that He endured, caused by our sin. We imagine the joy over discovering that He had risen from the dead, and the wonder of watching Him being carried up to heaven. Life would never be the same again after having come to know God's Son.

Maybe we believe that we are at a real disadvantage for not having been on earth while the Lord Jesus was here. If we'd met Him, surely our love for Him would be deeper, or we would better appreciate His attributes. If we'd known Him on earth, we'd be more devoted to Him. After all, if we love Him even though we've never seen Him, how much greater would our love be if we had seen Him?

He knew. Our Lord Jesus Christ was perfectly aware that a couple of thousand years down the line, you would be thinking those exact thoughts! Why do you think He told Thomas that those who have not seen and yet have believed would be blessed? Of course, these words were a lesson to Thomas. He refused to believe that the Lord was risen until he could not only see Him but touch His wounds. There's no record that he ever did put his finger into the nail prints. There was no need. One sight of the Saviour was enough to satisfy him. But through Thomas's lesson, we discover that believers like us are at no disadvantage. In fact, there is a special blessing for people who exercise faith in One whom they have never seen.

And one day we will see Him. If our love lacks anything now, it certainly won't then. These eyes of ours will gaze upon Him in all His splendour and majesty. We will fall before Him in wonder and worship, and spend all eternity praising the One who is worthy.

God created man in His own image... male and female created He them.

Genesis 1:27

"Who am I?" is a question that is often asked by those who are trying to understand themselves and their place in the world. It almost seems, however, that the oftener the question is asked, the greater the confusion about the answer. It doesn't help that many people disregard the Bible, God's guidebook for mankind, and attempt to live life by their own efforts and ideals, or by the rules and systems of men. It's no wonder they're confused. If we take God out, life ceases to make sense. After all, if we are only here by chance, what is the purpose of our existence?

My late father-in-law was a collector of old electronic gadgets, most of which are now without their instruction manuals. I have no idea what many of them are or how they work. In my hands, they are useless! For a machine to reach its full potential, it's vital to follow the instructions in the guidebook. This is also true when it comes to human beings. In the verse at the top of the page, we learn that it was *God* who made mankind, so He knows every little thing about us. He knows how we tick, what we need, and what's best for us – physically, mentally, emotionally, and spiritually.

We also read that man was made in the *image* of God – a reflection of Him. Animals weren't made in God's image, nor did they become living souls (Genesis 2:7). While God intended animals to be well looked after, He has given to mankind value and purpose which is vastly superior to that of animals.

Finally, we see that God made *male and female*. When you were born, probably the first thing the doctor or midwife announced was, "It's a girl!" or, "It's a boy!" There was no uncertainty about it – the chromosomes you were born with determined your sex. It's good to remember that God has different roles for male and female (for example, 1 Timothy 2:8-15; Titus 2:1-8). His design is always best.

With God's Word as our guide, we need not be in any confusion about our identity or purpose. After all, God has always known us better than we can ever know ourselves.

> Whether you eat or drink, or whatever you do, do all to the glory of God.
>
> 1 Corinthians 10:31 NKJV

You're at a wedding, or maybe at someone's house for dinner. A plate is set in front of you, laden with food – maybe piled high with roast beef and gravy, or a big juicy steak with pepper sauce and tobacco onions, heaps of chips or mashed potatoes, and only the vegetables you really like. The waiter or the host assures you that there is plenty more when you're ready for it.

What do you do? Do you gulp it all down and ask for the same again, or do you go pale at the thought of consuming so many calories, work out how much exercise you'd have to do to offset it, then pick through the dinner, eating as little as you can get away with?

Is one of these attitudes better than the other? Sadly, many people have unhealthy relationships with food – some overindulging and binging, and others trying to eat as little as possible in an effort to gain or maintain the 'perfect' figure.

Did you ever think that eating and drinking is something that can be done for God's glory? It can! When you sit down to a healthy breakfast before school, you're fuelling your body for the day ahead. That food will give you the energy, both mental and physical, that you need to do your best that day. And God wants you to do your best for Him. That glorifies Him.

Both overeating and undereating lead to unhealthy bodies. But more than that, they are underlying causes of a bigger problem. Both, believe it or not, have at their root the problem of self-control. It's easy to see that someone who can't resist food has this problem, but a person who cares so much about how they look that they don't eat what they should is also struggling with control over their obsession with calories and image.

Self-control is mentioned many times in the Bible, so it's obviously important to God. A Christian who is able to exercise self-control will please God and bring glory to Him. So next time you're offered food, stop and think, then eat in a way that brings glory to God.

The Lord is my light.
Psalm 27:1

At this time of year, where I live, it can seem as if we never see any daylight. When we get up, it's dark, when we go to school or work, it's dark, and when we come home, it's dark. Even when there is light, it seems muted and washed out. People who go out walking need high-visibility clothing. Our room lights are on more often than they're off. My hens call it a day mid-afternoon and climb up the ladder to roost for the night.

Unless we're at home, curled up by the fire, most of us don't really enjoy the darkness. It can be scary – what or who is lurking out there? Dangerous, too – without any light it's almost impossible to tell where we're going.

Back in June, the sun hardly seemed to go to bed at all but shone all day with a brilliant brightness from clear, blue skies. There was no darkness then, because the sun had dispelled it. All was clear and visible, and it was easy to find our way around.

The Lord is our light. Before we were saved, we were in darkness, but He has dispelled the gloom from our hearts. His presence brightens our way, and through His Word He shows us the path we should take. When it's dark, our imaginations can cause us to envisage all sorts of things that aren't really there, but in the light, we see everything for what it really is. It's the same with the light of the Lord's presence – when we are close to Him, we are better able to assess if what we are hearing or seeing is from God, or only from men. In His light, we'll be able to see danger and change direction – maybe to flee, like Joseph did when Potiphar's wife tried to seduce him to sin.

I don't need to tell you that light is one of the main conditions needed for growth, and growth is a sign of life. As Christians, when we are in the light, we will grow, and become more like Christ. And we will then be lights ourselves – as the Lord Jesus said to His followers, 'You are the light of the world' (Matthew 5:14 NKJV).

Forgetting those things which are
behind and reaching forward to
those things which are ahead, I press
toward the goal for the prize of the
upward call of God in Christ Jesus.

Philippians 3:13,14 NKJV

DECEMBER

22

This year, for the first time in ages, I made gingerbread men. Sadly, they were a little burnt, some of them were cracked, and the icing was so messy that my brother wondered if the ones I'd given him were the rejects. They certainly weren't perfect specimens of gingerbread men, that's for sure!

Isn't that sometimes how life is? We're coming to the end of another year and maybe you're looking back and noticing all the less-than-perfect moments, those times when things were a little messy, or you did something on impulse that you wish you hadn't. Maybe you took a risk and got burned, or someone said or did something that made you crack. You've got pain and regrets. Living in the past isn't hard to do. I know what it's like to relive situations over and over, to let them drag me down and hold me back.

The Bible, as always, has an answer for this. Look at the words at the top of the page, spoken by the apostle Paul. Paul knew that the best way to keep going forward is to stop looking back. Did you ever see someone at sports day, so intent on checking the progress of the people behind him, that he veers off course so badly he ends up coming last? We shouldn't dismiss what's happened in the past year. If we sinned, we should confess it to God. If someone wronged us, we should forgive. We should learn from experiences – and then move on. Look forward. There's a high goal to attain – the prize of the upward call of God in Christ Jesus. The focus of your life should be to live for God. Next year might not be great from an earthly perspective, but it could be an amazing year from a heavenly one. This could even be the year that we will be with Him! So let's face forward and press on, with the best goal in view.

And Mary said, "My soul doth magnify the Lord, and my spirit hath rejoiced in God my Saviour."

Luke 1:46,47

At this time of year, little children in many schools and church buildings across the world are playing their part in nativity plays, maybe as a shepherd, an angel, the innkeeper, Mary, or Joseph. Most of us have always known the 'Christmas Story' – Mary and Joseph travelling a great distance to Bethlehem, only to find no room in the inn. We all know that the Lord Jesus was born in an outside place, and announced by angels to the shepherds, who then visited and worshipped the One who was God manifested in flesh.

But have you ever thought about Mary? Back in those days, girls got married a lot younger than they do now in our modern, Western world. Mary was most likely a teenager, maybe around fifteen years old. Despite the fact she had to grow up pretty quickly, she had lived the same number of years on this earth as some of you! It was likely a hard life, full of busy work, without much free time. And yet this girl's knowledge of God and the Old Testament Scriptures (for remember that was all they had back then) was amazing. In her song in Luke 1:46-55, Mary recollected many parts of God's Word and wove them into an intelligent masterpiece of praise to God.

Ah, but Mary was special, you're thinking. *After all, she was chosen to be the mother of the Lord Jesus.* I agree there is something special about Mary, but only in the sense that she was a spiritual, yet simple and humble girl from a poor home. She was certainly not sinless – she recognised her need for a Saviour. And she hadn't been given anything 'extra' by God that no one else had. The knowledge of God that Mary had is exactly the knowledge that you and I can have today.

I don't know if Mary could read. In fact, even if she could, she likely only heard the Scriptures read by others – people didn't own whole copies back then. She probably had neither the ability nor the means to sit down and read God's Word. We have both. Let's not waste them. After all, God can do great and mighty things with teenagers who make the effort to know Him.

Bethlehem Ephrathah... out of you shall come forth to Me the One... from everlasting.

Micah 5:2 NKJV

DECEMBER

24

Ask anyone who is vaguely familiar with the 'Christmas story' where Jesus was born, and they'll answer "Bethlehem." They'll probably even be able to tell you that Mary and Joseph weren't living in Bethlehem but had to travel there because of a census. And they'd be right. But did you ever stop to consider what a significant fact this is? Was the location of the Lord Jesus Christ's birth one of those random happenings like those which occasionally place people in different areas of the country? Would it have made a difference if He'd been born in Nazareth where Mary and Joseph were from?

To answer, we need to turn to the Old Testament, to the prophecy of Micah, chapter 5. I've quoted part of the verse at the top of the page, but I recommend you read it all. As you read, consider who is being spoken of in the verse. It's obviously One with great power – a ruler. And One who is eternal. Could it be anyone other than the Messiah, the Lord Jesus Christ? We also find the location where He was to be born. The Bible is really specific. You see, there were two Bethlehems. One was only a few miles from Nazareth, but the other, Bethlehem Ephrathah, the Bethlehem mentioned in the prophecy, was in the south. It was the latter Bethlehem to which Mary and Joseph had to travel, a journey of up to ninety miles.

This journey involved much more than spending a few hours in the car or taking the train. It was not a trip they would naturally have considered or chosen to make, especially at this stage of Mary's pregnancy, had not Caesar Augustus decreed a census whereby each Jewish male had to register in the city of his fathers. Thus, they found themselves in Bethlehem Ephrathah, right at the time when the Lord Jesus was due to be born.

Isn't it remarkable that God moved the greatest leader in the world at that time, to decree a census in order to fulfil a prophecy hidden in the pages of His Word? We can learn two lessons from this – one is that the Bible is reliable and true; the other is that God's purposes will always come to pass.

For unto you is born this day
in the city of David a Saviour,
which is Christ the Lord.

Luke 2:11

Today, many people across the world will commemorate the birth of the Lord Jesus Christ. And although no one really knows when the Lord Jesus was born, taking time to think about Him and His coming into the world is always a good thing to do.

We have become so used to the story that we often fail to appreciate how amazing His coming really was. Just think – the One who was truly God, higher than the highest angel, whose dwelling place was the grandeur of glory, coming to earth. Not as a powerful ruler, but as a tiny baby. The place of His birth was neither a hospital nor even a house. Instead, it was a place where cattle were fed – a cave, or an open field. Mary, who was probably around the age of some of you, was her own midwife, and she wrapped her newborn Son in strips of cloth before laying Him in a feeding trough.

It was to shepherds – normal, humble, everyday people like you and me – that the angels were sent with the greatest message ever to reach human ears. For years, the Jewish nation had been watching and waiting for the Messiah, who had been promised as far back as Genesis 3. And now He had arrived! It's no wonder the shepherds were stunned. From everything they had known about the Messiah, they couldn't have imagined that He would arrive like this.

But there was more that they didn't understand. At this time, the Romans were ruling the land of Israel. The people felt that their need for a Messiah was greater than it had ever been. They were waiting and watching for a deliverer. But God's plan was better! Instead of saving them from Roman rule, the Messiah was going to save them from their sins. And what makes the birth of Christ so precious to us is that we were included too. He came to take away the sins of the whole world.

So on this busy and fun-filled day, don't forget to think about the Saviour's birth and what it means to you.

Won't heaven be wonderful? No sickness, no sadness, no separation! All the problems that troubled us on earth will be over, and we will be forever happy. Although the Bible has a lot to say about what isn't in heaven, it's still a mystery to us in many ways what it will be like to be there. What exactly will we spend our time doing? What will we look like? Will we still feel like ourselves? I can't give you the answers to these questions – we'll need to wait until we're there to find out.

I'm sure, though, that if we collected everyone's impressions of what heaven will be like, we'd end up with a variety of scenes. One scene that would probably occur frequently is that of being reunited with loved ones. Separation because of death is one of the most difficult things about living on this earth, and many of us have grandparents, parents, siblings, or friends that we're looking forward to meeting again when we arrive on the other side.

Maybe there are some reading this who don't belong to a large Christian family and you're wondering what heaven will look like for you. Will you be sitting in a corner by yourself while family reunions are taking place all around you? It's easy to feel like an outsider when you're in a roomful of people who all know each other and are talking and laughing, sharing inside jokes and secrets. Is this what heaven will be like? Of course not! As each person trusts Christ for salvation as an individual, so each of us will be in heaven as an individual through faith in Christ alone. Earthly ties will yield to our greater and fuller spiritual relationship with each other. Every single believer will be equally precious to us.

But more importantly, our gaze and focus will be centred on One alone – the Lord Jesus Christ, who loved us and washed us from our sins in His own blood. He will be the theme of our song and we will worship Him forever. Of all the wonderful things about heaven, being with Christ will surpass them all.

Keep yourselves in the love of God.

Jude 21

Where I live, we usually get a few falls of snow each winter. To be honest, most of the time I'd rather it stayed away! The problem is that our house has a sloping driveway, and when it snows it's impossible to drive up to it. So, unless I shovel the snow, or until it clears, we must park at the bottom of the hill and walk. During winter, I usually end up spending time and energy clearing the driveway, with no guarantee that even then the car will find enough traction to climb the hill.

There's something that's better than a shovel to clear the snow. It's sunshine! The warmth of the sun's rays can do a much better job than I can, and sometimes in far less time too.

The lane which stretches from the road to our driveway is a different story. On one side is a stream, and on the other is a hedge. It's not a particularly tall or thick hedge, but it's a sufficient barrier to prevent the sunlight touching the snow here. Last week, the snow had long melted from our driveway, but the lane stayed obstinately white.

The love of God is like sunshine – warm and powerful. When we let it shine, and bask in His wonderful love for us, demonstrated by sending His Son to pay the price for our sins, our hearts are softened and melted. There's nothing of ourselves to hinder or hold us back, and we can make progress on the hills of life.

But what happens when there are barriers – when we allow things to come between us and the love of God? Maybe it's a hobby or a habit that we cling to. Maybe it's something as simple as hitting 'snooze' and losing the time we could be spending in God's Word before we face a busy, challenging day. Are there hedges in your life, preventing the rays of God's love from warming your soul?

Pulling out the hedge isn't an option when it comes to our lane, but removing those things that are a hindrance to spiritual growth is vital. Let's take a look and find those shaded parts in our lives, and get the barriers removed!

But the end is not yet.

Matthew 24:6

This world is full of tears. From Abel right to this present day, over the history of this world, billions of people have been killed. Wars, genocide, and gang violence have been the cause of much heartache, each victim an individual with their own story and grieving family and friends. The collective pain of this world is incomprehensible. In such a hopeless, helpless, hurting world, you might ask, 'Where is God in all of this? Does He see? Does He care?'

Imagine that you are reading a book. You get partway through. Everything is going wrong for the poor characters and you can't see how they will ever extricate themselves from the situation they find themselves in. It's a total disaster, so you throw the book away in disgust. Do you? Of course not! You can't imagine how it will work out, but you can't help reading on. You're rooting for the characters, hoping they'll have a happy ending. And you know that by the last chapter everything will work out perfectly.

In the book of Exodus, the children of Israel had become slaves for the Egyptians. Their bondage was great. The burdens were getting heavier. The Egyptians made their lives bitter. I'm sure the Israelites asked where God was. Did He even see them? Hear them? Why wouldn't He deliver them? They hadn't read the last chapter. They didn't know that God had heard, He had seen, and He knew their sorrows. And, best of all, He was going to do something about it. Deliverance would come. Their groaning and pain wouldn't continue.

So it is with this world. We haven't reached the last chapter. We need to read the whole book – the Bible. This true-to-life book doesn't shy away from the pain we face, but throughout it there is hope – a bright promise of a day when all wrongs will be put right, when all sin will be judged, and the righteous Ruler will be on the throne. Those who have trusted Christ as Saviour will share in the great future that is ahead.

Would you like to know what we read at the end of this book? It's the best possible ending – 'There shall be no more death, neither sorrow, nor crying, neither shall there be any more pain: for the former things are passed away' (Revelation 21:4).

29
DECEMBER

My heart is inditing a good matter... my tongue is the pen of a ready writer.

Psalm 45:1

Does the name Philip P Bliss mean anything to you? If not, then what about the hymns 'I Am So Glad That Our Father in Heaven', 'Almost Persuaded', and 'Man of Sorrows'? These are only three of many wonderful hymns that Mr Bliss wrote and composed the music for, over his short lifespan.

Philip P Bliss was born in 1838 into a humble but godly home in Pennsylvania. At eleven years old, he left home to make a living for himself, and trusted Christ when he was twelve. His talents in singing and in composition were recognised and developed, and in 1874 he decided to leave his occupation and other interests in order to devote his time to the composition and singing of sacred songs for the Lord.

In December 1876, aged thirty-eight, Philip Bliss and his wife, Lucy, were returning to Chicago in a great snowstorm after spending Christmas with his mother, when they suffered a dreadful accident. As the train in which they were travelling was crossing a river, the trestle bridge gave way and the carriages plunged seventy-five feet into the ravine, before catching fire. Mr Bliss managed to escape, but when he realised his wife was trapped, he returned to save her. Tragically, he wasn't able to rescue her, and they both perished in the flames.

One source relates that the night before his death, he told his audience, "I may not pass this way again," before singing 'I'm Going Home Tomorrow'.[85] The words were truer than anyone realised!

Untimely deaths are always difficult to understand, especially of those who have been so useful in the service of the Lord. Someone stated that had he lived, he may have been the greatest songwriter of all time.[86] Possibly the last hymn that he wrote was 'I Will Sing of My Redeemer'. It finishes with the words 'He from death to life hath brought me, Son of God with Him to be.' On 29th December 1876, Philip P Bliss experienced the fulfilment of these words. Forevermore he will be singing of the wondrous love of his Redeemer.

---

85. From http://www.hymntime.com/tch/bio/b/l/i/bliss_pp.htm
86. From https://www.wholesomewords.org/biography/biobliss.html

> **The plans of the diligent lead surely to abundance.**
> Proverbs 21:5 ESV

Are you the sort of person who always makes New Year's resolutions? How do you get on? Do you work hard through the year to stick to your goal? Or perhaps you can hardly even remember what resolutions you made away back in January! Maybe you struggle with commitment, so you feel that the wisest course of action is not to make any resolutions in the first place.

I'm not sure what the statistics are, but my guess is that very few people who make New Year's resolutions are still going strong come 31st December. Everyone who fails to continue has their own reasons for what went wrong, but what is obvious, however, is that those who make resolutions are more likely to achieve their objectives than those who never make any resolutions at all.

So if you've decided to make New Year's resolutions for the coming year, here are a few pointers.

Make sure your goal is worthwhile. Our aim should be to live for the Lord Jesus Christ. Don't waste time and effort on things that have no eternal value.

Set realistic goals. It's good to challenge ourselves, but if we set extreme targets, we may become disheartened and give up.

Don't obsess on the external. We are to be good stewards of our bodies, but we should not make them objects of our worship. Any resolution which involves our appearance and our health should be moderated by the right motivation.

Plan! There is no point in setting a goal without a strategy; it will never work! Maybe this year you want to spend more time reading your Bible. This might involve sacrificing time you normally spend on sleep, the internet, or with friends. Determine when you are going to work towards your goal, set aside the time, and stick to it.

Keep the goal in mind. When things get tough, remember why you're doing it. Write it out on a sticky note and attach it somewhere you'll see it often, like your bedroom door.

Pray! This is the most important part of meeting our goals. If our New Year's resolutions have God at the centre, we can take our struggles and discouragements to Him, asking for His help to continue and knowing He will give us the necessary strength to keep going when things get tough.

In all thy ways
acknowledge Him, and He
shall direct thy paths.

Proverbs 3:6

Imagine the scene. It's a dark night – pitch black – with no street lights, moon or stars to give any illumination. You're standing at the side of a road. You know the road leads to the nearest town, where you want to be, but you can't see a thing. So you pull out your phone and turn on the torch. That's better! Now you can see some of the road in front of you, so you begin to walk. As you walk, the next part of the road becomes visible. You can't see the whole way to the town, but you know that if you move forward using the light that you have, eventually you will get there.

The road of life can be a bit like that. No matter how much we strain our eyes and stand on tiptoe, we can't see any further than that little bit right in front of us. If you're like me, you might start to panic. The unknown is scary! We know where we are eventually headed – to heaven – and we're sure of being there one day, but we don't know what the road looks like. We can't see the hills, the corners, or the potholes. We don't know if there will be forks in the road, T-junctions, or areas where the road isn't so obvious. We don't even know how long the road is!

That's why it's so good to remember that while the future is unknown to us, it's not unknown to God. He knows every single step we're going to take. He knows all about the difficulties and obstacles ahead. He's perfectly aware of the decisions we'll need to make. And He has promised to guide us, step by step, as we make our way along the road. We can't see the whole road – but we don't need to. Each little beam of illumination that God gives us is enough for now. And when we need more, we can be sure that He will give it.

One Year Further On...

It's been a full year since we started out on our climb together! We have learned lessons and proved God in ways that we'll never forget. I hope that what you have read has been helpful to you and has encouraged you as you live for God and aim to put Him first. Please don't think that I have reached the summit – I'm still climbing too, and much of what you've read in this book was written to myself.

As you pause to look back over the climb of the past year, remember what God has been teaching you, especially those lessons about Himself. Then face forward again, take a deep breath, and climb on!

Key Passages

Creation – Genesis 1

Inspiration of Scripture – 2 Timothy 3:14-17; 2 Peter 1:20-21

Attributes of God – Psalm 139; Isaiah 40

Deity of Christ – John 1:1-18; Colossians 1:15-19; Hebrews 1:1-14

Person of Christ – Philippians 2:1-11

Sufferings of Christ – Psalm 22:1-21; Isaiah 52:13 – 53:1-12; John 19

Sin and Salvation – Genesis 3; Romans 3:9-26

New Birth – John 3:1-21

Eternal Security – John 10:27-30; Romans 8:28-39

Church truth – Acts 2:41,42; 1 Corinthians 11; 1 Timothy 3:14-16

Future Events – Daniel 9; Matthew 24

Acknowledgements

A little boy once asked me, "How do you make a book?" With childish confidence in the ingenuity of adults, he believed that the book had been entirely produced – from the faint glimmer of early inspiration right through to the printed-and-bound substance – by yours truly! Those who are a little older and wiser will appreciate that my skills do not stretch so far, but what you may not realise is just how many people were necessary to help those early thoughts transform into the book you are reading today.

To those who planted the initial seed by suggesting I should write a teens' daily reading book, thank you! I feel honoured that you had confidence in me, and I hope this book fulfils your expectations.

For all my brothers and sisters in Christ, at home and right across the world, who prayed fervently as I wrote, eternity alone will reveal how vital your labours were. The knowledge that you were praying on the mountain while I was in the valley, doing battle at my laptop, kept me going when I would have otherwise admitted defeat. 'The effectual fervent prayer of a righteous man availeth much' (James 5:16). May God richly reward each one of you.

It's impossible to adequately thank those of you who sacrificed the time to read the manuscript and make many valuable and insightful suggestions and comments. These wonderful people include Samuel Chesney, Joanne Grattan, Margaret Moore, Phoebe Smyth, Eunice Wilkie, and David and Jennie Williamson. And although giving support, reassurance, and encouragement wasn't in the brief, you provided all of these abundantly just when I needed them most. I'm privileged to have such a fabulous team!

To those who read selected portions, made suggestions, and gave advice – a massive thank you. Jenna, John, Michael, Pamella, Phillip, and Priscilla – your contributions helped much more than you realise.

My grateful thanks to Alison, General Manager at John Ritchie Ltd., Bethany McClean who created the amazing artwork for the cover, and all those who worked hard behind the scenes in the design, production, and marketing of this book.

And to Samuel, my husband. Writing this daily devotional has often felt like flying through a thunderstorm, but I'm thankful that, on this flight, you were seated right beside me! I couldn't make this writing journey without your steady presence and loving support.

Above all, thanksgiving must go to the One who loved me, died for me, saved me, guides me, and keeps me. He is faithful.

Books

In this book, various topics have been mentioned that I haven't been able to expand upon because of limitations of space. If you'd like to know more about some of the issues mentioned, I suggest you read the following books, along with many of the resources mentioned in the footnotes:

Baptism – *Have You Gone Down in the 8:36?* is a booklet by Robert Plant, available from Ritchie Christian Media.

Christian life – *Following Christ in an Age of Confusion,* by Craig and Hannah Munro, published by John Ritchie Ltd in 2020.

Relationships – *Choosing Love in a Broken World,* by Heidi Johnston, published by 10Publishing in 2019.